# The Political Teachings of Shaykh Dr. Abdalqadir as-Sufi

# The Political Teachings of Shaykh Dr. Abdalqadir as-Sufi

Riyad Asvat

with three chapters on
trade and commerce by
Abdassamad Clarke

The Political Teachings of Shaykh Dr. Abdalqadir as-Sufi

| | | |
|---|---|---|
| Published by: | Iqra Agencies Ltd.<br>No 5 Laudium Plaza<br>Laudium, Pretoria<br>0037<br>South Africa | Diwan Press<br>311 Allerton Road<br>Bradford<br>BD15 7HA<br>UK |
| Website: | www.iqra.co.za | www.diwanpress.com |
| E-mail: | musa@iqra.co.za | info@diwanpress.com |



| | |
|---|---|
| Authors: | Riyad Asvat<br>Abdassamad Clarke |
| Editor: | Abdalhaqq Bewley |
| Cover: | Abdassamad Clarke |

A catalogue record of this book is available from the British Library.

ISBN-13: 978-1-914397-26-4 (paperback)
978-1-914397-25-7 (casebound)

# Contents

Preface xiii

Foreword xv

Shaykh Abdalqadir as-Sufi xvii

Muslims at a Crossroad xviii

Introduction xxii

PART 1 1

Islam – Its New Beginning 3

Chapter 1: Governance is a Divine Contract 5

The Miracle of Madīna 7

Emergence of High Civilisation 11

Chapter 2: The Linkage between Politics and Trade in Islam 15

(1) The selling in markets and the spread of the caravans 18

Protection of Trade Routes by the Political Authorities 22

(2) The welfare distribution of the annual *zakāt* 25

(3) The distribution of the booty as a last means of moving wealth among the people 28

CHAPTER 3: CAPITALISM, BANKING AND THE MODERN STATE 33

CHAPTER 4: THE FALL OF THE CALIPHATE 42

(1) The Arabian Peninsula 52

(2) Egypt 55

(3) The Anatolian and Salonikan regions of the Ottoman dawla 59

CHAPTER 5: THE RISE OF IDEOLOGY AMONGST MUSLIMS 64

CHAPTER 6: ATHEISTIC CAPITALISM: THE DOMINANT RELIGION OF OUR TIME 82

PART 2 89

CHAPTER 7: POLITICS 91

Stage One – The Machine 92

Stage Two – The Personnel 93

Stage Three – The Party 93

Stage Four – The Crisis 94

Stage Five – The Leader 95

Stage Six – The Money 96

CHAPTER 8: STATE CAPTURE 100

The Corporate State 101

How the State was Captured 105

(a) Civil Society 105

(b) Business 106

(c) Politics 108

CHAPTER 9: ECONOMICS 111

Economics: Science or Spin? 122

CHAPTER 10: SCIENTIFIC MATERIALISM 124

Scientism 124

Critique of Scientism 127

The End of Scientism – Apotheosis 129

CHAPTER 11: PUBLIC RELATIONS 131

The engineering of consent: how to fool all the people all the time 132

The alliance of democracy and consumerism 135

Consumer Politics 138

Resistance to consumer politics. 141

CHAPTER 12: THE NUCLEAR FAMILY 144

Pre-industrial households 144

The family and industrialism 145

The nuclear family 145

The family and banking 147

The Open Family 148

CHAPTER 13: EDUCATION 152

1) The adjustive or adaptive function 153

2) The integrating function 153

3) The diagnostic and directive function 153

4) The differentiating function 154

5) The selective or hygienic function 154

6) The propaedeutic function 155

The products of the school system 156

Corporate sponsors for compulsory schooling 157

Universities 159

Education in Islam – Futuwwa 161

Futuwwa Institutionalised 164

CHAPTER 14: MEDIA 174

Functions of Mass Media 174

Objectives of Mass Media 176

New Media 177

The Promised Utopia 178

The Dystopian Reality 179

Capitalism in Terminal Decline 181

The Wikileaks Phenomenon 182

PART 3 185

Chapter 15: The Institutions of Islamic governance 189

Institutions of Muslim Society 190

Postface 200

Chapter 16: Trade & Commerce in the Qur'ān 201

Sūra 2 al-Baqara – Spending, giving and *ribā* (usury) 202

Foundational *āyats* Prohibiting Usury 207

Qāḍī Abū Bakr ibn al-'Arabī in his *Aḥkām al-Qur'ān* 207

Sūra 2 al-Baqara – *Dayn* – credit/debt 208

Sūra 3 Āli 'Imrān – *ribā* continued 213

Sūra 4 an-Nisā' – *Farā'iḍ* – the fixed shares of inheritance 215

Sūra 5 al-Mā'ida – Contracts 216

Sūra 9 at-Tawba – "Take!" *Zakāt* 218

Sūra 42 ash-Shūrā – *Mīzān* – scales & justice 222

Sūra 65 aṭ-Ṭalāq – Provision 232

Sūra 73 al-Muzzammil – Traders 232

Sūra 83 al-Muṭaffifīn – the Stinters 237

Chapter 17: Trade and Commerce in the Sunna & Sīra 240

Time and the age 240

The New Inception 241

The Ancient World, Usury, Debt and Slavery 242

Ibrāhīm, the *Fiṭra, and the City* 245

The Messenger of Allah ﷺ, His Madīna and His Umma 246

The Ruler 252

The *Muwaṭṭa' – the blueprint for an illuminated city* 253

Ibn Khaldūn, the Bedouin and *'Aṣabiyya* 255

The Messenger of Allah ﷺ, trade and the market 257

Establishment of the market of Madīna 259

The *Khulafā' ar-Rāshidūn* and the Companions 261

CHAPTER 18: TRANSACTIONS – MU'ĀMALĀT 271

Context 272

The Heart 273

Gold Dinars and Silver Dirhams 275

The Prohibition of Going Out to Meet the Caravans – Forestalling 282

Hoarding or engrossing – Monopoly 283

Engrossing 286

*Gharar* – uncertain and risky transactions 286

Price fixing, whether by the state or a cartel 287

Undercutting and overpricing 287

Positive aspects of *mu'āmalāt* 290

*Qirāḍ/Muḍāraba* and Trust (*īmān*) 290

Caravans versus distribution 291

*Mushāraka* – Partnership 292

Guilds 293

*Murabāḥa* 294

A digression on terminologies 295

Land usage 296

Renting land for crops – *muḥāqala* 296

Bitcoin and cryptocurrencies 298

Blockchain 299

*Awqāf* endowments & the Commons 300

Islamic Banking – the Trojan Horse in the Heart of the Sharī'a, or, If the wolf pays the shepherd what hope is there for the sheep? 304

*Ḍarūra – exceptional need* 316

Dismantling the machine 318

Afterword 320

PART 4 321

CONCLUSION 323

The Modern Worldview 324

Capitalism – the religion of modernity 326

Allah's war on *ribā* 328

Consequences for the world 328

Consequences for the USA 329

The Messenger's war on *ribā* 331

Basis for Revival 332

Mu'āmalāt 343

The New Nomos 347

The cyclical nature of political power 348

Living in the moment 353

Endnotes 357

Index 407

# Preface

Ever since I met Shaykh Dr. Abdalqadir as-Sufi, may Allah be pleased with him, in 1984 it has been a matter of trying to catch up with his latest writings. He gave me *idhn* (permission) to write this book as he had done for *Sufism: The Living Tradition*. Writing them was no easy task because he was a prolific writer, whose literary output spanned well over sixty years. He was without doubt the most important Islamic scholar of the last hundred years as well as the most important Western intellectual during this period. The other difficulty that I faced was that he had the unique ability to unify the outward (physical), the inward (psychological) and hidden (spiritual) dimensions of reality whilst my university education trained me to do the opposite, that is, to divide, compartmentalize and analyse.

Shaykh Abdalqadir's writings on politics have been encyclopaedic, covering a vast range of subjects from political philosophy to systems of governance such as personal, monarchical, democratic and military rule as well as theocracy, totalitarianism and oligarchy. His greatest contributions to humanity have been: (1) his analysis of contemporary society; (2) his description of the original Islamic phenomenon; and (3) the steps he outlined for Islamic revival. The intention of this book is not to summarise what Shaykh Abdalqadir has already written. It is to reveal how the knowledge imparted by him has pragmatic value. Whilst others, who diagnosed the problems of the modern world, painted pictures of doom and gloom, Shaykh Abdalqadir provided solutions to the problems. He lifted us out of the abyss of despair and energised us, calling us to action and bringing out from within us nobility, dignity, courage and strength that we didn't know we possessed.

I have many people to thank. First and foremost my wife Fathima who has supported me from the time we met Shaykh Abdalqadir. Thanks also to Abdassamad Clarke for contributing three chapters on *mu'āmalāt* for the book. Many thanks to Hajj Hassim Dockrat for proofreading and his insightful suggestions. Special thanks to Hajj Mūsā Adam for publishing this book and for bringing Shaykh Abdalqadir to Pretoria which led to the establishment of the first South African Murabitun communities in Laudium and Soweto. My debt of gratitude extends to innumerable people and to all of them I say thank you for your help and companionship.

# FOREWORD

أَعُوذُ بِاللهِ مِنَ الشَّيْطَانِ الرَّجِيمِ

بِسْمِ ٱللَّهِ ٱلرَّحْمَٰنِ ٱلرَّحِيمِ

*Subḥānallāh walḥamdulillāh wa lā ilāha illallāh Allāhu akbar*
*Walā ḥawla wa lā quwwata illā billāhil 'Aliyyil 'Aẓīm*

*Alḥamdulillāhi Rabbil-'ālamīn waṣ-ṣalātu was-salāmu 'alā*
*Rasūlihil – Karīm 'alā*
*Sayyidil-Mursalīn wa 'alā 'Ālihi wa Ṣaḥbihi ajma'īn*

For readers to get to know the author of this excellent exposition on the political philosophy of Shaykh Abdalqadir as-Sufi *raḥimahu'llāh* it means going back in time to uncover the symbiosis between the author and his subject. Dr. Riyad Asvat was among a group of young men, who in the early nineteen eighties in Pretoria, South Africa was introduced to the primary writings of Shaykh Abdalqadir as-Sufi. This introduction was brought by Hajj Mūsā Adam, who at the time had just established his famous Islamic bookshop – Iqra Agencies.

Set during the heady days of political activism against apartheid in South Africa as well as the continuing rhetoric that flowed from the 'Islamic' revolution in Iran, there were some of us who innately searched for answers beyond the standard political and religious dialectics of the time. Since we knew that we were somehow trapped, on the one hand, within the arguments of the reigning ideologies, and on the other the orthodoxic *'aqīda*s that dominated the Muslim religious sphere. The early works of Shaykh Abdalqadir as-Sufi gave us a new conceptual understanding of the nature of politics and the existential reality of Islam both historically and within the context of the current ethos.

The discovery of this new understanding was up to that point quite academic until the auspicious physical encounter with the illuminated presence of Shaykh Abdalqadir as-Sufi in 1984. This encounter transitioned our early group of men beyond the zone of intellectual speculation through the door of *taṣawwuf.* This transition was significant because it was only through this door that the meaning of the reality of things, both political and religious became apparent.

Illuminated meaning bred certainty about how we viewed politics and Islam and how it is to be mapped from that moment onward. One of the defining actions of the fledgling community, which now called itself the Murabitun, in emulation of its historical namesake, was to establish Amirate. The first Amīr of this community was Riyad Asvat. Amirate being the cornerstone of governance in Islam, meant for those who understood its meaning to be the singularly most important expression of the politics of Islam. For Riyad Asvat this act of assumption was the culmination of one important milestone in his journey of spiritual and intellectual discovery. For those among us who took his hand it held a similar importance.

This milestone though, is an act centered in the existentiality of Islam. Its realisation is a testimony and confirmation of the teachings of Shaykh Abdalqadir as-Sufi and indeed underpins the entire essence of this book. Once the author made the decision to emigrate to Australia further milestones awaited him. Amongst these was the completion of his PhD at the University of Melbourne where he also served as a lecturer in Islamic Studies. His other milestones are to be found in his prolific published works on Islamic topics and a range of academic papers of similar import.

### Shaykh Abdalqadir as-Sufi

As Dr. Riyad Asvat states in his preface, Shaykh Abdalqadir's writings on politics have been encyclopaedic. Covering, over a period of half a century, a vast range of subjects on political philosophy, political analysis, historiography and proffering alternative socio-political models centred in tradition and scripture. Naturally as Shaykh of *ṭarīqa*, Shaykh Abdalqadir's teachings span the knowledge foundations of *taṣawwuf* and *sharī'a* and his exegeses, both written and verbal, cover the most critical elements required for the reestablishment of Islam in our time and indeed the survival of humanity and its coexistent ecology.

As the archetypal scriptwriter Shaykh Abdalqadir as-Sufi, through the gamut of his works, plots human events from the onset of the age of enlightenment to the post-modern era. In rendering this great play he begins with the nihilism of the emerging ethos, and within its unfolding visits, with dramatic effect, the decline of the Islamic hegemon. But this drama does not end in tragedy. For in the final theme of the play is the emphasis on hope and rebirth. This is the opposite of nihilism. This is Islam.

We must grasp the importance of Shaykh Abdalqadir as-Sufi in his role as *al-Quṭb ash-Shaykh* of this age. Similar in importance to the role of Shaykh Muḥammad ibn al-'Arabī in the 18$^{th}$ /19$^{th}$

centuries when the House of Islam lay besieged by the British East India Company in the East and the French and Spanish onslaughts on North and West Africa. In the teachings of Shaykh Abdalqadir as-Sufi is the key to the door of Islamic renewal, the unfolding of the *mu'āmalāt* in opposition to the onslaught of the current capitalist world order.

However, for any reader to truly comprehend the collected written works of Shaykh Abdalqadir as-Sufi, about politics and the *sharī'a*, remains a daunting task. Notwithstanding the literary sophistication of the Shaykh's analysis, one still finds simplicity of truth (*Ḥaqq*) in the concluding counsel.

In the light of the above remark, Dr. Riyad Asvat has succinctly and with academic proficiency and proposition superimposed Shaykh Abdalqadir as-Sufi's political philosophy within a simplified conceptual framework that serves as a template for ease of reading and understanding. In the context of prevailing perils it offers a blueprint for positive action.

This blueprint is contained in the final three chapters on *mu'āmalāt*. These chapters flow from the pen of another great intellectual icon of the Murabitun, Abdassamad Clarke. Himself, a prolific writer and academic of note. The subject matter in these chapters yet again rendered for ease of understanding and application.

### Muslims at a Crossroad

It would be fitting here to reference an important subject on the Modernists as raised by the author in this book. The encumbrances imposed upon the *umma* by both the modernist and traditionalist *'ulamā* since the closure of *sulṭāniyya* first in India and soon after the Khalifate in Turkey, has proven to be regressive for Islam. The modernist, in the absence of *amr*, had opened the door to *ijtihād*, and used this advantage as a tool to validate usury under the pseudonym of Islamic banking. The traditionalist, on the other hand, having closed the door of *ijtihād*, meant that they closed the books of *mu'āmalāt*. In doing so they denied themselves the ability to read adequately (intellectually and analytically) the unfolding of events and systemic order that would undermine the Muslim body politic and Islam. Between these two developments, and in the absence of Islamic *wilāyat*, the current Muslim diaspora finds itself at this critical crossroad. Between the abdication of the Modernists to capitalist technic and the zero-sum religious worldview of the traditionalists who have morphed into a clerical and insubstantive order.

This morphing has relegated Islam to the arena of private worship and morality. Abū Hurayra ﵁ reported: The Messenger of Allah ﷺ said, "Islam began as a something strange and it will return to being strange, so blessed are the strangers." The strangers are the *ṣāliḥūn*.

Shaykh Abdalqadir as-Sufi's actions went beyond literary discourse. In this regard he was master guide to the *sālik* (the seeker on the path of truth) under his aegis, and the foremost ambassador for Islam. He was passionately active in constructive engagement at a political level. In this regard Shaykh Abdalqadir never missed an opportunity to counsel kings, heads of state, politicians, army generals, revolutionary leaders and other important personages toward an Islamic reality based on *sulṭāniyya* and the just transaction in the market-place.

Having had the honour of serving as Shaykh Abdalqadir as-Sufi's political emissary for close onto a decade I could find no better example of the Shaykh's message as rendered in one of his many diplomatic letters, in this instance to the head of an important political movement active in South Asia. Herewith is an extract from the original letter delivered in November 1999:

> We must consider that the history of the last two centuries has seen

the power of the Muslim *Ummah* being eroded by a clearly defined set of strategies consisting of:

firstly the erosion of the wealth and then the sovereign integrity of the Muslim lands and its people.

and secondly the slavery and the maintenance of *kāfir* hegemony over the Muslims through modern banking and its instruments – usurious paper money and its political inventions namely constitutionalism, the nation state, fiscal government and the revolutionary dialectic.

In the light of this, there can be no such a thing as personality politics for the Muslims.

- Personality politics is what modern politics represent; personality politics is only for the media.

- The real issue in the modern age is the matter of money.

We must furthermore consider that both India and Othmany Turkey, were captured by trade and not military conquest. India was conquered by the East India Co.

In terms of power-political considerations – it must be remembered that trade has always preceded military conquests. In fact European military history was mitigated by trade.

It was categorically accepted by the great Ḥanafī Ulema of the Late Othmany period that paper money was *ḥarām* and one could not pay the *zakāt* with it.

Therefore the issue today is not of political considerations but of the weakening of the Muslims because of their abandonment of the *zakāt* on this basis. The intrusion of usurious paper money into the Muslim ethos has neutralised the *farā'iḍ* of *zakāt*.

> Dr. Erbakan of the Refah Party in Turkey has stated that the issue of money was the real issue for the Muslims today. He declared the gold *dīnār* and silver *dirham* the currency of the Muslims and he called it the atom bomb of the Muslims.
>
> If the Muslims of India had the gold *dīnār*, they would have India. Instead they have been relegated to the status of serfdom under the hindu empire.

The concluding counsel of this letter drives the point that the issue of money is not separate from the issue of morality. Meaning that the public arena (the matter of trade and the issue of money) is not separate from the private arena (the issue of morality). Therefore, by extension justice precedes morality. Viewed from this perspective the rejection of the issue of money and banking would mean the rejection of the fiscal state. The natural opposite of this rejection implies the establishment of sovereign power for the Muslims as defined in the Qur'ān and the *Sunna*.

The letter in its completeness encapsulates the political philosophy of Shaykh Abdalqadir as-Sufi. It encompasses all that he believed in and taught. In it, as with all his correspondence, lay the message of hope and care. It also serves as a fitting preamble to this significant work by Dr. Riyad Asvat.

With thanks
Hassim Ismail Dockrat

# Introduction

The current high prices of energy, food, rent and other essentials are attributed to the sanctions the US has imposed on Russia because of its war on Ukraine. Certainly, if Russian oil, gas and agriculture are excluded from the market there will be a shortage of supply and consequently prices will go up. That, however, is only part of the story. The real issue is inflation and whilst there are other reasons for inflation the primary cause is quantitative easing, that is, the injection into the economy of enormous amounts of money created out of nothing, otherwise known as fractional reserve banking. The creation of money out of nothing is no secret and just in case we have forgotten the statements made by the founder of the Bank of England, William Paterson in 1694, they issued another statement in 2014 stating that the most common assumptions of how banking works are simply wrong. In fact the statement continues to say that everything we know about banking is not just wrong, it's backwards. When banks make loans, they create money because money is really just an IOU. Our money supply, therefore, is a fraud (fractional reserve banking), *ribā* (usury/unjustified increase) and theft (fiat money inflates prices). Fiat money, which is the currency of modern states, is imposed on the populace by government regulation or law. With regards to the printing of paper money Shaykh Abdalqadir states that the process involves two elements that are prohibited by the *Sharīʿa* – the issuing of receipts over and above the deposits held and the lending of those receipts on interest. Both of these practices constitute unjustified increase, that is, *ribā*. The paper money created in this way is technically a promissory note, a promise to pay a debt and once again this practice is prohibited by Islamic law, which stipulates that a debt cannot be paid by a debt.

We are suffering the effects of inflation caused primarily by quantitative easing. Take for example the financial crisis of 2008 when the world's central banks, including the Federal Reserve, injected trillions of dollars of fabricated money into the global economy. This created a worldwide debt of $325 trillion, more than three times global GDP. The financial crisis consolidated the power of the central banks making them politically and economically stronger by allowing them and the world's largest financial institutions to fraudulently manipulate global markets and use fabricated or fake money to inflate asset bubbles for short-term profit. The economic crisis associated with the Corona virus pandemic of 2020 has also produced vast financial benefits for the investor class. During the Corona virus pandemic and the 2020 economic crisis, America's billionaires have seen their wealth soar by $434 billion. Their corporations received $500 billion in bailouts and they got $135 billion in tax breaks. The Treasury Department and the Federal Reserve are erasing the corporate debt they amassed over the last few years enabling the corporations to buy back their shares of stock. Meanwhile, Amazon, Google, Facebook, Walmart and other corporate giants are using their vast market power to make record profits. Central banks and governments have injected an estimated $15 trillion of stimulus to shield their economies from the Corona virus pandemic. This is money created out of thin air. This sum is about 17% of an $87 trillion global economy last year and this $15 trillion only covers the G10 group of major economies plus China.

Each time there is a crisis money is transferred from the poor to the rich. The rich get richer and fewer and the poor get poorer and more numerous. The wealthiest 1 percent of the world's population now owns more than half of the world's wealth. The total wealth in the world grew by 6 percent over the past 12 months to $280 trillion, marking this as the fastest wealth creation since 2012. More than half of the $16.7 trillion in new wealth was in the US, which grew $8.5 trillion richer. There are now 36 million millionaires in the world, and their numbers are expected to grow to 44 million by 2022. The most important issue in the modern age is the matter of money and the motor force that drives it – *ribā*. Shaykh Abdalqadir insisted that Islam is a market movement not a political movement and called upon us to put an end to the practice of ex nihilo money and re-establish a real-value exchange system in place of the fantasy numbers system. The Shaykh had outlined in great detail the way of putting an end to capitalism and re-establishing Islam. He pointed out the way for moving away constructively from the capitalist modalities of currency, banking and taxation to free exchanges between men and groups.

The first six chapters of the book cover Shaykh Abdalqadir's political writings in relation to: governance as a Divine contract: the linkage between politics and trade in Islam; capitalism, banking and the modern state; the fall of the caliphate; the rise of ideology amongst Muslims; and atheistic capitalism – the dominant religion of our time. Shaykh Abdalqadir had argued that nihilism, suicide and terrorism are not political doctrines but the failure of politics. They indicate an endgame and after it must come a new beginning, a new manifestation of Islam that will end nihilism. Islam is ready, yet again, to emerge into the wider arena of civic revival. Part one of the book outlines the Islamic view on governance, how capitalism came to be dominant and what has become of Muslim society as a result of the fall of the caliphate. Capitalism in its neo-liberal form, with usurious banking as its motor force, has come to dominate the Muslim world just as it has done in the rest of the world.

In part two of the book we will look at the pillars of the ideology that sustains capitalism and hides the fraud, scam, theft and deception that it is. It focuses on politics, state capture, economics, scientific materialism, public relations, the nuclear family, education and media. These are stratagems that have been devised by capitalism to enable the oligarchy to keep people in a state of passive subservience.

Part three of the book is dedicated to the *mu'āmalāt* of trade and commerce as the means of Islamic revival. As Shaykh Abdalqadir says: "We insist – Islam is not a political movement, but it IS a market movement." The battles in the war against capitalism will be fought and won in the market place, both physical and virtual. Shaykh Abdalqadir brought to our attention that the current world crisis of society and environment is none other than the collapse of capitalism and its fundamental principle – usury. The *dīn* of Islam advocates the principle of justice in governance and economic justice and demands the movement and equitable distribution of wealth in the society. Justice was manifest within the workings of the institutions established by Islam. Chapter fifteen addresses these institutions, namely, the caliphate, the wazirate, the *kuttāb*, the *muḥtasib*s, the judiciary, the *sūq*, the mint, the *bayt al-māl*, the *awqāf* and the *aṣnāf* that enabled the Muslim community to function. An Islamic *dawla* cannot exist without these institutions and a polity was defined as Islamic precisely because of the existence of them within it, whilst they functioned within the parameters of the *sharī'a*. Part three of the book will include three chapters (16, 17 and 18) by Abdassamad Clarke providing an overview of trade and commerce in the Qur'ān, the *Sunna*, *Sīra* and of transactions, rather than comprehensive accounts of them. The essence of what he is saying is that *zakāt*, being an act of worship undertaken by means of wealth, transforms our understanding of wealth itself and thus of the nature of our transactions in the world. This understanding reverses the disastrous misconception that changes the distinction between *'ibādāt* and *mu'āmalāt*, that is, worship and social transactions, into a religious versus secular dichotomy licensing the entire apparatus of the modern state and its legislation.

بسم الله الرحمن الرحيم

# PART 1

In this part of the book we investigate Shaykh Abdalqadir's political writings under the following chapter headings: governance as a Divine contract; the linkage between politics and trade in Islam; capitalism, banking and the modern state; the fall of the caliphate; and the rise of ideology amongst Muslims. The opening statement quoted below was made by Shaykh Abdalqadir.

## Islam – Its New Beginning

"Here, on the authority of the Noble Qur'ān and the *Sunna* of the Messenger, sallalahu 'alayhi wa sallam, and the known *'amal* of the city state of Medina.

Let us make a summary position on the emergent force of world Islam. Based on his blessed life and practice, and founded on the witness of his chosen Sahaba or Companions at the core of the Medinan phenomenon, there must be recognised that the divinely ordained social template was sent down on mankind.

The arrival of a new world *dīn* was confirmed by the divinely chosen change of *qibla* from Jerusalem to Makka. The abrogation of Judaism and Christianity indicated the end of their social systems, that is, tribalism – the unified bonding of the DNA blood group, and capitalism – the unified bonding of the financial elite by blood.

In short, the survival of the first, by taking on the priesthood of money dealing and the second, by a leadership of empire from Rome, to Europe and to America.

What occurred with the great event of *asabiya* of the core elite around the Messenger was the historic end of the DNA based family held power. The Shī'a counter-movement had a doomed determinism of those who wanted to reduce Islam, the new social template, to the old bloodline order.

The new social template, Islam, is based on trade and currency exchanges within which no shadow of usury (interest in the exchange) is allowed. In Imām Mālik's terminology 'to a blade of grass.'

The new *dīn,* like its profession of loyalty to the *shahāda*, has two parts.

The first involves the worship exchange of *'ibāda* (*ṣalāt, zakāt, ṣawm* and *ḥajj*).

The second involves the business exchange of worldly wealth.

Two contracts – one with Allah and one between believing men.

The state, according to Islam, which in its nakedness is taxation and its controls, is abolished. The state is an instrument of power by control and its method is structural and by political instruments of force.

The Islamic template is not ruled by constitutions and protocols. It implies a prior free commitment of obedience to the natural order of existence. Men and women, choosing worship and equality in the exchange, in place of coercion. The liberty of a republic or empire is based on the slavery of the others. Islam replaces false liberty with obedience and submission to Allah, that is, finally accepting our humanity, mortality and brotherhood."[1]

# Chapter 1

## Governance is a Divine Contract

*Khilāfa* or caliphate is "an honour which Allah, the Lord of the Universe, had decreed, appointed and determined to mark the leadership of the great Muslim community."[2] The Arabic word *khalīfa* means successor, deputy, vicegerent, inheritor, and substitute. It is used as the title of the leader of the Muslims who is the *khalīfa rasūl Allah*, successor of the Messenger of Allah ﷺ and his office and reign is known as *khilāfa*. The domain of the caliph is both in the *mulk* (the physical world) and the *malakūt* (the domain of unseen forms). As Shaykh Abdalqadir says: "the *Dīn* [life-transaction/way of life] of Islam of its nature being a Divine matter, neither a political programme nor a personal one. Unless life is lived not only as a progressive path of action and learning but of spiritual illumination it cannot be understood as the *Ṣirāṭ al-Mustaqīm* [the Straight Path]."[3] Al-Mawardī also makes this point: "Imāmate (leadership) is prescribed to succeed prophethood as a means of protecting the *dīn* and of managing the affairs of the world."[4]

Allah in the Qur'ān lays down the laws with relation to governance. They are firstly, Allah is the Sovereign; He is the Creator of the world. Allah has made laws by which human societies can function harmoniously and in peace. These laws also enable humans to coexist with each other and their environment. Secondly, in His "absence" Allah has placed representatives (caliphs) on earth to rule mankind on His behalf and the Prophets were Allah's caliphs in the world. Thirdly, the aims of the caliphate are to preserve social order and assure the prosperity of Allah's subjects. Fourthly, it is obedience to Allah that leads to successful governance. Inspiration for behaviour is not utilitarian or based on metaphysical speculation. It is the existential aspect of actions that is important – actions are to be in obedience and submission to Allah. Fifthly, the legitimacy of a government is dependent on its execution of justice. Government has to accomplish justice, fairness, equity, fair-mindedness, rightness and correctness.

Sixthly, the motivating factor for maintaining justice is accountability to Allah on the Day of Reckoning. The Qur'ān addresses the two selves of the human being, the physical and the spiritual or soul (*rūḥ*). The soul survives the death of the physical body and will have to face the consequences of its earthly actions. This includes all actions, be they personal, social, economic or political. There is no secular zone in Islam. At the Reckoning actions will be weighed on the scales of justice set up by Allah and those whose good actions outweigh their bad actions will be rewarded in paradise. Those whose bad actions outweigh their good actions will be punished in hell. Seventhly, the consequences of deviating from governing by Allah's just laws are either the destruction of the society or the replacement of the government by another.

Eighthly, the perfect model for correct governance is the Prophet Muḥammad ﷺ the last of the Prophets. Ninthly, after his death, political leadership passed on to the Prophet's followers, those who had imbibed the Qur'ānic message and governed by its precepts. Islamic governance is nomocratic, that is, law governed, as opposed to theocratic, democratic, autocratic, oligarchic, or timocratic. Tenthly, in order to maintain the integrity of the polity peace has to be established within the society and its frontiers have to be protected by force of arms. Eleven, since governing, that is the exercise of political power, is primarily associated with the production, distribution and consumption of resources, the circulation of wealth is guaranteed by the *sharī'a* and is the rationale for the existence of governance itself. Islamic law promotes the circulation of wealth and inhibits its stagnation.

### The Miracle of Madīna

Shaykh Abdalqadir shows the way by which Islam can be revived again; "The quickest way both to see what went wrong and to put it right is to turn to Islam when it was paramount and powerful. Shah Waliullāh[5] said that, given the assault on Islam in his time, the only way to recovery lay in starting from basics; by that he indicated that he meant the first great formula of the Islamic social nexus in Madīna – the *Muwaṭṭa'* of Imām Mālik, may Allah honour his high place." Madīna was a nomocracy governed by the Prophet Muḥammad ﷺ in accordance with the Qur'ān. Shaykh Abdalqadir explains that: "Limits of human behaviour remain decreed by the revelation until the end of the human situation. ... Thus all *ijtihād*[6] and all analogical extension of these basic elements must derive from the basic Islamic model of Madīna, during its phase when it functioned as the primary model for the future of mankind. The Madīna of the Salafī[7] community was neither a primitive nor a formative society but a complete blueprint for Islamic societies from then on. It is clear that in Madīna at the time of the Salafī communities man was at his greatest and the social contract at its healthiest and most balanced."[8]

After his migration to Yathrib the Prophet ﷺ renamed the city Madīna al-Munawwara (the Illuminated City). It was here that he was able to fulfil the Qur'ānic call for him to be the perfect model[9] for human behaviour and his society to be the standard for mankind.[10] In their writings, the great philosophers – Plato (*Republic*), Aristotle (*Politics*) and al-Fārābī (*The Virtuous City*) – presented their ideas of the ideal state, but such states were never practically realised. The Prophet ﷺ, however, succeeded in creating his Madīna al-Munawwara and it set the standard for all Muslim civilisations till the early twentieth century. Many of the features that al-Fārābī (870-950) outlined had already been achieved in the Prophet's Madīna.[11] Madīna was not a state like the contemporaneous Persian and Roman states – it was a nomocratic society led by Allah's representative (caliph), the Prophet ﷺ.

It was another great philosopher and jurist, Ibn Rushd (1128-1198), whose writings on Islamic law highlighted the richness of Madīna al-Munawwara. Explaining the *maqāṣid* (primary goals) of the *sharīʿa* he said that "the legal *sunan* (practices) pertaining to conduct have as their purpose the virtues of the believer". The four categories of human virtue he mentions are: the merit of chastity, the merit of justice, the merit of courage, and the merit of generosity. He added that "all kinds of worship (*ʿibāda*) are like conditions for the fulfilments of these merits." Elaborating on the merit of justice and abstention from tyranny Ibn Rushd said: "These are the categories of *sunan* that require the maintenance of a balance in financial dealings, and the maintenance of a balance in personal relations (physical contact)." With regards to the merit of generosity and the avoidance of meanness (*bukhl*) he said: "*Zakāt* is included in this category from one aspect, and is included in the communal sharing of wealth from another; the same is the case with charity (*ṣadaqāt*)." Relating to the merit of courage he said: "There are *sunan* laid down for social life, which is the essential condition laid down for human life, and the preservation of its benefits relating to conduct and knowledge, which are called statehood. It is for this reason that these *sunan* should be upheld by the leaders and the upholders of the *dīn* [religion]."[12]

In the *Muwaṭṭa',* Imām Mālik provided a composite picture of life in Madīna including the judgments of the caliphs, governors and scholars up until the time of its compilation in the middle of the second century AH (Islamic dating). For Imām Mālik, the actions of human beings are the "text" and the *Muwaṭṭa'* is a book primarily about *'amal* (action). Prof. Yasin Dutton points out that this view "allows us a fundamentally different perspective on Islamic legal history where the true expression of the law is seen as being preserved not in a corpus of texts but in the actions, or *'amal,* of men." A similar assessment is made by Abdalhaqq Bewley who says that for the Madinans the Qur'ān and *Sunna*[13] were a matter of direct transmission. They had been conscientiously and scrupulously preserved and passed down as a lived reality through the two generations after the Prophet ﷺ and his Companions. Abdalhaqq Bewley further says, "The textual sources were, for them, sounding boards or yardsticks against which their ongoing practice should be measured to make sure that there was no deviation and the road remained clearly delineated."

Islamic governance was upheld by the Prophet ﷺ who, in passing legal judgments, controlled the social nexus in all its aspects. The Prophet ﷺ ruled over the city of Madīna, and later the territory of Islam (*dār al-Islām*), and initially performed the functions of caliph, *qāḍī* (judge) and *muḥtasib* (municipal governance, including that of the market) himself. He ﷺ appointed officials as *amīr*s (governors), *qāḍī*s and *muḥtasib*s as the territories under his control expanded. As Allah's caliph one of his functions was the establishment of the *arkān al-Islām* (the pillars that support the edifice of Muslim society)[14], that is, the *shahāda* (bearing witness that there is no god but Allah and that Muḥammad is the Messenger of Allah), *ṣalāt* (the five daily obligatory prayers), *zakāt* (obligatory wealth tax), *ṣawm* (the obligatory fast during the month of Ramadan), and *ḥajj* (the pilgrimage to Makka). The *arkān al-Islām* encompass the most important social, economic and political dimensions of *ad-dawla al-Islāmiyya* (the Islamic polity). The absence of these tenets indicates the annihilation of Islamic law and governance.

The central function of *ad-dawla al-Islāmiyya* was the movement of wealth to all sections of the community. This was made possible through the pillar of *zakāt* and the condition of *ḥalāl* trade associated with it. In order to facilitate for *ḥalāl* trade the Prophet ﷺ established a new market. Certain transactions and contracts, relating to trade and commerce, deemed to be monopolistic or speculative were discouraged by the Prophet ﷺ. The following were categorically prohibited: dishonesty, theft, looting, arson, highway robbery, depriving others of their inheritance, defrauding customers in relation to weights and measures, betraying trusts, hoarding commodities and withholding them from circulation, and female infanticide.

An important aspect of *zakāt* was that it had to be paid on commodities such as gold and silver with gold and silver themselves, on crops with some of the crops and on livestock with some of those livestock. Currencies when used had to be commodities with intrinsic values. Paper receipts, like today's paper, plastic and electronic currencies, were prohibited because their values are subject to manipulation through *ribā* (usury). Hoarding, and by extension banking, were condemned and strongly discouraged.

Gambling and *ribā* in any guise or form were prohibited. Certain transactions, such as *muzāra'a*, *qirāḍ/muḍāraba*, and *mushāraka*, were encouraged. The Prophet ﷺ is also known to have encouraged the development of fallow land, with landlords who did not develop their land being asked to give it up to benefit those who could.

Madīna was established as the primary model for the future generations of Muslims in particular and the future of mankind in general. It was a complete blueprint pattern for human societies. The Prophet ﷺ had set up the Madīnan state as a functioning model to be emulated by future generations. The introduction of institutional changes enabled the Prophet ﷺ to eradicate oligarchy, that is, political control by the wealthy merchants of Arabia. In the subsequent history of Muslim societies the prototypal institutions and practices established by the Prophet ﷺ underwent further development.

## Emergence of High Civilisation

Out of the Qur'ānic injunctions arose the greatest of all civilisations, guided by the caliphates. They were the Khulafā' ar-Rāshidūn (the Rightly-Guided Caliphs i.e. Abū Bakr, 'Umar, 'Uthmān and 'Alī), the Umayyads, the Abbasids, the Ottomans, the South Asian caliphates including the great Mughals, the Malay Sultanates, and the African and European caliphates. Wherever the Muslims went they took with them high civilisation. What comes to mind when we hear of Islamic civilisation is science and technology. Although science and technology do not define a civilisation, how they are adopted is a reflection of the values of that civilisation.

What enabled the Muslims to produce their high civilisation was the attitude that Islam had towards knowledge. Knowledge is intended to achieve one aim, that is, worship of Allah. Since Islam insists that theory and practice are inseparable it means that worship of Allah is realised through practical action. Knowledge then is for the purpose of behaviour/action. Knowledge of what Allah has commanded, what He has recommended and prohibited, is obligatory on all human beings. In addition to the spiritual, Islam guides humanity in social, economic and political matters as well. According to Muslim jurists there are four fundamental activities without which chaos would rule the world: (1) agriculture for raising food-stuffs; (2) weaving for manufacturing clothes; (3) architecture for erecting houses; and (4) politics for establishing human relationships and society and for promoting co-operation in the control of the means of living.

This religious view of Islam led to the greatest flowering of knowledge the world had ever seen. Calculating prayer times and the direction of the prayer required knowledge of mathematics and astronomy as do computation of the calendar for fasting and the pilgrimage. Travel for the pilgrimage requires knowledge of geography, transportation etc. The Islamic attitude towards knowledge allowed for the appropriation, not destruction, of the knowledge of the ancients, despite the differing world views between, for example, the Muslims and the Greeks. Appropriated knowledge was however filtered through a process of reasoning and experimentation. According to historians: "What we call science arose in Europe as a result of a new spirit of inquiry: of new methods of investigation, of the method of experiment, observation, and measurement, of the development of mathematics in a form unknown to the Greeks. That spirit and those methods were introduced into the European world by the Muslims."[15]

Muslims, it must be remembered, have access to epistemological sources other than rationalism and empiricism which became dominant in Europe in the modern period. Ibn Rushd demonstrated that the use of reason, i.e. rational thinking and philosophy, is not only permitted by the *sharī'a* of Islam but is obligatory – within legal limits. In his *Kitāb faṣl al-maqāl*[16] he begins his argument by pointing out that the Qur'ān calls upon people to observe and reflect upon the phenomena of the natural universe in order to recognise how Allah manifests His power in it. This reflection must be conducted through demonstrative reasoning and a preliminary study of logic is required in order to master the art of demonstrative reasoning. After logic one can proceed to philosophy and science. Reflecting on *Kitāb faṣl al-maqāl* one finds logic, reason, wisdom and revelation linked together.

Ibn Rushd argued in the twelfth century that there is harmony between philosophy and religion and that philosophy (reason and logic in particular) is a valuable instrument in the application of the law and social development. Implicit in that argument is the acknowledgement that religion and philosophy (and by extension science) are mutually exclusive but not antagonistic. Ibn Rushd saw religion and science as supplementing one another. Asadullah Yate says of Ibn Rushd: "The time has now come for the Muslims to recognise this important precursor of modern, scientific and technological society. Ibn Rushd's message is simple, both in his *Bidāya* and in the great philosophical work underlying the *Bidāya*, namely, *Kitāb faṣl al-maqāl fī mā bayn ash-sharī'ati wal-ḥikmati minal-ittiṣāl*, in which he delineates the principles underlying the relationship between the *dīn*, in its strictest sense, and knowledge in general. Knowledge, he demonstrates, is a divine gift and as such may be used by Muslims, even if its source lies outside *dār al-Islām*, as long as it is contained by the *sharī'a* and as long as worshipping man and woman remain at the centre of Muslim society. The tyranny of the techno-socio-projects fuelled by the fiscal and banking entities of so-called 'islamic" countries is inconceivable in Ibn Rushd's ground-plan. As we can see from his final, tremendous words of the *Bidāya*, all activity must remain within the scope of the balanced human being, must be humanly possible and comprehensible."[17]

It was with this attitude that Muslims approached and excelled in law, *'aqīda* (belief/theology), *ḥadīth*[18], education, medicine, economics, politics, architecture, philosophy, astronomy, mathematics, alchemy and chemistry, geography, historiography, psychology, art, music, literature, poetry, bookshops and libraries.

# Chapter 2

## The Linkage between Politics and Trade in Islam

Politics and trade are inextricably linked due to the fact that governing, that is the exercise of political power, is primarily associated with the production, distribution and consumption of resources. We will look at the ways in which this linkage has manifested itself in the Islamic polity called *ad-dawla al-Islāmiyya.* Shaykh Abdalqadir says that *ad-dawla al-Islāmiyya* "is based on the movement of wealth, the sharing of wealth, and spending it in the Way of Allah."[1] In Shaykh Abdalqadir's commentary on the following verses he says: "In these two astonishing *āyat*s the whole dynamic of the Islamic financial practice is laid out."[2] The verses he was referring to are:

*"Whatever booty from them Allah has given to His Messenger -*
*And you spurred on neither horse nor camel in its acquisition,*
*But Allah gives power to His Messengers*
*over anyone He wills,*
*Allah has power over all things -*

*Whatever booty Allah gives to His Messenger from city dwellers*
*belongs to Allah and to the Messenger*
*and to near relatives and orphans*
*and the very poor and travellers,*
*so that it does not become something*
*that merely revolves between the rich among you.*
*Whatever the Messenger gives you, you should accept*
*And whatever he forbids you, you should forgo.*
*Have taqwā of Allah – Allah is severe in retribution.*
(Q. 59: 6,7)

Shaykh Abdalqadir says that three practices can be derived from these verses: "Firstly, the necessary activating factor of the movement of wealth is the presence of the Messenger, may Allah bless him and grant him peace. By extension, this implies the Khalif, for he then stands in as a substitute for the Messenger, may Allah bless him and grant him peace, in authority. ... Secondly, it establishes the given that the Muslim polity has constant obligation to *jihād*. ... *Jihād* is to fight the *kuffār*[3] in the Way of Allah, following their rejection of the invitation to enter Islam, with the intention that they should submit and then hopefully accept. In Clausewitz's classical definition, war is politics continued by other means. The Islamic definition, free of such hypocrisy, declares that *jihād* is trade carried on by other means, and from it takes a wealth, the booty, but at the same time it gives a wealth when by its victory the defeated choose to enter Islam. Thirdly, the distribution of the *ghanam*, booty, is clearly the same in principle as the distribution of *zakāt*. This allows us to say that there is a tripartite activity within the Muslim community. One, there is the selling in markets and the spread of the caravans. Two, there is the welfare distribution of the annual *zakāt*. Three, there is the distribution of the *ghanam* as a last means of moving wealth among the people."[4]

As mentioned before the Islamic polity is called *ad-dawla al-Islāmiyya*. In the interests of brevity we will use the term *dawla*. The etymological root of the word *dawla* is *d-w-l* meaning to rotate, to take turns, to alternate, and to circulate. In the above verse (verse 7 of *sūra* 59) Allah uses the word with reference to wealth which should *"not become something that merely revolves (dūlatan) between the rich among you."* This verse highlights the economic significance of the root word *d-w-l*. The word *dūlatan* here refers to a commodity that changes hands among people. It also denotes: to have currency, be in circulation, and passed (from hand to hand). The word also appears in verse 140 of the third *sūra* of the Qur'ān, where Allah says: "*We deal out (nudāwilu) such days to people turn by turn.*" The political implications of *dawla* are expressed by the term *nudāwilu*. *Dawla* here means rotation, turn of fortune, and dynasty. In this verse and in subsequent Islamic political history *dawla* is taken to mean the divinely granted turn in power.

The word in this verse is used in the context of politics and the changing of dynasties. The word in the previous verse is used in the context of wealth and therefore economics. The verses when taken together relate to government and how to govern. Since governing, that is the exercise of political power, is primarily associated with the production, distribution and consumption of resources, the message from Allah is that wealth should *"not become something that merely revolves (dūlatan) between the rich among you."* "We can deduce from this that the Islamic polity ... short-circuits the impulse of men to create an oligarchy of wealth."[5] This injunction is intended to eradicate the oligarchy which was predominant in pre-Islamic Arabia, the Roman and the Persian Empires at the time of the Prophet Muḥammad ﷺ. As Ronald Syme said: "In all ages, whatever the form and name of government, be it monarchy, republic, democracy, an oligarchy lurks behind the façade."[6]

Shaykh Abdalqadir says that the Prophet ﷺ abolished the political state. It was his destiny to create a new model of governance in response to the then prevailing state models of the Arabs, Romans and Persians. "Though this may shock some people it must be remembered that the historical definition of the state derives from the Romans, and the term automatically implies an adjective, in other words the legal social structure called the state is itself the fiscal state. The *kāfir* model of organised society is based on taxation."[7] Contrary to this the *sharī'a* guarantees the circulation of wealth. Islamic law promotes the circulation of wealth and inhibits its stagnation. This is achieved through *zakāt*, *awqāf* (charitable institutions), guilds, commercial contracts and free markets. Amongst the measures mitigating against the stagnation of wealth the most important one is the prohibition of *ribā*.

Let us take a closer look at the tripartite activity within the Muslim community as outlined by Shaykh Abdalqadir: (1) the selling in markets and the spread of the caravans; (2) the welfare distribution of the annual *zakāt*; and (3) the distribution of the booty as a last means of moving wealth among the people. It was the political authorities that had to oversee all of these economic activities.

### (1) The selling in markets and the spread of the caravans

Makka was one of the centres in a vast trading network that spanned Africa, Europe and Asia. The Arabs had been traders long before the advent of Islam with one of their most important products being frankincense which was used as medicine and as a fumigant by the Ancient Egyptians, Jews, Romans and Chinese, amongst others. Thanks to the rainfall on the south coast of the Arabian Peninsula huge surpluses of frankincense, myrrh, grapes, wheat, spices, dyes, camels, cattle and sheep were produced. This in turn facilitated the manufacture of aromatics, perfumes, cloth, metal products, and leather goods. These surpluses were traded, overland via the caravan routes, with the Fertile Crescent and the Mediterranean region.

The Incense Road, as it was known, ran along the southern coast of the Arabian Peninsula westwards towards Yemen and then north to Jordan. From there it split with one route going north to Syria and the other west to Egypt. The Incense Road also carried products, such as gold, silk, gems and spices from India, Southeast Asia and China which landed at the port of Aden. Makka was an important stop for the trade caravans besides being the place of pilgrimage for tribes from all over the Peninsula. The trade and pilgrimage made the Incense Road one of the most coveted routes attracting the attention and machinations of the Assyrians, Greeks, Romans and Byzantines. This was the route taken by the Prophet ﷺ with his uncle Abū Ṭālib to Syria and then when he became a trader himself travelled it in the service of his wife Khadīja رضي الله عنها.

As mentioned before, the Prophet ﷺ renamed the city of Yathrib, after his migration to it, Madīna al-Munawwara. In order to establish freedom of trade the Prophet ﷺ founded a new market in Madīna. There were to be no fees levied in the market and it was to be tax-free. There was a dispute between the Prophet ﷺ and Kaʿb ibn al-Ashraf, the chief of the Jews, over the setting up of this market. Kister remarks that: "The clash with Kaʿb b. al-Ashraf seems to indicate that Kaʿb considered the establishment of the new market as competition to the existing one of the Banu Qaynuqa. The story of the market supplies us with an additional aspect of the contention between the Prophet and the Jews in Madīna."[8] It indicates that the opening of the new market was essential for the establishment of the new *dīn*.

Up until then the Jews of Madīna monopolised commerce, trade, industry, agriculture, knowledge and learning in the city.[9] The market of the Prophet ﷺ spelt the end of that dominance. It was clearly understood by the antagonists that the Islamic market was the most important instrument for political transformation of the society. As mentioned before the central function of *ad-dawla al-Islāmiyya* was the movement of wealth to all sections of the community. This was made possible through the pillar of *zakāt* and the condition of *ḥalāl* (permissible) trade associated with it. The new market of the Prophet ﷺ facilitated for *ḥalāl* trade where certain transactions and contracts, relating to trade and commerce, deemed to be monopolistic or speculative were prohibited.

*Expansion of Trade after the Prophet* ﷺ

Abū Bakr ؓ, the first caliph after the Prophet ﷺ, emphasised the *sharī'a*'s intention for the movement of wealth amongst the members of society when he declared war on the tribes who refused to pay *zakāt*.[10] It was 'Umar ibn al-Khaṭṭāb (r. 634-644) the second caliph who, due to the rapid expansion of the *dawla* in his time, initiated numerous administrative measures that related to financial matters. He had conquered Damascus in 635, Jerusalem in 637, Babylon in 641 and Alexandria in 642, and large parts of Syria, Persia, Egypt and North Africa came under his control. The administrative measures he introduced included: policing; the army; land surveying; regional development; appointment of judges in different cities; the *dīwāns* (registers to organise the pay of the fighting forces, public records and official bureau); *bayt al-māl* (the treasury); maritime transportation; department of amenities; civil engineering; *awqāf*; and taxation. 'Umar renovated buildings, built cities, dams, bridges and canals. It was 'Umar ؓ who defined the legal weights of the currency, i.e. the *dīnārs* and *dirhams*, and, according to Maqrīzī, 'Umar was the first to issue

Islamic coins in 18 Hijra (640). 'Uthmān ﷺ added Libya, Cyprus, Armenia, Azerbaijan, and Afghanistan to the territories he already ruled. Islam had also reached Abyssinia, East and Central Africa. 'Alī ﷺ added parts of Sistan to the caliphate and his navy went as far as Kohan, near Bombay in India in 38 A.H.

After the seventh century the Mediterranean became a 'Muslim Lake' and Western Europe was a tiny outcrop lying on the edge of a vast African and Asian economy. Islam also spread into Europe – Spain between 711 and 1492 and Sicily in 902. Eastwards Islam spread to India, Southeast Asia and China and southwards into sub-Saharan Africa, an expansion largely brought about by commercial influence. Naval ports on the shores of the Red and Arabian seas enabled trade with Africa and India. Muslim ships carrying cargo sailed down the East African coast as far as Sufalah in Mozambique and Madagascar. There was gold-mining in Ethiopia and Zimbabwe, and the Tanzanian city of Kilwa was the principal port facilitating the import, export, collection and distribution of goods. East African ports had commercial relations with Aden, Suhar and Siraf. This long-distance trade helped stimulate trade into the African hinterland, and West African hubs such as Sijilmassa (in Morocco) and Awdaghast enabled the interlinking of the eastern and western coasts in both the northern and sub-Saharan regions.

The Middle East has been described as the "Bridge of the World."[11] In the "Golden Age" of Islam (during the Abbasid caliphate) Baghdad stood as the key cross point where the most heavily travelled land and sea routes intersected. Iraq was described as situated near the centre of the world and the most prosperous country in the world. The Muslim Abbasid state was the greatest centre of science, arts and civilisation in the world during its time. That came to an end when the Mongols invaded most of the Abbasid caliphate, sacked

Baghdad and executed the caliph al-Musta'ṣim on 20 February 1258. Ibn Khaldūn noted that the Mongol invasion had destroyed the Abbasid economy.

### Protection of Trade Routes by the Political Authorities

What was previously called the Incense Road became known as the Silk Road and contained the busiest trade routes in the world. It was a network of Eurasian trade routes that spanned some 8000 kilometres from China in the east through Central Asia, present day Iran and Turkey to Portugal and Africa in the west. Active from the second century BCE till mid-fifteenth century it facilitated trade, political, cultural and religious ties between Asia, Europe and Africa.

The middle route began in Yemen, went up through the Arabian Peninsula to the Mediterranean coast of Syria/Palestine, crossed the Mesopotamian plain to Baghdad and then divided into a land and sea route. The land route continued across Persia to Transoxiana and then either south-eastward to India or eastward to Samarkand and then to China. The sea route linked Baghdad, the Abbasid capital, to the Persian Gulf, via the Tigris River, and this route fanned out through the Indian Ocean and into the South China Sea and the East China Sea passing the trading kingdoms of Oman, Siraf and Hormuz.

Whilst a significant proportion of that trade constituted agricultural products such as spices, manufactured goods were also central to it. It shows that methods of mobilising labour and organising work processes, within the various centres of the network, were advanced enough to produce surpluses for export over and above those required for local consumption. The wide varieties of merchant communities spoke Arabic, Greek, Latin and Mandarin Chinese. Whilst currencies were not the same (for example, silver was favoured in Europe, gold in the Middle East and copper in China) goods were transferred, prices were set, exchange rates were agreed upon, contracts were made, credit was available, records kept and agreements honoured.[12]

The southern route linked the Alexandria-Cairo-Red Sea complex with the Arabian Sea, the Indian Ocean, Southeast Asia and China. From the thirteenth to the sixteenth century Egypt controlled the major gateway to Asia setting the terms of trade for Europe. Egyptian power was enormous controlling 80% of all trade that passed to Asia. With the fall of Baghdad Cairo became a pivotal centre for global trade and Delhi became the centre of the Islamic world.

In the thirteenth century, the northern route through the Mongol Empire linked China, Central Asia, the Middle East and Europe into a continuous trading space. The so-called *Pax Mongolica* (peace and stability across the Mongol Empire) enabled long distance trade between China and Europe. This route began to decline towards the end of the fourteenth century, primarily due to the conquests of Timur when he ruled from 1370 to 1405. The unification of the Eurasian landmass under the imperial authority of the Mongol Empire provided conditions for commercial growth and the development of commercial relations in Europe that would later become a dominant feature of the modern capitalist world system.[13]

The Ottomans[14] crossed into Europe in 1354 and a century later Mehmed II conquered Constantinople bringing an end to the Byzantine Empire. During the period between 1453 and 1606 the Ottoman caliphate emerged as a world power and directly challenged Spain in the Western Mediterranean. They supported the emerging nations of north-west Europe whilst at the same time projecting their power in the Indian Ocean all the way to

Sumatra to aid the Muslims of the region against the Portuguese. For six centuries until World War 1 the Ottoman Caliphate was at the centre of intercontinental trade, stretching from the Balkans and the Black Sea through Anatolia, Syria, Mesopotamia, the gulf of Egypt and North Africa.

During the reign of Suleyman I, the Ottomans were the most powerful empire in the world. Suleyman's revenue was twice that of his rival Charles V of the House of Hapsburg, the Holy Roman Emperor. Whilst the Ottomans were regarded as an existential threat by the Hapsburg Empire and the Italian city-states, the backward parts of Europe, that is, England, the Netherlands and France received Ottoman support. During the Abbasid and Mongol periods of dominance, Europe had an interdependent commercial relationship with the rest of the world even though it was peripheral to world trade. The flourishing of commerce and the cultural renaissance that accompanied it in Europe were directly connected to the reestablishment of peaceful lines of communication and international trade that followed the consolidation and expansion of the Ottoman Empire.

The *Pax Ottomana* (peace and stability across the Ottoman Empire) lowered commercial protection and transaction costs, established uniform trading practices and increased the speed of trade. The Ottomans built roads and canals to facilitate inter-regional trade. Ottoman rule was crucial to safeguarding traders from piracy on the seas and banditry on land. *Pax Ottomana* linked trade between Russia and Central Asia with Europe via the Black Sea. It also linked the Levant and North Africa to the Indian Ocean where most of Euro-Asian trade was conducted. The Ottoman Caliphate was before a pivotal centre which connected the economies of Europe with those of Asia.

The engines of the economic boom in the 15$^{th}$ century, such as Venice, Marseilles and Ragusa depended on the Ottoman Caliphate for both luxury and bulk goods. In the course of the 16th century France, England and the Low Countries (Netherlands, Belgium, Luxembourg and French Flanders) relied on Ottoman raw materials. European imports, such as spices, silk, wheat, rice, cattle, timber, wool, mohair, cotton and hides from North Africa, the Middle East and Asia, were facilitated by the Ottomans. Trade and communication between the Ottomans and Europe assisted the transmission of social and technological knowledge into Europe and Ottoman traders introduced their business methods, such as their system of credit, *simsar* (brokerage) associations and partnerships into their transactions with Europeans.

### (2) THE WELFARE DISTRIBUTION OF THE ANNUAL *ZAKĀT*

The Prophet ﷺ said: "There is no right to a person's wealth other than *zakāt*." Abū'l Ḥasan al-Mawardī's comments that Muslims have no obligation to pay tax other than *zakāt* are noteworthy. He wrote: "Tax in Islam is known as *ṣadaqa* and *zakāt*, and the latter is the same as the former; the names are different but the issue is the same and the Muslim has no other obligation to pay tax than this tax on his wealth."[15] The effectiveness of *zakāt* is explained as follows: "No poor person would ever go hungry, lack clothing or be hard-pressed if the wealthy paid their *zakāt*, but it is admitted that there is no obligation more demanding than the payment of *zakāt*."[16]

Islamic law prohibits taxation on income but the following taxes on wealth are allowed: 1. *kharāj*, the tax on produce from lands not confiscated from the inhabitants of conquered or surrendered lands; 2. *ghanīma*, booty captured from the enemy; 3. *jizya*, the poll-tax taken from non-Muslims in the Muslim *dawla*; 4. *'ushr*, one tenth of the harvest of agricultural produce (one twentieth if the land has been irrigated by human endeavour); 5. properties with no known owner; 6. properties of apostates; 7. estates of deceased persons; 8. revenues from state lands; and 9. judicial fines. Revenue from these sources went into the *bayt al-māl* which is literally the 'house of wealth' institutionally developed to become the treasury of the Muslim *dawla*. The origin of this institution can be traced back to the time of the Prophet ﷺ when the revenues that came into it were distributed almost immediately. It maintained similar characteristics during the time of the first caliph Abū Bakr ؓ but developed into a complex institution in the time of the second caliph 'Umar ؓ when huge amounts of wealth were acquired by Muslims after Persia, Syria and Egypt were conquered by them.

The economic implications of *zakāt* are enormously significant. Firstly, not only does *zakāt* have to be paid but it also has to be paid on wealth that is earned in a *ḥalāl* way.[17] Secondly, the *zakāt* on held wealth has to be paid with gold and silver, which are of intrinsic value. The consequences of this stipulation are immensely profound with regards to fiat currencies, that is, currencies created through fractional reserve banking. Currencies have got to be commodities with intrinsic value. Thirdly, *zakāt* has to be assessed and taken by *zakāt*-collectors who are appointed by the *amīr* (leader of the Muslims).

With regards to the first condition, that *zakāt* has to be paid on wealth that is earned in a *ḥalāl* way, we have already outlined above in the establishment of the market and permissible transactions.

Let us briefly look at the second point that *zakāt* has to be paid with commodities which have intrinsic value. For Muslims not only is the production, distribution and exchange of goods and services governed by Islamic law but currencies as well. There is a vast corpus of literature dealing with currencies and money substitutes. After the caliphate/sultanate, al-Qurṭubī in his legal commentary of the Qur'ān, regarded the mint (and its minting of *dīnārs* and *dirhams*) as one of the seven most important institutions in Islam.[18] Ibn Khaldūn deals extensively with the minting of currencies in his *al-Muqaddima*. Referring to the *dīnār* and *dirham* he said: "The Revelation undertook to mention them and attached many judgments to them, for example, *zakāt*, marriage, and *ḥudūd*, etc.; therefore within the Revelation they have to have a reality and a specific measure for assessment [of *zakāt* etc.] upon which its judgments may be based rather than on the non-*shārīʿī* [*dīnārs* and *dirhams*] that have become common."[19]

The third condition, that *zakāt* has to be assessed and taken by *zakāt*-collectors, is of crucial importance to Muslim governance. Although all the obligatory duties of Islam are connected with the central authority, *zakāt* "cannot be divorced from active Muslim governance."[20] This is amply verified by the Qur'ān, the *Sunna*, and *fiqh* of the four Sunnī *madhāhib* (*madhhabs*). Abdalhaqq Bewley wrote that: "As long as the *Dār al-Islām* remained a unified political reality, *zakāt* retained the possibility of playing its integral role in the economic fabric of Muslim society. With the fall of the khalifate, however ... the dismemberment of the Muslim *umma* was completed and the *sharīʿa* lost its central position in Muslim society. One of the major casualties of this was the institution of *zakāt*."[21]

The *fiqh* of *zakāt* is clearly outlined by the *fuqahā* (jurists) but it is important to note that the recipients of *zakāt* are specified in the Qur'ān. "*Zakāt is for: the poor; the destitute; those who collect it; reconciling people's hearts; freeing slaves; those in debt; spending in the Way of Allah; and travellers. It is a legal obligation from Allah. Allah is All-Knowing, All-Wise.*"[22] No person would ever go hungry, be homeless, lack clothing or be destitute if the wealthy paid their *zakāt*. Shaykh Abdalqadir says that the abolition of the caliphate "had shattered the chain of command on which an Islamic society was founded – that is, a Leader in whose name the Jumu'a is celebrated, and by whom the fast and 'Eids are determined, and the *Zakāt* Collectors are appointed. Very quietly the Third Pillar of Islam was lowered to the ground, in its place came a voluntary personal gift. *Zakāt* was abolished. The abolition of *Zakāt* rent asunder the Qur'ānic Command which bonded *together Ṣalāt* and *Zakāt*. Look at the Divinely ordained sequence on which the *Dīn* is set up. Amīr – he commands the appointed Collectors to collect the *Zakāt* after assessing it. Collectors – they in turn must take from the Muslim they are taxing the gold and silver Dīnār and Dirham – a *Sunna* of *Nabawiyyat*. There can be no *Zakāt* on pieces of paper, themselves promissory notes. The restoration of the pillar of *Zakāt* must precede the re-adoption of the *Shari'at* of Islam. ... When the Muslims ... are led by the strongest among them, who in turn take public *Bāy'at* then take *Zakāt* from the community through Collectors – then at that point the usury epoch will fall to pieces, doomed by Allah, the end of an age. Islam will have re-awakened and ancient promises will have been fulfilled."[23]

### (3) THE DISTRIBUTION OF THE BOOTY AS A LAST MEANS OF MOVING WEALTH AMONG THE PEOPLE

Booty is property of non-Muslim enemies of the Muslim *dawla* appropriated by the Muslims during or after warfare. The goods taken by force during and after a battle are called *ghanīma*. *Ghanīma* includes property as well as enemy persons, such as captured women and children and prisoners of war. Three other terms need to be mentioned in relation to *ghanīma*, namely *fay'*, *'abd* and *jizya*. Property acquired without the use of force, such as the evacuation of the enemy from their land or by virtue of the terms of a peace treaty is called *fay'*. *'Abd* means slave. Captured women and children and prisoners of war are taken into slavery by the Muslims. *Jizya* is a poll tax levied on all non-Muslim adult males living under Muslim rule.

Modern people who regard these matters as belonging to our historical past have forgotten that the Muslims have been conquered by the non-Muslims, our lands have been colonised and looted (their way of extracting the *ghanīma*) and we are paying the *jizya* (through fractional reserve banking[24]). The most striking example of these phenomena is the colonisation the Mughal *dawla* by the British East India Company. At the height of Mughal power the Sultan Aurangzeb ruled over nearly 150 million people, almost a quarter of the world's population at the time. The Mughal *dawla* had ushered in the era of industrialisation and in the 17th century Mughal India was the world's largest economic and manufacturing power. By the 18th century they produced about 25% of the world's industrial output. Mughal manufactured goods and cash crops, such as wheat, rice and barley were sold all over the world. The key industries included textiles, shipbuilding and steel. Manufactured products included cotton textiles, yarn, thread, silk, jute products and metalware. Food products included sugar, oils, butter, spices and peppers.

A royal charter from Queen Elizabeth I on December 31, 1600, laid the foundation for the English East India Company as a joint stock company of London merchants. It had the monopoly for all trade from England to Asia and was permitted to carry bullion out of the country to finance its trade. The first ship of the company arrived at Surat in 1608. Sir Thomas Roe, an English emissary of King James I approached the Mughal Sultan Jahangir (1605-1627) for a *firman* (royal edict) in 1615 to establish a factory at Surat.

Granted this *firman*, the English started trade in India by the setting up of the first factory in Surat which was then followed by factories in Madras in 1639, Bombay in 1668, and Calcutta in 1690. In 1687 Bombay become the headquarters of the west coast after shifting from Surat. The three ports of Calcutta, Bombay, and Madras allowed the East India Company to have a monopoly over the trade routes in the Indian Ocean. The company started trade in cotton, silk, indigo, saltpeter and spices. In 1711, the company began commerce in tea and established itself in China and by the end of 1715 trading activities of the company expanded trade in the Persian Gulf, Southeast and East Asia.

By 1883 the Company had a private army of 260,000 which was twice the size of the British army and it gradually took over the Mughal *dawla* through threats, intimidation, bribery and outright war. The Company's rule over the Mughal *dawla* began in 1757 and lasted till 1858. Following the Indian Rebellion of 1857 the Government of India Act was passed in 1858 giving the British Crown direct control of the Indian subcontinent. Eminent Indian economist Utsa Patnaik estimates that Britain robbed India of $45 trillion between 1765 and 1938. It is also estimated that 1.8 billion Indians died due to deliberate deprivation under the British (1757-1947). The impact of British occupation of India continues today 71 years after Independence, with 4 million people dying avoidably due to deprivation each year in India.[25] Muslim servitude today is achieved by means of capitalism, banking and the modern state.[26]

Shaykh Abdalqadir says: "Now the rhetoric and position of the *kuffār* on the issue of slavery, loaded as it is with emotional and theatrical appeals to humanity and justice, is one of a set of values which this monstrously inhuman society uses to control the thinking and reason of its members while all the time claiming justice and reasonability. It must be clear to the Muslim that the so-called abolitionist position is a highly political stance. It should be recalled that the same men who were purportedly fighting for the freeing of all slaves were at the same time planning and executing the colonial policy which led to the complete disintegration of West Africa and northern Nigeria. Abolitionism was the arm of a militant Christianity which saw that slavery – and remember the *kāfir* slaving is not in any way comparable to the slavery of the Muslims who are under strict injunctions of the *shari'at* – on an individual level was anachronistic when the industrial society opened the way to a much more extensive and all controlling form of slavery, that of the technological society, that is the concentration camp, the gulag, and indeed, the work nexus of the machine society. In short, slavery was their humanism and they saw it as outmoded by the slave-society that was modern industrialism."[27]

This brings us to "the humane conditions of Islamic law" in the context of slavery. Shaykh Abdalqadir says that the Islamic "view of slavery is that it is part of the human condition, and what is at issue is that it be practised with compassion and with regards to the *Sunna* in right treatment and in dealing with the slaves and their rights in marriage and so on."[28] The teachings of the Qur'ān and *Sunna* appeal to people to show respect for slaves, to have the same meals as them, to provide them with clothing similar to their owners, to be moderate in the work assigned to them, not to punish them excessively if they go wrong, to forgive them seventy times a day. Freeing slaves is highly recommended as charity and expiation for missed fasts. Allah will free from hellfire a person who frees a slave. A man will receive a double reward in paradise for educating his slave girl, freeing her and marrying her.

Before leaving this discussion it is appropriate to note again that the Muslims have been conquered by the non-Muslims, our lands have been colonised and looted (their way of extracting the *ghanīma*) and are paying the *jizya* (through fractional reserve banking). The significance of *jizya*, the poll tax levied on all non-Muslim adult males living under Muslim rule, puts all these matters within their proper context. Abdalhaqq Bewley said *jizya* "puts everything in its right place, affirming the supremacy of Islam as the final Divine Revelation for all mankind but permitting the continued existence of previous religions in the subservient position which their supersedure[29] by Islam demands. The only way to order human society is in accordance with the extent to which people acknowledge their Creator and agree to live by the laws which He has prescribed for them which alone can ensure a justice and balance for the human race. Allah makes the position abundantly plain a few *āyat*s after his command to take *jizya* when He says, in conclusion to that particular passage: '*It is He Who sent His Messenger with guidance and the Dīn of Truth to exalt it over every other dīn, even though the idolaters hate it.*' (9: 33)"[30]

# Chapter 3

## Capitalism, Banking and the Modern State

In chapter one we looked at governance being a Divine Contract and in chapter two saw how economics and politics are linked in Islam. In this chapter we will study capitalism, banking and the modern state. This is a necessary step for understanding the fall of the caliphate in chapter four.

Capitalism is defined as an economic system that determines how goods and services are produced and traded. Its key features are that property is owned by individuals; goods and services are exchanged in a free market; and capital is invested in businesses to make a profit.[1] Capitalism is a system that came to dominate the world and transformed the way people lived and worked. In order to maximise their profits businesses sought out new and cheaper ways of manufacturing an ever increasing number of new products. In order to do this they promoted mechanisation and technological innovations claiming that capitalism generates material progress as a result of the pursuit of profit.[2]

Essential to the genesis of capitalism is the modern state. Pierson lists the stages of historical transition from traditional to modern state forms in Europe, the birthplace of capitalism, as: (a) traditional tribute-taking empires; (b) feudalism: systems of divided authority; (c) the polity of estates; (d) absolutist states; and (d) modern nation states.[3] He adds that the modern state is best understood by its political structures, institutions and practices. Of these the essential ones are: (1) monopoly and control over the means of violence; (2) territoriality; (3) sovereignty; (4) constitutionality; (5) impersonal power; (6) the public bureaucracy; (7) authority/legitimacy; (8) citizenship; and (9) taxation. Furthermore, a variety of features have been identified with the transition to modernity. The following is a list of features as identified, again by Pierson: industrialisation; demographic transition; commercialisation and commodification of economic relationships; rise of capitalism; social division of labour; rise of scientific modes of thought; transformation of conceptions of reality; transformation of modes of communication; urbanisation; and democratisation.

Industrial capitalism has transformed into finance capitalism, which makes wealth through fractional reserve banking, interest, debt leveraging and rent-extraction. It has to be noted that none of this wealth creation is created through new investments and employment. Explaining the connection between politics and economics in the modern period and how the power nexus moved from the political to the economic, Shaykh Abdalqadir says that: "... the primal model is to be found in the Napoleonic state. The event of the Revolution could not have been accomplished without the creation of the Assignats, the paper money printed by the Revolutionary State and devoid of collateral. One of the key institutions Napoleon founded was the Banque de France."[4]

The 19th century witnessed the emergence and evolution on the world stage of banking. The bankers took advantage of the great technological advances that were taking place around them and banks evolved from being usurious clearinghouses of currencies into powerful institutions of technological project investment. They acted as middlemen between governments and these technological projects. Governments gave privately owned Central Banks control over the money supply on the condition that they guaranteed government expenditure. Credit money or fiat money is the currency of modern states that is imposed on the populace by government regulation or law. There are two parties involved in the creation of the money supply: the government on one hand and the privately owned banking cartels known as Central Banks (called the Federal Reserve System in the US) on the other. Governments benefit from this arrangement because it allows them to create an unlimited amount of money out of nothing without having to burden the tax payer with direct taxes. The banking cartel benefits by being able to create a perpetual flow of unearned wealth in the form of interest on money made out of nothing.

At this point the power nexus of states moved from the political to the economic. The operational model of political economy became oligarchy with liberal democracy acting as the public relations interface for it. The national state and its institutions, both executive and judiciary, have no access to or control over the financial system. In order to receive a loan the recipient country must adhere to the political programs designed for them by the IMF and the World Bank, the financial oligarchs. Shaykh Abdalqadir explains that such a view as described above is not a conspiracy theory. Rather, oligarchy is a continuously existing historical fact. It was the same in pre-Islamic Arabia and it is no different in China where the world's biggest banks are owned by the Communist Party. Thanks to capitalism and globalisation the wealthiest 1% of people in the world today has more than double the wealth of 6.9 billion people combined.

The creation of money out of nothing is no secret and, just in case we have forgotten the statements made by the founder of the Bank of England, William Paterson in 1694, they issued another statement in 2014 stating that "most common assumptions of how banking works are simply wrong." The statement continues to say: "In other words, everything we know is not just wrong – it's backwards. When banks make loans, they create money. This is because money is really just an IOU."[5] The US dollar has become, *de facto*, the world's reserve currency because it is underwritten by oil which is the most important source of energy for all industrial societies. The price of oil is denominated in dollars.[6]

The history and foundations of the modern state are inextricably linked to modern currencies. As stated before, the prototype for the modern state and its money system is the French Revolution and the Napoleonic state.[7] No comprehension of modern money and the modern state is possible without understanding the interconnection between politics and economics and these events (the French Revolution and the establishment of the Napoleonic state) best illustrate this connection. The three stages in the evolution of paper money, as outlined by Umar Vadillo[8], were clearly manifest during the French Revolution. They are: "(1) A promissory note backed by gold or silver; (2) A process of unilateral devaluation leading to a complete revocation of the contractual agreement; (3) A piece of paper not backed by any specie, whose legal value is determined by the compulsion of the State Law."

With regards to Vadillo's first point, using the French Republic as the model, we see that paper money and public banking were necessitated by the financial crisis experienced by the state[9].

The purpose of issuing paper assignats in large and small notes was that they "would give the treasury something to pay out immediately, and relieve the national necessities; that having been put into circulation, this paper money would stimulate business; that it would give to all capitalists, large or small, the means for buying from the nation the ecclesiastical real estate,[10] and from the proceeds of this real estate, the nation would pay its debts and also obtain new funds for new necessities ... ."[11] These assignats although not backed by gold or silver but by land[12] formerly owned by the Church) "would soon be considered better than the coin now hoarded, and will bring it out again into circulation."[13]

In April 1790 the revolutionary government of France issued four hundred million *livres* in paper money – the assignats using the confiscated property of the Church as security. White says that: "No irredeemable currency has ever claimed a more scientific and practical guarantee for its goodness and for its proper action on public finances. On the one hand, it had what the world recognised as a most practical security – a mortgage on productive real estate of vastly greater value than the issue. On the other hand, as the notes bore interest, there seemed cogent reason for their being withdrawn from circulation whenever they became redundant."[14]

With regards to Vadillo's second point (that of devaluation) the French government continued to issue paper money year after year and then month after month. This was due to the fact that within five months of the first issue the government had spent all the money and was in difficulties again. The effects of these issues were inflation, depreciation and economic ruin.[15]

The third point raised by Vadillo was that the legal value of paper money "is determined by the compulsion of the State Law." The full force of the law was used to ensure that the assignats were a success. Anyone who sold the assignats for less than their nominal value would be imprisoned in chains for twenty years and those making investments in foreign countries would face the death sentence. The Reign of Terror of the French Revolution extended into trade and commerce.[16]

This attempt at public banking was a complete failure and the government destroyed the machinery for printing assignats on February 18, 1796. The engraving apparatus for the mandats (a new currency issued to rescue the government) was destroyed in accordance with the decrees and orders of February 4 and 14, 1797. The riots in Paris in April and May 1795 opened the way for the rise of Napoleon. Having witnessed the failure of public banking – that is the issuing of paper money (the assignats and mandats) by the government – Napoleon decided that the control of money supply by private banking was better for financial stability. He established La Banque de France (the Bank of France) in 1800.[17]

Central or reserve banking, the foundation upon which the modern state is built, was entirely paper based before the appearance of plastic and electronic currencies. Public and private banking, based on paper money issued during the French Revolution, illuminate the processes generally involved in banking both past and contemporary. The system of banking that existed during the French Revolution is the same as today's global banking system under which all countries function including the USA[18]. The three stages in the evolution of fiat currencies as outlined by Vadillo, clearly manifested during the French Revolution, are visible everywhere today, including the Islamic states.

This process of creating the money supply through fractional reserve banking is, in Islamic legal terminology, usurious, that is, it involves *ribā*. In this process the countervalue of the currency in circulation is not equivalent to the value of collateral held by the banks. Since the political and social realities of the modern state are subsumed under economics, and the financial system is dependent on the medium of exchange, i.e. the currency, then if the currency is illegitimate the model of the modern state is also unlawful and therefore not viable.

The modern state is based on income tax and banking. Fractional reserve banking, that is, the printing of money with no backing of real wealth, creates inflation which is a hidden tax. These two elements together allow for wealth to be concentrated in the hands of oligarchic elites. Banking and *ribā* are precisely what Allah has prohibited in the Qur'ān. The paper money created in this way is technically a promissory note, a promise to pay a debt, and once again this practice is prohibited by Islamic law, which stipulates that a debt cannot be paid by a debt. As such the money supply is, in Islamic terms, fraudulent (fractional reserve banking), *ribā* (usury/unjustified increase) and theft (fiat money inflates prices for everyone and is stealing from future generations). With regards to the printing of paper money Shaykh Abdalqadir states that the process involves two elements that are prohibited by the *sharī'a*[19] – the issuing of receipts over and above the deposits held and the lending of those receipts on interest. Both of these practices constitute unjustified increase, that is, *ribā*.

Different opinions about the relationship of the state to the economy have "helped to define what is probably the single most important cleavage in the political opinion of the past two hundred years. On one side there have been those, now best represented by the neo-liberals, who have argued for a minimal state and the greatest possible autonomy for an economy founded upon the private ownership of economic resources. ... On the other side have been those 'traditional' socialists (not all of them Marxists) who have seen private ownership in a market economy not as a solution, but as the core problem which the state has a duty to address."[20] What has been glossed over by the majority of political theorists is the fact that there is something more fundamental than these two positions.

Currencies are the life-blood of economies. Currencies are essential to economic activity and without them economies could not function. With regards to the economy the currency that is used in trade and commerce is of paramount importance. The legitimacy and integrity of currencies form the basis of economies and take precedence over the question of whether the means of production, distribution and exchange are owned privately or by the state. Both camps (rightist and leftist) of the debate do not give this issue the weight it deserves. The political and social realities of the modern state are subsumed under economics and the financial system is dependent on the medium of exchange i.e. the currency.

The currencies of Islamic states in general, and the oil producing states such as Saudi Arabia in particular, are linked to the US dollar.[21] As stated before, these currencies, that is, the money supply, are fraud, *ribā* and theft. Again, as stated before, the printing of paper money involves the issuing of receipts over and above the deposits held and the lending of those receipts at interest. Both of these practices constitute *ribā*. *Ribā* is condemned in the strongest terms. The insidious nature of *ribā* is graphically illustrated in the Qur'ān. "*You who have belief! have fearful awareness of Allah and forgo any remaining ribā if you are believers. If you do not, know that it means war from Allah and His Messenger (ḥarbin minallāhi wa rasūlihi). But if you repent you may have your capital, without wronging and without being wronged.*" (Q. 2: 277-8) People who do not abandon *ribā* are threatened with war from Allah and His Messenger ﷺ (*ḥarbin minallāhi wa rasūlihi*). The legal implications of this verse are that practising usury and making use of it are major wrong actions in Islam.[22] Those who take it, those who pay it, its scribes and its witnesses are all regarded as guilty, and it is the leader of the Muslims who is responsible for ensuring that they are punished.

In order to prevent *ribā* entering into the currency itself the Prophet ﷺ used gold *dīnār*s and silver *dirhams*. The consequences of the practice of *ribā* are immensely profound with regards to fiat currencies, that is, those created through fractional reserve banking and imposed on us by government legislation. Currencies must be commodities with intrinsic value. The issuing of receipts (paper money) through fractional reserve banking is usurious (based on unjustified increase) and the exchange of unequal amounts of gold and silver is also a manifestation of *ribā*. The *dīnār* (gold) and *dirham* (silver) currency demanded by Islam are fundamental in preserving stable currencies that fluctuate in value but are not subject to inflation. Islamic *dīnār*s and *dirham*s are not subject to inflation because they cannot be substituted by inflated credit money, credit money being not valid in Islamic law.

# Chapter 4

## The Fall of the Caliphate

The exploration of new sea routes and the "discovery" of the Americas in the $15^{th}$ century enriched the opponents of the Ottomans (1299-1924) and made it difficult for them to challenge the European powers. The flow of cheap American silver through Europe into the Ottoman domain contributed to financial turmoil, particularly since the Ottomans used silver for their coinage. The industrial revolution strengthened Europe financially and technologically and the Ottomans could not match them in the fields of armaments and weaponry. As a result tools, weapons, naval and military technology and know-how were imported by the Ottomans from Europe. The invention of the steam engine, for example, in the eighteenth century, profoundly changed transportation. Adoption of modern transport technologies, for both land and sea, meant increased foreign involvement in the Ottoman economy. Modern transport technologies involved foreign enterprises capitalised in Europe and built by Western engineers. Government borrowing on domestic and international markets was from financiers who charged interest on the loans. The Ottoman foreign debt reached phenomenal levels leading to the establishment of the Ottoman Public Debt Administration (OPDA) in 1881. As a result of which some of the major sources of revenue of the state were handed over to the OPDA and consequently Ottoman finances fell under almost total European control.

From the 16th century onwards there grew up in Europe a new world economy which was able to consolidate itself and develop the capitalist mode of production and the inter-state system which was the structural correlate of that world economy. As this capitalist world economy expanded it incorporated the Ottoman Caliphate and by the 20th century it had incorporated the entire planet. Incorporation meant the establishment of links between the production processes of the Ottoman Caliphate with Europe, which was the locus of production and consumption. It also meant the integration of the political structures of the Ottoman Empire into the interstate network of the world system. Once established, these links irrevocably bound the Ottoman caliphate into the capitalist world economy and as a result it ceased to exist as an independent unit.[1]

This process, by which the Ottoman Empire was reduced from being, for centuries, the greatest superpower in the world[2] into being the "Sick Man of Europe", was achieved through economic and financial control. Pamuk succinctly remarked: "The development of European financial control of the Ottoman Empire into one of the most striking forms of imperialist penetration short of *de jure* colonialism, and the abundance of primary source materials as a result of that control have helped turn this subject into one of the most studied aspects of recent Ottoman History."[3] The instruments of European economic control were banking and interest-based financing. As Shaykh Abdalqadir points out: "Clearly the Khalifate fell not to an enemy sword and not to a historical depassement[4] by a higher civilisation. It fell to an unsurpassable, mathematically unmeetable usury-debt, whose interest payments alone prevented achieving release from the capital sums of original endebtment. Loans to pay interest on debts – these alone might have failed to destroy this greatest of civilisations – but for the inescapable deception: that the technical project came bonded and liased to interest debt mechanisms and institutions which made two phenomena seem one."[5] Importation of Western technology was attached to financing which inevitably led to debt and bankruptcy.

The actions of thc Ottomans reveal their lack of understanding of *ribā* and its profound consequences. Shaykh Abdalqadir describes this phenomenon as the: "inexperience of the Osmanlı in dealing with the modalities of usury finance and its instruments".[6] The Ottoman scholar Birgevi Mehmed Effendi (d. 1573) noted: "most of the *waqf* administrators are ignorant and don't recognise pictures of usury in the Book".[7] The non-*shārīʿī* (to use Ibn Khaldūn's term) currencies of the modern state are based on (a) *ribā* (b) debt and (c) imposed by government fiat. As such they violate Islamic law. Due to the importance of this issue let us very briefly review the legal arguments for each of these categories:

(a) Money supply is created through fractional reserve banking. More money is issued than the actual reserves that are held. This "unjustified increase"[8] and "unjustified increment"[9] is clearly defined as the prohibited practice of *ribā*.

(b) Paper money is a promissory note or a debt to be discharged by the one who issued it, in this case the bank. To use paper money as a medium of exchange involves the transfer of debt between individuals. When debts are transferred Islamic law requires that the first contract be liquidated and another private contract be created. A promissory note, therefore, cannot be used a money.[10]

(c) Islamic law does not permit any currency to be imposed on people as the medium of exchange. Governments in modern states have laws of legal tender giving the banks a monopoly for issuing money. These laws at the same time restrict the use of other forms of payment. In Islam, on the other hand, all merchandise can be used as money.[11]

The demise of the Ottoman caliphate in many respects resembles the pattern by which monarchy was eliminated during the French Revolution and was supplanted by liberal democracy, constitutionalism, capitalism, paper money, and banking. This process came into sharp focus from 1839 onwards. The period between 1839 and 1878 became known as the *Tanzimat* (era of modern reform).

In the preceding century the Ottoman caliphate had been in decline when compared to the Western European states, particularly its immediate neighbours the Austrian and Russian empires. With the aim of preserving the caliphate and strengthening it the Ottoman's first response was to improve the armed forces. Efforts were also made to strengthen the central government and to increase control over the outlying provinces. The Porte (the central authority of the Ottomans) initiated representative government by establishing government councils, even including members of the non-Muslim minorities in some of them. Bureaucracy was considerably expanded and government functions normally restricted to the administration of justice, collection of taxes and maintenance of the armed forces were expanded to include matters such as education that had traditionally been in private hands. "Almost all the reforms involved a greater or less degree of Westernisation. At times, specific Western models were adopted or adapted. French institutions supplied the usual examples, except for army and navy. The French language became more widespread in the empire, especially among the leading reformers. Westernisation inevitably implied secularisation. Particularly in law and education, secular institutions developed that paralleled Muslim institutions. This dualism was matched by another – the increasing tendency for the Porte to treat all the sultan's subjects simply as individuals, while at the same time preserving the corporate organisation of the non-Muslim *millets* [religious groupings], from which individuals traditionally derived their own identity."[12]

Umar Vadillo points out that the *Tanzimat* entailed a number of measures and laws "consisting mainly of a process often called 'westernisation', but in fact explained more accurately by a different name: 'state-isation'; the transformation of government into state – always accompanied the transformation of trade into usury. The Europeans had evolved this hybrid institution called the state. The state was the amalgamation of government and banking. The institution of government had been finally captured by the extraordinary power of banking, banking being an evolved form of usury that included the lending at interest, not of money, but of substitutes of money. ... Nobody was able to ignore this new power, and those who did were punished. And nobody was able to find a way around it. Not even the Muslims."[13]

Three documents defined the *Tanzimat*: (1) the *Hatti-Sherif Gulkhane* of 1839; (2) the *Humayun* of 1856; and (3) the constitution of 1876. The authorisation of paper money came from the *Hatti-Sherif Gulkhane.* This movement for reform led to the formulation of the constitution of 1876, which anticipated the parliamentary regime that came into force in 1908. The installation of a parliament and the emergence of the Committee of Union and Progress eventually led to, what is commonly called, the abolishment of the sultanate and the caliphate.[14]

The sultanate and the caliphate have been decreed by Allah and cannot be abolished. We are now in an interregnum.

Shaykh Abdalqadir says that the "return of the Khalifate is inevitable."[15] Caliphate has been decreed by Allah in the Qur'ān, and

Shaykh Abdalqadir says that caliphate is "an honour which Allah, the Lord of the Universe, had decreed, appointed and determined to mark the leadership of the great Muslim community."[16] It belongs to the *fiṭra* of the human being, it is part of one's natural predisposition. *"It is Allah Who made the earth a stable home for you and the sky a dome, and formed you, giving you the best of forms, and provided you with good and wholesome things. That is Allah, your Lord. Blessed be Allah, the Lord of the worlds."*[17] Shaykh Abdalqadir explains that *"the best of forms"* means that human beings are imbued with *fiṭra* which is defined as an inborn natural[18] predisposition which cannot change and which exists at birth in all human beings.

The destinies of all things in the universe, including human beings, are predetermined by their life-form. Allah has said *"I am putting a caliph on the earth."*[19] Shaykh Uthman dan Fodio outlined the *fiqh* of caliphate under the heading 'Clarification of the fact that the Muslims are not permitted to remain leaderless without giving allegiance to an *amīr*': "I say, and success is by Allah, that it is an obligation for every Muslim to give allegiance to the Amīr of the Believers, if he exists. Muḥammad ibn 'Abdu'l-Karīm al-Maghīlī said in the *Answers* he gave to the questions of the Askia[20] that it is not *ḥalāl* for a group of Muslims to remain leaderless. Allah says, *"Hold fast to the rope of Allah, all together, and do not split up."* In the *Ṣaḥīḥ* of Muslim, Ibn 'Umar said that the Messenger of Allah, may Allah bless him and grant him peace, said, "Whoever withholds obedience will have no excuse when he meets Allah on the Day of Rising. Whoever dies without having given allegiance dies the death of the Days of Ignorance."[21]

One of the greatest of all Ottoman caliphs Sultan Abulhamid II was deposed on April 27, 1909 after ruling for 33 years.[22] He was put under house arrest in Selanik (Thessaloniki) but brought to Istanbul in 1912 where he lived at the Beglerbegi Palace until his death on February 10, 1918. Sultan Abdulhamid had sensed that the nature of his people had been transformed by modernism and foresaw that the office of *Sulṭāniyya* and *Khilāfa* "shall both cease to be of any importance. It seems to me as if I will be the Last Khalif."[23] Indeed, the two caliphs who came after him were both without power.

Externally, he had to contend with Germany, Austria, Russia, France, Italy and Britain. The foreign policy of the Sultan "consisted of causing rivalry among the Western nations in matters pertaining to himself, of having the Western powers contradict themselves and quarrel with each other, and then seizing hold of them by the weak points of their domestic and foreign affairs in order to bring about their failure."[24] He was able to achieve this through having a thorough understanding of the West and looking at it with the eye of someone who considered himself superior to it.

His domestic politics has been summarised as follows: "To clean the country of the viruses which always appeared claiming to cure and heal. To establish a material civilisation built on a sound spiritual base. To assimilate the West along with its positive sciences while avoiding the evil effects of its spiritual influence; to stay true to the character and dignity of the East while carefully protecting its traditional origins. To awaken in the body of the Devlet[25] and government a spirit which would have as its main consideration moral, economic and social superiority. To see all perfection and the means to perfection as residing in the *Dīn*, to recover true passion and love for the *Dīn* after its centuries-old degeneration. And to reinstate these as the overriding impulses of life, both at the individual and social level."[26]

Sultan Abdulhamid's achievements were many but in the interests of brevity let us mention two of them. Firstly, he reduced the National Debt, which he inherited, to one tenth from 300 million

Lira to 30 million. Secondly and this is his greatest achievement, he saved his people from the bloodbath that comes with revolutions. When the forces of insurrection, the Hareket Army entered Istanbul to dethrone the caliph, Sultan Abdulhamid ordered the forces under his command not to open fire under any circumstances and not to cause any bloodshed. Why was there an insurrection against such an extraordinary leader? His biographer Ustad Necip Fazıl provided the answer as follows: "So what is the truth about this incomprehensible aversion to him, and from which source did it come? The answer is simple. He was, of the thirty-four Osmanli Padishas[27] including himself, the most religious and the one whose Islam manifested as a wholesome, complete worldview; and each and everything during his period had been aligned with Islam. This is the reason why the Jews, masons, Young Turks, admirers of the West and agents of imperialism – the treacherous Turks, the typical Jews and the wicked people from among the Europeans – surrounded him hand-in-hand in a circle of enmity."[28]

How did these subversive forces bring about his downfall? Shaykh Abdalqadir says: "The Osmaniya was not defeated and destroyed by war. It was infiltrated and eroded over 150 years with a quite new and dazzling deception. Thinking that it was somehow winning for itself 'modernity' – that is, technique – it signed away its wealth. It agreed to pay the price. The price was a whole civilisation, built on superior, truer lines."[29] Technique is an all-encompassing system, including politics, economics, scientific materialism, technology, statism, public relations, the nuclear family, education and media. We will investigate all of these in the second part of this book but for our immediate purposes let us take a closer look at technology. Technology is a key part of the system of technique and was the "Trojan horse" that brought down the Ottoman caliphate. Shaykh Abdalqadir says that the "other side of the underneath of technology" is "dirty money."[30] We previously quoted the following lines from Shaykh Abdalqadir: "Loans to pay interest on debts – these alone might have failed to destroy this greatest of civilisations – but for the inescapable deception: that the technical project came bonded and liased to interest debt mechanisms and institutions which made two phenomena seem one."[31] The money that was borrowed is "dirty money," that is, money that is *ḥarām* (prohibited).

What Shaykh Abdalqadir is referring to is fiat money, which is the currency of modern states that is imposed on the populace by government regulation or law. As mentioned before there are two parties involved in the creation of the currency, the government on one hand and the privately owned banking cartels known as Central Banks (called the Federal Reserve System in the US) on the other. Governments benefit from this arrangement because it allows them to create an unlimited amount of money out of nothing without having to burden the tax payer with direct taxes. The banking cartel benefits by being able to create a perpetual flow of unearned wealth in the form of interest on money made out of nothing. As such the money supply is fraudulent (fractional reserve banking), *ribā* (usury/unjustified increase) and theft (fiat money inflates prices for everyone and is stealing from future generations).

With regards to the printing of paper money Shaykh Abdalqadir states that the process involves two elements that are prohibited by the *sharī'a* – the issuing of receipts over and above the deposits held and the lending of those receipts at interest. Both of these practices constitute unjustified increase, that is, *ribā*. The paper money created in this way is technically a promissory note, a promise to pay a debt and once again this practice is prohibited by Islamic law, which stipulates that a debt cannot be repaid with a debt.

Coming back to the financiers to the Ottomans and their dirty money, the bankers took advantage of the great technological advances that were taking place around them and banks became powerful institutions of technological project investment. They acted as middlemen between governments and these technological projects. Shaykh Abdalqadir explains that at the beginning of the story there was Moses Hirsch and his son Jacob. Jacob's son Joel created one of the first mortgage banks in 1835 with the Rothschilds as majority shareholders. Joel's brother Joseph was appointed court banker to Ludwig I in Munich. One of Joseph's sons Maurice de Hirsch was apprenticed to the banking house of Bischoffsheim and Goldschmidt. In 1868 Hirsch got the concession for the East Hungarian Railway in association with the Anglo-Austrian Bank. Hirsch thereafter instigated the Orient Railway project to link Vienna with Istanbul, a distance of 1000 miles.

For this project to be feasible there had to be unification of not only the rail gauge but also, more importantly, the financial system. Hirsch was granted the Orient Railway concession by an Imperial Firman on October 7, 1868. It was to run from Istanbul to Edirne, Plovdiv, Sofia, then through Serbia and Sarajevo and onto the Austrian Sudbahn (Southern Railway). "Over the 19th century up until the 1873 Depression, the Porte had been encouraged to borrow in order to cover interest payments and deficit. By 1875 Mahmut was forced to declare a moratorium on the Porte's £200 million debt."[32] The Western Powers then declared Turkey bankrupt and appointed an International Commission to represent foreign bondholders. Shaykh Abdalqadir's book *The Return of the Khalifate*[33] describes the machinations of the bankers in the Ottoman *dawla* at the end of the 19th century.

To summarise these developments Shaykh Abdalqadir says: "The continuing intrigues – I do not suggest conspiracy merely that continuing series of protocols and contracts around the building of the railroad – involved the Sultan, Grand Wazir Ali Pasha then Grand Wazir Mahmud Nedim Pasha and Ralph Anstruther Earle of the East Hungarian Railway. The technical projects of modernity, far from being concrete, physical modules, rationally executed, were simply the licences for the movement of non-national, non-specie, abstract numbers encoded in so-called currencies onto paper documents called stocks and bonds."[34] As a consequence: "The price of reducing a seven day journey from Vienna to Istanbul to a forty hour one was to lead to the inevitable destruction of the Islamic Khalifate."[35]

By the time Sultan Abdulhamid II, who ruled from 31 August 1876 to 27 April 1909, came to power, the Ottoman *dawla* "had reached a state of utter helplessness after having lost all its power."[36] Shaykh Abdalqadir in his book on the Ottoman caliphate outlined the series of events that culminated in the dethronement of Sultan Abdulhamid. The three regions of the Ottoman *dawla* in which these events transpired were (1) the Arabian Peninsula (2) Egypt and (3) the Anatolian and Salonikan regions of the Ottoman *dawla*.

### (1) The Arabian Peninsula

The main Islamic lands, including parts of present day Saudi Arabia, came under Ottoman control in the sixteenth century. Ottoman authority was established in the Hijaz province, including the cities of Makka and Madīna, and extended along the Red Sea coast down to Yemen in 1517. Ḥasā province voluntarily submitted to the Ottomans in 1550 but the interior province of Najd never did come under Ottoman control. In the absence of an official Ottoman presence the towns and oases of Najd were ruled by local *amīr*s and the Bedouin tribal confederations maintained their independence and autonomy. Muḥammad ibn Sa'ūd (r. 1742-1765), a member of the

Sa'ūdī clan, was the *amīr* of Dir'iyyah, a "small settlement in Najd with a mixed population of farmers, merchants, artisans, minor *'ulamā* and slaves."[37] Najd produced very little surplus of dates and livestock and its merchants travelled to distant places like Basra and India to supplement their income.

Strategically, the destiny of the Sa'ūd dynasty changed with their adoption of the Wahhabi doctrine of the religious reformer Muḥammad ibn 'Abd al-Wahhāb (1703-1792). On arriving in Dir'iyyah in 1744 he formed an alliance with the local *amīr*, Muḥammad ibn Sa'ūd. "According to this arrangement, Ibn 'Abd al-Wahhāb was responsible for religious matters and Muḥammad ibn Sa'ūd was in charge of political and military issues."[38] This alliance resulted in the expansion of the Wahhabi doctrine and the establishment of the Sa'ūd dynasty in much of the Arabian Peninsula. The Kingdom of Sa'udi Arabia, formed in 1932, is the last in a series of three Sa'udi states. The first existed between 1744 and 1818 and the second lasted from 1824 to 1891.

It was through the military conquests of Muḥammad ibn Sa'ūd's son, 'Abd al-'Azīz (1765-1803), that Riyadh, Kharj and Qasīm fell to the Sa'ūdīs in 1792. Al-Ahsa, Qatar and Bahrain followed. Overcoming the robust opposition of the Sharīf of Makka, Sa'ūd ibn 'Abd al-'Azīz (1803-1814) gained control of Ṭā'if in 1802, Makka in 1803 and Madīna in 1804. In the north-east the Sa'ūdī expansion reached Mesopotamia and in 1802 the city of Karbala was sacked. In revenge for the treatment of the Shī'a in Iraq the Sa'ūdī leader 'Abd al-'Azīz was assassinated in 1803. He was succeeded by his son Sa'ūd ibn 'Abd al-'Azīz. The Ottoman Sultan dispatched his viceroy in Egypt Muḥammad 'Alī to regain control of the Sa'ūdī territories. The death of Sa'ūd meant that his son 'Abdullāh had to tackle the forces of the Sultan. It was Muḥammad 'Alī's son, Ibrahim Pasha, who finally took control of Madīna in 1812, then Makka and Ṭā'if in 1813. The sacking of Dir'iyyah in 1818 brought to an end the first Sa'udi state and the Sa'ūdī leader 'Abdullāh ibn Sa'ūd was sent to Istanbul where he was executed.

When the Egyptian forces had withdrawn, Turkī ibn 'Abdullāh the son of the executed leader, captured Riyadh with a small force in 1824. From there he extended his authority over the surrounding regions with Ḥasā recognising Sa'ūdī authority in 1830. Turkī was assassinated in 1834 at the instigation of his cousin Mishārī, the governor of Manfūḥah. With the help of the *amīr* of Hā'il, 'Abdullāh ibn Rashīd, Turkī's son Fayṣal defeated Mishārī to become the imam of the second Sa'ūdī-Wahhabi state. It was under him that the state saw its most successful stage between 1843 and 1865. "Fayṣal acknowledged Ottoman overlordship through the payment of an annual tribute, and in return achieved recognition of his own position."[39] Civil war finally led to the collapse of the state with the capture of Riyadh by Ibn Rashīd in 1887. By 1891 'Abd ar-Raḥmān, the son of Fayṣal and main claimant to the leadership, was forced into exile in Kuwait with his son 'Abd al-Azīz. In 1902 'Abd al-Azīz, popularly known as Ibn Sa'ūd, returned from his exile in Kuwait and captured Riyadh. Almost all of Najd was under Ibn Sa'ūd's control by 1906, al-Ḥasā in 1913, 'Asīr in 1920 and the Hijaz in 1926. "The country, first known as the Kingdom of Najd, Hijaz and its Dependencies, formally adopted the name Kingdom of Saudi Arabia in 1932."[40] Some former Yemeni territory was added to the Kingdom after the Saudi-Yemeni war of 1934.

The ideas of national independence reached the Arabs through British crown agents and Muḥammad ibn 'Abd al-Wahhāb himself is said to have travelled the Arabian Peninsula with a British agent. Shaykh Abdalqadir explains this phenomenon as follows: "The political dismemberment of the Khalifate was dependent on the clinical surgery which removed the Hijaz[41] from the Islamic body.

The instrument of this operation was the criminal family of Ibn Saud. The English spy, Shakespeare informed the Foreign Office, 'The Wahhabi Amīr is a weapon to fight the Turks with.' Their task was, 'to render the position of the Turks on the Arabian coast of the Gulf untenable.' The Ibn Saud family were undoubtedly puppets of British imperialism."[42]

The Sa'ūdī dynasty transferred their allegiance from the Ottomans to the British and finally to the USA whose primary interests lay in exploiting the country's oil and gas reserves. Ibn Sa'ūd gave his allegiance to the Ottoman Sultan by signing the treaty of 15th May 1914. Article 2 of the agreement states that: "The Vilayet of Najd is to remain in charge of Abdul Azīz Pasha Al-Saood so long as he is alive, according to the Imperial Firman. After him it will go to his sons and grandsons by Imperial Firman, provided that he shall be loyal to the Imperial Government and to his forefathers, the previous Valis."[43] On 26 December 1915 Ibn Sa'ūd reneged on his allegiance to the Ottoman Sultan and signed a treaty with Britain. "On signing the treaty Ibn Sa'ūd received 1,000 rifles and a sum of £20,000. In addition the treaty granted a monthly subsidy of £5,000 and regular shipment of machine guns."[44]

### (2) Egypt

Shaykh Abdalqadir writes: "The man who cleverly linked rebellion against Khalifate with colonial rebellion against Europe was the notorious Jamāl ad-Dīn al-Afghānī, the Shī'a activist from Iran. A dedicated mason, he recruited the young *'ālim*, Muḥammad 'Abduh into his Lodge in Cairo where he in turn met and befriended the banker-governor, Lord Cromer, of the Baring family. His student, in turn, was Rashīd Reda, who issued a string of *fatwās* accommodating Islamic law to Western imperatives, social and financial. In turn, from him stem the key figures of sub-Shī'a modernism, Maududi and Ḥasan al-Bannā. From al-Bannā, Sayid Quṭb who opposed

Nasser. It must in turn be recalled that Nasser's deadly enemies were Israel, France and Britain. Nasser nearly achieved the expulsion of the British-installed Saudis in Arabistan."[45]

Modernist Muslims have devised legal methodologies to justify involvement in the capitalist system. David Johnston writes: "I argue here that an epistemological shift has taken place in the twentieth century *uṣūl al-fiqh*: away from the classical/orthodox Asha'rī position, in which the human mind simply discovers the divine law and extends it to new cases on the basis of consensus (*ijmā'*) and analogical reasoning (*qiyās*), and toward a position in which reason is empowered to uncover the *ratio legis* [reason for the law] behind the divine injunctions... This shift has been accompanied by a privileging of universal ethical principles (*kulliyyāt*), now identified as the aims of the Law (*maqāṣid ash-sharī'a*), over the specific injunctions of the text (*juz'iyyāt*) – a hermeneutic strategy that has often favoured public interest (*maṣlaḥa*) as the chief criterion for developing fresh legal rulings in the light of new socio-political conditions. The main theoreticians discussed here are Muḥammad 'Abduh, Muḥammad Rashīd Riḍā, 'Abd ar-Razzāq Sanhūrī, 'Abd al-Wahhāb Khallāf, Muḥammad Abū Zahra, and Muḥammad Hāshim Kamālī."[46]

'Abduh had blamed the *'ulamā* for their impervious judicial outlook which "fostered the misconception that Islam by its very nature is incapable of coping with the growing complexity of modern life, and Muslims had therefore to have recourse to foreign laws".[47] 'Abduh's methodology called for a return to the original sources of the law. He claimed that this was necessary in order to "liberate" thought from the shackles of *taqlīd*[48] and thereby unleash the ability for exercising *ijtihād*[49]. *Taqlīd* is referred to pejoratively by him as blind imitation and involves the unquestioning and uncritical conformity with decisions made by past *mujtahids*.

In order to bring out the latent dynamism of the *sharī'a* 'Abduh promoted *istiṣlāḥ* (public interest) and *talfīq* (legal eclecticism). Riḍā went further and spoke of the need for *ishtirā'* (legislation). He takes the division that the *sharī'a* makes between *'ibādāt* (devotional and ritual acts) and *mu'āmalāt* (social transactions) and proposes legislation in the *mu'āmalāt*. All administrative, juridical, political and military acts are therefore subject to man-made legislation. Riḍā claimed that the foundation of his methodology leads to legal dynamism. The evidence, however, indicates that, contrary to his claim, this methodology ends up in the abandonment of Islamic law.

With regards to the Egyptian reformers, which include 'Abduh and Riḍā, Layish points out that their legal reforms are deliberately secular legislative acts, which were carried out in a traditional medium but outside Islamic law. He contends that although the source of inspiration for the reforms is in the West, "technical resemblance to the *ijtihād* may create the illusion that they are an internal overhaul of the *shari'ah*."[50]

Riḍā's thinking promoted secularism, constitutionalism, democracy, legislation and capitalism. Riḍā was the conduit linking the ideas of Jamāl ad-Dīn al-Afghānī (1838/39-1897) and his disciple 'Abduh to Ḥasan al-Bannā (1906-1949), who went on to become the founder of the Muslim Brotherhood (*al-Ikhwān al-Muslimūn*). In her book entitled *An Islamic Response to Imperialism* Keddie has shown that the aim of al-Afghānī was to subvert the Islamic ethos.[51]

The method that the modernists use in order to achieve their goals is called *islāḥ*, which is the Arabic term for reform. Reform calls for new interpretations of Islam due to changing historical and social realities. Reform, they say, has to be achieved through changes in the laws of Islam. The legal techniques used by the religious reformers for effecting changes in law were *maṣlaḥa* (considerations of public interest) and *siyāsa shar'iyya* (administrative regulations). The stated objective of the modernists is "to rid the Muslim *umma* of a centuries-long mentality of *taqlīd* (blind imitation) and *jumūd* (stagnation), to restore Islam to its pristine form, and to reform the moral, cultural and political conditions of Muslims."[52]

They also claimed that they desired to free Muslims from political despotism and foreign domination. Despite making these claims, the reality is that the modernists accept the entire political and economic methodology of democracy and capitalism. Their political philosophy includes such Western concepts as statism, nationalism, constitutionalism, democracy, parliamentarianism, capitalism, banking, the International Monetary System, and the United Nations Organisation. It should be noted here that these concepts are commonly accepted by Sunnī, Shī'ī and Wahhabi modernists and this includes the Ottoman modernists. There is a considerable philosophical and political affinity between them. All modernists, through their principle of reformism, played a major role in the secularisation of Islamic law.

The net result, however, of this "islamisation" process was that capitalism and the modern state did not become "Islamised", on the contrary the Muslim countries and people continued to modernise and continued to be incorporated into the global capitalist network. As Shaykh Abdalqadir writes: "Muḥammad 'Abduh, student of the dubious Shī'a, Jamāl ad-Dīn al-Afghānī, who was in fact Irani, is considered the founder of modern 'fundamentalist' theory. He was appointed Grand Mufti in 1899, by Lord Cromer (of the Baring's Bank family) in order to legalise banking. Cromer said of him: 'I suspect my friend Abdu was in reality an agnostic.' And of his Salafī movement: 'They are the natural allies of the European reformer.' In Cairo the Post-Office Savings Bank was established in 1900 and the Agricultural Bank in 1902. (*Modern Egypt*, Cromer, Vol. 2,

1908)"[53] Encapsulating the goals of the modernist movement Shaykh Abdalqadir says: "Basically the disastrous *muwahid*[54] doctrines, strongly allied to and financed by the Saudi usurpers, have in this century plunged the Muslims inexorably into political disaster and collapse. Their final cynical achievement was the establishment of so-called 'Islamic Banks' siphoning off the wealth of the Muslim peoples into the worthless *ḥarām* system of usury banking and usury instruments of number-based exchange. The collapse of the falsely named 'Islamic Movement' from Algeria and Egypt to Pakistan is parallel to its Masonic mother's and modernist/nationalist father's demise."[55]

### (3) The Anatolian and Salonikan regions of the Ottoman dawla

There were many people from the Ottoman *dawla* who travelled to Europe and were impressed by what they saw. Some took on rationalism and scientific materialism[56], the hallmarks of modernism, unaware that the roots of modernity were to be found in the Reformation, which in reality was the subversion of religion, and most of the reforms were initiated through Freemasonry. Shaykh Abdalqadir writes: "Lord Curzon declared: 'Turkestan, Afghanistan, Persia – to me, I confess, they are pieces on a chessboard upon which is being played out a game for the domination of the world.' At the turn of the century a most active and virulent freemasonry was at work, demonstrably so, and beyond the modern attempts to psychologise the view that it posed a political threat. The lodges of Salonika and Anatolia, lay at the heart of resistance to the Khalifate. They in turn linked directly to the grand lodges of India. India was connected from 1839 with the lodges of Basra. The Shaykh of Kuwait, then as now, was Grand Master of all Mesopotamian freemasonry, and closely linked to the criminal rebel family of Abdalaziz ibn Saud."[57] With regards to the masonic system's attack on the caliphate Shaykh Abdalqadir adds that: "The crucial element is that the Salonika lodges, in preparing their Young Turk coup d'état, were at the same time linked to the Young Azharis, the rebel modernist *'ulamā* of Al-Azhar."[58]

Today, freemasonry has lost the role it had played at its birth in 1717 with the foundation of the Grand Lodge of London. The reason for this is that it has now achieved its goals and overcome opposition to it from Christianity and Judaism. One of the most important factors contributing to the neutralisation of the opposition to incipient freemasonry, whose roots lie much earlier than its official foundation, was the Reformation. The dominant voice of reform in Germany was Martin Luther (1483-1546) and in Switzerland, then France and Britain it was John Calvin (1509-1564). The Reformation was the start of Protestantism which challenged the religious and political authority of the Catholic Church. Freemasonry achieved the following goals that it had set out to achieve: multi-confessionalism[59], secularism, constitutionalism, democracy, capitalism, the legalisation of usury and banking, human rights, the brotherhood of mankind, and globalisation.

Freemasonry made deep inroads into the Ottoman *dawla* with the introduction of a number of measures and laws aimed at modernisation or westernisation called the Tanzimat reforms, which were promulgated between 1838 and 1876. The key reform decrees were the Gulkhane Hatti-Cherif by Sultan Mahmud's successor Sultan Abdulmajid on November 3rd 1839 and the Khatt-I Humayun of 1856. They led to a conscripted army, introduction of paper money (Caime-i-Muthebere-i-Nakdiye), the banking system (capitalism), decriminalisation of homosexuality, the replacement of religious with secular law, territorial nationalism and the replacement of the guilds with factories.

Shaykh Umar Vadillo says: "In the last days of the Ottoman Khalifate the freemasonic lodges were working assiduously by planting their own people inside the established institutions of Islam and throughout the journalistic profession. The people attacked Islam through insidious, sweet words, smiling faces, financial help and flattery. They said that all people, religious or irreligious, were brothers and that religious obligations were not necessary."[60] Freemasonry first penetrated the Ottoman *dawla* via lodges established by Europeans. From the mid-19th century more and more freemasonic organisations founded lodges in the main population centres of the Ottoman *dawla* through their European residents. European economic involvement and influence led to the establishment of many lodges, for example, the first lodge in Jaffa was set up by French railway engineers in 1891. By the end of the century there was hardly any town or city of importance without one lodge. Natives, foreigners, Christians, Jews and Muslims mingled freely in these lodges.

The latter part of the 19th century was the golden age of Ottoman masonry. Many Muslim masons were strategically placed, liberals such as Prince Murad, son of the Ottoman Sultan Abdulmajid, Prince Abdulhalim, son of Muḥammad Ali Pasha, and Mustafa Rashīd Pasha, one of the most important Ottoman reformers of the century and grand *wazīr* repeatedly from 1848 until his death. Namik Kemal, who was influential in the formation of the Young Ottomans and their struggle for political reform in the Ottoman *dawla* during the Tanzimat period, was also a mason. The Tanzimat reforms, which were promulgated between 1838 and 1876, introduced a number of measures and laws aimed at modernisation or westernisation. Namik Kemal was inspired by the French Third Republic and the constitution of the United Kingdom.

The reformer Mehmed Ali Pasha, five time grand *wazīr* to Sultan Abdulmajid and Sultan Abdalaziz, himself a freemason, brought Jamāl ad-Dīn al-Afghānī to Istanbul. These lodges served as nuclei for anti-establishment and revolutionary political activity, for example early in the 20th century Masonic lodges served as a cover for the meetings of leaders of the Young Turks. Then we have Midhat Pasha who was trained under the patronage of the masons Muḥammad Ali Pasha and Mustafa Rashīd Pasha. This champion of constitutionalism was convicted for the murder of Sultan Abdalaziz.

Sultan Abdulhamid had a *fatwā* issued against masonry declaring it to be an instrument of *kufr* to destroy Islam. "The large number of masons among leading members of the Committee of Union and Progress (CUP) that dethroned Abduhamid after the revolution of 1908 led the French historian Thierry Zarcone to call the resulting regime 'the masonic state.'"[61] It must be remembered that the freemasons were instruments that were used by the bankers. Referring to the bankers, Ustad Necip Fazıl said: "The whole palace, the Supreme Porte, the nobility and then, as a consequence, the whole nation became as playthings in the hands of these characters. These people very rarely showed themselves on the front-line but rather manoeuvred within the most vital areas of finance. When they did appear they appropriated the image of the oppressed and the condemned for themselves. They were the obedient agents of Western imperialism, ready to strike from inside, ready to prepare the way for their masters. But despite this, neither Ali Pasha, nor Fuad Pasha, nor Mithat Pasha, nor Shinasi, nor Namik Kemal nor Ziya Pasha were really aware of this situation."[62]

The British spy, Mark Sykes, who worked at the British Consulate in Istanbul said, in his appraisal of the removal of Sultan Abdalhamid: "The fall of Abdulhamid has been the fall, not of a despot or tyrant, but of a people and an idea. In the place of theocracy, imperial prestige and tradition, came atheism, Jacobinism, materialism and license. ... In an hour, Constantinople changed. Islam, as understood by the theologians, as preached in the mosques, as the moral support of the people, as the inspiration of the army, died in a moment. The Caliphate, the clergy, the Qur'ān, ceased to hold or inspire."[63]

# Chapter 5

## The Rise of Ideology amongst Muslims

In the last chapter we outlined the series of events that culminated in the dethronement of Sultan Abdulhamid. Shaykh Abdalqadir notes that the three regions of the Ottoman *dawla* in which these events transpired were (1) the Arabian Peninsula (2) Egypt and (3) the Anatolian and Salonikan regions of the Ottoman *dawla*. What we found was that whilst each region was subjected to methodologies specific to them, these methodologies became ideologies which were then applied to other Muslim countries and were adopted by Muslims in non-Muslim countries. These ideologies were Wahhabism from the Arabian Peninsula, Islamic modernism from Egypt and secularism from Anatolia and Salonika. They evolved into systems of belief, ideas and ideals that formed the basis of economic and political theory and policy. These ideologies have been adopted by the Muslim mainstream and have become the everyday reality of all Muslims.

As mentioned before, Ali Pasha, Fuad Pasha, Mithat Pasha, Shinasi, Namik Kemal and Ziya Pasha were used by the bankers but were unaware that the whole nation had become playthings in their (the bankers') hands. The ideologies of Wahhabism, Islamic modernism and secularism as well as democracy, capitalism and communism merely provide a smokescreen for the banking elite that govern the world. As Shaykh Abdalqadir observes: "We are tyrannised, enslaved and endebted to an entirely un-elected elite whose names we do not even know. Upholding humanism, it could be said that they have no human loyalty. Insisting on their compassion they uphold the Rights of Man, sure in the certainty that the upholding of that empty rhetoric will distract you from ever attempting to refrain from their monetary system and live without banking. They are an oligarchy."[1]

Shaykh Abdalqadir notes with great insight why it was that the *'ulamā* were unaware that they had become the instruments of the bankers. He says that the confusion of the "*'ulamā* has been their misreading of the nature of modern 'technique,' of technological process, due to their being indoctrinated by the outmoded 'modernism' of men who had themselves been seconded to *kāfir* ideas and organisations in Egypt and the Middle East. To place the demands of a machine culture over the survival of man, and to prefer systems control over human transactions, is against *Kitāb wa Sunna* in a clear and demonstrable way. The Messenger of Allah, blessings of Allah and peace be on him, did not create machines, but rather he left behind men who were in their time, and have been ever since, lights to inspire and demand following by men of heart and intellect. We would indicate, therefore, that the cause itself of the false dialectic above is the false dialectic, which sets the rules of 'system technique' over and above 'basic technique' or primitive technology, while aligning truly Salafī[2] Islam with the world of primitive or basic technique. It has been this trick which embarrassed and deceived educated – in this technical sense –

Muslims to 'buy' the modernist dismantling of Islamic governance, transposing, in the process the true pattern of Islamic society – amirate ruling the people and *fuqahā* ruling the *amīr* – by defining *sharī'a* limits, not by cult of personality – but with the myth of an Islamic 'state', which is a systems concept deriving from the subversion of existing western modes that preceded the industrial revolution."[3]

The long passage I have quoted above contains several terms that need to be investigated in greater detail. These terms are: the nature of modern technique; technological process; modernism; machine culture; system technique; basic technique; primitive technology; systems concept; political ideology; industrial revolution; and monetary system. They all relate to our way of thinking, which then leads to our way of understanding the world, which in turn leads to the way we act and the institutions we adopt in our social interactions. Although the passage refers directly to reformist *'ulamā* we have noted above that the various strands of their thinking have created the ideologies of Wahhabism, Islamic modernism and secularism. These ideologies evolved into systems of belief, ideas and ideals that formed the basis of economic and political theory and policy that have been adopted by the Muslim mainstream and become the everyday reality of all Muslims.

To understand the terminology used by Shaykh Abdalqadir we have to first look at the way we think. The way of thinking that we have been brought up with from school, university and through the media is scientific thinking. Scientific thinking has its roots in philosophy which is the enquiry of the 'what,' 'where' and 'how' of things. Thinking this way requires us to define all entities as things. In this way we form a concept of things, which means an idea that is connected to those things. In this way of thinking we do not know the things, we can only describe them. The thing itself and the idea (or description) of it are two completely different things.

This thinking has been with us for a long time; it was initiated by the Greek philosopher Plato (428-348 BC) who is considered the founder of Western philosophy. Philosophy also took to defining human beings and God. René Descartes (1596-1690) built on Plato's ideas and defined humans as rational beings. He came up with the famous saying '*cogito ergo sum* – I think, therefore I am.'[4] Descartes along with Benedict Spinoza (1632-1677) and Gottfried Wilhelm Leibniz (1646-1716) became known as rationalists and took the view that humans were rational. It was Immanuel Kant (1724-1804) who went on to explain how the process of how thinking works.

According to Kant the human being is the subject who observes the objects around him or her. The three fundamental powers of our minds are: the capacity to receive sensory data, the ability to conceptualise, think and judge – that is intellectually process the data and understand it – and lastly the ability to draw valid conclusions, to reason. This rationalist definition reduces the human being to being a thing amongst other things. The division between mind and matter led to the belief that the universe was a mechanical system consisting of separate objects, which in turn were reduced to fundamental building blocks whose properties and interactions completely determined everything. This view was extended to include all living organisms, which were regarded as machines constructed from separate parts. It was Isaac Newton (1643-1727) who developed a complete mathematical formulation of the mechanistic view of nature which has formed the foundation of science from that time on. Such a conception of the world formed the basis of all the sciences influencing all aspects of life.

The transition from the medieval to the modern modes of thought and practices was supported by rational methods in all fields of inquiry. Galileo Galilei's (1564-1642) heliocentrism (*Dialogue Concerning the Two World Systems*, 1632) and Isaac Newton's mechanics (*Principia Mathematica*, 1867) set the agenda in physics and René Descartes' (1596-1650) '*cogito ergo sum* – I think therefore I am' (*Principles of Philosophy*, 1644) and Immanuel Kant's (1724-1804) theory that objective experience is constructed by the functioning of the human mind (*Critique of Pure Reason*, 1781) did so in philosophy. The foundations for biological and psychological thought and practice were laid by Charles Darwin's (1809-1882) evolutionary theory (*On the Origin of Species*, 1859) and Freud's (1856-1939) psychological building blocks (*The Ego and the Id*, 1923).

The social sciences adopted the paradigm of mechanical science, with its belief in the objectivity and universality of scientific knowledge and method, as the model for morality, law and government,[5] epitomised by Adam Smith's (1723-1790) economic free market (*The Wealth of Nations*, 1876) and Thomas Hobbes' (1588-1679) theory of the social contract in political theory (*Leviathan*, 1651). It is on the epistemological foundations of sciences based on the above writings, together with others in a similar vein, that the new model of humanity took shape. The French Revolution (1789), with its Reign of Terror, and the Napoleonic state that followed, determined the future course of modernity. Developments in science and technology in Europe led to the Industrial Revolution and the Voyages of Discovery to Africa, the Americas and Asia.

According to Shaykh Abdalqadir the confusion of the Wahhabi, Islamic modernist and secularist *'ulamā* "has been their misreading of the nature of modern 'technique,' of technological process, due to their being indoctrinated by the outmoded 'modernism' of men who had themselves been seconded to *kāfir* ideas and organisations in Egypt and the Middle East." They were unable to see that the culture and institutions of liberal democracy with its capitalist system, and totalitarianism with its communist economy (state capitalism) developed from these modernist visions of reality. The legal, educational, and healthcare systems and the modes of recreation of these societies were born out of modernism. The institutions that eventually developed to facilitate the goals of global capitalism were the United Nations Organization (UNO), the World Trade Organization (WTO), the International Monetary Fund (IMF) and the World Bank. Finally humankind had achieved one global world state, one world government (UNO) and one currency, the US dollar.[6]

The Wahhabi and Islamic modernist and secularist *'ulamā* have adopted the eurocentric worldview. Eurocentrism assumes that the West and the East are separate and different entities and it asserts an inherent superiority of the West over the East. According to this worldview the West became what it is due to ingenious scientific rationality. The other qualities that the West has, according to eurocentrism, are discipline, order, self-control, sanity, sensibility, and it is mind-oriented, paternal, independent, functional, free, democratic, tolerant, honest, civilised and morally and economically progressive. As a result of these qualities the West occupies the centre stage of progressive world history, both past and present. According to eurocentrism the East, and by extension all non-Western societies, are imitative, ignorant, passive, irrational, superstitious, ritualistic, lazy, chaotic/erratic, spontaneous, insane, emotional, body-oriented, exotic and alluring, childlike, dependent, dysfunctional, enslaved, despotic, intolerant, corrupt, savage, barbaric, morally regressive and economically stagnant.

The term 'outmoded modernism' used by Shaykh Abdalqadir in the above quoted passage is referring to the physical sciences, philosophy and social sciences of the modern age, and they are outmoded because they have been transcended through advances in these areas since the early twentieth century. The science and philosophy of modernity have been shattered and its institutions have failed and are in terminal decline. The towering figures of the new thinking were the scientist Werner Heisenberg (1901-1976), the philosopher Martin Heidegger (1889-1976), the jurist Carl Schmitt (1888-1985) and the poet and novelist Ernst Jünger (1895-1998). Referring to them Shaykh Abdalqadir writes that by mid twentieth-century "only a quartet of individuals stood apart from the mass ethos, insisting not just that a whole system was, in Malaparte's final diagnosis, 'Kaputt', but the time was moving towards an utterly renewed world order."[7]

Shaykh Abdalqadir says that Heisenberg's "most important contribution was to insist that thinking be in terms of a dynamic world of fusion and fission as understood in nuclear physics. The Newtonian model was of a world where the laws of gravity affirmed the billiard-ball solidity of the atom. In the coming ethos the cosmos had to be understood as a realm of whirling matter which if viewed one way was particles and if viewed another way was waves. The Kantian world of categorical imperative and fixed terms bounded by logical processes had given way to paradox; and precision had yielded to models of 'fuzzy' mathematics. The new order could not be a retro-impulse going back to the past. It had to be grounded in the present."[8]

Shaykh Abdalqadir says that Heidegger's masterwork *Sein und Zeit* has towered over the philosophical scene and, along with his *Nietzsche* book, has dominated Western thought.[9] Nietzsche and Heidegger had seen, like Hegel before them, that the greatest event to affect Western civilisation was what they called "the death of God" and its consequence, nihilism. The idea that God is dead, points to the gradual demise of Christian theism as a major cultural force. This process was and continues to be brought about by many forces. Since Descartes, the philosophical traditions of the West have undermined Christian doctrines by positing science as an explanation of reality without reference to God. Other factors that undermined Christian theism were industriousness as an end in itself, materialistic pursuits and democracy.

The loss of belief in God and the collapse of the values that were built upon that belief led to the rise of nihilism, which is a repudiation of value, meaning, knowledge, desirability, truth, virtue and art. Heidegger explained that philosophical thinking in the West began with the thought of the post-Socratic[10] philosophers and terminated with the nihilistic hegemony of technology – a technology that is sustained by scientific or instrumental rationality and which in turn underlies the industry, bureaucracy and other structures of modern society. The use of technology was initially seen as an instrument under the control of humanity whose aim was the subjugation of nature through human reasoning. Humankind however, was not liberated through the use of technology but was instead subordinated by it, in its drive for world domination.

For Heidegger, understanding the human being entails a proper understanding of the Being of everything else. He named the human being '*Dasein*' the entity whose being discloses and understands the Being of itself and that of other entities. Shaykh Abdalqadir points out that: "To break through to a new situation Heidegger goes to the depths of the dynamic of our thinking and questions metaphysics and thinking itself. In his view, it is not enough to negate metaphysics but rather to confront its core and so be free of its overpowering grip on man. To do this, Heidegger engaged in a lifelong discourse on the nature of the human being (*Dasein*) as a project directed entity and Being itself."[11]

Heidegger believed that Plato (424/423 BC – 348/347 BC) distorted the meaning of Being as it was understood by the pre-Socratic philosophers (particularly Parmenides (b. 540 BC or 515 BC) and Heraclitus (535 BC – 475 BC)), thereby initiating 'nihilism' in Western philosophical thinking. For Heidegger this meant the beginning not only of metaphysics but also of philosophy as we know it. He said: "Therefore metaphysics begins with Plato's interpretation of 'Being' as idea. For all subsequent times, it shapes the essence of Western philosophy, whose history from Plato to Nietzsche is the history of metaphysics."[12] Heidegger's thinking was aimed at overcoming Plato's metaphysics and as such it signified a shift from metaphysics to ontology. The study of metaphysics focuses on beings whilst ontology focuses on the Being of beings. For Heidegger the task of philosophy was to bring metaphysics to an end and it is upon this end that the overcoming of nihilism was dependent.

Heidegger's critique of metaphysics leads to a new way of thinking. The old scientific, technological, calculative and rational way of thinking is blind to Being or Truth because, as Heidegger says, "Science does not think."[13] Truth (*aletheia*) for the pre-Socratic philosophers, particularly Parmenides and Heraclitus, meant unconcealment, from the Greek '*a*', meaning not and '*leth*', to escape notice or to be concealed. The human being was understood as being "the locus of the self-disclosure of Truth" and not a rational animal (a mistranslation of *zoon logon echon*). Heidegger redefined human beings as *Dasein*, which in German means 'being-there'. *Dasein* is the clearing for the disclosure of Being, that is the locus where Being manifests. There is an abyss between thinking and science, between Being and being and between a human being as a rational animal and a being who is the locus for the self-disclosure of Truth. Between these two modes there is no bridge.

Heidegger stated: "By way of a series of lectures, we are attempting to learn thinking. The way is long. We dare to take only a few steps. If all goes well, they will take us to the foot-hills of thought. But they will take us to places which we must explore to reach the point where only the leap will help further. The leap alone takes us into the neighbourhood where thinking resides. The leap will take us abruptly to where everything is different, so different that it strikes us as strange."[14] Shaykh Abdalqadir states that Heidegger needed to make the leap himself but failed to do so. Although Heidegger was a great admirer of Goethe (1749-1832)[15] he did not take the leap, which Shaykh Abdalqadir avers that Goethe had taken by becoming Muslim. Taking the leap into Islam for Heidegger required engaging more profoundly with the philosophical issues that were raised by Goethe, Nietzsche and Ernst Jünger (1895-1998) whose writings he was so familiar with during his life.

In 1932 Jünger saw the inescapable power of the phenomenon of technology. He recognised that technology did not represent a complex set of tools that were there for the use of human beings. He thought of technique or technology as a new power with its own inner logic which rendered human beings subservient. Jünger used the concept of *Gestalt*[16] to characterise the worker. Modern human beings are under the *Gestalt* of the worker each one of them defined within the all embracing system of technique. Shaykh Abdalqadir points out that, "It is in this sense that Heidegger declared Jünger to have defined nihilism for our time."[17] The unstoppable movement of technology has ended in a world state with the global power of technique forming an imperial unity. There are no classes because everyone is living under the domination of technique. Social identity is defined by the use of technology, such as electricity consumers, train users, television watchers, road users etc. The state that rules the infrastructure rules over the individual. All people have become slaves and they vote to install their slave drivers. There is no place on earth that will be able to resist this phenomenon "which from a long time ago has carried the seal of a great barbaric invasion."[18] This phenomenon has manifested itself through colonisation, exploration of deserts and forests, extermination of indigenous peoples, elimination of laws and religions and the destruction of social groups and nations.

This human being – the worker – this passive receptor of all technological procedures can however, recover his or her deepest power. Jünger did not propose a withdrawal from technique. He calls on people to accept the vast wave of technology engulfing the time and prepare not only for survival and escape but ultimately victory over it. The *Gestalt* of the worker can take on a new image argues Jünger. He says: "Nothing may exist which cannot be conceived of as work. Work is the rhythm of the arm, of the thoughts, of the heart, the life of night and day, science, love, art, faith, ritual, war. Work is the vibration of the atom and the force which moves the stars and the solar systems."[19] Human beings are free once they accept that they are indeed the workers. There are two types of individuals: the ordinary individual, the television watching single unit of the mass who votes away his or her freedom and the other is *Der Einzelne*, the isolated one – not differentiated from the masses – who becomes the transformative force in existence.

Once the limited nature of resources and technique is grasped, the transformation begins. When a person is aware of his or her *Gestalt* that person becomes aware of other *Gestalt*s and their relationships with one another. The *Gestalt* contains more than the sum of its parts. For example a human being is more than the sum of atoms, limbs, organs, and humours of which he or she is composed. Jünger explained that: "It is in the *Gestalt*, independent from every appreciation, that there resides innate value, immutable and imperishable, its existence the highest and most profound confirmation. The more we engage in movement, the more we become intimately persuaded that hidden behind it is a Calm Being, and that every acceleration of speed is only the translation of an original, imperishable language. ... The vision of the *Gestalt* is a revolutionary act in as much as it recognises a Being in the complete and unitary plenitude of his life."[20]

Jünger is suggesting here that the way of freedom lies in plunging into reality, taking it on and, by a new *Gestalt*, going beyond it. The above quote suggests the development of the *Waldgänger* (lit. Forest Walker) who can encounter a greater power. In Jünger's *Heliopolis* the hero of the novel Lucius says: "The game [of technique] must have exhausted all its possibilities. Then only can one dare the impossible."[21] Lucius is here referring to the *Waldgänger*, an individual who acts in every situation. He or she does not need theories or laws "cooked up by party legalists."[22] These individuals know what is right through the purity within them.

Jünger calls the encounter with a superior power the great experience of the Forest, which is "the encounter with one's own self, the invulnerable core, the essence, from which the temporal and individual phenomenon originates."[23] Shaykh Abdalqadir explains that the central *Gestalt* of the mythology[24] created by Jünger is that of the one who goes into the Forest, which Jünger defines as the non-temporal, inner zone where the conscious break is made with the horrific reality of the contemporary social contract. The *Waldgänger* is not an anarchist but he or she is free and sovereign. When uncovered as a spiritual outsider he or she is forced to flee society to preserve his or her autonomy. The flight to the Forest makes him or her a *Waldgänger*.

Jünger says in *Der Waldgang*, "Man sleeps in the forest. When he awakens and realises his power, then order is reconstituted."[25] Jünger's hero, however, never outlined the parameters of his or her behaviour within society. On the occasion of the installation of Jünger as Doctor *Honoris Causa* of Literature in the University of Bilbao in 1989, Shaykh Abdalqadir presented a paper whilst Jünger was present. Referring to Jünger's words "*Freiheit ist Existenz*" Shaykh Abdalqadir says: "*Freiheit ist Existenz*. Freedom is Existence. Which means that there can be no submission except to the Divine. This is called Islam."[26] To know God requires that you first be in harmony with the destiny of your life form. In Qur'ānic terminology this harmonisation is called service or worship. In other words in order to know God one has to submit to the Divine.

Jünger's great contribution was that he went beyond Marx's critique of capitalism. In *Der Arbeiter*, Jünger was taking on a very deep theme when he wrote: "It remains to destroy the legend that the essential quality of the worker is an economic quality."[27] Jünger argued that economics is an industrial process in itself and part of the total system that is technique. One of the consequences of this process is that, "Bourgeois society is condemned to death."[28]

The last of the quartet of intellectuals we are discussing is the jurist Carl Schmitt. We have to agree with Tracy Strong's observation of Schmitt as "being the Martin Heidegger of political theory" albeit for reasons other than hers.[29] Schmitt, the political theorist of the quartet, said as early as 1963 that the modern state had lost substantive power. In his words: "the model of political unity, which embodied the monopoly of political decision, the State, this work of art made in a European mould and with Western rationalism, is dethroned."[30] Shaykh Abdalqadir points to Schmitt's *Der Begriff des Politischen*[31] as the text in which he explains depoliticisation and renunciation of the state.

With the collapse of the Soviet Union and Deng Xiaoping's embrace of capitalism the interest of the social sciences is once again centred on the relationship between the state and democracy. Schmitt made a clear distinction between politics and the political which are in a dialectical tension with each other. What is meant by dialectic in this sense is the examination and discussion of opposing ideas in order to find the truth. In the 19th and early part of the 20th centuries the state was the political and it had political monopoly. The state was on one side and society on the other. Citizens demand that the state protect them. However, with the adoption of liberal democracy, post World War II, the political elites claim that the market will do that on its own.

Tihomir Cipek says that the "functions of the state have been taken over by international arbiters of power which are not democratically elected and are not subject to democratic control such as the World Bank, the International Monetary Fund, and various expert commissions and courts. At the same time, the neo-liberal ideology claims that the state is something bad because it prevents the free operation of the market. The argument is that politics is an unnecessary obstacle to the economy and that the state should be reduced to a minimum, because everything will be resolved by the market. On the other hand, it is quite clear that democracy is historically and institutionally tied to the state. We thus find ourselves in a paradoxical situation in which the political is at the level of the state, but the public policies are at the supranational level ... Essentially we are talking about a process of depoliticization."[32] Neo-liberalism has established a one-world state (the UNO), a one-world economic order (global capitalism) and a one-world currency (the US Dollar). Schmitt regarded this as an unworkable phenomenon because it would lead to world-wide civil war.

This is exactly what happened. Schmitt defined the political as a friend/enemy relation. "In contrast to the various relatively independent endeavours of human thought and action – particularly the moral, aesthetic, and economic – the political has its own criteria which express themselves in a characteristic way. … Let us assume that in the realm of morality the final distinctions are between good and evil, in aesthetics beautiful and ugly, in economics profitable and unprofitable. … The specific political distinction to which political actions and motives can be reduced is that between friend and enemy."[33] In his theory, the enemy is more important than the friend because it is only with regard to the enemy that a nation can be formed as a homogeneous unit. The enemy of one state is another state or states. Only the state wields the amount of power to make a decision for going to war. Within its borders, the state guarantees peace, while outwardly it can wage war. When there is one global state there is no outside enemy. "A world state would therefore be apolitical, an enormous consumer and production community, some kind of a global super-market, but not a state."[34] This hybrid state then turns against its own citizens, in other words, there is civil war.

For Schmitt the state is always solely and only a nation state and no global and universal state is possible. He insisted that there has never been a world state there have only been empires and no empire encompassed the entire world. The world's dominant empire is the USA which has been at war for 225 years out of its 246 year history.[35] Charles Perkins defines empire as a "nation-state that dominates other nation-states and exhibits one or more of the following characteristics: 1) exploits resources from the lands it dominates; 2) consumes large quantities of resources – amounts that are disproportionate to the size of its population relative to those of other nations; 3) maintains a large military that enforces its policies when more subtle measures fail; 4) spreads its language, literature, art, and various aspects of its culture throughout its sphere of influence; 5) taxes not just its own citizens, but also people in other countries; and 6) imposes its own currency under the lands under its control."[36] On all these counts the USA is an empire.

The USA represents less than 5% of the world' population but it consumes more than 25% of the world's resources. It maintains the largest and most sophisticated military in the world. Until 2017 the number of US foreign military interventions stood at 188 and, up to 2016, the world superpower had tried to change other countries' governments 72 times. The English language and American culture are pervasive throughout the world. The US Dollar is the world's reserve currency and inflation is the hidden tax the rest of the world has to pay. Pilger says of the US empire and illusory one-world state: "On the surface, it is instant financial trading, mobile phones, McDonald's, Starbucks, holidays booked on the net. Beneath the gloss it is the globalisation of poverty, a world where most human beings never make a phone call and live on less than two dollars a day, where 6,000 children die every day from diarrhoea because most have no access to clean water."[37]

In Shaykh Abdalqadir's reflections on the American empire he says: "For Lucan,[38] civil war is the final political abyss of men. If the United States of America began with at least a pretension to being a republic it soon took a predictable path; from Constitution and Senate it soon gained great wealth. The path to Empire was swift but it was preceded by a continent-wide civil war. Faulkner, one of America's profounder writers, insisted that the American civic project could never work, built as it was on an indigenous community enslaved in Reservations and a community transformed from the slavery of possession to the slavery of poverty. Thus the history of America from a Lucanian perspective is simple. A people, who fought their own people to be free, promptly massacred and then enclosed the remnant of the indigenous people in Reservations, that is, village prisons. Burgeoning wealth turned the Americans into a nation divided by civil war."[39] Empire soon followed with the occupation of Hawaii and Puerto Rico and a colonial presence in Panama and Cuba. The great expansion came in the two world wars with America blanket bombing Dresden, Hamburg and Berlin and nuclear-bombing Hiroshima and Nagasaki. By the end of last century their forces all but obliterated Baghdad and followed that with a decade-long occupation of Afghanistan.

Schmitt saw the establishment of a new *nomos*[40] as the way to end the world-wide civil war. Shaykh Abdalqadir argues that nihilism, suicide and terrorism are synonyms. They are not political doctrines but the failure of politics. They indicate an endgame and after it must come a new beginning, a new *nomos*. Islam, said Shaykh Abdalqadir, is the *nomos* that will end nihilism. "The new *nomos* has not vanished from the earth. It has survived. Now it is ready yet again, to emerge into the wider arena of civil revival. It is by the networking of groups of the noblest of youths and the finest women, bonded together in worship of the Lord of the Universe, that the plastic and polluted cities will be cleansed. The political class will die away. ... Their mere two hundred year rule is over."[41]

Shaykh Abdalqadir saw that the 'outmoded modernism' of the Wahhabis, modernists and secularists had been deconstructed since the early twentieth century and that the science and philosophy of modernity had been shattered and its institutions had failed and were in terminal decline. There were many intellectuals engaged in this new thinking but the towering figures amongst them were without doubt the scientist Werner Heisenberg, the philosopher Martin Heidegger, the jurist Carl

Schmitt and the poet and novelist Ernst Jünger. Yet the ideologies of Wahhabism, Islamic modernism and secularism still dominate the thinking of the Muslim world. The common factor that unites them is capitalism, the dominant doctrine of our time.

# Chapter 6

## Atheistic Capitalism: The Dominant Religion of Our Time

Shaykh Abdalqadir indicates that the revival of Islam, the new *nomos*, will spell the end of atheistic capitalism. This will entail moving away "constructively from capitalist modalities – currency, banking, taxation – to free exchanges between men and groups."[1] He reminds us that "physical and military opposition are the lifeblood of capitalist atheism." Therefore the "revival of Islam is dependent on step by step turning away from *kufr* and finally, submitting to the natural religion." The face of modern *kufr* is capitalism and its public relations interface is either democracy or communism. In China it is state capitalism and in the rest of the world oligarchy masquerades as democracy. This oligarchy entails the rule of the financial, commodities (including the military industrial complex) and media elites over governments and countries. Capitalism is the religion of the modern world with its priesthood, temples and worshippers. Shaykh Abdalqadir's critique of capitalism and its relation to the modern state comes from an Islamic perspective.

It was in Europe that the dominant modernist worldview, that now pervades the entire world, including Muslim society, developed. Capitalism was the end result of modernity. It developed an elaborate ideology and a range of institutions that enabled it to function. Besides Shaykh Abdalqadir's views on the processes by which capitalism came to dominate the world, there are two other prominent narratives. One, we will refer to as the Weber/Taylor narrative and the other as the Benjamin/McCarrarher narrative. After briefly noting these views we will proceed to see how Shaykh Abdalqadir's differs from theirs and, more importantly, he shows that Islam and capitalism are antithetical to each other.

The sociologist and historian Max Weber spoke of the disenchantment of the world. This meant that with the advent of modern society there was a radical break from the pre-modern, to use Catholic philosopher Charles Taylor's expression, "context of understanding". In pre-modern society the presence of God was seemingly undeniable. The natural world displayed order, design, divine purpose and action. The fertility of the earth, abundance of sustenance and fresh water, shelter from the elements, as well as floods, earthquakes and forest-fires were all seen as acts of God. Kings ruled in the name of God and society was ordered in ways that involved revealed guidance and worship. The existence of God and His direct involvement in the cosmos was apparent. Europe went through various phases on its way to its present modern worldview. The transformation of pre-modern Christian society involved the eclipse of God's control of individual and social action. It also involved the rise of the belief in the power of the human self to morally organise society. This is the basis of Humanism, which resulted in the secularisation of society. The world, according to this view, lost its wonder and enchantment.

In the Benjamin/McCarrarher narrative capitalism is a religion. "Christianity in the time of the Reformation did not encourage the emergence of capitalism, but rather changed itself into capitalism" wrote Walter Benjamin.[2] Eugene McCarrarher argues that, far from being an agent of disenchantment, capitalism has been a technique of enchantment and "renaming of our intrinsic and inveterate longing for divinity."[3] McCarraher says that the animating spirit of capitalism is money, its theology is philosophy and its cosmology is economics and its sacraments are the material culture of production and consumption of commodities and technologies. Its moral codes are contained in management theory and business journalism. Its priests are the corporate intelligentsia made up of economists, executives, managers and business writers. Its icons consist of advertising, public relations, marketing and product design. For McCarraher: "Under capitalism, money occupies the ontological throne from which God has been evicted."[4] In other words for capitalists Money is god and ecstasy can be bought with it, in spite of the fact that capitalism sanctions the printing of counterfeit paper money.

Shaykh Abdalqadir says: "The Osmaniya was not defeated and destroyed by war. It was infiltrated and eroded over 150 years with a quite new and dazzling deception. Thinking that it was somehow winning for itself 'modernity' – that is, technique – it signed away its wealth. It agreed to pay the price. The price was a whole civilisation, built on superior, truer lines."[5] In 2011 Shaykh Abdalqadir pointed out that capitalist society is rapidly collapsing. He said that the very frame, structure and pattern of society, which had until now seemed actual, solid and founded on material itself has now begun to disintegrate and collapse. As it fragments, a further condition is revealed, which is that the structure and pattern of society is itself illusory. Shaykh Abdalqadir tells us that capitalism is not a system, it is a psychosis. Psychosis means to lose touch with reality, that is, to perceive the world and how it works in a way that is delusory. Mediating between ourselves and the reality of the world around us is our brain, that is, our intellect. The intellect creates a series of structured pictures by which we understand the world around us. We view ourselves and the world around us through the prism of capitalism. The foundation of capitalism is banking and fractional reserve banking.

We have previously noted that the most important of the oligarchic elites are the bankers and that money is actually created out of nothing through fractional reserve banking. The processes of capitalism are fraudulent, deceptive and illusory. If we believe that money is real, when it in fact is not, we are being psychotic. If money supply, the foundation of capitalism, is in itself not real then capitalism is in fact an illusion. This illusion is perpetuated through an elaborate ideology backed up by highly developed institutions. Defining the capitalists Shaykh Abdalqadir says: "These people have acquired the world's wealth by a deception, by a theft."[6] The institutions of capitalism do exactly the opposite of what they claim to be doing. The World Bank, the International Monetary Fund and the World Trade Organisation do not in reality look after the poor and deprived; they further the interests of the oligarchy. The national state is a façade that allows the oligarchs to have legislation passed in their favour and the United Nations Organisation does not even try to conceal the charade that it actually is.

The pre-modern Muslim background, or the context of our understanding of the world, was never like this. It was not like this as long as the sultanates and caliphates continued to exist. In pre-modern Islamic society this "background" understanding allowed the believers to function in a way in which there was no distinction between experience and its construed meaning. The presence of Allah was undeniable. The natural world displayed order, design, divine purpose and action. Caliphs ruled in the name of Allah and society was ordered in accordance with the guidance of the Qur'ān and *Sunna*. Atheism was almost inconceivable in a world which had these features as its background understanding. It was taken for granted that the mercy and compassion of God would repel the forces of evil.

Religion was something that was related to action rather than thought. It was action/behaviour that enabled one to deepen the perception of the heart. This, it was understood, could not be acquired through reason. Knowledge of Allah came only through dedicated practice and lay beyond thoughts and concepts. Knowing about Allah was different from knowing Allah. Knowing about Allah was the subject of *'ilm al-kalām* or *'aqīda*, that is, "theology", whereas knowing Allah was the subject of Sufism, because the experience of God cannot be contained within the dogmas of theologians or the hypotheses of scientists or the speculation of philosophers. Allah is beyond space and time and human imaginings.

It was in Europe that the dominant modern worldview, that now pervades the entire world including Muslim society, developed. Modernist epistemology took the form of mechanism, materialism and structuralism. The assumptions that underpinned modernisation were secularism, individualism and a commitment to progress through science and technology. Development was defined as the control of nature for the benefit of human beings, according to the principle of liberal market forces. Modernity in turn led to the establishment of nationalism, capitalism and democracy and the end of the age of faith.

The religious worldview was supplanted by the modern worldview over a period of time, the chronology of which is disputed by historians. The transition from the medieval to the modern modes of thought and practices was supported by rational methods in all fields of inquiry. Empiricism and rationalism became the primary sources for the acquisition of knowledge. Rationalism is the belief that phenomena are best understood through logic and reason and empiricism is the belief that knowledge is based on sense experience. Much of the modernisation process outlined above was made possible through the development of science.

The worldview fostered by science came into direct conflict with that of religion and in order to make "science possible, religion's claim to hegemony over the mind had to be broken."[7] Challenging the hegemony of the Church, both in its Catholic and Protestant forms, was fraught with danger. It was in this environment that the champions of science insisted that the scientific method was merely an objective endeavour using rationalism and empirical measurements to test hypotheses. Scientific procedures involved experimentation, observation, reasoning and review. Success in terms of this methodology was evaluated in terms of the application of scientific discoveries to technology.

The universe as understood by science turned out to be radically different from how it was understood by Christianity. Science thrived in circumstances of doubt, scepticism and revision. Such ideas were anathema to Christian theological orthodoxy and culminated in the burning of many scientists at the stake by the Church. Thinkers such as Galileo Galilei, René Descartes, Francis Bacon, Marin Mersenne and Pierre Gassendi found ways of separating science and religion. They implied that religion dealt with spiritual matters and science dealt with the material world.

This attitude opened up a debate about the relation of the one to the other, with the ultimate triumph of the scientific attitude over religious belief as the final arbiter over thought and action. It was the victory of atheism over religion. Once the power of God over individual thought and social action is denied, religion ceases to be a vital factor in human life, even though some belief in God may subsist. In other words, as expressed in the philosophy of Nietzsche, God dies. It is in this sense that Shaykh Abdalqadir argues: "At the centre of this ruined world is the lack of recognition of the Divine. The age is both atheist and bankrupt. Man has been reduced to being a debtor when the world is rich and full. The atheist is at the core of the disaster, having mistaken the idea of god for Divinity. Rightly he rejects theism. So too, do the Muslims. The reality of man is that he has a dynamic opening to the Divine."[8]

# PART 2

Shaykh Abdalqadir says: "The horror of this modern age is not the annihilation of millions in Nazi Death Camps and Stalin's Gulags, nor is it the obliteration of a whole society in Iraq and Afghanistan. It is not the slaughter and torture of the innocents. The horror of this age is the somnambulistic helplessness of the masses to ACT to stop the global holocaust. It is this unarguable condition of mankind which permits us to define the technic society as a psychosis."[1] In this part of the book we will look at the pillars of the ideology that sustains the psychosis of capitalism and hides the fraud, scam, theft and deception that it is. These stratagems have been devised by capitalism to enable them to fool all the people all of the time into passivity. Shaykh Abdalqadir says that our civic reality is a "socially structured psychosis."[2] This socially structured psychosis is created through politics, state capture, economics, scientific materialism, public relations, the nuclear family, education and media.

# Chapter 7

## Politics

It is claimed, by its proponents, that finally, with democracy, society was being established on rational principles. Democracy meant that the struggle of centuries was over and we had achieved the ultimate purpose for mankind. "The future was free of conflict, in its place came shopping and limitless sexual practice, meaningful and guiltless. History had come to an end."[1] The idea that a country can be run by any other system than political democracy, specifically party democracy, is the anathema of this new thinking. Aisha Bewley says: "Modern democracy provides freedom – freedom for the pursuit of one's own interests, but subject to the tyranny of the majority. This is the will of the majority – or more precisely as expressed by many – the tyranny of the majority. In other words, if you do not agree with the herd as a whole, you are a wolf – and must be removed or silenced."[2] The herd is so well programmed that it is unaware of the reality, which is that "political democracy is the obedient servant of the financial oligarchy, a public relations branch of an un-elected elite."[3] Shaykh Abdalqadir outlines six stages in the development of democracy.

Stage One – The Machine

Political democracy is a machine which functions by interfacing with the public through the media and by opening up its parliamentary sessions, thereby enabling the public to observe the deliberations of the assembled representatives of the people. They have been elected from an electoral roll defined by geographical district and the time of their tenure is limited to around four to five years. These representatives belong to political parties proposing a political agenda. Two adversarial parties are preferred but sometimes, when they fail to gain a working majority, they form coalitions with minor parties or rely on independents. The party members are incapable of financially sustaining their parties and depend on donations. The left wing parties depend on trade union contributions, left wing newspaper tycoons and "socialist" millionaires. The right wing parties tend to receive their funding from large corporations, right wing newspapers and right wing billionaires.

We can see from this arrangement that the representatives are controlled by their parties, their financial sponsors and lastly by the rules and regulations of the assembly in which they sit. It has to be borne in mind that no modern state could survive with a complete change of leadership over such a swift cycle of time (around four to five years), and it is the civil service, the bureaucracy behind the scenes, that is the bureaucracy that in the end does the deciding, governing and dictating. The idea that it is the people's representatives that govern is an illusion. Shaykh Abdalqadir in his later analysis of democracy goes on to show that beyond the elected representatives and bureaucracy "we will find that the trail of authority leads even further down the dark corridors of power to a hidden elite."[4]

Stage Two – The Personnel

It is only a certain kind of person who can submit to the requirements and punishments of the machine of political democracy. There was a time when politicians had the confidence to speak up with effective and persuasive rhetoric. Now they speak in an exalted and idealistic rhetorical style only to conceal their irrelevance. There is a general agreement among people that politicians are corrupt, unprincipled and hypocritical. "The politician must toe the party line. The politician must unprotestingly accept demotion. In other words he must be without honour. His loyalty is never to principles but to pragmatism. In other words, an altogether despicable creature."[5]

Stage Three – The Party

The bicameral parliamentary assembly in its modern form is derived from the founding assembly in Paris before and after the death of Louis XVI. The two main political factions crystallised during the momentous events of the revolution from 1789 to 1792. This is when the Right and the Left were born and the resulting rivalry has, in the last two hundred years, seen the opposing parties, "hurling everything from invective to the explosive device"[6] at each other. Party A assumes power on the grounds that Party B has ruined the economy and brought strife to the nation. Once in power they explain that the reason that they were unable to fulfil their election promises was because they were cleaning up the disastrous errors of the previous administration. At the next election they are flung out of office. Once in power the opposing party renege on their promises to undo the disasters of the last government. They tell the people they had no idea what a disaster they were inheriting until they took office. "What is intriguing," Shaykh Abdalqadir writes, "is that if the People are so smart that they can choose those who will govern them, why do they continue to choose a system and individuals who have cyclically proved to bring utter failure upon the society?"[7]

STAGE FOUR – THE CRISIS

Democracy is not, as is taught to the masses, just, people-governed and an evolutionary end-station. The reality is that the democratic state is not the fantasy procedure of the ballot box but rather it represents the state as machine. Political leaders are operative command modules each one representing a variant model of the modern state as designed by Napoleon. A module is one of a set of separate parts or units that can be joined together to make a machine. What Napoleon did was expertly design and set in place a new machine of modern statism. It is part of the essential nature of democracy that breakdown and crisis are inevitable. Due to the inevitable nature of crises in the capitalist system it is false to make a distinction between dictatorships and democracies "since in political and existential terms these two modes are synonymous. For example it should be pointed out that state control and access is now almost total. The modern State can freeze the funds of an individual, examine in minute detail the character of their expenditure, and trace their movements inside and outside state boundaries. ... In democracy dictatorship is either latent or active. It is simply one of its modes."[8]

Shaykh Abdalqadir explains crisis management as follows: "The procedures which gave legality, and indeed were the legality on which Terror[9] was founded, have not in any way been surpassed in more recent democratic political procedure and practices. A constitutional instrument of power is itself a dynamic which can move into special modes, crisis policies, emergency powers, rules of exception. Such powers, far from being rare, are constraints of 'democratic' governance, which allows us to say, however illogical it demonstrably is, that totalitarian edict and Terror are both built into, and necessary for, the continuance and survival of the same democratic system."[10] The old saying, as famously stated by Winston Churchill, is: "Don't waste a good crisis." This is exactly what happens again and again, as we have seen in 2001 (terrorism), 2008 (global financial crisis) and 2020 (Covid pandemic).

### Stage Five – The Leader

The true nature of democracy is war, fighting in the streets, the hooligans, race riots, school children murdering their classmates and the poll-tax riots. To stop the battle of the adversarial parties spilling over into internecine warfare, citizen against citizen, democracy has to find an equilibrium. Peace at home is guaranteed by war on the frontier. Peace requires the cabinet, committee and the theatre of debate. War needs a leader who will maintain peace internally and, once the war is over, the leader has to be discarded as with the execution of Mussolini. No such demise was necessary for Hitler; he committed suicide. If the war-time leader is not replaced the truth, that democracy is itself dictatorship, is laid bare. The elected government and the leader represent the lowest common denominator of the masses.

Shaykh Abdalqadir takes examples of leaders and shows that they had extreme deficiency of character and, in some cases, personalities that were split right down the middle. Hitler was a genocidal maniac but, at the same time, he was vegetarian, loved his Alsatian dog, cowboy novels and afternoon tea with scrumptious cream cakes. His brilliant creation was the Nazi party apparatus. Stalin was a student of the Orthodox Seminary and his modernisation plans were his technical achievement. He was also a compulsive drinker who went on to murder millions of people. Napoleon had the capacity to design the architecture of a modern state and the technical procedures of mass battles but "His very assumption of Empire has in it an inescapable vulgarity. The Empire style is not the image of glory but somehow seems to be the perfect décor of the Pigalle night club."[11] What can be observed from these leaders is that alongside an extremely developed technical ability they were unsavoury characters.

### Stage Six – The Money

Democracy has proved to be the instrument of mass exploitation by the financial oligarchs. As Shaykh Abdalqadir says: "Political Democracy in this new epoch has been reduced to being nothing more than a political front for banking."[12] To illustrate the truth of this statement let us see how this link between government and banking works in the USA. The relation between Wall Street and the Treasury is effectively a "revolving door" from Wall Street to the Treasury Department to Wall Street. Private bankers who take up appointments in the Treasury ensure that all the resources and policies Wall Street needs are granted with the least hindrance from citizens, workers or taxpayers. They ensure that the highest priority is given to the survival, recovery and expansion of Wall Street profits. They block regulations or restrictions on bonuses and loopholes in the financial system. These Wall Street executives gain a reputation from being in the Treasury and then return to the private sector in higher positions than they held before. A Treasury appointment is a ladder up the Wall Street hierarchy and they return as senior advisers and partners in Wall Street firms. Approximately 774 officials departed from the Treasury between January 2009 and August 2011.[13] Having provided beneficial services to their future Wall Street bosses they re-enter private finance at a higher more lucrative position.

It is clear that elections, parties and electoral campaigns have little to do with democracy and more to do with selecting the president and legislators who then appoint un-elected Wall Street executives to make the strategic economic decisions for all the people of the US. The Wall Street/Treasury alliance has been a boon for finance capital. Despite universal condemnation of Wall Street by the vast majority of the public for its swindles, bankruptcies, job losses and mortgage foreclosures, the Wall Street/Treasury alliance publicly backed the trillion dollar bailout after the 2008-2009 financial crisis. They dumped the entire "free market" doctrine that justified profits based on risk and imposed the new dogma of "too big to fail", in which the state treasury guarantees bailouts even when companies face bankruptcy, providing they are billion dollar firms.

They also abandoned the principle of "fiscal responsibility" in favour of hundreds of billions of dollars in tax cuts for the corporate-financial elites, running up record peace-time budget deficits and then blaming the social programs that are supported by popular majorities. On top of all that the Treasury and the Federal Reserve (US Central Bank) provide near zero interest loans that guarantee big profits to private financial institutions which borrow at these low rates from the Federal Reserve Bank and then lend at high rates (anywhere from four to ten times the interest rates they pay) even including back to the government, especially in purchasing overseas government and corporate bonds. It is the taxpayers who are providing an enormous subsidy for Wall Street speculation.

In other words speculative activities are now insured by the federal government under the "too big to fail" doctrine. It must be noted that increased productivity and profitability is not, as governments and central banks claim , the result of innovation. It is a product of a state labour policy that deepens inequality by holding down wages and raising profit margins. There are fewer workers producing more commodities and no refinancing for households and small and medium size firms, leading to bankruptcies, buyouts and "consolidation" that is, greater concentration of ownership. This results in the stagnation of the mass market whilst corporate and bank profits reach record levels. According to financial experts the Wall Street/Treasury alliance has created a "new order" in which "bankers are a protected class who enjoy bonuses regardless of performance, while relying on the taxpayer to socialise their losses."[14]

Shaykh Abdalqadir draws attention to the inability of the general population to identify the motor forces of the social reality in which they live. He points out that in 1913 the US Supreme Court Judge, Louis Brandeis (1864-1941) said that the "dominant element in our financial oligarchy is the investment banker."[15] From 1947 onwards the new oligarchy introduced a set of complex instruments and measurements (i.e. technical terms and practices), which for over half a century were adopted globally, encompassing world markets. Detailed studies were published with regards to instruments such as securitisation, high yield debt, arbitrage trading, derivatives, credit default swaps and interest rate swaps. Research around financial concepts, structures and theories produced the Black-Scholes model, deregulation doctrines and efficient market hypothesis.

In the last decade of the twentieth century the financial elite exercised very significant influence over politicians, winning for the banks extended powers and banking deregulation. In the US the Riegle-Neal Act of 1974 removed restrictions on interstate banking. The Gramm-Leach-Bliley Act of 1999 demolished remaining barriers between commercial and investment banking and the Commodity Futures Modernisation Act of 2000 prohibited Federal regulation of over-the-counter (O.T.C.) derivatives. One of those who introduced the Gramm-Leach-Bliley Act of 1999 for legislation to the US Senate was Senator Phil Gramm who became

Vice-Chairman of the Investment Bank Division of UBS AG after retiring from the Senate.

In the Spring of 2009 the following C.E.O.s of thirteen of America's leading banks met with the US President: Ken Chenault of American Express, Ken Lewis of the Bank of America, Robert Kelly of the Bank of New York Mellon, Vikram Pandit from Citigroup, John Koskinen of Freddie Mac, Lloyd Blankfein of Goldman Sachs, Jamie Dimon from JP Morgan Chase, John Mack of Morgan Stanley, Rick Waddell from Northern Trust, James Rohr of PNC, Ronald Logue from State Street, Richard Davis of the US Bank and John Stumpf from Wells Fargo. Shaykh Abdalqadir comments that: "The important thing to recognise is that these names would have remained completely hidden and unknown to the masses. It was only the financial collapse of 2008 that forced the oligarchic chiefs into the open. It must also be taken into account that they were responsible for the loss of billions of dollars."[16]

# Chapter 8

## State Capture

The modern state, being the institution that we are born into, has become so commonplace that little thought is given to its significance in our daily lives. The distinction between government and state has become blurred. A state is a geographic area while a government is the entity that administers or manages that area. The government has legislative, executive, and judicial powers to enforce the laws of the state. One reason for our complacency with regards to government and state is that it is generally believed that all questions relating to the state have been resolved. It is assumed "that power in Western societies, is competitive, fragmented and diffused; everybody, directly or in organised groups, has some power and nobody has or can have too much of it. In these societies, citizens enjoy universal suffrage, free and regular elections, representative institutions, effective citizen rights, including the right of free speech, association and opposition; and both individuals and groups take ample advantage of these rights, under the protection of the law, an independent judiciary and a free political culture."[1]

In this view, therefore, governments respond to the demands of competing interests. From this democratic-pluralist perspective it is a political system in which the voices of all active and legitimate groups can make themselves heard at some crucial stage in the decision-making process. Political scientists who hold this view, however, do agree that economic, social, political, administrative and professional elites do exert pressure on the state, and that the role of the state is to accommodate and reconcile the conflicting lobbying of these organised groups and interests. This is what we are expected to believe but the reality, however, is very different.

## The Corporate State

Joel Bakan said: "Over the last decade, our society as a whole has now taken on the operating principles that define the corporation. We are no longer a society that has corporations within it, but we have become a corporate society. ... We have become less able to constrain the harmful consequences of the corporation and, in fact, our governments and public institutions have increasingly become even more beholden to, and dominated by, business corporations."[2]

The true era of the corporate form began with the construction of railways in the USA and Britain. Railways required large sums of money to lay tracks, manufacture rolling stock (trains etc.), and operate and maintain systems. The industry came to rely on corporate financing. In England between 1825 and 1849 the amount of capital raised rose from £200,000 to £230 million mainly through joint-stock companies. In the USA more than one hundred thousand miles of track were laid between 1865 and 1885. At this stage in the development of the corporation the person investing in a corporation was personally liable, without limits, for the company's debts. The investor's assets would be exposed to claims by creditors if a company failed. Business leaders and politicians, however, began to change the law in order to limit the liability of shareholders to the amounts they invested in a company.

In England limited liability became part of corporate law in 1856 as it did later that century in the USA. In order to attract corporate investments into their jurisdictions, states (both at federal and provincial levels in the USA) began to discard restrictions from their corporate laws. They repealed the rules that required businesses to incorporate for only narrowly defined purposes, for limited durations and to operate in particular locations. Controls on acquisitions and mergers were loosened and the rule that one company could not buy stock in another company was abolished. This launched the era of corporate capitalism and within a few decades economies, in which there had previously been individually owned companies freely competing with each other, became dominated by relatively few huge corporations each owned by many shareholders.

By the end of the $19^{th}$ century the law courts had transformed corporations into legal persons with identities separate from the people who were its owners and managers. Corporations were empowered, like real people, to conduct business in their own names, employ workers, acquire assets, pay taxes, and defend their own rights and actions in court. Corporations were viewed as free individuals with rights to the due process of law. Naturally, with these protections in place the size and power of corporations grew.

Corporations have always relied on "externalities" for the maximisation of their profits. An externality, as an economic term, means the effect of a transaction on a third party who has not consented to, or played any role in, the transaction itself. In other words corporations make others pay for their expenditure. Corporations, for example, rely on governments to provide infrastructure, education and research and development for their commercial activities. For corporations, externalities also include the harm caused to others, that is, workers, communities and the environment. These include air, water and noise pollution, climate change, industrial farm animal production, overuse of antibiotics, processed foods, and passive smoking to name but a few.

Governments have put legislation in place in order to limit the exploitation of people and environmental damage by corporations. However, through lobbying, public relations campaigns and political donations, corporations and their leaders have turned the political system and public opinion against adopting these regulations and, as a result, the ability of the law to protect people and the environment from harm has suffered. In the US: "Another significant change in corporate-government relations since the 1970s has been the expanded role of corporate donations within the electoral system. In the mid-1970s the Supreme Court extended First Amendment constitutional protection to corporate financing of elections, a decision that opened the door to corporations' near-complete takeover of the electoral process."[3] Corporate donations fuel the political process and form the core strategy for influencing government support for business campaigns.

Over the last 150 years corporations have risen from relative obscurity to become the world's dominant economic institution. Today corporations determine what we eat, watch, wear, where we work and what we do. Their culture, iconography and ideology surround everything. Increasingly corporations have gained the power to influence government decisions and to control domains of society once well-established within the public sphere.

In 2000 Charles Derber, by amalgamating the words corporation and democracy, called the political system we are living in a global corpocracy. He explained it as follows: "The commanding role of business has become the key element of the new system. This partly reflects the astonishing new size and global reach of transnational corporations, the largest being virtually world empires in their own right, with their own global rules and private armies. The biggest global corporations are each far larger, economically speaking, than most countries in the world. General Motors' annual sales are larger than the gross domestic product of Denmark. Walmart is bigger than Poland, Ford is larger than South Africa, and Daimler/Chrysler is bigger than Greece. Phillip Morris's sales are greater than the GDPs of 148 countries. Of the hundred biggest economies in the world – counting both corporations and countries – fifty one are global corporations. The top ten alone in terms of sales – GM, Walmart, Ford, Exxon Mobil, Daimler/Chrysler, Toyota, GE, Royal Dutch/Shell, IBM, and BP Amoco – are each larger than about 140 of the 190 nations of the world. The top five corporations are each bigger than 182 of 190 countries."[4]

There are more than 45,000 corporations worldwide with 300,000 affiliates, and the sales of the top 200 account for more than 25 percent of the entire output of the world. These top 200 hold 90 percent of the world's patents; they grow, refine, and sell much of the world's food; they supply nearly all the energy for transportation and for domestic, commercial and industrial use; they operate the global media and entertainment companies that reach billions of people; and they create most of the world's software and manufacture the computers it runs on. "They build the airplanes and cars we travel in, make most of our clothes, provide most of the world's banking and financial services and, increasingly, dominate services from health care to financial services to retailing. Finally the top 200 produce nearly all the weapons that cram the arsenals of nations everywhere."[5]

## How the State was Captured

In academia, corruption within the state is termed state capture, regulatory capture and crony capitalism. State capture is defined as systemic political corruption whereby private interests influence the decision making processes of the state to their advantage. There is corruption in all countries but the most corrupt countries in the world are in North America and Europe – in countries that claim to be advanced democracies. The most unjust example of corruption has been the passing of legislation permitting fractional reserve banking and fiat money. Governments are complicit in these crimes, i.e. those of fractional reserve banking and fiat money. Shaykh Abdalqadir says: "All the crimes of all the criminals in the world do not amount to the enormity of this crime that they daily commit through their continued application of the usury system."[6] In more recent times the Enron scandal and the 2008 financial crisis provide ample evidence of state capture by corporations. Let us look at three areas in which corruption takes place: civil society; business; and politics.

### (a) Civil Society

In his investigation into media reports G. McMahon found cases of regulatory capture amongst: officers of the court; medical researchers; auditors; police; criminal investigators; archbishops; environmental protection authorities; insurance regulators; health bureaucrats; and even a Commission of Enquiry. He explains that: "The last decade in Australia [another so-called advanced democracy] has seen many demonstrations of the phenomenon of 'regulatory capture', that is, capture of 'regulators' by the regulated. By 'capture' is meant behaviours, active and passive, by responsible authorities, which behaviours act to protect the same illegal, unethical, immoral or anti-public interest practices that those authorities are charged with 'policing'. ... This phenomenon of 'capture' has been visible with respect to the regulation functions carried out within Australia's private sector organisations, within professions, and within State and Federal public sector authorities. Australian experience has been matched in recent times by spectacular examples of regulatory capture in other democratic countries."[7]

(B) BUSINESS

Corruption is endemic in companies in all of the economically developed countries. Until the 1999 OECD Convention on Combating Bribery of Foreign Public Officials in International Business Transactions, bribery was legal and could be claimed as a tax deductible expense.[8] Even though it is illegal in the countries that have signed up to the Convention, the crime of bribery continues unabated. According to a report from Transparency International released on 12 September 2018, almost all of the world's most powerful export markets are failing to punish corporations paying bribes overseas. The countries and territories reviewed in the report are responsible for more than 80 per cent of world exports. China, the world's biggest exporter, was also evaluated in the report as were India, Singapore and Hong Kong, which are not signatories to the OECD Convention but are parties to the UN Convention against Corruption.

The report featured case studies of five companies operating in the sectors of aerospace, construction, mining and oil: Airbus, Odebrecht, Rio Tinto, SBM Offshore and Sinopec. The Rio Tinto case study also makes reference to China Sonangol and China International Fund. The report revealed that "an alarming proportion of world trade occurs in a consequence-free environment for foreign bribery and makes specific recommendations to governments and the international community for improving enforcement."[9] In an article entitled:

"Foreign Bribery Rages Unchecked in Over Half of Global Trade", Transparency International wrote: "There are many losers and few winners when companies bribe foreign public officials to win lucrative overseas contracts. In prioritising profits over principles, governments in most major exporting countries fail to prosecute companies flouting laws criminalising foreign bribery. What is missing is active enforcement."[10]

Companies bribe in order to gain mining rights, contracts for major construction projects, purchases of planes and other deals. One of the most shocking examples is the massive foreign bribery scheme carried out by the Brazilian construction conglomerate Odebrecht involving about US$788 million in bribes to government officials and political parties in at least 12 countries. The Oderbrecht example, however, is dwarfed by the case in which French, UK and US authorities announced that Airbus would pay record penalties for foreign bribery, after the European aerospace manufacturer reached a €3.6 billion corporate plea deal to end a long-running corruption probe. This case shows that bribery of foreign officials in the public and private sectors was part of a major multinational corporation's business model. French prosecutors said the violations that they uncovered increased Airbus's profits by one billion Euros.

Foreign bribery has a pernicious and devastating effect on the countries where the bribes are paid because governments pay higher prices for lower quality goods or incomplete services. They also waste millions on unnecessary procurements due to which essential services like education and healthcare are deprived of much needed funds. In poorer countries the impact can be a matter of life and death. Limited resources are diverted to benefit a few individuals while citizens are denied vital services, such as access to clean water, safe roads or basic health services.

(c) Politics

Shaykh Abdalqadir says that there are two ways of writing the history of a democratic regime. The first rests on the legal state, on declared principles, public programs, the model well presented: on stage as it were. The second consists of not looking at what is on stage, but rather looking at what is happening off-stage, in the wings, "that is to say not the façade of official history but the practice and the real history of democracy."[11] The democratic political process is manipulated by political professionals, a new kind of managerial elite, and the mechanism of the political process is "so specialised that access to it is correctly limited to its own professionals ... to that handful of insiders who invent, year in and year out, the narrative of public life."[12]

A spectacular example of state and regulatory capture is provided by the American Legislative Exchange Council (ALEC). Summing up this organisation Alan Greenblatt says: "For decades, the American Legislative Exchange Council has been a force in shaping conservative policies at the state level. Today, its impact is even more pervasive. Its legislative ideas are resonating in practically every area of state government, from education and health to energy, environment and tax policy. The group, which brings together legislators with representatives from corporations, think-tanks and foundations to craft model bills, has rung up an impressive score. Roughly 1,000 bills based on ALEC language are introduced in an average year, with about 20 percent getting enacted."[13]

In his book *State Capture How Conservative Activists, Big Businesses, and Wealthy Donors Reshaped the American States – and the Nation,* Alexander Hertel-Fernandez says ALEC's model bills focus on corporate-friendly priorities. The most common proposals ALEC advances lift environmental, health, safety, and economic regulations on business; cut taxes on wealthy individuals and companies; and privatise state programs and agencies.[14] As well as making these proposals ALEC works at setting policies that increase corporate profits. State governments are also battlegrounds where businesses can have important advantages. State legislators are attuned to corporate demands, especially when businesses threaten layoffs or relocating to other states.

Another advantage for business is that most Americans do not pay much attention to what happens in state legislatures. This lack of scrutiny gives businesses more opportunities to shape policy with almost no opposition. ALEC has boasted a membership of around 200 of the largest and most prominent companies throughout the country. Its corporate backers have included businesses such as Amazon, FedEx, Google, UPS, Facebook, Kraft Foods, McDonald's, Visa, Walmart, and State Farm Insurance. ALEC's corporate members provide for the group's annual budget of some $6 million to $10 million. Many private companies also sponsor ALEC such as those owned by the Koch brothers. ALEC has been an ideal way to advance the policy priorities of the political parties.

Alexander Hertel-Fernandez has shown through his research that political scientists have struggled to show a clear link between corporate political spending and policy outcomes. It is always challenging to detect a clear-cut relationship between the weight of interest groups and their ultimate policy successes and losses. "One important reason why it is so difficult for scholars to pin down exactly how business shapes policy is that corporate interventions often occur early on in the legislative process, shaping the agenda of alternatives that are considered by lawmakers and specific language that is drafted within a bill. That means studies focusing on the later stages of policymaking, and especially roll call votes, will have difficulty detecting traces of business power."[15]

Hertel-Fernandez was able to take advantage of the operation of ALEC to pin down precisely how policy proposals, including many corporate drafted priorities, end up in state law. ALEC relies on model bills to lobby state legislatures and these can be compared with actual legislation to see when and where state lawmakers borrowed text from ALEC proposals. This process offers a much richer picture of where businesses, operating through ALEC, got their way in state policy. It underscores the importance of looking beyond traditional measures of business clout, such as disclosed campaign contributions from businesses, as evidence for enduring relationships between individual lawmakers and organisations, like ALEC, that grant corporate managers access to the policymaking process.

US businesses keep their most controversial and ideological political participation off the public's radar as a deliberate strategy on the part of businesses to shield themselves from consumer or investor backlash. Researchers who look at companies' public involvements, like political action committee contributions or disclosed federal lobbying expenditures, will necessarily miss out on corporate participation in groups like ALEC. Many of the largest and most prominent Fortune 500 companies with relatively unremarkable electoral giving are also heavily supporting ideologically-supercharged bodies such as ALEC.

# Chapter 9

## Economics

Economics, masquerading as a science, is first and foremost the ideological tool concealing the chicanery that is capitalism. Economics is defined in textbooks as a social science and it is claimed that a major task of economists is to discover how the economic world works. In order to achieve this goal economists claim to use scientific methods to study: the impact of technological change; determinants of income; role of government; causes of unemployment; origins of increases in the level of prices; gains from trade with the rest of the world; and sources of growth.[1]

Contrary to that view the economist Ha-Joon Chang argues that economics is not a science; it is an ideology. He wrote: "Economics is a political argument. It is not – and can never be – a science; there are no objective truths in economics that can be established independently of political, and frequently moral, judgments. Therefore, when faced with an economic argument, you must ask the age-old question 'Cui bono?' (Who benefits?), first made famous by the Roman statesman and orator Marcus Tullius Cicero."[2]

Shaykh Abdalqadir says: "There is an all-powerful junta of financiers who do effectively govern human affairs and they were appointed by no known franchise."[3] He explains this statement in detail as follows: "Another deliberate over-simplification of the *kāfir* banking system is that banking operates in some kind of economic vacuum. While it has its own rules and systems, it is utterly interactive with other networked institutions of the *mushrik*[4] anthropology. ... We have no choice but to characterise the whole monetary system as usurious. That is to say that the whole interactive networked system of banks and megabanks (IMF, World Bank, etc), stock exchanges and all forms of trading conducted under their protocols, are nothing other than the true face of usurious power control which openly governs the world through its own organisations and personnel. They, in turn, are dispersed over the banking system as such, and are interlocked with the vassal systems of so-called democratic governments and their agencies on the one hand, and the puppet dictators who rule the debtor client nations on the other."[5]

Shaykh Abdalqadir states quite clearly that the dominant element in the financial oligarchy is the investment banker.[6] When seen in the context of historical and geographic reality this becomes apparent. We will attempt to do this very briefly. Modern capitalism, known as mercantilism, emerged in the early modern period between the 16th and 18th centuries. It evolved through the phases of colonialism, European imperialism and neo-colonialism into its present form of neo-liberalism. In order to understand neo-liberalism David Harvey's definition is particularly useful: "Neo-liberalism is in the first instance a theory of political economic practices that proposes that human well-being can best be advanced by liberating individual entrepreneurial freedoms and skills within an institutional framework characterised by strong private property rights, free markets, and free trade. The role of the state is to create and preserve an institutional framework appropriate to such practices. The state has to guarantee, for example, the quality and integrity of money. It must also set up those military, defence, police, and legal structures and functions required to secure private property rights and to guarantee, by force if need be, the proper functioning of markets. Furthermore if markets do not exist (in areas such as land, water, education, health care, social security, or environmental pollution) then they must be created, by state action if necessary. But beyond these tasks the state should not venture. State interventions in markets (once created) must be kept to a bare minimum because, according to the theory, the state cannot possibly possess information to second-guess market signals (prices), and because powerful interest groups will inevitably distort and bias state interventions (particularly in democracies) for their own benefit."[7]

Almost all states have turned to neo-liberalism in their political and economic practices and thinking since the 1970s. The proponents of neo-liberalism occupy positions of influence in education, media, corporate boardrooms, financial institutions, treasury departments, central banks, the International Monetary Fund (IMF), the World Bank and the World Trade Organisation. Neo-liberalism has become hegemonic as a mode of discourse. It has pervasive effects on ways of thought to the point where it has become the common-sense way people interpret, live in, and understand the world.

Neo-liberalism adopted the political ideals of human dignity and political freedom as the central values of civilisation so as to appeal to the intuitions, instincts, values and desires of human beings.

These values, it was stated, were threatened not only by fascism, communism and dictatorships, but also by all forms of state intervention. Neo-liberals adhere to the free market principles that are aimed at displacing the classical economic theories of

Adam Smith, David Ricardo and Karl Marx. At the same time they promote Adam Smith's view that the hidden hand of the market is the best device for controlling even the basest of human instincts such as gluttony, greed and the desire for wealth and power. Neo-liberal doctrine is deeply opposed not only to Marxist inspired centralised state planning but to all forms of state interventionist theories. State decisions on matters of investment and capital accumulation, they believe, are bound to be wrong because the information available to the state will never equal the information that the market possesses.

The manifestation of neo-liberalism as an economic orthodoxy at a state level began in 1979 in Britain with the election of Margaret Thatcher and in the USA with Paul Volker, chairman of the US Federal Reserve Bank. Ronald Reagan's election in 1980 provided the political backing for further deregulation, tax cuts, budget cuts, attacks on trade union and professional power in the US. This began the impetus for the momentous shift towards greater social inequality and the restoration of economic power to the finance, media and commodities elites.

During the OPEC oil price hike in 1973, the US forced the oil producing countries of the Middle East to recycle their vast amounts of petrodollars through the New York investment banks. Many governments in the developing world happily borrowed but this required secure conditions for lending. To secure conditions for lending the investment banks looked to the US imperial tradition to open new investment opportunities and to protect their foreign operations. The US government would find a local strongman and provide economic and military assistance to him, his family and immediate allies, so that they could repress or buy off opposition whilst accumulating wealth and power for themselves. In return these regimes, once in power, would open up their countries to US capital and promote US interests in their countries and abroad. In places where US influence could not be bought, covert operations and military force were deployed.

In 2004 John Perkins published his book, *Confessions of an Economic Hit Man*, and in it he described his career of convincing heads of state to adopt economic policies that impoverished their countries and undermined democratic institutions. These policies helped enrich tiny, local elite groups while filling the pockets of US-based transnational corporations. He worked for a private consulting company where his job, as an economist, was to generate reports that justified lucrative contracts for US corporations, whilst sinking vulnerable nations into debt. Countries that did not cooperate had the screws tightened on their economies. For example, President Richard Nixon famously called on the CIA to "make the economy [of Chile] scream" to undermine the democratically elected president, Salvador Allende. In a recent interview Perkins said: "Back in my day we were pretty much limited to what we called the third world, or economically developing countries, but now it's everywhere. And in fact, the cancer of the corporate empire has metastasized into what I would call a failed global death economy. This is an economy that's based on destroying the very resources upon which it depends, and upon the military. It's become totally global, and it's a failure."[8]

Eric Lipton at *The New York Times* noted that in the Trump administration we continue to see "the merging of private business interest with government affairs." As an example, the billionaire investor Carl Icahn was named special adviser to the president but, since he was not officially a government employee, he was not subject to conflict of interest divestment requirements. As a consequence, Icahn retained his majority holdings in an oil refinery whilst advocating for rule changes that would benefit his refinery.

"We have reached an apotheosis of concentrated wealth running government for their interests – Trump's cabinet had more wealth than one-third of American households, and Icahn is wealthier than all of them combined."[9]

Violence, intrigue and economic power could not by themselves attain success for neo-liberalism. The question that arises is: how then was it accomplished? What the capitalists did was to construct politically and economically a neo-liberal market-based populist culture of consumerism and libertarianism. In August 1971, just prior to his appointment to the Supreme Court, Lewis Powell sent a memo to the US Chamber of Commerce stating that: "It is time for American business – which has demonstrated the greatest capacity in all history to produce and to influence consumer decisions – to apply their great talents vigorously to the preservation of the system itself. ... The role of the National Chamber of Commerce is therefore vital. Other national organisations (especially those of various industrial and commercial groups) should join in the effort, but no other organisations appear to be as well situated as the Chamber. It enjoys a strategic position, with a fine reputation and a broad base of support. Also – and this is of immeasurable merit – there are hundreds of local Chambers of Commerce which can play a vital supportive role."[10]

He was suggesting that the Chamber of Commerce should lead the assault on the major institutions of society, that is, political, economic, legal, educational, media and publishing, in order to transform what people thought about corporations, the law, culture and the individual. What influence the Powell memo had is impossible to assess but it gives us an insight as to what really happened in the decades that followed. What did happen was the 'construction of consent' throughout large parts of the world.

The model for the neo-liberal paradigm was New York City. The New York City fiscal crisis "pioneered the way for neo-liberal practices both domestically under Reagan and internationally through the IMF in the 1980s. It established the principle that in the event of a conflict between the integrity of the financial institutions and bondholders' returns on the one hand, and the wellbeing of the citizens on the other, the former was to be privileged. It emphasised that the role of government was to create a good business climate rather than look to the needs and well-being of the population at large."[11] Capitalist restructuring and de-industrialisation had for years been eroding the economic base of New York City and rapid suburbanisation had left much of the central city impoverished. The gap between revenues and expenditure in the City budget was already large due to extravagant borrowing over many years. With recession escalating, the gap increased considerably.

Financial institutions were at first prepared to finance the deficit, but in 1975 a powerful cabal of investment bankers refused to roll over the debt and pushed the city into technical bankruptcy. The bailout amounted to a coup by the financial institutions against the democratically elected government of New York City. New institutions were created to take over the management of the city budget. They had first claim on city tax revenues and what was left went for essential services. This effectively curbed the city's powerful municipal unions. Wage freezes were implemented as were cutbacks in public employment and social provision (education, transport services and public health) and, for the first time, tuition fees were imposed on the City University of New York system, and municipal unions had to invest their pension funds in city bonds. The consequences of the New York City fiscal crisis and the actions taken by the investment bankers on the working class and ethnic immigrants of the city were devastating. They were ignored only to be ravaged by racism and drug addiction which left many young people dead, homeless, imprisoned or annihilated by AIDS.

The New York investment bankers seized the opportunity to restructure the city in ways that suited their agenda, which was the creation of 'a good business climate.' Public resources were used to build infrastructure for business, particularly in telecommunications. Subsidies and tax incentives were offered to business enterprises. The investment bankers restructured the city's economy around financial activities and ancillary services. They promoted diversified consumerism with an emphasis on gentrification and neighbourhood restoration. The governance of the city was taken to be an entrepreneurial entity and the democratic and representational functions of local government were diminished. There is an uncanny concordance between all of this and the memo sent by Lewis Powell to the US Chamber of Commerce.

The New York City fiscal crisis not only pioneered the way for neo-liberal practices domestically but it did so internationally as well through the IMF. As already mentioned, during the OPEC oil price hike in 1973 the US forced the oil producing countries of the Middle East to recycle their vast amounts of petrodollars through the New York investment banks. Many governments in the developing world happily borrowed this money. The bedrock of the world monetary system is private banks, with states, including their central banks and treasuries, acting as guarantors for them – the IMF works on their behalf. Susan George said: "As watchdog and messenger, the IMF helps to ensure that overexposed banks will be repaid, that even major borrowers like Mexico will be prevented from destabilising the system as a whole. As alibi, it allows the major industrialised countries and their banks to off-load the consequences of their own short-sighted policies and financial recklessness on to the Fund's shoulders. The IMF helps them to consolidate their power over poor nations. At the same time, and in exchange for co-operation, it generally allows the elites of these same nations to maintain their affluence and perks at the expense of the majority of their fellow citizens. The IMF is a sort of Godfather figure – it makes countries offers they can't refuse."[12]

Let's take a closer look at what this means in practice. At the end of 2012 the financial aid, investment and income from abroad to poor countries was a little over $2 trillion. In the same year $5 trillion went from the poor countries to the rich ones. There was a net outflow of $3 trillion dollars. This outflow consists of: payments on debt[13]; and repatriation of profits from foreign investors[14]. Developing countries have lost a total of $23.6 trillion through capital flight since 1980[15]. Multinational corporations pull out about $138 billion from developing countries in the form of tax holidays each year. Remittances sent home by immigrant workers are reduced by high transaction fees, costing families about $33 billion each year. Add volatile aid disbursements, the 162 million acres of land grabs in the global South since 2000, the $571 billion per year loss due to climate change to the above, and the phenomenal outflow of wealth from the poor countries to the rich countries becomes clear. But there is more – add to that repatriated profits from European and American investors, through pension funds etc. There are also foreign patent payments in order to access technologies and pharmaceuticals.

The debt crisis, however, has also overtaken Western countries. In her article 'Debt, austerity, devastation: it's Europe's turn' Susan George says: "Like plague in the 14th century, the scourge of debt has gradually migrated from South to North. Our 21st-century

Yersinia pestis isn't spread by flea-infested rats but by deadly, ideology-infested neo-liberal fundamentalists. Once they had names like Thatcher or Reagan; now they sound more like Merkel or Barroso; but the message, the mentality and the medicine are basically the same. The devastation caused by the two plagues is also similar – no doubt fewer debt-related deaths in Europe today than in Africa three decades ago, but probably more permanent harm done to once-thriving European economies."[16]

During the financial crisis of 2008, the world's central banks, including the Federal Reserve, injected trillions of dollars – called quantitative easing – of fabricated money into the global economy. This created a worldwide debt of $325 trillion, more than three times global GDP. The money was hoarded by banks and corporations and loaned by banks at predatory interest rates. It was used to service interest on unpayable debts and spent on buying back stock thereby accruing millions of dollars for the financial elites. The money was not invested in the real economy and no products were manufactured and sold. Workers were not reinstated into jobs with sustainable incomes, benefits and pensions and no infrastructure projects were undertaken. The financial crisis consolidated the power of the central banks making them politically and economically stronger by allowing them and the world's largest financial institutions to fraudulently manipulate global markets and use fabricated money to inflate asset bubbles for short-term profit.

The economic crisis associated with the Corona virus pandemic of 2020 has produced vast financial benefits for the "investor class."[17] During the Corona virus pandemic and the 2020 economic crisis, America's billionaires have seen their wealth soar by $434 billion. Their corporations received $500 billion in bailouts and they got $135 billion in tax breaks. The Treasury Department and the Federal Reserve are erasing the corporate debt they amassed over the last few years enabling their corporations to buy back their shares of stock. Meanwhile, Amazon, Google, Facebook, Walmart and other corporate giants are using their vast market power to make record profits. The corporate looting includes wage theft through mis-classifying employees as independent contractors and denying workers the overtime pay they are due.

The most profitable corporations in America are looting billions in taxes through loopholes, write-offs, and special exemptions. Amazon paid just a 1.2 percent tax rate on $13 billion in profit in 2019 and companies, including Chevron, Halliburton, and Netflix, have not paid a cent in federal taxes in years. The US loses nearly $70 billion a year in tax revenue because corporations loot America by shifting their profits to tax havens overseas.[18] The above figures provided by Robert Reich are understated. Central banks and governments have injected an estimated $15 trillion of stimulus to shield their economies from the Corona virus pandemic. This is money created out of thin air. This sum is about 17% of an $87 trillion global economy last year.[19] The $15 trillion covers the "G10" group of major economies plus China.

Both public and private debt, far from being a threat to the capitalist economy, lie at the very core of the neo-liberal project. As Maurizio Lazzarato says in *The Making of the Indebted Man*: "The debtor-creditor relation, which is at the heart of this book, sharpens mechanisms of exploitation and domination indiscriminately, since, in it, there is no distinction between workers and the unemployed, consumers and producers, working and non-working populations, between retirees and welfare recipients. They are all 'debtors,' guilty and responsible in the eyes of capital, which has become the Great, the Universal, Creditor."[20]

### Economics: Science or Spin?

We began our discussion on neo-liberalism with Harvey's definition. Let us look at what conclusions he arrived at by the end of his study. He wrote: "Neo-liberalism has not been very effective in revitalising global capital accumulation, but it has succeeded remarkably well in restoring, or in some instances (as in Russia and China) creating, the power of an economic elite. The theoretical utopianism of neo-liberal argument has, I conclude, primarily worked as a system of justification and legitimation for whatever needed to be done to achieve this goal. The evidence suggests, moreover, that when neo-liberal principles clash with the need to restore or sustain elite power, then the principles are either abandoned or become so twisted as to be unrecognisable."[21]

If economics was a science it would have developed ways of recognising error and correcting it. Any science must have criteria for validating and substantiating its claims. Worldviews, frameworks and paradigms are not immutable. For five decades now economists who plan economic growth and design development models have seen the disastrous results of their plans and models. Economic growth and development must be for the benefit of all human beings – not only for well-off and well-fed elites. Economists have failed to recognise, correct and avoid their errors. Jason Hickel points out these errors as follows: "If people begin to accept that, despite many decades of development, poverty has been getting worse, and the divide between rich and poor countries is growing rather than closing, then it will become clear to all that there is something fundamentally wrong with our economic system – that it is failing the majority of humanity and urgently needs to be changed. The official success story has helped keep people on board with our existing system for a long time. If that story falls apart, so too will their consent."[22]

Why do they not acknowledge that they have failed to achieve the supposed goal of their plans and models, which is, human welfare? The dominant development model has always been for the most part, the handiwork of economists, whilst sociologists, historians, anthropologists, ecologists etc. have contributed little to its formation. It has been largely funded and controlled by Western-controlled political institutions and most development economists must accept, consciously or not, subservience to the goals of those who now dominate the world economy and derive the most benefit from it. "Although in no sense the result of a conspiracy, the reigning paradigm does reflect a convergence of world views, a shared vision of a desirable society and a keen, common perception of economic and political self-interest. In sum, it is riddled with ideology."[23] This certainly allows us to say that economics is a political argument and not a science and there are no objective truths in economics that can be established independently of political requirements.

# Chapter 10

## Scientific Materialism

This chapter focuses on those aspects of knowledge which are required for the understanding and interpretation of the meaning of reality. Beliefs and their justification in relation to knowledge lead to certain values and these values lead to the institutionalisation of specific types of behaviour. The institutions which develop around these values form the core of cultures and civilisations. It is claimed that the inspiration for the modernist paradigm came firstly, from a desire to escape the tyranny and irrationality of the Catholic Church and secondly, from the desire to overcome the squalor, disease, poverty, starvation and brute labour of the European Middle Ages.[1] Prior to the modern age, the worldview in Europe was that of scholasticism, which was a harmonisation of Christian theological thinking and the classical philosophical tradition of Ancient Greece. In pre-modern Europe, people's lived experience was within a Christian context of understanding.

### Scientism

The modern worldview, based as it is on reason and sense perception, i.e. rationalism and empiricism, can be described as scientistic, that is, based on "scientism". It is claimed that scientism puts too high a value on natural science in comparison with other branches of learning or culture.[2] Scientism asserts that science, modelled on the natural sciences, is the only source of real knowledge.[3] It holds the view that "the characteristic inductive methods of the natural sciences are the only source of genuine factual knowledge and, in particular, that they alone can yield true knowledge about man and society."[4]

The roots of scientism are to be found in what has come to be known as the scientific revolution of the 16th and 17th centuries. The architects of the modern worldview made the assumption that those things that could be weighed, measured, and counted were true whilst those that could not be quantified were not true.[5] People like Francis Bacon (1561-1626) and René Descartes (1596-1650) claimed that we could master nature and possess it by studying how the physical world worked. In this way humans could overcome hunger, eliminate disease and improve the quality of life through technology and industry. As this thinking gained ground, the outlines of scientism began to emerge. The use of reason and logic was elevated and other human faculties were denigrated.

Descartes depicted the universe as a giant machine and Bacon said: "Those therefore, who determine not to conjecture and guess, but to find out and know; not to invent fables and romances of worlds, but to look into and dissect the nature of this real world, must consult only things themselves."[6] For Bacon truth came to mean scientific truth. Existence, which had previously been considered a unity of spiritual and material dimensions, became split into two. The truth of religion and the truth of science were now two separate domains. God, according to Bacon, works in nature only by secondary causes. Scientism under the guise of natural philosophy came to replace theology as the supreme form of knowledge.

The beginning of modern philosophy is often attributed to Descartes who is famous for his dictum "*cogito ergo sum* – I think, therefore I am."[7] On this narrow foundation Descartes was convinced that he himself existed, that he had certain ideas and that God existed. Whilst the idea goes back to Aristotle and Plato, Descartes is recognised as the first person to have formulated the body/mind dichotomy as we know it today. He regarded the body and the mind to be as distinct from each other as two separate substances. He regarded the body as material and its essential property being that it exists spatially. Secondly he held that the mind was an immaterial substance that thinks. Descartes, however, was unable to resolve this dichotomy which later came to be known as the body-mind problem.

The other achievement of Descartes was his famous scientific method, the starting point of which was that the human being is the observer of the phenomena around him. "Thus he made his own rationality, and by extension human reason in general, the ultimate arbiter of what is true or not true. What Descartes left us with is a picture of the human being as a mind enclosed in a body looking out as subject/observer on an objective/separate world surrounding him which had to be brought under control and made to serve him."[8]

The philosopher Thomas Hobbes (1588-1679) supplemented the thinking of Descartes by claiming that anything other than material existence is not real. If something cannot be proved empirically it is to be disregarded. For Hobbes mechanico-materialism was accepted as an exhaustive account of reality and any spiritual dimension of existence was denied altogether. The social and political implications for Hobbes, of this way of understanding the universe, were that the government and not God was the absolute authority. This idea led him to devising the theory of social contract in political theory.

The astronomer Copernicus shattered the traditional view of the universe, which held that the earth was the stationary centre of the universe around which the sun, moon, the planets and galaxies revolved in their various orbits. In the Copernican system the earth and several planets orbited the sun and this solar system was one among countless others in an unimaginably vast universe. Mankind was now seen as an insignificant species living in limitless space. Galileo's (1564-1642) invention of the telescope enabled him to demonstrate the validity of Copernicus's theory.

Isaac Newton (1643-1727) formulated what he called the law of universal gravitation and the three fundamental laws of mechanics. His writings proved to be fundamental for the whole of modern science and people's perception of the universe. Everything could now be explained as particles and mutually dependent, internally self-consistent and interactive forces. "After Newton there was no longer any need for God; everything was perfectly explicable without positing Divine intervention. God had been expelled from the physical universe."[9]

Immanuel Kant (1724-1804) explained how objective experience is processed by the functioning of the human mind. The foundations for other aspects of modernist thought and practice were laid by Adam Smith's (1723-1790) economic free market, Charles Darwin's (1809-1882) evolutionary theory, and Freud's (1856-1939) psychological building blocks. It is on the epistemological foundations of sciences based on the above writings, together with others in a similar vein, that the new model of humanity, based on scientific materialism, took shape.

### Critique of Scientism

This modern worldview, based as it is on rationalism and empiricism, has been criticised throughout its development. As argued by Massimo Pigliucci, science is a particular ensemble of epistemic and social practices built on a faulty system of peer review. What we have now is quite different from "science" as it was done by Aristotle, or even by Galileo. There is continuity, of course, between its modern version and its historical predecessors, but "when scientistic thinkers pretend that any human activity that has to do with reasoning about facts is 'science' they are attempting a bold move of naked cultural colonisation, defining everything else either out of existence or into irrelevance."[10]

In his paper entitled "Statistical Procedures and Human Values" delivered at the II Islamic Countries Conference on Statistical Sciences in Kuala Lumpur, Shaykh Abdalqadir speaks about the modern structuralist defence of scientism, which goes by the names of philosophy of science or logical empiricism. Martin Heidegger's publication in 1927 of his magnum opus, *Sein und Zeit – Being and Time* was an event of the greatest importance. It meant a total transformation of the intellectual climate which had a lasting effect on almost all the sciences. "What Heidegger has done, far from implying an invalidation of science, is establishing a transvaluation of the scientific evaluation. He has taken it out of the hieroglyphics of mathematical logic, where it lay enshrined and inaccessible and world-destroying, and placed it firmly within the hermeneutics of a restored human discourse. Heidegger's lifelong dismantling of the Kantian frame, and, in his pure objectivity, his inescapable removal of the mythic subject, could not have succeeded without his also redefining man. In naming man as a being oriented towards Being-itself, and in recognising Being not as the passive category either of Kant or Aristotle but as Event, he moved his phenomenological ontology to the limits of discourse. Confirming and re-appraising Nietzsche, he declared the end of metaphysics. The encounter with Being in his final years had taken on the character of what we as

Muslims recognise as a confirmation of *tawḥīd*, not at all in the modern manner of the rationalist educated Egyptians who come after Abduh, who can only confirm divinity as idea, their idea ..."[11]

The worldview of scientific materialism is now ubiquitous throughout the world. Where modern Muslims are concerned, Abdalhaqq Bewley has said that their understanding of *tawḥīd* has been weakened and corrupted by the dominant worldview. "Like almost everybody else the modern Muslim has in reality separated Allah from direct involvement in natural processes, seeing them only in terms of secondary causation. He too views existence through a Galilean telescope and sees a Newtonian mechanistic universe with a mind permeated by Cartesian dualism."[12]

### The End of Scientism – Apotheosis

Scientism and the worldview and institutions generated by it have failed, bringing in its wake an apocalypse.[13] In 1932 Jünger saw the inescapable power of the phenomenon of technology. He recognised that technology did not represent a complex set of tools that were there for the use of human beings. He thought of technique or technology as a new power with its own inner logic which rendered human beings subservient. The unstoppable movement of technology has ended in a world state with the global power of technique forming an imperial unity. There are no classes because everyone is living under the domination of technique. Social identity is defined by the use of technology, and the state that rules the infrastructure rules over the individual. All people have become slaves and there is no place on earth that will be able to resist this phenomenon. Jünger did not propose a withdrawal from technique. He calls on people to accept the vast wave of technology engulfing the time and prepare not only for survival and escape but ultimately victory over it.

Jünger is suggesting that the way of freedom lies in plunging into reality, taking it on and going beyond it. We have arrived at the apotheosis of modernity, the extreme point of its development beyond which it cannot survive. Modern society is self destructing. We had to reach this point to force us to re-evaluate everything that we believe and do. As Jünger said: "The game [of technique] must have exhausted all its possibilities. Then only can one dare the impossible."[14] On the occasion of the installation of Jünger as Doctor *Honoris Causa* of Literature in the University of Bilbao in 1989, Shaykh Abdalqadir as-Sufi presented a paper whilst Jünger was present. Referring to Jünger's words *"Freiheit ist Existenz"* Shaykh Abdalqadir as-Sufi said: *"Freiheit ist Existenz.* Freedom is Existence. Which means that there can be no submission except to the Divine. This is called Islam."[15]

# Chapter 11

## Public Relations

Shaykh Abdalqadir writes: "It was only the financial collapse of 2008 that forced the oligarchic chiefs into the open. It must also be taken into account that they were responsible for the loss of billions of dollars. Yet how can men lose something that was not there in the first place? It was lost but cannot be found. It never had substantial existence, only numerical traces indicating a possibility of existence, which proved worthless. This dilemma which involves the greater mass of modern men is the deepest and penultimate matter in this affair. It implies that the quotidian social nexus is itself a psychosis."[1] As stated previously, Shaykh Abdalqadir argues that our civic reality in society today is a socially structured psychosis. Modern money has no intrinsic value, oligarchy presents itself as democracy with politicians having no substantive power over the economy, and the citizen is expected to believe that the system works whilst it patently has failed. That system is capitalism.

The signs of the failure of capitalism and its servant, democracy, have become very clear to us. Banks have been involved in generating bogus money; the state has been captured by corporations; there has been flagrant tax avoidance by corporations and increasing surveillance of the communications of citizens; the gap between the poor and the rich grows ever wider; blatant lies have been told for going to war in Iraq, Syria, Libya, Afghanistan and elsewhere; and the worldwide refugee crisis shows no sign of abating. All this is clear to everyone but nobody can do anything to change it. The structure of power remains the same, that is, oligarchy masquerading as democracy. All that remains is the theatre of the political class. Shaykh Abdalqadir says that the "horror of this age is the somnambulistic helplessness of the masses to ACT to stop the global holocaust."[2] Why are people helpless? How can the oligarchy fool all the people all the time?

### THE ENGINEERING OF CONSENT: HOW TO FOOL ALL THE PEOPLE ALL THE TIME

This is the legacy of Edward Bernays (1891-1995). He was born in Vienna and moved to New York in 1892 where he received his school and university education. He was the nephew of Sigmund Freud, his mother Anna was Freud's sister and his father's sister Martha was married to Freud. Bernays was the first person to take Freud's ideas and use them in economics and politics, that is, in marketing and public relations.

Freud developed a theory called psychoanalysis which proposed new ways of understanding what he called the unconscious. Psychoanalysis explores the human psyche: a term originating from Greek mythology that referred to the soul. In psychoanalytic terminology soul is not used in the religious sense. The psyche is the mental apparatus as it is defined in contrast to the body or the soma. Psychoanalysis, through reading dreams, daydreams and slips of the tongue, provides a way of unlocking the symbolism and multi-meanings relating to the workings of the human mind. For Freud the unconscious is primarily the store of instinctual desires and needs. "Freud's theory, psychoanalysis, suggested new ways of understanding, amongst other things, love, hate, childhood, family relations, civilisation, religion, sexuality, fantasy and the conflicting emotions that make up our daily lives. Today we all live in the shadow of Freud's innovative and controversial concepts. In their scope and subsequent impact Freud's writings embody a core of ideas that amount to more than the beliefs of a single thinker. Rather they function like myths for our culture; taken together, they represent a way of looking at the world that has been powerfully transformative."[3]

Since the end of the 19th century the US had become an industrial society with millions of people clustered together in cities. It had come out of World War II rich and powerful and the system of mass production had flourished during the war with enormous amounts of goods pouring off production lines. The corporations were afraid that there would be an overproduction of goods and there would come a point in time when people would have enough of what they needed and stop buying the goods. Up to then goods had been marketed and sold to people on the basis of need. The aim of advertising was to promote products in functional terms, for their durability and practical virtues.

Paul Meiser of Lehman Brothers, a leading Wall Street bank, understood exactly what was required to solve the problem of over-production. He wrote: "We must shift America from a needs to a desires culture, to want new things even before the old has been entirely consumed. We must shape a new mentality in America. Man's desires must overshadow his needs."[4] This was the kind of thinking that gave birth to American consumerism and Bernays was the man at the centre of shaping the new mentality. Bernays applied psychological theory to further the interests of the corporations.

In the early 1920s the New York banks financed the establishment of chains of department stores across the USA. Change had come over US democracy: "It is called consumptionism. The American citizen's first importance to his country is not that of citizen but that of consuming."[5] Bernays' first success in marketing was for the American Tobacco Corporation in persuading women to smoke. Prior to this there was a taboo against women smoking. "The psychoanalyst A.A. Brille told Bernays that cigarettes were a symbol of the penis and male sexual power. He told Bernays that if he could find a way to connect cigarettes with the idea of challenging male power then women would smoke because then they would have their own penises."

At the Easter day parade in New York in 1929 a group of rich young women lit up cigarettes at a signal from Bernays who then informed the press that the cigarettes symbolised "torches of freedom" for them. From then onwards the sales of cigarettes to women began to rise. He had made cigarettes socially acceptable with a single act. Bernays had created the idea that if a woman smoked it made her more powerful and independent. He realised that it was possible to persuade people to behave irrationally if you link products to their emotional desires and feelings. Although the idea that smoking made women freer was completely irrational it did make them feel independent and it meant that irrelevant objects could become powerful emotional symbols of how you wanted to be seen by others.

Bernays created techniques of large scale consumer persuasion. He set out to create a new type of customer and the technique he used was that of the focus group.[6] He originated the idea that the customer was not just buying a product but was engaged personally and emotionally with the product or service. It was about how the product or service made you feel. He showed that products and services can also be powerful emotional symbols for enhancing one's self-image and one's image in the eyes of others. The growing wave of consumerism that arose out of this type of marketing helped create a stock-market boom and Bernays promoted the idea that ordinary people should buy shares by borrowing money from the banks that he represented. He soon became famous and millions of people followed his guidance. His clients included politicians, government agencies, major corporations and not-for-profit organisations.

### THE ALLIANCE OF DEMOCRACY AND CONSUMERISM

The publication of the works of Freud in the US by Bernays drew the attention of journalists, intellectuals, politicians and planners. They were fascinated by the idea that deep within human beings lay hidden and dangerous irrational fears and desires. They became convinced that unleashing these instincts would produce frenzied mobs as happened in the Russian Revolution in 1917. In other words human beings could not be relied on to make rational decisions. The leading political writer of the time, Walter Lippmann (1889-1974), said that it was time to rethink democracy since human beings were motivated by unconscious irrational forces. He believed that it was necessary to have an elite group which would manage the 'bewildered herd'. This would be done through psychological techniques that would control the unconscious feelings of the masses. Bernays was fascinated by Lippmann's ideas and he wrote a series of books in which he argued that he had already developed the techniques that Lippmann was suggesting. He called these techniques the engineering of consent, that is, by stimulating the inner desires of people and then sating them with consumer products he was creating a new way of managing the irrational forces of the masses.

According to Stewart Ewan: "Both Bernays' and Lippmann's concept of managing the masses takes the idea of democracy and turns it into a palliative. It turns it into giving people some kind of feel-good medication that will respond to an immediate pain or immediate yearning but will not alter the objective one iota. The idea of democracy at its heart was about changing the relations of power that had governed the world for so long. Bernays' concept of democracy was one of maintaining the relations of power, even if it meant that one needed to stimulate the psychological lives of the public. And in fact, in his mind, that is what is necessary; that if you can keep stimulating the irrational self then leadership can basically go on doing what it wants to do."[7] President Hoover (1929-1933) was the first politician to promote the idea that consumerism would become the motor of American life. After his election he told a gathering of advertisers and public relations men: "You have taken over the job of creating desire and have transformed people into constantly moving happiness machines. Machines that have become the key to economic progress."[8]

Bernays was part of the team that attended the Paris Peace Conference after World War I. After his return he opened up a public relations business in New York and taught a course on public relations at the same time. These are regarded as pioneering events in the field of modern public relations. In 1939-40 Bernays directed public relations at New York's World Fair which he called 'democricity'.

When American soldiers returned from World War II it was found that a large percentage of them were emotionally unstable, suffering from anxieties and fears. Psychoanalysts were convinced that they understood these hidden forces and could control them. The ideas of Bernays and Freud's daughter Anna, a psychoanalyst in her own right,[9] were used by the US government, corporations and the CIA to develop techniques to control the minds of the American people. According to them, in order to create a stable society in which democracy would work, it was necessary to repress the savage barbarism that lay hidden within human beings. They cited

Germany as an example where ordinary citizens were complicit in the mass killings of their fellow countrymen and women. The ruling class believed that these forces could easily break through and overwhelm democracy.

In 1946 President Truman signed the National Mental Health Act the aim of which was to deal with the invisible threat to society. It was the first time that mental illness was officially regarded as a national problem. Thus in the 1940s the vast project of applying the ideas of psychoanalysis to the general population began across the US and as psychoanalytic ideas became widespread a new elite began to emerge in politics, business and social sciences. As Ellen Herman explained: "They actually believed that the elite were necessary because individual citizens were not capable, if left alone, of being democratic citizens. The elite were necessary in order to create conditions that would produce individuals capable of behaving as good citizens and also behaving as democratic citizens. They didn't see their activities as anti-democratic, as undermining the capacity of individual citizens for democracy. Quite the opposite, they understood they were creating the conditions for democracy's arrival in the future."[10]

In the late 1950's the CIA poured millions of dollars into the psychology departments of universities across America. They were in reality funding experiments of how to alter and control the inner drives of human beings. Some of these experiments were carried out by Ewan Cameron the head of the American Psychiatric Association. Cameron, like many psychiatrists of his time, was convinced that inside human beings were dangerous forces which threatened society and that it was possible not only to control them but to actually remove them. The CIA's chief psychologist (1950-1974), John Gittinger, was very clear as to what their goals were: "The image of the human beings that was being built up at that particular time was that there was a great deal of vulnerability in every human being and that vulnerability could be manipulated to program somebody to be something that I wanted them to be and they didn't want to be. That you could manipulate people in such a way that they could be automatons, if you will, for whatever your own purposes were. This was the image that people thought was possible."[11]

### Consumer Politics

During the economic crisis in the UK in the mid-1970s consumer spending fell dramatically and corporations turned to advertising agencies for help. The marketing agencies insisted that the only way companies could survive was to find more effective ways of advertising. They brought in Americans to run focus groups with British housewives. Edward Bernays' ideas and techniques came with the Americans and these ideas and techniques took over politics. Margaret Thatcher in the UK, like Ronald Reagan in the US, encouraged business to take over from government the role of fulfilling the needs of the people. Consumers were encouraged to see the satisfaction of their desires as their most important priority and the satisfaction of these desires should form the basis of a better form of democracy.

Robert Reich explains that: "Ronald Reagan and Margaret Thatcher both embraced an economic philosophy that says that the unit of judgment was not only the individual but it was the individual's personal satisfaction, the individual's own unique happiness and wellbeing. It was in a sense the triumph of regarding individuals as purely emotional beings who have needs and wants and desires that need to be satisfied and can be satisfied unconsciously. It goes way back to the early part of the twentieth century, to Freud, to notions of the unconscious, the assumptions that in terms of our rational minds we are little corks bobbing around on this great sea of hopes and fears and desires of which we are only dimly aware and that the role of the marketer, the role of somebody selling something, including a politician, is to appeal to this great swamp of desire, of unconscious desire."[12]

In the 1980s the Labour Party had lost election after election and a growing number of its supporters were convinced that for them to regain political power they would have to come to terms with the new individualism. Phillip Gould, an advertising executive, became part of a group of modernisers around Labour politician Peter Mandelson. Their aim was to reconnect lost voters back to the Labour Party. To achieve this goal Gould turned to the technique of the focus group. He commissioned focus groups in suburban areas throughout the country with voters who had switched to Thatcher's Conservative Party. Gould found that there was a fundamental shift in the relationship that people had to politics. They saw themselves as individuals who could demand what they wanted from politicians in return for paying taxes. He found that people had become consumers and wanted politics on their own terms. They saw themselves as powerful and autonomous individuals entitled to the best of goods and services in health, education etc. Gould then set out to convince the Labour Party to make concessions to the new aspirational classes as he called them.

In 1994 Tony Blair became the leader of the Labour Party (and the reformist group around Peter Mandelson) and the desires and fears of the aspirational classes began to shape Labour Party politics. The philosophy of their campaigns was to concentrate on swing voters and conduct focus groups with them to find out what they wanted and what would appeal to them. Once these things were ascertained they were relentlessly pushed in the campaigns. The Party started to drop policies that would not benefit swing voters, even if it meant sacrificing its fundamental principles. Clause Four of the Party constitution, whose aim was to use the collective power of the people to challenge the unfettered greed of business, was dropped. The swing voters saw themselves as individual consumers who were given their identities by what business delivered to them. Consequently the new Clause Four promised not to control the free market and to let it flourish. Derek Draper, assistant to Peter Mandelson, explained that what the Labour Party did was to fit in perfectly well with the people who exert power in society, not through the democratic political system, but big business, entrenched interests and the status quo – the very things that the Party was a counter-force to.

Not surprisingly the Labour Party won the elections just as Bill Clinton had done before in the USA using the same strategies. Robert Reich, US Secretary of Labour from 1993 to 1997, says of this phenomenon: "Fundamentally here, we have two different views of human nature, we have two different views of nature and of democracy. You have the view that people are irrational, that they are bundles of unconscious emotion. That comes directly out of Freud, and businesses are very able to respond to that. That's what they have honed their skills to and that's what marketing is really all about – what are the symbols, the images, the music, the words that will appeal to these unconscious feelings. Politics must be more than that. Politics and leadership are about engaging the public in a rational discussion and deliberation about what is best, and treating people with respect in terms of their rational abilities to debate what is best. If it is not that, if it is Freudian, if it is basically a matter of appealing to the same basic unconscious feelings that business appeals to, then why not let businesses do it? Business can do it better, business knows how to do it. Business after all is in the business of responding to those feelings."[13]

### Resistance to consumer politics.

The counterculture of the 1960s resisted this worldview. It was an anti-establishment cultural phenomenon that developed in Western countries in the 1960s until the mid-70s. An array of social issues came to the fore during this period. Some of these included: civil rights; movements against military intervention in Southeast Asia; nuclear disarmament; sexuality; human rights; women's rights; traditional modes of authority; freedom of speech; freedom of assembly; anti-poverty campaigns; industrialisation and its effects on the environment; environmentalism; pollution; and the use of psychoactive drugs.

One of the main targets of the counterculture was business corporations. They were accused of brainwashing the public with the aim of not only making money through consumerism but also keeping them docile. Docile citizens made it possible for governments to pursue all manner of illegal and violent acts such as the US war in Vietnam. Herbert Marcuse (1898-1979) was a source of inspiration for the intellectuals of the counterculture. The excitement caused by Martin Heidegger's *Being and Time* led Marcuse to a life-long engagement with philosophy and he began reading it in 1927. The impact of Heidegger was so great on him that Marcuse went to Freiburg in 1928 to study philosophy with Heidegger and Edmund Husserl. Marcuse also studied psychoanalysis and was a fierce critic of the Freudians. He said that they had contributed to create a world in which people were reduced to express their identities and feelings through mass produced objects. The psychoanalysts had become the corrupt agents of the ruling class in the US.

In 1950-51 Marcuse gave a series of lectures at the Washington School of Psychiatry. The result of this seminar was one of Marcuse's most famous books, *Eros and Civilisation: A Philosophical Inquiry into Freud.* Marcuse's book was a response to the pessimism of Freud's *Civilisation and Its Discontents* (1930). Freud paints a bleak picture of the evolution of civilisation as one of greater and greater repression from which there seems to be no escape. The death and life instincts are engaged in a battle for dominance with no clear winner in sight. Marcuse argued that that human instincts or drives are not merely biological and fixed, but also social, historical, and malleable.

Marcuse said that in advanced industrial societies there is no longer a problem with acquiring the resources needed for existence, or even the most favourable life, for members of those societies. The problem is the unfair and unjust distribution of resources. The concept of scarcity in this age functions ideologically and supports the domination of the worker by the capitalist. Marcuse said: "It was one of the most striking phenomena to see to what extent the ruling power structure could manipulate, manage and control not only the consciousness but also the subconscious and unconscious of the individual. And this took place on the psychological basis, by the control and the manipulation of the unconscious drives, which Freud stipulated."[14]

The counterculture created a generation that rebelled against the conformity which was imposed by consumerism. They believed that the self was inestimable and people could be anything they wanted to be. This liberation of the self would create new kinds of people free of social constraint. People who were free to create an identity for themselves and to change the world into whatever they wanted it to be. As always business would find a way to cater for this new type of customer – the self-actualising individual. In fact they would become the motor of the new economy. Corporations had worked out that it was in their interests to encourage people to feel that they were unique individuals and then offer them goods and services to express that individuality. The vast array of differing individual desires was catered for through changes in industrial production. Computers made it possible for manufacturers to economically produce short runs of consumer goods. The fear that corporations would produce too many goods no long worried them because, with this generation of self-actualising individuals, consumer desire had no limits. Business used the ideas of Sigmund Freud to develop techniques to read the inner drives of individuals and then design and promote the products that will satisfy those drives.

# Chapter 12

## The Nuclear Family

The predominant family formation today is the nuclear family. The modern nuclear family was solidified as an institution during the industrial revolution of the 19th century. The Industrial Revolution brought about the change from what had till then been an agrarian and handicraft economy to one dominated by industry and machine manufacturing. It began in Britain and then spread to the rest of the world.

### Pre-industrial households

In pre-industrial society individual families were mostly centres of economic production, organised through the male head of household. Domestic production was geared towards manufacture or agriculture and the work of women was central to it. In pre-industrial society the family played a central role and one of its essential characteristics was that of being a unit of production. Most economic activity took place within the household based on sophisticated methods of production and distribution. Goods were produced for home consumption but also for selling and trade in the market-place. Family production was not limited to agriculture but also included manufacturing and providing services. Women performed tasks such as spinning, childcare, cleaning or agricultural work in and around the home and all these things were considered productive and necessary work. Labour became necessary at times and this was provided by members of other households who possessed the required skills or were experiencing financial difficulties.

### THE FAMILY AND INDUSTRIALISM

With the advent of industrialisation goods previously produced in the home, such as food, drinks and clothing, came to be produced in factories and mills. Together with men, women and children worked in factories and mines and were exploited in barbaric conditions. The consequence of this was the destruction of family life. Working people, however, began to fight for protections for themselves in the workplace and gradually did win their struggles for shorter working days and the introduction of child labour laws. At the same time, the nuclear family, with father as the head of the household and mother at home caring for children, became the norm. This happened despite the fact that the so-called family wage, which was paid to men so that women could stay at home and look after children, was never adequate for working class families. As a result, in order for the family to survive, working class women were forced to seek employment outside the home, usually in low-paid jobs.

### THE NUCLEAR FAMILY

A nuclear family is made up of a group of people consisting of the mother, the father and their children, united by marriage and parenthood. This arrangement, in which the income of only the parents is supposed to finance and maintain the lives of four or more people, is what drives the economy and maintains capitalism.

By separating citizens into small families supported by only two adults, capitalism is able to force employees to accept undesirable working conditions. By creating a society that is divided in this way capitalism guarantees a continuous supply of workers at all times. A survey conducted in 2016 by the Bureau of Labor in the USA revealed that in 48% of married-couple families, both the husband and wife were employed. This statistic is so high out of necessity because nuclear family guardians do not have the economic freedom to choose if or when they want to work.

The nuclear family structure is set up to ensure that there will always be labour for the system. "Each nuclear family is a miniature replica of the major capitalist structure that we live in; this is necessary for our capitalist society to run as it currently does. If the structure of the family were to change and become malleable, citizens would have more freedom, especially in regards to their supply of labor."[1] Apart from being the cause of high rates of domestic violence and sexual abuse against women and children, the nuclear family functions as a unit of consumption. It grooms children to spend their lives toiling under oppressive conditions in order to buy commodities they do not need.

Representative democracy and capitalism are presented as mutually inseparable and both are tied to the fate of the nuclear family. The family is constructed and organised explicitly to link family policy to the survival of democratic capitalism. Nuclear families make economic expansion possible by saving money and they also teach children the values upon which savings are built. "Attitudes toward work are formed in the family. Families which teach that effort results in gain prepare skilled and energetic workers who are the engine for democratic capitalism. In contrast, if children are taught that effort is to no avail that 'the deck is stacked', nothing is more likely to undercut achievement. Without employees, investors, and entrepreneurs nurtured in families and instilled with the work ethic, democratic capitalism fails."[2] Enacting government family policies does not mean that the family itself is the ultimate object of concern. Family policy is always an instrument, whether overt or covert, to implement social control. Policies promoting the family as worthy of support are regarded as the best way for safeguarding capitalism.

### The family and banking

Shaykh Abdalqadir says that the abolition of the family was a consequence of modern banking. In 1926 Wyndham Lewis wrote: "It is round the question of the family that all the other questions of politics and social life are gathered. The break-up of the family unit today is the central fact of our life: it is from its central disintegration – both in fact and in our minds – the consequent readjustments of our psychology – that all other revolutionary phases of our new society radiate. The relations of men to women, of the child to the parent, of friendship and citizenship to the new ideals of the state, are all controlled by it."[3] The abolition of the family has been the deliberate program of evolved banking.

Shaykh Abdalqadir explains that the popular saying, "the Greeks have a word for it" does not apply when it comes to modern banking. They did not have a word for it so their popes proposed as a translation for "bank" the word "trapeza", literally "table". That word was chosen because it was the only bank they had known. It was on the household table that the family would lay out their profits and wages and they would then sort out the family expenditure. When the table is bare the family is dispersed and abolished.[4] The overwhelming majority of modern families are in debt.

To compensate for the loss of economic freedom people were offered sexual liberty. The "tactic from the quite astonishing effulgence of banking-finance and banking itself becoming both the fuel and the machine of world trade, was specific, individual, and directed at the psychological identity of the urban individual. Rome, to divert the Plebeians from the burgeoning wealth of the elite, gave the masses bread and circuses. The modern version was as follows: to distract people from desiring economic freedom, the right to choose your medium of exchange, freedom from purchase tax, interest, credit profile, something intrinsically human had to fill the void created by their financial slavery. In place of it they were offered sexual liberty. Bonded and enslaved by debt, mortgaged, and crippled by interest rates, the individual was offered sexual liberation. Basically the human creature was free to 'explore his or her sexuality'. Anything was permitted. Unfortunately for the world, the removal of all sexual taboos opened up an anomalous forbidden zone, the molestation of children. 'Unfortunately', because, given the nature of man and thus the lie of Humanism, once something is forbidden, it becomes desirable."[5]

## The Open Family

Shaykh Abdalqadir brings to our attention another family structure – the open family – based on Islamic practice. Referring to the collaborative couple, husband and wife, he says: "The superior collaborative woman will require the social freedom of the multiple wife family in order to carry out her higher spiritual task. The superior collaborative man will require the multiple wife family as a human and open non-Oedipal base for the next generation."[6] The reference to 'non-Oedipal base' is related to the Oedipus complex which is a concept of psychoanalytic theory introduced by Sigmund Freud. Here Shaykh Abdalqadir speaks of the Oedipus complex in the familial context. The collaborative woman is able to inspire her husband by preventing the primal Oedipal process from taking place.

In her reflections on this matter Rabea Redpath said in reference to the Oedipal model: "In the enclosed bourgeois marriage there are two larger than life presences from which the child absorbs everything in his or her psyche. The mother, who is disappointed in her marriage and has no greater goal, transfers all her love and nurturing away from her husband solely onto the child. The male child projects onto the mother a connection which stops his transference into the adult state. The necessary separation never takes place. Therefore the fantasy life of the grown man will always have an unconscious yearning for his mother which no other relationship can fulfil. He turns his wife into his mother and this ends with him punishing the woman for not being the mother. So this is the Oedipal/primal drama that cannot be escaped."[7] The collaborative woman breaks this cycle which in turn enables the renewal of society.

In the other context, the social context, Shaykh Abdalqadir says that the state "institutionalises the Oedipal conflict by constructing a rigid frame, a stasis, and a neurotic condition that proposes an ideal of developed, mature, reality that will take place in the future. The ideal state, which is proffered by the politicians, is deferred because everything is in chaos and therefore they say, 'We are going to give you the ideal state after the five year plan, after we've dealt with the problems.' All the while you are passive and not dealing with these problems. The state is dealing with them."[8] Shaykh Abdalqadir explains that the dynamic of the totalitarian state is usury or interest debt and the state does not allow freedom of expression because it cannot allow this matter to be examined.

The only dynamic response to the mass society which is controlled by a structured information system is a re-educated society, which is active and collaborative. "The non-Oedipal man, that is the differentiated man, will place his life project above his personal life. Do you see what I'm saying? As long as man considers his project as earning a living in this enslaved system from which he cannot escape and therefore never comes out of the family system, he is not only punishing and destroying his wife, he is destroying the human situation in its totality. As long as he remains inside this trap he is not a man. He is not a man until his project for life is a higher purpose than his own family gratification. Until a man is prepared to get up and fight, for something higher and nobler (and not for himself in selfishness), women will be the victim. This implies a still centre to the human creature male and female, concerned with meaning and divine knowledge."[9]

Marcuse, Laing, Deleuze, Guattari and others, have criticised Freud for limiting the libido to sexual drives and containing them in the narrow categories of the nuclear family. As we have already noted, Marcuse was a fierce critic of the Freudians. He said that they had contributed to the creation of a world in which people were reduced to expressing their identities and feelings through mass produced objects. The psychoanalysts had become the corrupt agents of the ruling class. Deleuze and Guattari endorse Sigmund Freud's explanation of desire in the form of the libido, agreeing that the libido is primary in the subject's relationship to his or her world. However, they accuse Freud of limiting the libido to sexual drives.[10]

According to Deleuze and Guattari, desire enters directly into the social field, into politics, history, communities and mythologies, and also into objects and events. It affects whole spheres of non-familial attachments that begin with the child's earliest experiences. They insist that desire is invested into capitalism itself. The capitalist works not for himself or his children but for the immortality of the system. People do not need to be deceived into supporting capitalist forms of social domination, people come to desire capitalism, and that desire is an essential part of the system's perpetuation. Reproduction of capitalism is not an ideological problem, it is a problem of desire, and desire is part of the infrastructure. "Deleuze and Guattari thus stress that the nuclear family is a specific historical formation tied to the political and cultural demands of industrial capitalism in the West, rather than a universal social structure that might be 'discovered' in other societies or within other historical junctures."[11]

# Chapter 13

## Education

Theorists from Plato to Rousseau have realised that childish and childlike people are far easier to manage than accomplished critical thinkers. To keep people childish and childlike they would have to be cloistered in a society of children, stripped of responsibility and their inner lives would have to be deprived of the wisdom of historians, philosophers, novelists, and religious leaders. Furthermore, the inevitability of suffering and death would have to be removed from their consciousness and replaced with emotions such as greed, envy, jealousy, anxiety and fear. If all these goals could be accomplished then people, especially the young, could be easily manipulated and supervised. In this way people would be turned into 'human resources' to be used by governments and corporations for political, social and economic efficiency. The ways of achieving these goals were clearly outlined by Assistant Professor of Education at Harvard University, Alexander James Ingles (1879-1924) in *The Principles of Secondary Education*.[1]

The six principles or functions of education as outlined by Ingles are: the adjustive or adaptive function; the integrating function; the diagnostic and directive function; the differentiating function; the selective function; and the propaedeutic function. The goal of the education system is to have students meet these functions which are supposedly meant to produce students who will be happy and prosperous adults.

### 1) The adjustive or adaptive function

The adaptive or adjustive function correlates with measures of academic achievement, that is assessing and grading students. A more important criterion, however, for assessment is non-academic behaviour in a community setting, such as employment status. This means that the purpose of education is to prepare students to enter the economy and workforce. School creates fixed habits of reaction to authority figures and this precludes critical judgment as well as eliminates the need to teach any kind of useful or interesting material in the educational field.[2]

### 2) The integrating function

Through the integrating function teachers are expected to create an equally accepting environment for all students irrespective of ethnicity, customs, cultures and background. It is impossible in the public school environment to challenge students and encourage them to succeed on their own. Having to pay individual attention to each student, which would challenge students and encourage them to succeed on their own, is not part of the curriculum of public schools.

### 3) The diagnostic and directive function

Modern society is organised into different classes which determine the economic status and occupation of people. The public school system is mainly used as a basis for determining which jobs students will end up doing, the resources available to them, and their status in society. The ability to determine which students will not be entering certain fields of study gives public schools an enormous amount of control over future generations. School determines each student's proper social role by monitoring the performance of students both mathematically and anecdotally in cumulative records.

4) The differentiating function

Children, as much as possible, are made indistinguishable, undifferentiated and identical. As egalitarian as this may sound, its purpose is to assist the market and governments to achieve their goals, which is to create people who are conformist, predictable and easily manipulated. As is well-known, within the capitalist system, there are diverse economic classes and the possibility of people transitioning to a higher class perpetuates a sense that there is a probability for economic success in life. Whilst upward mobility seems to be in decline for the majority, the ranks of the upper-classes continue to grow because of the quality of their social status and private education. It tends to be easier for the rich to reach the next class and increase their wealth, whilst for the majority it is extremely difficult or impossible to move up from one economic class to another. In the public educational system what is achieved is conformity.

5) The selective or hygienic function

The selective or hygienic function is a standardised pathway used by the education system to evaluate students based on their educational performance. This is supposedly meant to help create the pathway for students to pursue successful careers. This selection process, used by the educational system, is based on the theory of evolution, including natural selection as suggested by Charles Darwin in his *The Origin of Species by Means of Natural Selection or the Preservation of Favoured Races in the Struggle for Life*. Without competition, according to Ingles, we would not be able to develop or progress in our business, politics, sports and education. This type of selective function looks at the different levels of education that students will pursue and the part it plays in the workforce. Through the selection process, there are students who will fill the low-skilled jobs "due to a less ambitious educational path. Social status is no longer based on family or group membership but it is acquired in the labour market on the basis of merit."[3]

Gatto wrote that the fifth function, which Ingles calls the hygienic function, "has nothing to do with bodily health. It concerns what Darwin, Galton, Ingles, and many important names from the past and present would call 'the health of the race'. Hygiene is a polite way of saying that school is expected to accelerate natural selection by tagging the unfit, so clearly they will drop from the reproduction sweepstakes. That's what all those little humiliations from first grade onward, and all the posted lists of ranked grades are really about. The unfit will either drop out from anger, despair, or because their likely mates will accept the school's judgment of their inferiority."[4]

6) The propaedeutic function

Propaedeutic is: "A fancy Latin term meaning that a small fraction of kids will quietly be taught how to take over management of this continuing project, made guardians of a population deliberately dumbed down and rendered childish in order that government and economic life can be managed with a minimum of hassle."[5] The propaedeutic function focuses on the need for an elite group of caretakers in society. Children enter the classroom divided into different groups. The dominant group are those who enter the classroom well prepared to succeed. They are from wealthy families and share common factors such as modes of speech, the style in which they were taught and the way they interact between themselves. For the children who come from poor families school is a hostile environment. It is culturally and socially different from the world they are accustomed to in their families and communities. Whilst the children from the dominant class make progress, the other children have difficulties with learning and most likely will fail to reach the higher levels of education. As a consequence they will not enter the higher echelons of business or the administrative, judiciary or executive branches of government.

### The products of the school system

School can be seen as a conditioning laboratory that makes children susceptible to authoritarian command, marketing and public relations. If children are trained to surrender their personal judgments and free wills to political and commercial persuasion, it is a boon for corporate profits and governments. For a system of industrial mass production to flourish, with enormous amounts of goods pouring off production lines, the society had to be transformed from a needs culture to a desires culture and for people to want new things even before the old had been entirely consumed. This is what we call consumerism today, where the logic of Adam Smith's ideas on supply and demand are subverted through psychological manipulation of susceptible populations. If people want something there is no need to market it to them and there will be no need for marketing. It is easy to sell ice in places where the climate is very hot but very difficult to sell ice to people who live at the North Pole.

Marketing strategy is designed to overcome resistance to buying and it is an art. How can it be turned into a science? Gatto explained how it is done: "By isolating children far from the everyday world, by isolating them with total strangers in strange, sterilized environments where various inputs could be studied, where growing children could be scrutinized, labelled and numbered for different future utilisations. And where data collected from these children could be passed on to other levels of authority for evaluation. Out of this flow of information, materials toward a science of marketing and a science of management would inevitably arise."[6] Gradually habit-control schooling was turned to serve the emerging mass production business empires.

The founders of compulsory schooling aimed at collectivising and socialising the population not through force but through the inculcation of dependency habits in children. Educational institutions executed a plan to extend childhood well beyond its natural limits. This was done by removing young people from home and neighbourhood associations and placing them with people utterly unknown to them or their parents. Stripped of any effective authority, the teachers were under the comprehensive direction of faraway school administrators such as state education departments, ministers etc. Schools are also beholden to local industries and foundations. "In this amazing fragmentation of control resides the immense stability of institutional schooling – nobody knows how to get anything much done without breaking the law, written or unwritten."[7]

Students graduating from the school system are people who are less intellectually developed, less sophisticated, shallow, superficial, trivial and frivolous. They are also demoralised, divided from one another, alienated from themselves, deprived of deep relationships and conformist, easily manipulated and accepting of authoritarianism.

## Corporate sponsors for compulsory schooling

After the American Civil War a corporate economy began to expand across the USA. The prospect of acquiring wealth through industry and financial manipulation led to the destruction of the old economy. The old economy had as its goal an independent livelihood for all, based on competence, resourcefulness, self-reliance, frugality and stoicism from its adherents. The new corporate economy, on the other hand, demanded childishness from its employees and from its consumers alike. It was, therefore, not surprising that corporations sponsored academic research into education. For example, the principal patron of John Dewey, the noted educational reformer, whose reputation came from his tenures at the University of Chicago and Columbia Teachers College, was none other than John D. Rockefeller himself.

In the US the transformation of education methodology into mass schooling was an undertaking of industrial titans like Andrew Carnegie and J.P. Morgan, John D. Rockefeller, Henry Ford, Vincent Astor and Commodore Vanderbilt amongst others. They understood that a commercial/industrial economy depends upon conspicuous consumption; that is, on people who define themselves by what they buy and who become dissatisfied almost instantly with what they have bought so that they, therefore, discard it and purchase something else. With the arrival of conspicuous consumption the problem of production had been solved. Accumulation of capital in the hands of industrialists and financiers, together with unlimited fossil fuel energy which was developed in the second half of the 19th century, made the idea of an industrial utopia a possibility for society.

However, certain impediments had to be removed for the industrial utopia to be established. Individuality, personal liberty and conventional morality, to begin with, had to be banished and most people would have to surrender the dream of an independent livelihood. The majority of people would have to become socialised into a dependence on centralised management. Family tradition, religion and the wisdom of elders had to be replaced by the authority of the business and political state. A task as huge as this –

the creation of a new world order – had to begin with the children and the age of arrival of maturity had to be delayed. Preparing the ground for the scientific management of a vast population required: extending the period of childhood; controlling the environment of children; placing children under the custodianship of teachers who followed orders minutely; dividing the children from one another through assessments; and setting them into meaningless competitions so that the natural bonds of sociability among them were strained to the breaking point.

"There were other agencies of socialisation for mass society, too, of course. Think only of the federal income tax, which comes about in the first flush of universal forced schooling. It takes a minute's reflection to see that it isn't an instrument of revenue for the central government – the government creates the currency it needs – but instead a mechanism of mass surveillance, of behavioural regulation, and of intimidation. Or think of the concentration of power over the mass instruments of communication which took place early in the 20th century and has continued ever since. Through newspapers, magazines, television, radio, song, websites and more, a relentless wave of propaganda washes over us morning to night, building and reinforcing attitudes and opinions, gushes of information we have no way to gauge the accuracy of, no way at all. The contents of our minds, in some important fashion, are built upon a foundation of faith not very different in kind from religious faith, if we depend upon media for our opinions. Think of Enron, Global Crossing and World.com if you doubt it."[8]

### Universities

Shaykh Abdalqadir says that a completely new worldview was laid down in Western universities during the fifties. This entailed not only the discrediting of the great masters of the European discourse, Wagner, Goethe, Rilke, but poetry, music and thinking itself. By the method of so-called critical analysis a whole culture was dismantled and by the techniques of dialectical method a new evaluation was set in place. This was done to ensure the slavish acceptance of the monetarist social model founded on the new acquiescent society that declared human rights and democracy as absolutes. To achieve this quite massive shift in view, the new leaders of intellectual life dismantled the foundations of the pre-1945 cultural ethos. Shaykh Abdalqadir insists we must free ourselves from the dead weight of structuralism in all its inhibitive and divisive effects.

Modernism and its reformist versions have as their core the lie that humans can be reduced and controlled by the pseudoscientific methodologies of sociology, psychology, political science and economics. Shaykh Abdalqadir says that this is an age of intellectual bankruptcy in which all "literature published today is obliged, whether the authors know it or not, to be absorbed into a total culture module whose tentacles stretch round the whole world. The Peking Academy, the Russian university system and the Western academic community basically share the same worldview and accept the same central thesis that exalts the continuing tyranny of speculation, (defined as a 'freedom') the myth of research, the cult of system, and the priesthood of the doctorate."[9]

Shaykh Abdalqadir explains that the methodology which was set in place in 1945 was the advanced stage of market-forces monetarism, and the creation of a new set of super-states, super-currencies and a whole series of newly empowered international institutions. The banks had seized political power, while the state became the service industry of the bank, the debt collector, debt receptor, and policeman. This new world order is continuing towards its goals of implementing a one world currency, a one world bank and a one world state. Shaykh Abdalqadir says that when the dust of dialectics and critical analysis has cleared, "what can be seen is that all this orthodoxy [i.e. the methodologies that had been set in place in 1945] has ever stood for is the enthronement of the world state controlled by an un-elected, indeed anonymous elite of bankers. The democratic has been forced ineluctably into the hands of the oligarchic."[10]

Shaykh Abdalqadir writes in his book *Kufr: an Islamic Critique* that: "The campus is the most carefully structured free-space in society. It is a completely monitored environment with its actions and rituals more carefully programmed than any other section of society. Since youth is volatile and therefore, due to its transformative energy, dangerous for the dominant group, students come into university young and they go out mature. They are trained to go out having agreed to keep the deception going. The control of the campus "can be recognised as creating an arena of staged social debate, planned anarchy, a coherent vocabulary of social change without access to the social reality, musically scored outbursts of revolutionary activity, even carefully cast martyrdoms (Kent State), so that student life may stand, both in experience and retrospect, for the fun, glory and MISTAKEN nature of youthful energy."[11] The point of study at university is to develop a certain point of view. In other words education is a means to total indoctrination of the student.

### Education in Islam – Futuwwa

Shaykh Abdalqadir says: "The rebirth of *futuwwa* in our time is incumbent on us."[12] *Futuwwa* is the foundation for the education of the Muslim. *Futuwwa* comes from the word *fatā* meaning young man (plural *fityān*; feminine *fatya*; feminine plural *fatāyāt*). The first and foremost quality of the *fatā* is refusal to submit to anyone or anything other than Allah. The second is dismantling of the *nafs* (self). The third is service.

*1. Refusal to submit to anyone or anything other than Allah*

With regards to the first quality of the *fatā,* Allah, the Almighty, says in Sūra al-Anbiyā (21) verse 60: "*They said, 'We heard a young man (fatā) mentioning them. They call him Ibrāhīm.'*" This is referring to the Prophet Ibrāhīm ﷺ when he broke the idols that his father and his people worshipped. Shaykh Abdalqadir says that from the Qur'ānic verses (Q. 21: 51-67) we derive three vital elements of *futuwwa*: that the Prophet Ibrāhīm ﷺ was a youth; that he teaches by action; and that the intellect follows the action.[13] From the reference to *fatā* in the young men who took refuge in the cave in Sūra al-Kahf (Q. 18: 10) we can deduce that illumination precedes action and action precedes intellect. The Prophets receive *waḥy*, revelation, from Allah and the young men who took refuge in the cave received *'ilm al-ladunī*, direct knowledge from Allah, or in the terminology of *taṣawwuf* – *tajalliyāt*, illumination into their hearts. *'Ilm al-ladunī* is a possibility for all human beings. From these two references in the Qur'ān we know that these *fityān* were constrained to worship other-than-Allah but they chose not to do so and to die rather than to worship something other than Allah.[14]

Shaykh Abdalqadir notes that *futuwwa* is, in a sense, alongside *tawḥīd*. *Futuwwa* is a kind of nobility and relates to the highest capacity or quality possible in knowledge for the servant of Allah.[15] As Imām as-Sulamī said: "All praise is due to Allah Who has opened the path of *futuwwa*, which leads to the most beautiful form of the fulfilment of our duties to Him, and Who has cleared and cleansed the path from all errors and all evil and raised its level to the highest. The Prophets whom He has sent and the chosen servants who are close to Him are on this path. All of those to whom the path to Truth has been opened and whose names are written as pure in the Book of Righteousness have learned to follow this path and attained the noble level of those who embody *futuwwa*."[16]

*2. Dismantling of the Nafs*

The second quality of the *fatā* is dismantling of the *nafs* (self). Allah says in verse 58 of Surah 21: "*He broke them in pieces, except for the biggest one, so that they would have it to consult.*" Shaykh Abdalqadir tells us that in Sufi commentaries (*tafsīr*) on the words "*he broke them in pieces*" the Prophet Ibrāhīm ﷺ is also teaching about the true nature of Allah's absolute unity and uncompromising power. If we take, for example wealth, fame and power to represent idols that can be "easily" smashed we are still left with the "*biggest one*" which is one's self (*nafs*). Shaykh Abdalqadir says that for the Sufis the breaking of the idols is also the breaking of aspects of character such as freewheeling and free operating and thinking that one can deal with the world as one wishes.

He adds that "you cannot make good character just by not being mean, not saying bad things, not being suspicious. That is not enough. You see for *birr*, for true right action, the man of knowledge has to know that his *nafs* has to be disintegrated. This is what the Sufis call *fanā fillāh* (annihilation in Allah). He has to lose the big idol and then he knows that things are not as they seem in experience. And then he understands the true nature of Allah's absolute unity and uncompromising power over him and everybody. This is the essence of *futuwwa* and it means a different way of experiencing reality."[17]

*3. Service*

The third quality of the *fatā* is service. When the Muslims migrated to Madīna, the Prophet ﷺ instituted brotherhood and guardianship (*muwālāt*) binding the Muslims together in solidarity and support for each other. Allah speaks of brotherhood in the Qur'ān (49:10) "*The mūminūn (believers) are brothers, so make peace between your brothers and have taqwā (fearful awareness) of Allah so that hopefully you will gain mercy.*" Imām al-Ghazālī listed the following eight duties of brotherhood: material assistance; personal aid; holding one's tongue; speaking out; forgiveness; prayer; loyalty and sincerity; and informality.[18]

In relation to *muwālāt* Allah says in the Qur'ān (9: 72): "*The men and women of the mūminūn (believers) are friends (awliyā) of one another. They command what is right and forbid what is wrong and establish ṣalāt and pay zakāt, and obey Allah and His Messenger. They are the people on whom Allah will have mercy. Allah is Almighty, All-Wise.*" The *walī* (singular of *awliyā*) accepts total responsibility for looking after someone else. Whilst *muwālāt* can be fulfilled by the father, the next of kin and ruler of the Muslims, it also means a unique relationship that bound the Muslims into a unit much closer than that of a close-knit family. *Muwālāt* has very wide social, political, economic and legal implications.

Shaykh Abdalqadir says that the Prophet ﷺ laid down the fundamental elements of a new order "for a new social ethos, grounded in *'ibāda* for Allah and love of the Messenger ﷺ. We have been given these four orders: You are not *mūmin* (a true believer) until you love Rasūl ﷺ more than your family and the whole of mankind. You are not *mūmin* until you want for your brothers what you want for yourself. If you believe in Allah and the Last Day you will treat your neighbour with kindness. And if you believe in Allah and the Last Day you will show hospitality to the guest."[19]

### Futuwwa Institutionalised

The qualities/values of *futuwwa*, namely the refusal to submit to anyone or anything other than Allah, the dismantling of the *nafs* and service, were institutionalised in *ad-dawla al-Islāmiyya*, the military, *ṭarīqas*, guilds and in the circles of teaching. Discussing each of these would be too extensive for the purposes of this book.

We will look at *futuwwa* as it came to be institutionalised in the military because Shaykh Abdalqadir has written on the subject.

The term *futuwwa* has been used interchangeably with that of the Arabic term *furūsiyya,* and *fatā* (young man) with that of *fāris* (horseman). The term *fāris* embodies bravery (*shajā'a*), gallantry (*shahāma*), manliness (*murūwwa*) and generosity (*sakhā*). These values were extolled in Arabian society from pre-Islamic times.[20] *Ḥilf al-Fuḍūl* was a pact which was witnessed by the Prophet ﷺ in pre-Islamic times about which he stated "I witnessed a pact of justice in the house of 'Abdullāh ibn Jud'ān that was more beloved to me than a herd of expensive red camels. If I were called to it now in the time of Islam, I would respond." In another narration, the Prophet ﷺ said, "Make such pacts to restore rights to their owners and that no oppressor has strength over the oppressed." In his biography of the Prophet ﷺ Ibn Hishām said that members of his ﷺ family "promised and pledged that they would not find any wronged person among their people, or anyone else who entered Makka, but that they would support him. They would stand against whoever oppressed them until the rights of the oppressed were restored."[21] *Futuwwa/Furūsiyya* permeated Muslim society throughout the Islamic period and *furūsiyya* writings developed along two branches: noble *furūsiyya* (*al-furūsiyya an-nabīla*) and military *furūsiyya* (*al-furūsiyya al-ḥarbiyya*).

Noble *furūsiyya* was a state institution which consisted of the training from childhood of the male members of the Abbasid family and the sons of notables in the eighth and ninth centuries. Their training included horsemanship, the use of weapons, archery, polo and hunting. Al-Manṣūr (754-75), the Abbasid caliph, being too old to engage in these activities, used them to prepare the ground for his son and heir al-Mahdī (775-85). Al-Mahdī was the first crown prince to be brought up according to the values of noble *furūsiyya,* which thereafter became a prerequisite for the caliphate. As al-Jāḥiẓ wrote: "None of the descendants of al-'Abbās mounted the throne without having fully mastered the arts of *furūsiyya*."[22]

In his references to military *furūsiyya* Shaykh Abdalqadir speaks of Sultan Ṣalāḥ ad-Dīn Ayyūbī's battles against the Crusaders. Sultan Ṣalāḥ ad-Dīn (1137-1197), the founder of the Ayyubid dynasty, ruled from 1174 to 1193. He was sent to Egypt to accompany his uncle Asad ad-Dīn Shirkuh, a general of the army, by Amīr Nūr ad-Dīn (r. 1146-1174) the Seljuk governor of Aleppo. Their task was to help reinstate Shawar as the *wazīr* of the teenage Fatimid caliph al-'Āḍid li-Dīn Allah (r. 1160-1171). After the death of Shirkuh and Shawar, Ṣalāḥ ad-Dīn was appointed *wazīr* by al-'Āḍid. With the death of al-'Āḍid, Ṣalāḥ ad-Dīn declared himself the sultan of Egypt. Amīr Nūr ad-Dīn instructed Ṣalāḥ ad-Dīn to align himself with the Abbasid caliphate in Baghdad. Within days the *khuṭbas* in Cairo and al-Fusṭāt acknowledged, the Abbasid, al-Mustaḍī' ibn Yūsuf al-Mustanjid (r. 1170-1180) as caliph.

Not only did Sultan Ṣalāḥ ad-Dīn study the Qur'ān and the sciences of Islam, including law, but he was well versed in Euclid, *The Almagest* and arithmetic. He had knowledge of the genealogies, biographies and histories of the Arabs as well as the bloodlines of Arabian horses. He spoke Kurdish and Arabic and had memorised the *Ḥamāsah* of Abū Tammām, a ten volume anthology of Arabic poetry. Sultan Ṣalāḥ ad-Dīn had an illustrious military career with the capture of Jerusalem from the Crusaders in 1187 being his greatest achievement.

He took as his guide the greatest scholar of his time, the Sufi Shaykh, 'Abd al-Qādir al-Jīlānī (1078-1166). "Many people may not be aware, however, that one of the dimensions of Shaykh 'Abd al-Qādir's greatness and his profound influence on the Muslims of his time was that he strove to produce a new generation of Muslims, not just to revive true Islam but to defeat the Crusaders in Palestine and Greater Syria. The victories of Nūr ad-Dīn Zanjī and his general Ṣalāḥ ad-Dīn Ayyūbī and the re-conquest of Jerusalem also stand as a testimony to the efforts of al-Quṭb al-Ghawth 'Abd al-Qādir al-Jīlānī and the thousands of upright men and women that appeared with that new generation. ... When Shaykh 'Abd al-Qādir appeared at the age of 50 in 1127 after 32 years of preparation, he appeared with tremendous intellectual and spiritual power. The great Ḥanbalī scholar Ibn Rajab says of him: 'He won the complete acceptance of the people ... and the kings hold him in fear and awe, not to mention those who were less powerful.' It is not mere coincidence that the year Shaykh 'Abd al-Qādir appeared in Baghdad was the same year that the great *mujahid* king and *shahīd* 'Imād ad-Dīn Zanjī came to the city's rescue and was then followed by his son Nūr ad-Dīn and then by their general Ṣalāḥ ad-Dīn, all of them stood with Shaykh 'Abd al-Qādir – just as he stood with them."[23] Sultan Ṣalāḥ ad-Dīn learnt to be honest, truthful and the importance of being in harmony with his destiny from Shaykh Abd al-Qādir al-Jīlānī.

More than fifty poets contemporary with Sultan Ṣalāḥ ad-Dīn demonstrate his strong faith in Allah as the most quintessential aspect of *futuwwa* that he lived up to. They celebrate his piety, fear of Allah, trust in Him, his loyalty to Allah and the fact that he was a devoted believer in the teachings of Islam. What was apparent to the poets was that Sultan Ṣalāḥ ad-Dīn's *'ibāda* accounted for his success as a warrior and how his fear of Allah inspired him to improve the political, financial and educational circumstances of Egypt between 1164 and 1174. Sultan Ṣalāḥ ad-Dīn's used his power to protect women and the weak, support right against wrong and confront evil fearlessly and then destroy it.

After the Third Crusade (1189-1192) Western historians embraced Sultan Ṣalāḥ ad-Dīn as a chivalrous knight famous for his bravery, status, honesty, truthfulness, justice, generosity and fair treatment of women.[24] His treatment of his enemy, King Richard I of England, is exemplary. In one of his battles with the Crusaders he initiated one of his prisoners, who was put up for ransom, into the ethos of *futuwwa*. He then paid for his ransom and released him so he could transmit to his fellow knights the roots in *futuwwa* of Islamic conduct in war and peace.

Shaykh Abdalqadir points out that chivalry in European civilisation has its roots in Islam. He says that: "Islamic *futuwwa* pre-dated and pre-designed the christian rules of chivalry which created the whole of European civilisation in the Middle Ages."[25] In his discussion on English history Shaykh Abdalqadir says that the Tudor dynasty, which lasted 118 years (1485-1603), can be seen as the "triumphant high point of English society."[26] To grant legitimacy to his reign Henry VII promoted chivalry and its medieval sports, which in turn inspired a new aristocracy loyal to the Tudor throne. "As a result of this chivalric ethos, which brought honour, nobility and loyalty to the nation's elite, he established an iconography of family identity and connection. Heraldry became an instrument of political power. ... However, the unfolding of the applied laws of legitimacy, inheritance and conquest is not merely a monolinear system of genealogical hegemony – essential to it, not just a civic background but as living dynamic, is the rise, growth and demise of a way of life and evaluation called chivalry."[27]

Chivalry began and evolved as a secular organisational procedure, which, after its triumphant flowering, was infiltrated by the Church and eventually deconstructed. Shaykh Abdalqadir says that the sources and evaluations of chivalry were not Christian. Chivalry was involved in the formation of a brotherhood under arms bonded together by high moral behavioural values. Its honour was delineated outwardly by the science of heraldry which indicated the bloodline of the participant and the military allegiance of the knight. Inwardly it was preserved by the membership of a chivalric order which demanded from its members high moral practices. The most famous of these were the Order of the Garter, Order of the Star and the Order of the Golden Fleece. As these Orders came into the public domain, involving both Church and State, "we can discern a quite discrete system uniting a hidden Order of a very different kind that set itself at odds with the Roman Church and its belief systems."[28] The vowed obligations of the chivalric knights were: prowess, loyalty, largesse (generosity in bestowing money and gifts on others), courtesy, franchise (nobility), martial training, jousting and keeping the company of other knights.

The emergence of the rites and practices of chivalry took place against the background of a Europe oriented towards a program of Crusades. The Crusader ethos ran through the thinking, the practice and the imagining of several generations. The militant conflict between the Papal Church and the Muslim community, however, implied a mutual familiarity between the two parties. "Both sides saw prisoners, taken, ransomed and sometimes absorbed. By the end of the chivalric age the great writers of Europe were utterly conversant with Islam, its beliefs and its people. From Dante to Shakespeare and Marlowe there is on record a remarkable grasp of the enemy religion. Over these centuries is a trail of intellectual exchange, marriage, trade and diplomatic agreements."[29] There was a harmony between the chivalry of the Christians and the *futuwwa* of the Muslims and there was amity between the two warrior elites. However the Papal Church was opposed to this harmony and "ruthlessly rewrote and redesigned anything that might point towards the adoption of the Islamic model."[30] Nevertheless, the super-state of European Papal Christendom was infiltrated and taught the lessons of Islamic brotherhood and leadership, through the inevitable meetings between Muslims and Christians during the Crusades.

The plays of Christopher Marlowe demonstrate that, by the time of the Tudor Dynasty, there was an intellectual grasp of Islam in Europe both as *dīn* and social nexus. Over the five centuries from Sultan Ṣalāḥ ad-Dīn to the Tudors, the aristocratic leadership of Europe had developed a completely independent and opposite religion to that of Papal Rome. The Church, however, persisted in penetrating this other religion, both by execution and torture and by smothering its heraldic displays with crosses, crucifixes and Saints-days. Most abhorrent to the celibate and misogynistic priesthood was the honour given to women by the new elite brotherhood of warriors. Women were seen as pure by nature and not, as the priests claimed, corrupted vessels of flesh dragging men down to damnation. Part of chivalry was having respect for good women and protecting them from danger and slander.

Similar to the numerical composition of the Companions of the Cave, the disciples of the Messenger of Allah 'Īsā ﷺ and the ten Companions of the Prophet Muḥammad ﷺ who were promised the Garden, the chivalric Orders always comprised of a small number of knights, usually ten or twelve or some other small number. "In all of this we can discern a dynamic form, not just of a brotherhood elite but of a key qualitative bonding, which is at the same time the core of the Divine transaction set up among peoples and also the core evaluation of which civilisation itself is the by-product."[31] It is from the Qur'ānic and Islamic pattern "that are derived the chivalric Orders of Knights and the *Ahl al-Futuwwa* and this in turn allows us to recognise that the essentials of pure original nature, *fiṭra*, have to be sustained, honoured and protected against the entropic forces of humanness and the passage of measured time."[32]

During the Plantagenet period (1154-1399) the structural grid on which the society depended was the dynamic collaboration and conflict between the king and the aristocracy. The king was upheld by a vibrant and active aristocracy who in turn were strong and unified by the chivalric values that they imposed on themselves. King John had tried to upset this order but the barons forced the king to observe the chivalric obligation to protect the poor and maintain the balance of society. The King was forced to sign the Magna Carta[33] but subsequently asked the Pope, Innocent III, to annul the Charter who, in turn, declared it illegal and threatened anyone who observed it with excommunication. The Magna Carta stood for the chivalric order against the Papal system. What began in the Plantagenet period was brought to completion by the Tudor Dynasty with the abolition of Papal rule under Henry VIII (1491-1547). Throughout his reign he kept alive the chivalric honours and courtesies at court and in battle.

The deep power network of chivalric power withered as a new system began to emerge during the reign of Elizabeth I (1533-1603) that set the stage for the confrontation of two fundamental doctrines of political power. As a result of this confrontation, power was transferred from the monarch to a new political class, and the legend of Elizabeth the Virgin Queen became essential for the subsequent development of the modern state. The opposing forces in this transition were on one side the Cecils (Lord Burghley and his son, Sir Robert Cecil) and on the other Robert Devereux (1565-1601), the Earl of Essex. It manifested as "a crystallisation and impact of one ancient and natural ethos, biological and anthropological, with a new emergent model of human society that had natural philosophy as its foundation and structuralism as its identity."[34]

Robert Devereux, the scholar and soldier, embodied the noble chivalric qualities of generosity, heroism, bravery and justice. He was knighted after his first military excursion to the Low Countries in 1586. On the $25^{th}$ February the Earl of Essex was sworn in as a member of the Privy Council of Queen Elizabeth I. During the years 1593 and 1597 he was held in high esteem by King Henry IV of France and King James VI of Scotland for his activities as a protean statesman. "Essex held the firmest conviction that political events for their fruition required not only men of action but men of *futuwwa*, noble brotherhood."[35]

At a privy council meeting in 1598 the debate over the appointment of a governor for Ireland got so heated that Essex rose angrily from the table and in effect turned his back on his Sovereign. The Queen sent Essex to Ireland with the mission of subduing the revolts led by Hugh O'Neill, the Earl of Tyrone. After a series of inconclusive battles, Essex signed a truce with Tyrone and returned to England. In June 1600 Essex was deprived of his offices and in February 1601 Essex and his supporters planned to seize the court, the tower and the city in order to force the Queen to change the leaders of her government, especially Robert Cecil. The rebellion resulted in the execution of Essex on February 26th 1601.

As Shaykh Abdalqadir observes, this event marked the end of an era: "In the great cycle of chivalry, or more exactly of *Futuwwa*, that is of bonded men of honour and nobility held together by their belief in the Divine and the obligation to service, to protecting women and to raising up the poor, the end of its epochal achievement is the execution of the great Earl."[36]

The Earl of Essex's honour, nobility and political philosophy can be gleaned from his letter to his young cousin Roger Manners, the 5th Earl of Rutland: "Clearness of judgment makes men liberal for it teacheth to esteem the goods of fortune not for themselves, for they are but jailors to them for their use, where we are in truth lords over them; and it makes us know that it is *beatius dare quod accipere* [it is more blessed to give than to receive], the one being a badge of sovereignty, the other of subjection. Also it leadeth us to fortitude, for it teacheth us that we should not too much prize life which we cannot keep, nor fear death which we cannot shun; that he that dies nobly lives forever, and he that lives in fear dies continually; that pain and danger be great only by opinion, and that in truth nothing is fearful but fear itself; that custom makes the thing used natural as it were to the user. I shall not need to prove these two things, since we see by experience it holds true in all things, but yet those that give with judgment are not only encouraged to be liberal by the return of thankfulness from those to whom they give, but find in the very exercise of that virtue a delight to do good. And if custom be strong to confirm any one virtue more than another, it is the virtue of fortitude, for it makes us triumph over the fear which happily we have encountered and hold more dear the reputation of honour which we have increased."[37]

Our present situation in the West dates back to the collapse of *futuwwa* among the knightly elite at the end of the Elizabethan Age and the European wars, specifically the failure of the Essex coup d'état. With the collapse of the chivalric code came the evolution of the structuralist state, the rise of the new elite of bankers and the nationalisation of monarchism. The age of the corporation and bank, controlled by an un-elected personnel, had begun. The masses were given elected democratic governments and preoccupied with taxation whilst the corporation-financiers seized the world's wealth in total immunity.

# Chapter 14

## Media

Mass communication media are comprised of communication outlets used to store and deliver information through print media, radio, television, publishing, photography, cinema and digital media.

### Functions of Mass Media

The stated functions of mass media are: information and education; socialisation; entertainment; political awareness; cultural transmission; and a catalyst to development.

Information and Education: The core of the media's information function is performed by news which is supposed to carry accurate, objective, and complete information. After finishing their formal education, members of society depend on mass media for updated educational content on a wide variety of subjects and the newest trends in their surroundings.

Socialisation: Mass media functions as an agency for socialisation by empowering people to acquire norms and experiences of the group as a whole, to maintain cultural consensus and communal harmony. The supposed aim of this information is the creation of common values for creating an integrated society.

Entertainment: All media have entertainment content to supposedly break the monotony of daily life. Newspapers, for example, publish cartoons, comics, puzzles and special supplements. Television and cinema have become big industries comprising motion picture companies, music firms, theatre groups and game developers.

Political Awareness: Most of the content of mass media, especially news, be it television or newspapers, is centered on politics. Political leaders are seen to advocate better living conditions for the population and journalists appear to expose corruption and condemn or praise political activities considering their merits. All this is supposed to make people believe that they have a vibrant democracy. Thus mass media assume a key role in setting the agenda for the political system and of policy-making by influencing public opinion on various issues. We will see later how this agenda-setting ability of media is misused by various interest groups.

Cultural Transmission: Mass media have become the bridge between the past and present. Cultural traditions are learnt from history and media have become the transmitters of past history. Today's news reports become the historical record that shapes the future. Media have therefore assumed the role of introducing new lifestyles, values and fashions.

Catalyst to Development: You might have seen reports in newspapers urging the authorities to build new roads and bridges in your locality or campaigning for the betterment of the living conditions of underprivileged people. Mass media report on problems faced by people and make the administrators aware of them. This might be in relation to infrastructure, goods or services and this function of media is termed Development Communication.[1]

### Objectives of Mass Media

The main objectives of mass media are: information; education; entertainment; and persuasion.

Information: The main objective of mass media is to give information to people in the form of facts, news and basic information about events that have occurred. Sadly information has become the only link for modern society. Thus, mass media not only informs about events and conditions of the society and the world but they also indicate, or more properly, suggest relations of power and facilitate innovation, adaption, and progress.[2]

Education: Education means the creation of awareness through a well though-out interpretation of information. Thus, mass media communication is designed to steer people as to what course of action to take both in crises and other times.

Entertainment: Many people are dependent on mass media for entertainment. Reports indicate that there has been unprecedented growth in the entertainment industry in recent times.

Persuasion: Last, but most important of all, is that persuasion "which brings about change in the human mind, human personality, and human character. ... In fact, persuasion is the ultimate objective of any mass media, which brings about reformatory change by informing, educating, and entertaining people. Hence, persuasion is that point at which information, education, and entertainment merge together. Therefore, it totally depends on the skills of the communicator to mix information, education, and entertainment in such a proportion that it becomes persuasive."[3]

## New Media

The invention of the Internet and the World Wide Web opened up several new avenues for mass communication. These include e-mail, websites, podcasts, e-books, blogging, social networking sites, Internet Protocol Television, Internet radio etc. Social networking is a major facility enabling users to create a profile and build a personal network connecting users around the world. The new media facilitates instant interaction between senders and receivers enabling access to the latest events without any delay. New media facilitates the convergence of the various types of content like audio, video, text, image and data on a single device. The new media was used by Julian Assange, the founder of Wikileaks, which revealed that mainstream media acts as a protector for the established powers and is not an independent restraint on them. The Wikileaks phenomenon will be discussed later in this chapter.

Hassim Dockrat says that social media is rapidly becoming an agent for positive change in the way people assess situations and events. He argues that the uncontrollable evolution of social media platforms, in form and function, has become the breach in the armour of the capitalist agenda, which is desirous of optimum control and regulation of information and its use. The new media format has certainly contributed to information overload. From this perspective it simultaneously projects the good and the bad, mediocrity and substantiveness. On the flip-side its positive spinoffs are proving to be far greater, offering alternative news, views and opinions. No man-made system is fail-safe even by design. This has therefore proven to be a double-edged sword for both the user and the powers that be or controlling agents. Corporations and government agencies use social media platforms and its related technologies to put society under microscopic conditions of scrutiny, to be observed as organisms needing control, psychic and emotive manipulation and genetic re-engineering spelling the end of privacy and the end of secrecy. "However, by the very bipartisan nature of this technical system, the organism itself has become an observer, able to telescopically observe the primary observer. Big brother may be watching but I am watching big brother too. In one sense the handset and PC have unwittingly restored a semblance of individuality and personal identity to the perceived herd called humanity. It is a condition of nature that things are by their opposites. Existential relevance of a thing finds itself in its opposite or contrast. The inability of the capitalist world order to grasp this fundamental principle of existence ultimately remains its failing. Social media and the internet are merely one component propelling it toward that inevitability. Whatever our view may be of the evolution of media platforms, what is certain is that people are becoming more aware, more socialised (through screen imaging and chat groups) and more expressive in a meaningful way than ever thought possible fifty years back, even if literary skills are reduced to a new form of hieroglyphics."[4]

### The Promised Utopia

We have been told by the media that capitalism gives everyone a fair and equal opportunity to make a living or even to amass a fortune if you want to. The educational system is there to help you develop your full potential and capabilities so that you may excel at what you wish to do. The health system is there to help you maintain your wellbeing and keep you at your optimum capacity. The democratic system allows you to determine who will represent your interests in the political processes. Legislation will be in your best interests and will be adjudicated by the legal system which will guarantee justice for you. Police will guarantee that the law is implemented and that you will be safe. The army will keep you secure from external threats. Institutions developed to facilitate the goals of global capitalism were the United Nations Organisation, the World Trade Organisation, the International Monetary Fund and the World Bank. Finally humankind had achieved one global world state, one world government (UNO) and one currency, the US dollar.[5]

We are also told that the multitude of benefits that were to result from globalisation were that: the nation state would wither away; power would lie with global markets; economics and not politics would shape human events; global markets would establish international economic balances; boom-and-bust cycles would end; waves of trade would generate economic prosperity all over the world; dictatorships would turn into democracies and governments would become debt-free.[6] With the fall of the USSR it was declared that the end of history had arrived and what we were possibly witnessing was not just the end of the Cold War or the passing of a particular period of post-war history but the end point of mankind's ideological evolution and the universalisation of Western liberal democracy as the final form of human government.[7] In reality this is all spin. It is all a lie concealing the biggest crime in the history of mankind. It is a public relations exercise. The results speak for themselves. Capitalism is a fraud, a dishonest scheme (scam) and a malicious deception (hoax). Capitalism and democracy, its public relations interface, have failed.

### The Dystopian Reality

In fact they, that is, capitalism and democracy, do the opposite of what they promise. One percent of the world's population owns fifty percent of the world's wealth. Democracy provides nothing more than an interface between corporate power and the people. It is a public relations exercise. Global results for capitalism obtained from the United Nations agencies are as follows:

1 Nearly ½ of the world's population – more than 3 billion people – live on less than $2.50 a day. More than 1.3 billion live in extreme poverty – less than $1.25 a day.

2 1 billion children worldwide are living in poverty. According to UNICEF, 22,000 children die each day due to poverty.

3 805 million people worldwide do not have enough food to eat.

4 More than 750 million people lack adequate access to clean drinking water. Diarrhoea caused by inadequate drinking water, sanitation, and hand hygiene kills an estimated 842,000 people every year globally or approximately 2,300 people per day.

5 In 2011, 165 million children under the age 5 were stunted (reduced rate of growth and development) due to chronic malnutrition.

6 Preventable diseases like diarrhoea and pneumonia take the lives of 2 million children a year because they are too poor to afford proper treatment.

7 As of 2013, 21.8 million children under 1 year of age worldwide had not received the three recommended doses of vaccine against diphtheria, tetanus and pertussis.

8 ¼ of all humans live without electricity – approximately 1.6 billion people.

9 80% of the world population lives on less than $10 a day.

10 Oxfam estimates that it would take $60 billion annually to end extreme global poverty, that is less than ¼ the income of the top 100 richest billionaires.

11 Hunger is the number one cause of death in the world, killing more than HIV/AIDS, malaria, and tuberculosis combined.[8]

On the other hand, according to a Credit Suisse report the wealthiest 1 percent of the world's population now owns more than half of the world's wealth. The total wealth in the world grew by 6 percent over the past 12 months to $280 trillion, marking this as the fastest wealth creation since 2012. More than half of thc $16.7 trillion in new wealth was in the US, which grew $8.5 trillion richer. The world's millionaires are expected to do the best in the coming years. There are now 36 million millionaires in the world, and their numbers are expected to grow to 44 million by 2022. The US still leads the world in millionaires, with 15.3 million people worth $1 million or more. Japan ranks second with 2.7 million millionaires, while the UK ranks third with 2.2 million. China ranks fifth with 1.9 million millionaires, but its millionaire population is expected to hit 2.8 million by 2022.[9]

### Capitalism in Terminal Decline

Shaykh Abdalqadir categorically states that "the monetarist system has in effect collapsed, its theoretical foundations cannot sustain rational critique, cannot pretend that 'business' can continue using these instruments, institutions and protocols."[10] John McMurtry regards capitalism as a life-threatening disease that is a danger to the human species and explains the role of the media in perpetuating it: "The failure of our social immune system to recognise or respond to the cancerous form of capitalism is understandable once we realise that the surveillance and communication organs of host social bodies across the world, as they now function, are incapable of recognising the nature and patterns of the disease. That is, capitalist-organised media and information systems select for dissemination only messages that do not contradict the capitalist organisation of social bodies. Consequently, whatever exposes the systemic disorder of this social organisations structure (such as this essay) is normally refused transmission through its communications media. In this way, our social immune system has been gravely compromised by the accelerating control of multinational capital conglomerates over most of the recorded information produced and exchanged around the world – mass communications, the production of textbooks and educational resources for higher learning, and the biotechnology for reproducing and adapting life-forms themselves."[11]

Even a cursory investigation into global media ownership shows the veracity of McMurtry's analysis. The world's media is highly concentrated and dominated by a small number of firms which include Bertelsmann, National Amusements, Sony Group Corporation, News Corp, Comcast, The Walt Disney Company, Time Warner, Discovery, Fox Corporation, Hearst Communications, MGM Holdings Inc., Grupo Globo and Lagardere Group. The biggest six are Comcast (valued at $148.2 billion), Disney ($88.1), Time Warner ($60.6 billion), News Corp ($56 billion), National Amusements ($43 billion) and Sony Group Corporation ($34.1 billion).

### The Wikileaks Phenomenon

Prior to Wikileaks, computer hackers[12] generally accessed and acquired information for either personal viewing or showing off. Few people had the political will to disseminate that information to the public and a mass audience on the internet had not yet developed. Wikileaks is an international not-for-profit organisation that publishes news leaks and classified media acquired from anonymous sources and between 2006 and 2015 it released 10 million documents online. Julian Assange the founder of Wikileaks was born in 1971 in Townsville, Australia and went on to study Physics at the University of Melbourne. In 2010 he was arrested in London and since then has been under house arrest, in the Ecuadorian embassy, where he sought refuge, and in prison. In July 2022 the British government approved his extradition to the USA to face charges for which he can be sentenced to life imprisonment.

Jason Ferriman of Dallas House wrote that: "The Wikileaks phenomenon has revealed that mainstream media acts more as a guardian for the entrenched power domains than as an independent check on their power. As Assange succinctly asked, 'How is it that a team of five people managed to release to the public more suppressed information, at that level, than the rest of the world press combined?' The core to understanding the Wikileaks effect is that it revealed a fissure crack in the power nexus – its inherent structuralism. The truth is that all the leaked information that Wikileaks has revealed is neither that revelatory nor groundbreaking, and to focus on this information is to misunderstand its political effect (and why Assange is being attacked from the strangest of corners and with the most egregious of methods – his Swedish rape trial, previously thrown out by the Swedish judiciary). It is that Wikileaks has exposed the inherent structuralism in today's power nexus. Since the French Revolution, structuralist-rule has dominated people-rule, with Napoleon, the great architect of the modern State, and the Financial elite, the successors to the Church."[13]

Wikileaks had exposed the structuralism of the US State Department's SIPRnet program. It is estimated that there are 854,000 people who hold top secret security clearances since the Cold War epoch and its successor the War on Terror. The public is unaware of how much money the program costs, how many programs exist within it or how many agencies do the same work. "The result of this classification-structuralism is the division into two distinct groups: those who are privy to the actual conduct of American policy, but are forbidden to write or talk about it, and the uninformed public. Wikileaks merely broke this division."[14]

# PART 3

This part of the book is dedicated to the *mu'āmalāt* of trade and commerce. It will include three chapters (16, 17 & 18) by Abdassamad Clarke, which function as overviews of trade and commerce in the Qur'ān, in the *Sunna* and *Sīra*, and of transactions, rather than as comprehensive accounts of them. For the transactions in particular one must have recourse to the standard works of *fiqh*. The essence of what we are saying is that *zakāt*, being an act of worship undertaken by means of wealth, transforms our understanding of wealth itself and of the nature of our transactions in the world, thus reversing the disastrous misconception that changes the distinction between *'ibādāt* and *mu'āmalāt* into a religious versus secular dichotomy, licensing the entire apparatus of the modern state and its legislation. *Mu'āmala* – behaviour is the singular and *mu'āmalāt* – transactions the plural. It has been said that the *dīn* IS *mu'āmala*, and that has been ascribed to the Prophet ﷺ himself.

Shaykh Abdalqadir says: "We insist – Islam is not a political movement, but it IS a market movement."[1] He explains that Islam is transactional. "The *dīn*, as it is declared in a renowned *ḥadīth*, is *MU'AMALAT*. In other words Islam, while making supreme governance *khilāfa*[2], as categorically insisted on by Imām al-Qurṭubī, leaves the issue of local governance an open matter. What is non-negotiable is the *dīn* itself. And the *dīn* is *mu'āmalāt*."[3] What the Shaykh refers to here is *mu'āmala* – behaviour, whose plural *mu'āmalāt* means transactions. The *dīn* is comprised of *'ibādāt* (worship) and *mu'āmalāt* (social transactions), and what this *ḥadīth* is emphasising is that the *dīn* is not only *'ibādāt*, but is one's behaviour in the widest possible sense. If the *dīn* were only *'ibādāt*, that would be secularism, which is alien to Islam. *Mu'āmalāt* are an integral part of the *dīn* and have to be conducted according to the *fiqh*[4]. Shaykh Abdalqadir explains that: "All *'ibāda*, the first half of the *dīn*, is expressed in fiduciary metaphor, debt, profit, gain, loss – all these indicate the spiritual transaction. All *fiqh* regulates every single fiduciary event as a spiritual metaphor. It is in its totality a socio-financial system devoid of usury, abhorring stored wealth, inviting expenditure, and looking on debt as dreadful."[5]

Shaykh Abdalqadir states that "the monetarist system has in effect collapsed; its theoretical foundations cannot sustain rational critique, cannot pretend that 'business' can continue using these instruments, institutions and protocols. However, the fundamental principle – usury – is not, apparently cannot be, confronted, let alone abolished. It is for us to determine whether we can claw back the moral power to put an end to the monetarist (money *ex nihilo*) practice and re-establish a real-value exchange system in place of a fantasy numbers system."[6] In fact the Shaykh outlines in great detail the way of putting an end to capitalism and reestablishing Islam. The first steps to Islamic revival are:

> "Firstly, the *jamat* must form itself into a legal entity like the rebel humans did with trade unions, but this is step one to a new life.
>
> Secondly, the local leaders, by their wealth and influence in the land, have to be taken, enjoining them to right action. Islam has no priesthood, imams take prayer, governance is a social capacity.
>
> Thirdly, move constructively from capitalist modalities – currency, banking, taxation – to free exchanges between men and groups.
>
> Fourthly, remember physical and military opposition are the lifeblood of capitalist atheism. The revival of Islam is dependent on step by step turning away from *kufr* and finally, submitting to the natural religion.

Fifthly, this program of life will be founded on the movement from money as pure electronic stored units of numbers to real wealth – gold, silver and commodities. This will lead to the abolition of capitalist supermarket distribution, that is, of goods and paper money, and the restoration of hand to hand trade locally and usury free container caravans around the world. The abolition of value added tax, of sales tax, would be the first indication of the *kuffār* abandoning their hypocrisy. The gold Islamic *dīnār* and the silver Islamic *dirham* are the signs of our emergence."[7]

# Chapter 15

## The Institutions of Islamic governance

The modern state, in all its modes, has been captured through the takeover of their governments by the oligarchs. The Prophet ﷺ abolished the state. Madīna was the model of government without a state and the greatest expression of it can be found in the caliphate of 'Umar ibn al-Khaṭṭāb ؓ. Shaykh Abdalqadir writes that the task of the coming century is the abolition of the fiscal state.[1] "The irrational function within the societal system which was the instrument which upheld tyrannical statism was usury. Destroy usury and you destroy the unjust structuralist state."[2]

Since the act of governing is primarily associated with the production, distribution and consumption of resources, the Islamic *dawla* has to guarantee justice and equity in the financial affairs of its citizens. The central function of governance in the Islamic *dawla* is to facilitate the movement of wealth to all sections of the community and this circulation of wealth is guaranteed by the *sharī'a*. In economic terms Islam demands equity, freedom and justice in trade and commerce. Islamic law promotes the circulation of wealth and inhibits its stagnation, thereby impeding the development of oligarchy.[3] The application of the *sharī'a* should, therefore, result in prosperity for society. The Islamic *dawla* established by the Prophet ﷺ in Madīna was a law-governed society, a nomocracy,[4] in which free trade and the movement of wealth to all sections of the community were central to the establishment of justice.

The institutions of governance that were set up by (a) the *Khulafa al-Rashīdun* (the Rightly-Guided Caliphs i.e. Abū Bakr, 'Umar, 'Uthmān and 'Alī ﷺ), (b) the Umayyads, (c) Abbasids, and (d) the Seljuks (e), the Ottomans (f), and the sultanates that lay outside of the central Islamic lands, were adaptations of those established by the Prophet ﷺ in Madīna. As mentioned before Madīna was established as the primary model for the future generations of Muslims in particular and the future of mankind in general. It was a complete blueprint pattern for human societies, and all subsequent caliphates were an approximation to that model. The institutions that developed from the Madīnan model in subsequent Islamic history were the caliphate, the wazirate (vizierate), the judiciary, the *bayt al-māl* (the treasury), *ḥisba* (administration of the city), the mint, the *sūq* (market), the *awqāf* (charitable endowments), the *aṣnāf* (guilds), the *shurṭa* (police) and the army (*jaysh*). These institutions, regulated by Islamic law, provided the means by which Muslim societies functioned.

## Institutions of Muslim Society

### *Caliphate*

Throughout the history of Islam political authority has been based on personal rule.[5] Islamic political thought pertains primarily to the problems of governance, especially to the conduct of the ruler. From the perspective of the *sharī'a* the functions of the caliph include: continuity of the goals and functions held by the Prophet ﷺ and previous caliphs; establishment of the rule of law; defence of the territorial integrity of the polity; management of a free market economy; collection and distribution of taxes; maintenance of public order; construction and maintenance of physical infrastructure and public works relating to land, water and civilisation; and delegation of tasks as a means of helping him in the "surveillance of affairs and the scrutiny of circumstances such that he may execute the policy of the *umma* [society] and defend the nation."[6]

*Wazirate*

The *wazīr*, the deputy and representative of the caliph, became under the Abbasids the highest ranking civil official after the caliph. He was the chief or prime minister of the state. His financial functions included the disposal of treasury funds and the management of the *dīwāns* (registers) of the army (*al-jund*) and land tax (*kharāj*).[7]

*Amirate*

An *amīr* is a governor of a province or a town appointed by the caliph. His clearly defined tasks are: ordering the armies and provisioning them; payment of the soldiers; applying the law; appointing judges and magistrates; execution of punishments following the judgments made in the courts; appointment of *zakāt* collectors and the collection and distribution of *kharāj* and *zakāt*; protection of the *dīn* from modification and deviation; leading the congregational prayers; protection for the pilgrims; and war against the enemy if his territory is adjacent to that of the enemy; and subsequent distribution of the booty.

*Kuttāb*

It was from the ranks of the *kuttāb* (secretaries) that the *wazir*s were appointed. The *kātib* (scribe or secretary) was a specialist in administrative and financial matters whose functions were the maintenance of the *dīwān*s and correspondence. He was not simply a collaborator of the caliph and *wazīr* but at times determined the course of events through the skill of his communications. As Imām al-Ghazālī noted: "If the sword and the pen did not exist, the world would not stand on its feet. These two are rulers over all things."[8] The Prophet ﷺ had many scribes and secretaries e.g. Abū Bakr, 'Umar, 'Uthmān, 'Alī and Zayd ibn Thābit ﷺ.

*Ḥisba*

Public order and governance of the city is the responsibility of the *muḥtasib* who is the most important functionary of the caliph. The *muḥtasib* has to investigate unacceptable behaviour in order to discourage it and renew good behaviour that has been abandoned. He has assistants in order to discharge his duties. He may impose punishments for misdemeanours as long as they do not exceed the limits set for the *ḥadd*-punishments (specific fixed penalties laid down in the *sharī'a*). Although the *muḥtasib* has certain judicial powers these are conditional. If his appointment includes the power to compel others through his own *ijtihād* (the use of independent reasoning to arrive at new legal judgments in the absence of any clear precedent) and judgment he must be a *mujtahid* (one capable of *ijtihād*). If that is not part of his brief he should, nevertheless, be aware of the legality of the disputed matters.

The task of the *muḥtasib* covers all spiritual, political and economic considerations and reflects the unity that Islam has always sought to achieve between *al-mā'ash* and *al-mā'ad* – the Muslim's material and spiritual life. It is customary to divide the *muḥtasib*'s duties into two categories. The first, those relating to the "spiritual" life of the city, include: the arrangements for the Friday-prayer, the *Eid*-prayer, the five daily prayers, the *adhān* (the call to prayer) at the time of prayers; maintenance of mosques and public baths. He is also responsible for the supervision of the fast of Ramadan, the breaking of it and the *zakāt al-fitr* (a small tax paid at the end of Ramadan for the benefit of the poor enabling them to also participate in the festivities). The *muḥtasib* is charged with the responsibility of helping people have their rights and claims fulfilled and their overdue debts repaid. He has to ensure that guardianship of minors is undertaken in accordance with the conditions stipulated by the *qāḍī* (judge).

He is to make certain that the guardianship of women regarding their marriage is properly discharged and see to it that the *'idda* (a period after the death of her husband or divorce during which a woman must wait before re-marrying) is completed. He ensures that masters respect the rights of their slaves. The *muḥtasib* may be asked to intervene in cases where the authority of *zakāt* collectors does not extend. He must control the teaching of *fiqh*, *tafsīr* (commentary and explanation of the meaning of the Qur'ān) and *ḥadīth* so that they are not taught by people unqualified to do so. It is his task to examine the *imam* who leads the prayer and to supervise the selection process. He also assesses the abilities of the *mu'adhdhin* (one who calls to prayer), *mu'allim* (teacher or master of a craft) and *mu'addib* (schoolmaster) ensuring that excessive punishment is not meted out. The *awqāf* (charitable foundations) were also under his purview. The *muḥtasib*'s duties included the enforcement of the law with regard to the consumption of alcohol, gambling, fortune-telling, as well as "the countless examples of wrongdoing that are possible."[9]

The second category of his duties deals with the physical environment of the city (the heart of which is the market) and comprehensively covers trade and commerce. In this sense he is also the ombudsman charged with the responsibility to guarantee that all goods and services that enter the market place are good for society and the environment. His economic functions included: "1. ensuring the supply of necessities (foodstuffs, etc.); 2. supervision of industry (product standardisation, arbitration, minimum wages, etc.); 3. supervision of services (professional services – medical practitioners, pharmacologists, teachers, etc.); 4. supervision of trading practices (weights and measures, product quality, enforcing laws against forbidden practices, etc.); 5. civil and municipal functions (public safety, business locations – even enforcing anti-pollution rules)."[10]

The civil and municipal duties of the *muḥtasib* with regards to trade and commerce included the maintenance of the markets; free access to public thoroughfares (that they are not invaded by merchants' booths); public safety and hygiene; contamination of foodstuff; pollution; supervision of trading practices; control of weights and measures; coinage; the monitoring of fraudulent transactions, unlawful sales and collusion; and elimination of *ribā* (usury) in all its guises. The *muḥtasib* had to see to it that illegal and fraudulent sales/transactions were punished.

*Judiciary*

The judicial powers of the Prophet 🕌 were assigned to him by Allah in the Qur'ān.[11] Judicial authority was in turn delegated by him to Muʿādh ibn Jabal and ʿAlī ibn Abī Ṭālib 🕊 each of whom was sent as *qāḍī* to the Yemen.[12] After the death of the Prophet 🕌 the first caliphs administered the law personally in Madīna. With the expansion of the conquered territories under the Caliph ʿUmar 🕊, judges were appointed for the expeditionary forces and eventually the provinces and this arrangement remained in place till the Ottoman period.

*Mint*

The minting of coins was the prerogative of the caliph and a symbol of his authority. In subsequent history this right was exercised by governors as well. The currencies that the Muslims used in their commercial transactions were gold (*dīnār*) and silver (*dirham*) coins. The office of the mint was responsible for standardising the quality of the coins and guarding against their falsification (clipping). The ruler's mark on the coins indicated their good quality and purity.

*Market*

*Sūq* (market) refers to both the place where commercial transactions take place and the commercial exchange of goods and services itself. Markets existed long before the Prophet's ﷺ experience of them in Makka and Madīna. After capturing Makka the Prophet ﷺ appointed Sa'id ibn Sa'id ibn al-'As ؓ as 'ā*mil as-sūq* (the proto-*muḥtasib*).[13] A woman named Samra bint Nuhayk al-Asadiyya was appointed in this post by the Prophet ﷺ in Madīna. Another woman, ash-Shifā bint 'Abdallāh, was employed in Madīna by the Caliph 'Umar ؓ for the same task some time later.[14] The market was an open space situated adjacent to the mosque and no buildings were to be constructed in it.

Ghazanfar summarises certain key characteristics as to the functioning of economic/business activities, that are found in the writings of the early jurists, as follows: "1. ... markets evolve as part of the 'natural order' of things in an interdependent, competitive environment ... 2. Demand and supply forces are fundamental determinants of prices ... 3. ... greed in human affairs is shunned and profits are not to be 'excessive'. 4. While economic pursuits are part of one's divinely ordained duty ('calling'), the production of necessities is specifically viewed as socially obligatory. 5. A society's welfare function is defined in terms of a tripartite hierarchy of mutually reinforcing individual and social utilities: necessities, conveniences or comforts, and refinements or luxuries ... 6. Money as a medium of exchange evolves as a social necessity, for without it barter results in problems such as lack of a common denominator, the double-coincidence of wants and lack of indivisibility. And hoarding of money for its own sake is against divine rules, as would be counterfeiting and debasement. Further, as with the Judaeo-Christian tradition, usury is 'sinful', for money in itself is useless and sterile."[15]

The economic principles outlined above had the force of the law behind them. The caliph, the *amīr*s, the judiciary and the *muḥtasib*s were responsible for their practical implementation. Much of the administration of economic matters was the duty of the *muḥtasib*, for example, the giving of full measure and weight, proscribing fraudulent business practices, ensuring the legality of contracts, prohibiting improper gain like *ribā*, and arbitrary manipulation of the market like hoarding of necessities.[16]

*Bayt al-Māl*

Literally the 'house of wealth' institutionally developed to become the treasury of the Muslim *dawla*. The origin of this institution can be traced back to the Prophet ﷺ when the revenues that came into it were distributed almost immediately. It maintained similar characteristics during the time of the first caliph, Abū Bakr ؓ but developed into a complex institution in the time of the second caliph 'Umar ؓ when huge amounts of wealth were acquired by Muslims after Persia, Syria and Egypt were conquered by them. The revenue that went into the *bayt al-māl* was from the following sources: 1. *zakāt*; 2. *kharāj*; 3. *ghanīma*; 4. *jizya*; 5. *'ushr* – one tenth of the harvest of agricultural produce (one twentieth if the land has been irrigated by human endeavour); 5. properties with no known owner; 6. properties of apostates; 7. estates of deceased persons; 8. revenues from state lands; and 9. judicial fines.

*Craft, Artisan and Trade Guilds*

Craft, artisan, and trade guilds were variously known as *aṣnāf, ṭā'ifa* and *futuwwa* in the Muslim world. The guilds were integrated into an economic milieu that included the professions, markets and the physical localisation of each profession in their own quarters in the market. Economic activity varied according to the size and importance of each city. Guilds were autonomous organisations in which members "of the same craft got together, elected a head (*shaykh*) from among their ranks, and appeared in the law court to have their nominee endorsed by a *qāḍī*."[17] The *muḥtasib* supervised the guilds, checking weights, measures, quality and prices.

The two aspects relating to the internal organisation of the guilds are administrative and professional. The professional ranks were apprentice (*al-ājir* or *al-mubtadi'*), journeyman (*aṣ-ṣāni'*) and master (*al-mu'allim* or *al-ustādh*). An apprentice was an adult but could be pre-adolescent. A contract, which had to be legalised in a court of law, had to be signed between the apprentice and the master. The contract had to stipulate length of contract and remuneration. Apprentices were in due course promoted to the rank of journeymen who were the most productive and most numerous members of the guild. This could be because their promotion to master entitled them to have their own workshops and the opportunities to open new workshops were limited. The master had to buy or rent premises. If the land on which his workshop stood was *waqf* (a charitable endowment) property he could buy only the structure (the walls and roof) that was built on it. He was also expected to buy or rent equipment for use in the workshop and seek prior permission to use it there. He earned his living from his work but did retain a portion of the apprentice's remuneration for his (the apprentice's) upkeep.

The Islamic guilds displayed four distinctive qualities: 1. they developed spontaneously from the craftsmen themselves and not in response to state needs; 2. the masters, journeymen and apprentices did not develop into different economic and social classes; 3. membership was not restricted to Muslims; and 4. they possessed an inner spiritual life.[18] The guilds provide a good example of how the political, economic, social and spiritual dimensions of human nature are welded together.

Guilds formed the dominant economic and social institutions in Muslim lands and Rafeq notes that the stability of economic and social life can be attributed to the guilds. "For the craftsmen the *ṭā'ifa*s ensured an organised way of work, a balanced income, a minimum of competition, and, more importantly, a high standard of work ethics cutting across religio-ethnic barriers. In short, the *ṭā'ifa*s helped perpetuate the stability of the social and economic fabric of the country." [19] Three economic functions performed by the guilds are noteworthy here: inhibiting monopoly capitalism, providing social security and protecting the integrity of the bi-metallic currency. The use of debased coins was frowned upon as a grave sin and their withdrawal from circulation was obligatory.

### *Awqāf*

A *waqf*, the singular of *awqāf*, is a charitable endowment, that is, "a property, an amount of wealth etc. dedicated to the benefit of the created to please the Creator. The dedicated assets are put in possession, ownership of Allah eternally. The establisher of a *waqf* no longer has any right of ownership regarding the said wealth or property. The motive for establishing a *waqf* is solely to obtain the pleasure of the Creator, hoping only for His reward."[20] The deed of trust (*waqfiyya*) is ratified by the *qāḍī* who records it in a register (*sijil*). The *waqfiyya* states: what wealth or property is dedicated; who will administer it; how the revenue will be spent; who the beneficiaries are; the number of employees; and salaries of the administrator and employees.

Islamic society was financed through the *waqf* system.[21] Prior "to the twentieth century a broad spectrum of what we now designate as public or municipal services e.g., welfare, education, religious services, construction and maintenance of the water system, hospitals, etc. were set up, financed and maintained almost exclusively by endowments ...."[22] *Awqāf* supported so many sectors of the economy that the evolution of Islamic civilisation is incomprehensible without taking them into account. Before the founding of the Republic of Turkey in 1923, three-quarters of the country's arable land belonged to *awqāf*. Around the same time, one-eighth of all cultivated soil in Egypt and one-seventh of that in Iran was *waqf* property and, in the middle of the 19th century, one half of the agricultural land in Algeria, and, in 1883, one-third of that in Tunisia was owned by *waqf*s. After Greece broke away from the Ottoman Empire in 1829 its new government expropriated *waqf* land that composed about a third of the country's total area. "At the end of the 18th century, it has been estimated, the combined income of the roughly 20,000 Ottoman *waqf*s in operation equalled one-third of the Ottoman state's total revenue, including the yield from tax farms in the Balkans, Turkey, and the Arab world."[23]

In Maksudoğlu's list[24] the wide variety of *awqāf* included those dedicated for: mosques; *muṣallas* (places set aside outside the towns for Eid); *madrasas* (schools); libraries; *zāwiyas* (gathering places for Sufis); tombs; fountains; cisterns; ponds; wells; lakes; roads; caravanserais; hospitals; cemeteries; meadows for weak cattle and sheep to graze; the upkeep of the holy cities of Makka and Madīna; the Masjid al-Aqṣā in Jerusalem; pilgrims; teachers; recitation of

Qur'ān, *ḥadīth*, *Dalā'il al Khayrāt*[25] and *Mawlid*[26] in mosques; serving dates, olives and water in mosques at the time of breaking the fast of Ramadan; food hampers for the poor; soup kitchens; providing house utensils and bride's trousseaus for poor girls; funerals; purchasing clothes for the poor at Eid; the replacement of broken crockery; wayfarers; setting slaves free; writing of Qur'ān and other books, purchasing, repairing and binding them. Kuran lists other objectives for *waqf*s, such as: "delivering water to a locality, defending a town, paying a neighbourhood's taxes, supporting retired sailors, supplying fruits to the children of a community, organising picnics for a designated guild, subsidizing the cultivation of rare roses, and operating commuter ships, among hundreds of other purposes of varying social significance. One even finds *waqf*s for the benefit of non-humans, including donkeys and storks."[27]

## POSTFACE

The caliphate, the wazirate, the *kuttāb*, the *muḥtasib*s, the judiciary, the *sūq*, the mint, the *bayt al-māl*, the *awqāf*, and the *aṣnāf* were the institutions that enabled the Muslim community to function. The *dīn* of Islam advocates the principle of justice in governance, and economic justice demands the movement and equitable distribution of wealth in society. The principle of justice was manifest within the workings of the institutions. Belief in the principle of justice cannot be disconnected from acting justly because Islamic law does not permit the separation of belief and practice. Islamic law is the means that prevents the disconnection between theory and practice and thinking and action. An Islamic *dawla*, therefore, could not exist without these institutions and a polity was defined as Islamic precisely because of the existence of these institutions within it and whilst these institutions functioned within the parameters of the *sharī'a*.

# Chapter 16

## Trade & Commerce in the Qur'ān

*"I have not created jinn and men but to worship Me."* (51:56)

Mujāhid[1] commented, '...to know[2] Me.'[3]

*I do not require any provision from them*
*and I do not require them to nourish Me.*
*Truly Allah, He is the Provider, the Possessor of Strength, the Sure.*
(51:57-58)

Apropos of trade and commerce in the Qur'ān we will develop an overview by picking up elements of our theme, working from the beginning of the Qur'ān to near to the end. In that endeavour and in orienting ourselves in the world today with regards to this issue, we feel more than anything the need for guidance: about the nature of the world we are in and our circumstances, the nature of our law and how we should proceed in our affairs.

Seventeen times a day at the least Muslims stand in *ṣalāt* and repeat the Fātiḥa, in which, after praising Allah, we acknowledge to Him that it is Him alone we worship and Him alone we seek aid from. Then we ask for guidance, specifically discounting two paths, that of those on whom there is anger, the Jews and their ilk, and that of those who are astray, the Christians and their ilk. These two parties in collusion have given the world the usurious religion of capitalism that is rampaging without reason or limits.

Guidance (*hudā* and *hidāya*) is twofold: clarification (*bayān*) – such as making clear or explaining the difference between good and bad – and actually showing someone the way (*irshād*).

The word *sharī'a* comes from a root denoting road, and a road is wide with two edges. Provided one is somewhere between the two edges one is clearly on the road, contrary to what those who have made it their imperative to get everything exactly right in every detail claim. The two edges are the obligatory and that which is prohibited. In *fiqh*, they become five-fold gaining another set of opposites – the desirable and undesirable, with the permissible an almost neutral mid-point. But everything that is between the two edges of the obligatory and the forbidden is in fact permissible.

### Sūra 2 al-Baqara – Spending, giving and *ribā* (usury)

In its second *sūra,* Sūra al-Baqara, Allah's Book almost immediately states that it is guidance, but for a specific group of people, the people of *taqwā,* meaning literally "those who protect themselves". If we are not as yet sure what that quality consists in, the subsequent *āyats* amplify its meaning. First, the Book is guidance for the people who believe in the Unseen. In other words, it is the opposite of the dominant paradigm which is based on the assumption that the physical existence that presents itself to our senses is all that exists. Those who believe in the Unseen establish the *ṣalāt,* the most striking aspect of which is that, if they are able to, they do that together in mosques five times a day. And, germane to our study, Allah continues His description of the people for whom His Book is guidance by saying: *"And out of that which We have provided them they spend,"* introducing here one of the dominant threads of the *sūra*. If we had expected the coupling of *zakāt* with *ṣalāt*, which is what we usually find, here is a matter of some interest. The word "spend"[4] will be echoed throughout the rest of the *sūra* and most particularly around the pivotal *āyats* on *ribā*. Spending is the opposite of *ribā*.

*Ribā –Uusry*

Cicero tells of Cato being asked: "What do you think of lending at usury?" Cato answered, "What do you think of murder?"[5]

For our definition of *ribā* we resort to one of the oldest most respected dictionaries of the Qur'ān, that of ar-Rāghib al-Aṣfahānī, who says: "*Ribā* is increase over the capital,"[6] and Qāḍī Abū Bakr ibn al-'Arabī said: "Our *'ulamā* have said that, 'Linguistically, *ribā* means increase." Note: there is no mention of "excessive" or "extortionate" increase. *Ribā* subdivides into *ribā al-faḍl,* which is the unjustified increment in an exchange, and *ribā an-nasī'a,* which involves a delay, such as exchanging a number of *dīnār*s for the identical number of *dīnār*s, even if the delay is to the extent of, "I'll just go to my house and get them." Exchanges of gold for gold, silver for silver and gold for silver, and by extension any exchange of anything that is considered money, must be immediate, "hand to hand".

About this spending, al-Qurṭubī says:

> The word for "those who spend" (*yunfiqūn*) means "to bring something out". "Spending" is to give out money with the hand. The verb *nafaqa* with regard to a sale means to transfer money from the hand of the buyer to the hand of the seller. ... Scholars disagree about what is meant by the giving of provision in this instance. It is said that it refers to obligatory *zakāt*. That is related from Ibn 'Abbās and is because the prayer accompanies it. It is said that it refers to what a man spends on his family. That is related from Ibn Mas'ūd because that is the best type of expenditure. Muslim related from Abū Hurayra that the Messenger of

Allah ﷺ said, "Out of a *dīnār* which you spend in the way of Allah and a *dīnār* which you spend on freeing a slave and a *dīnār* which you give to a poor person and a *dīnār* which you spend on your family, the one with the greatest reward is the one which you spend on your family." It is related from Thawbān that the Messenger of Allah ﷺ said, "Is not the best *dīnār* a man spends the *dīnār* which he spends on his family and the *dīnār* which he spends on his mount in the way of Allah and the *dīnār* which he spends on his companions in the way of Allah?" Abū Qilāba said, "He began with the family," and then he continued, "What man could have a greater reward than someone who spends on a young family to keep them virtuous, or Allah gives them the benefit of him and he enriches them?"...

Aḍ-Ḍaḥḥāk said, "Spending was, at first, a kind of sacrifice by which a person drew near to Allah Almighty according to his effort in it until Allah revealed the obligations of *zakāt* in *Sūra at-Tawba* which abrogated that." ...[7]

We customarily expect *zakāt* to be coupled with *ṣalāt*, and it is easy enough to almost dismiss this mention of "spending" by interpreting it as *zakāt*, which indeed is one of the interpretations offered. However, the *āyat* relating to the eight categories who are eligible to receive *zakāt* is contained in Sūra at-Tawba, much of which was revealed around the time of the military expeditions to Ḥunayn and Tabūk, both of which occurred after the *Fatḥ* of Makka in the eighth and ninth years after the *Hijra* respectively.

Al-Qurṭubī continues:

It is said that its meaning is general and that is a sound position because Allah praises all kinds of spending out from what we are provided with. In that case the meaning is that they pay the *zakāt* obliged by the *Sharī'a* and also spend in other ways in which it is recommended for them to spend. It is said that *"believe in the Unseen"* is the portion of the heart, *"establish the prayer"* is the portion of the body and *"spend from what they are provided with"* is the portion of wealth. This is evident. Some early scholars said in their interpretation of the words of Allah Almighty: *"they spend from what We have provided them,"* that they refer to people teaching others some of what Allah has taught them. Abu Naṣr 'Abd ar-Raḥīm ibn 'Abd al-Karīm al-Qushayrī related that.[8]

Thus spending extends to maintenance of a family, to the pillar of *zakāt*, and on to general spending in the way of Allah. Its opposite is *ribā*, usury, as Allah says, placing them in opposition: *"Allah obliterates ribā but makes ṣadaqa grow in value!"* (2:276) Perhaps the key *āyat* on usury is: *"But Allah has permitted trade and He has forbidden ribā."* (2:275) Although permission and prohibition are a set of opposites, another opposition is given by the *āyats*: *"Those who give away their wealth by night and day, secretly and openly, will have their reward with their Lord. They will feel no fear and they will know no sorrow. Those who practise ribā will not rise from the grave except as someone driven mad by Shayṭān's touch."* (Sūra al-Baqara 2:274-5) In other words, spending and giving away are opposite to *ribā*. And if we are to talk legally, to address the parameters, then it is *zakāt* that is the opposite of *ribā*, because *zakāt* is obligatory and *ribā* is prohibited. Just as *ribā* is corrosive of civil authority, since it is the job of the latter to prohibit usury and to govern the market, *zakāt* is dependent on its being collected by a civil authority, and its purity is dependent on barring usury from the market.

We must note almost in parentheses that because of the familiarity one has with the topic of *zakāt* and the effort that every Muslim will undoubtedly make to ensure they have paid it, it is far from obvious to many that in fact it is a 'fallen pillar' as in the work by Abdalhaqq Bewley *Zakāt – Raising a Fallen Pillar*.[9] Restoring it authentically according to its genuine parameters as practised in the first community and for much of history right up until comparatively recently is a genuinely momentous act, which must be undertaken purely for the sake of Allah and not solely to defeat usury, but which nonetheless has immeasurable consequences. This is not the place to develop this theme, which will come up again later in this book.

Both processes, spending/giving and usury, are exponential in nature. The exponential[10] effects of usury produce the story of technical banking culture, from its roots in Europe to its global hegemony of today. Most people think of exponential growth in terms of the astonishingly precipitous rise and increase at its end, but more important is the long initial stage of the exponential curve during which there is no apparent change whatsoever. The banking culture has reached the impossibly precipitous ascent phase and so can now only collapse. The time has come for the exponential rise of the giving/spending culture, but its very undramatic beginnings are vital to grasp or people raised on scientific causality will quickly give up because they see no apparent results.

The reasons for exponential growth in the case of usury are simply in-built in the mathematics of compound interest, remembering that in the end all interest compounds. The exponential growth of the spending/giving culture takes place because it works through personal relationships, personal experience, and because it always starts with the few. The few have few personal relationships, and everything personal is organic and takes its time. It cannot be hurried. However, since there is success built-in, it's in harmony with God and the natural processes He has created, these few will inevitably have success. Indeed, Allah, exalted is He, concludes the pivotal first *āyats* of Sūra al-Baqara we have been looking at saying: "*They are the people guided by their Lord. They are the successful.*" (2:5) He, exalted is He, doesn't limit that success to either worldly or other-worldly success.

Much of Sūra al-Baqara, particularly the *āyat*s preceding the *Āyat al-Kursī* and the significant section after it containing the prohibition of usury, is about the importance of spending. On this pivotal theme of spending, Allah says: *"But anything you expend will be replaced by Him,"* (34:39) as Moroccans customarily remind each other when buying and selling, even when it is something so trivial as groceries in a small local shop. Allah says: *"anything"*.

### Foundational *Āyats* Prohibiting Usury

### Qāḍī Abū Bakr ibn al-'Arabī in his *Aḥkām al-Qur'ān*

Qāḍī Abū Bakr introduces the issue of the *mu'āmalāt* in considering this *āyat* of Sūrat al-Baqara, His words, exalted is He:

> *"Do not devour one another's property by false means nor offer it to the judges as a bribe, trying through crime to knowingly usurp a portion of other people's property,"* (Sūrat al-Baqara 2:188)

He says that, "respecting which there are nine issues:

> First issue: this *āyat* is one of the pillars of *mu'āmalāt*, and the foundations of mutual exchanges are based on them, which are fourfold: this *āyat*; and His words, exalted is He, *"And Allah has made trade ḥalāl and has made ribā ḥarām"*; the *ḥadīths* concerning *gharar* – transactions that are unclear and undefined; and taking *maqāṣid*[11] and matters of benefit into account." ...
>
> Fourth issue: His words, *"false means"* means 'that which is not *ḥalāl* in the *sharī'a* and does not fulfil one of the *maqāṣid*,' because the *sharī'a* forbids it and prevents it and makes mutually exchanging it *ḥarām*, such as *ribā* and *gharar* and the like. '*False means*' are those things in which there is no benefit."[12]

So let us proceed to looking at two of the key *āyats* on usury:

> *You who believe! be fearful of Allah and forgo any remaining usury if you are believers. If you do not, know that it means war from Allah and His Messenger.* (2:278-9)

Al-Qurṭubī says: "Ibn 'Abbās also said, 'If someone insists on usury and does not desist, it is a duty for the leader of the Muslims to ask him to repent. If he still does not desist, he strikes off his head.' Qatāda said, 'Allah threatened the people of usury with killing and made it lawful to kill them wherever they are found.'... Ibn Khuwayzimandād said, 'If the people of a land think usury to be lawful, they are apostates and the ruling regarding them is the same as that regarding the people of apostasy, and it is permitted for the ruler to fight them. Do you not see that Allah Almighty has announced that when He says: "*...know that it means war from Allah and His Messenger*"?'"[13] It is well to note here that Allah does not merely announce war on usury, but He, exalted is He, announces war from Himself and His Messenger ﷺ on those *mūminīn* who do not forgo usury. It is also important, however, to remember that the above legal judgment is for the situation where there is a polity in which the *sharī'a* is in place, since it is only the *sulṭān* who can carry out legal punishments or wage war. Where that does not pertain, then these remarks in *tafsīr* serve as a stern reminder of the gravity of usury as a crime.

### Sūra 2 al-Baqara – *Dayn* – credit/debt

The *āyats* on spending begin with making it one of the preconditions for receiving guidance from the Noble Book. They culminate in the longest *āyat* in the Qur'ān, which is about debt and credit transactions, that comes immediately before the astonishing final two *āyats* of the *sūra*, about which the people of *tafsīr* have said that they were uniquely revealed without the intermediary of the angel Jibrīl directly to the Messenger of Allah ﷺ during his Night Journey and Mi'rāj.[14]

Because of the transformation of Islam into a private "religion", we almost always hear the *āyat*s on *dayn* as being about personal debt, called in Arabic *qarḍ ḥasan* (a goodly loan), which is undoubtedly also a part of its meaning. But the implications of it are really for the two types of credit transaction: paying in advance for goods to be delivered later, and paying later for goods already received, it being understood that the command to record these transactions is a recommendation.

A great many transactions are payment in advance for something to be received later, from a humble bus ticket to the great number of purchases made online. In the commercial world much trade is based on delivery of goods on credit terms ranging from a week, 30 days to as much as 60 and 90 days. Both of these types of credit transaction are covered by the *āyat* and were part and parcel of the commercial life of the Muslims, a world culture spanning from Morocco and West Africa to India, China, and Indonesia for over a thousand years. But in the writing and recording of these credit and debt transactions, it is not permitted for chits or dockets pertaining to foodstuffs to become objects of trade. As Imām Mālik said, "It is not lawful to sell food before receiving it in full since the Messenger of Allah ﷺ forbade that."[15] There is, therefore, no possibility of futures markets in foodstuffs, for it is such markets that siphon off people's wealth from before the planting of crops until their sale, benefitting no one but a parasitical class of speculators.

Al-Bukhārī narrated that Ibn 'Abbās ﷺ said the *āyat* was revealed about the *salam* contracts of the people of Madīna in which they paid in advance for harvests. He said, "The Prophet ﷺ came to Madīna when they used to pay two and three years in advance for fruits,[16] and so he said, 'Pay in advance for a known measure of fruits and for a known period of time.'"[17]

Thus the purchaser secured the crops, and his funds helped the cultivator finance his work and pay for his living expenses. What is prohibited is for that person who has paid in advance for something to sell that purchase of his to another before taking possession of it. In other words, futures contracts are impermissible.

Muslim society was an intricate web of interconnected finance of this nature that obviated the need for institutions and removed the opportunity for usurers to take advantage of people's neediness. Muslims were paying in advance for goods to be delivered later and they were buying goods on credit to be paid for later at a specific time. And they had their contract witnessed and wrote it down.

This produced a very extensive and sophisticated commercial civilisation that traded globally, until Muslims were beguiled and deceived into adopting bank loans in order to gain new technologies using debt-based monetary systems employing paper, and later digital-currencies. But for such a system to work again, as it did for centuries, two elements are needed in addition to knowledge of the *fiqh* of commercial transactions: trustworthiness and legal redress when people fail to be trustworthy or when things simply go wrong through no ill-will or wrongdoing. The latter is possibly achievable today through existent arbitration systems, since most of our commercial transactions could be enforceable by modern courts if the contract is drawn up correctly.

Not only were credit transactions widespread but people had a positive attitude to debts if they were undertaken with a serious intention to repay them. 'Abdullāh ibn Ja'far said: "The Messenger of Allah ﷺ said, 'Allah is *with* the debtor until he settles his debt as long as it is not for something which Allah dislikes.'" On the basis of this *ḥadīth*, 'Abdullāh ibn Ja'far used to say to his treasurer, "Go and get something for me on credit, for I dislike to spend a night without Allah being *with* me."[18]

Conversely, the stern warnings against debt, particularly when engaged in carelessly without the intention of repaying it, or dying and leaving no funds to pay it, are too well-known to need citation here.

With respect to the the importance of this theme in history, Niall Ferguson writes: "The evolution of credit and debt was as important as any technological innovation in the rise of civilization, from ancient Babylon to present-day Hong Kong. ..." but then he adds, "Perhaps, too, it will be a financial crisis that signals the twilight of American global primacy,"[19] writing in the year of the global banking crisis, 2008, whose effects are still working themselves out, particularly with the enormous sums of credit subsequently created during the pandemic through quantitative easing. His passage draws attention to two things: the importance of debt and credit for trade, and the perils of its unregulated use as is inbuilt in usury economics. Muslim trade had always availed of a limited and regulated degree of credit and debt, but leaving no space for the creation of credit in the way fractional-reserve banking and the issuance of fiat currencies do.

*Tijāra – trade*

Retracing our steps to the early *āyats* of Sūra al-Baqara, we find the first occurrence of the word for trade itself, *tijāra*, when Allah ﷻ says about those who say: "*'We believe in Allah and the Last Day,' when they are not believers*" (2:8), among whom are the Jews and the hypocrites: "*Those are the people who have sold guidance for misguidance. Their trade has brought no profit; they are not guided.*" (2:16) It is not accidental that the first mention of the words 'sold', 'trade' and 'profit' is metaphorical, highlighting a trade that is much more profound and has far greater impact than buying and selling goods in the market. This point is underlined by the Prophet ﷺ in the famous *ḥadīth*, "Everybody goes out in the morning and sells his self, then he either frees it from slavery or destroys it."[20] This important metaphor will resonate throughout the Book and the *ḥadīth* literature.

Apropos the literal rather than the metaphorical meaning of trade, in the earliest glossary of Qur'ānic terms ar-Rāghib al-Aṣfahānī defines it thus: "*Tijāra* is to transact with capital seeking profit,"[21] using *ra's al-māl* (capital) unequivocally. So how is that not capitalism? Capitalism in our age is marked by the great exorbitant capital fortunes of oligarchs and others – massive amounts of money gained and employed without regard for *sharīʿa* or any nomos or natural justice. These mega-capital fortunes were arrived at in three ways:

First: inherited capital of the old royal and aristocratic families. This was gained by conquest and perpetuated by means of primogeniture – the principle by which the first-born son inherited all, and other sons and daughters were disinherited or received minor inheritances. This has been modified greatly over the generations – women can now inherit all – but the principle of keeping the fortune intact remains. It famously has a serious defect, called the second-son problem. They were sent off to earn their own fortunes as best they could. Think Crusades.

Second: banking. Here the fortune was accumulated by the exponential growth powers of usury. And that was also done by families, some Christian such as the Barclays and Lloyds, and some Jewish such as the Warburgs and others. They were often able to take over part of the first group's capital, occasionally being ennobled in the process, although without understanding the social responsibility inherent in noblesse oblige.

Third: the state. By its tax gathering powers, the state entered the field as a capitalist entity.

There are permutations and cross-fertilisations between these three, which interweave promiscuously.

The *sharīʿa* laws of inheritance break up such fortunes and return to the loose-cannon second and third sons, and to the daughters, their rightful shares, thus shrinking the fortunes generation by generation. The *sharīʿa* forbids banking and thus the great capital sums that banking houses accumulate. Islam has no fiscal state, and there is no place for the state as a capitalist entity. Its collection of *zakat* is not allowed to linger in the *bayt al-māl* becoming standing capital. Other income such as the *jizya* and *kharāj* taken from the people of the Book is spent on the welfare of Muslims and non-Muslims. Capitalism as an abstraction is not the issue. The issue is the oligarchs empowered by their gargantuan wealth, and by the ground-rules of capitalism today, to pervert the course of people and government.

We have, however, seen that the role of capital is acknowledged in one of the core books of Islam, but with the placing of restrictions on it that protect against the evil in the unmitigated and unrestricted sort of capitalism that we suffer from today.

### Sūra 3 Āli 'Imrān – *Ribā* continued

The theme of usury recurs in Sūra Āli 'Imrān right in the middle of the *āyats* on the Battle of Uḥud, when Allah ﷻ says: "*You who believe! do not feed on ribā, multiplied and then remultiplied. Have taqwā of Allah so that hopefully you will be successful.*" (3:130) A false interpretation of this *āyat* claims that the prohibition of usury only applies to compound interest and not to simple interest. This is easily dismissed by returning to the *āyats* in Sūra al-Baqara prohibiting *ribā* in which Allah, exalted is He, says: "*But if you repent you may have your capital, without wronging and without being wronged.*" (2:279) You may have your capital back, and the capital excludes both simple and compound interest, not just the latter. That is borne out by the words of Ibn Mas'ūd ؓ in the *Muwaṭṭa'*,[22] "If someone makes a loan, they should not stipulate better than it. Even if it is a handful of grass, it is usury."[23] A handful of grass is not only simple interest but it is almost the smallest amount conceivable.

About its interpolation in among the *āyats* on Uḥud (3:130), al-Qurṭubī says:

This is a prohibition of consuming *ribā* interpolated into the story of Uḥud. Ibn 'Aṭiyya said, "I do not recall anything transmitted about that." Mujāhid said, "They used to sell on credit and, when the term came, they would increase the price for a delay and so Allah revealed: '*You who believe, do not feed on usury multiplied and then remultiplied.*'

Usury is singled out among acts of disobedience because it is that against which Allah has declared war when He says: '*If you do not, know that it means war from Allah and His Messenger.*' (2:279). War allows killing, and so it is as if He were saying, 'If you do not fear usury, you will be defeated and killed.'"[24]

Another reference to usury with the word *ribā* in the Qur'ān is in Sūra an-Nisā' (4:161) which is about how the Jews[25] had been prohibited usury but nevertheless received it. It is beyond the scope of this book to look into the origins of usury among the Jews and its adoption among the Christians. Ammar Fairdous shows the essential agreement between Judaism, Christianity and Islam on the nature of the laws governing commerce and the strict prohibition of usury, and the identical ways that those who wished to do so found to circumvent those laws, saying: "Attempts to evade the prohibitions of interest are as various in form as they are many in number, to be found in the Islamic, Jewish and Christian traditions alike."[26]

Allah mentions *ribā* one more time in Sūra ar-Rūm: "*What you give with usurious intent, aiming to get back a greater amount from people's wealth, does not become greater with Allah. But anything you give as zakāt, seeking the Face of Allah – all who do that will get back twice as much.*" (30:39) Again, we see *ribā* and *zakāt* placed opposite each other.

The treatment of this theme is further proof that the revelation of the Noble Qur'ān and the Sunna of the Messenger ﷺ are precisely for this very age. They are not *ancient* or *pre-modern* thus requiring elaborate *ijtihād* to work in our 'modern' world but are all too modern and fitted for the very issues that we experience today.

## SŪRA 4 AN-NISĀ' – *FARĀ'IḌ* – THE FIXED SHARES OF INHERITANCE

Having pursued the theme of usury in the first *sūras* of the Qur'ān, we come, in Sūra an-Nisā', to a different theme where there are *āyats* dealing with a topic whose significance is too little appreciated in the context of trade and commerce and the growth of oligarchic capitalism: the obligatory shares of inheritance (*farā'iḍ*). This profound set of judgments is treated as if it were merely "Islamic personal law" when its implications, socially and economically, far exceed that definition.

It is when we understand the importance of primogeniture in European culture – the exclusive inheritance of the first born and the arbitrary designation or disinheritance of other heirs – in the rise of predatory oligarchic capitalism that we realise the profound wisdom in these *āyats* of the Noble Book that share out at least two-thirds of the deceased's estate in algebraic amounts, a half, quarter, third, a sixth, an eighth and so on, to specified near relatives. It was what led to al-Khwārizmī inventing the science of algebra (*al-jabr*). In *al-Kitāb al-mukhtaṣar fī ḥisāb al-jabr wa-l-muqābala* he uses algebra to work out a large number of cases from the laws of inheritance. The lack of this distribution of inheritance shares in Christendom was one of the main causes of the formation of the great capitalist fortunes and their perpetuation from generation to generation.

A side issue but one of considerable importance, to which the popular genres of detective and murder mystery fiction bear eloquent testimony, is the considerable familial strife occasioned by arbitrary designation of some heirs and disinheritance of others. It is the laws of inheritance, along with *zakāt,* that shape Muslim culture and make it much more horizontal, flattening out the differences between the extremely wealthy and the poor, a point lost in our age where once-Muslim lands are disposed of at will by obscenely wealthy oligarchs, who are sometimes themselves even "Muslims". The laws of inheritance prevent the emergence of self-perpetuating oligarchic families, which is one of the worst aspects of usury capitalism.

Moreover, the laws of inheritance result, not in a rigid 'socialist', totally egalitarian society, but one in which the excessive extremes of wealth and poverty are reduced. There is room for those who pursue wealth to do so, and, if they pay *zakāt*, to enjoy their wealth without guilt, just as there is room for poverty not to entail avoidable misery.

### Sūra 5 al-Mā'ida – Contracts

Continuing our journey through the Qur'ān, we come next to the theme of contracts. Like proper management of credit and debt, and application of the fixed shares of inheritance, if paid attention to, care in contracts will contribute to bringing about a new nomos free of the ills of capitalism.

Allah says, *"You who believe! fulfil your contracts."* (Sūra al-Mā'ida 5:1) Ibn Juzayy al-Kalbī says: "It has been said that the contracts referred to here are the ones people make with each other, such as sales, marriage, setting slaves free and the like. It has also been said that it refers to to the acts of obedience someone has contracted with his Lord to fulfil, such as *ḥajj*, fasting and the like. And it has been said that it is the contract Allah has made with them concerning judging what is to be *ḥalāl* and *ḥarām* in His *dīn*."

The command is repeated later in Sūra al-Isrā': *"Fulfil your contracts. Contracts will be asked about."* (Sūra al-Isrā' 17:34) Ibn Juzayy al-Kalbī clarifies, "It is in general about contracts both with Allah and with people." Note that Ibn Juzayy did not say, "... and with Muslims," because that might have given rise to the false assumption that it is fine to cheat non-Muslims. The problematic issue then arises of contracts made with corporations and mega-entities. The very nature of contracts has been changed entirely. A contract was originally a verbal agreement between two or more parties, witnessed by people of integrity, and recorded in writing so that there would be no doubt about it if later people should remember it differently and argue about its terms. Today the whole process has become automated and the emphasis has shifted from the agreement of persons to the written record. This extends from the very nature of money itself to the countless transactions that each one undertakes daily with state, corporations and banks.

If asked whether we have read the terms and conditions and agree to them, we quickly click YES, because we certainly do not have the time to read even one of these sets of terms and conditions, and, even if we did, we strongly believe that nothing we could say about them would have any effect in any case. So such documents are not agreements entered into by two free contracting parties, although freedom is the basis of true choice. Choice in these terms is entirely illusory, and the exception of those brave souls who take on the corporate world in litigation proves the rule. Thus the very idea of a contract is fatally undermined, purely for the sake of automating the process of earning money. Are such contracts valid? I leave that as an open question.

Lest it be thought that only legal contractual matters are of interest, the core or essence of the matter is addressed repeatedly throughout the Qur'ān: truthfulness, justice and trustworthiness, which we will look at it in more depth when we come to Sūra al-Muzzammil.

Contrary to the impression some have that the *sharī'a* places restrictions on Muslims that make them uncompetitive in the modern world, simple things like avoiding intoxicants give people, including employees a distinct competitive advantage and makes working with Muslims very attractive, and in the increasingly dog-eat-dog world of modern capitalism, people who keep their word and fulfil their contracts are esteemed greatly in trade. These qualities are winning out, in spite of the ubiquity and seeming unavoidability of corruption. That is not to mistakenly imagine that all 'Muslims' are great paragons of virtue, but whereas those who grab quick returns have a fleeting benefit, the slower returns of honesty are more solid and reliable.

### Sūra 9 at-Tawba – "Take!" Zakāt

Although *zakāt* is not one of the *mu'āmalāt*, it is clear how fundamental they are to it, and it is to them. Here I want only to attend to one of the aspects that is now neglected with respect to *zakāt*: that it should be taken by those in authority. Allah says:

> *Take Zakāt from their wealth to purify and cleanse them and pray for them. Your prayers bring relief to them. Allah is All-Hearing, All-Knowing.* (9:103)

Shaykh Dr. Abdalqadir as-Sufi first reminds us of one instance of the numerous *āyat*s which command us to: '*...and pay zakāt,*' (2:277), a command which every Muslim certainly endeavours to obey according to his understanding. He says:

> 3. ...This third injunction for the complete restoration of the Deen of Islam in our time comes with our decision to restore the fallen pillar of the deen, *Zakāt*. In order for this to happen, every aspect of it must be in strict obedience to what has been laid down by Allah and His Messenger, may Allah bless him and grant him peace. Firstly, *Zakāt* is not given. It is a taken *ṣadaqa*. This is in obedience to the order of Allah, glory be to Him, in the Qur'ān, when He says, 'Take!'[27]

The Shaykh means, and Allah knows best, that the person who "pays *zakāt*" does not take it upon himself to distribute it to people in need and the other categories mentioned in Sūra at-Tawba, but he gives it to the *zakāt* collectors authorised by whoever is in authority who thus "takes" it. The Shaykh continues:

> This in turn indicates the true organic nature of the Deen al-Fitra. As our great Qadi, Ibn Khaldūn, has pointed out, Islam, as at its very beginning, can grow from the smallest group to the greatest empire.[28]

In other words, the situation is the same whether the one in authority rules three people or a million. Imām Ibn al-Humām, the great Ḥanafī scholar said:

> The apparent meaning of His words, exalted is He, "*Take zakāt from their wealth.*" (9:103) necessarily requires the absolute right of the Imām to take the *zakāt*, and the Messenger of Allah ﷺ and the two *khalīfa*s after him were based on this. Then when 'Uthmān ؓ was appointed and the changes that had taken place in people became obvious, he disliked the *zakāt* collectors to investigate people's hidden wealth[29] and thus he entrusted the payment to the owner who would undertake it on [the *khalīfa*'s] behalf, and none of the Companions disagreed with him about that. This does not invalidate the [right of the] Imām to demand it. For this reason, if he knows that the people of a certain land do not pay their *zakāt*, he demands it from them."[30]

This makes clear 'Uthmān's judgment and the consensus of the Companions on its correctness. That does not mean, as the Imām explains, that the practice of the Prophet ﷺ and the first two *khalīfa*s has been abrogated. Notice that the point that is mentioned here is the dislike of the man in authority intrusively investigating people's private wealth holdings. This is the matter that people fear: the creation of a state that surveils people. Although I think few would today object to people in authority investigating the wealth of the super-wealthy and insisting on their paying their due. This point is clearly resolved in the following two passages. In the *Mudawwana* Saḥnūn said:

['Abd ar-Raḥmān ibn al-Qāsim] said: And Mālik said, 'If the Imām (leader) is just it is not permissible for a man to distribute his *zakāt* on hard cash (*naḍḍ*) or anything else, but he pays the *zakāt* on hard cash to the Imām.'[31]

Furthermore, Saḥnūn also cites in the *Mudawwana:*

Ibn Wahb said: Men among the people of knowledge informed me that 'Abdullāh ibn 'Amr ibn al-'Āṣ, 'Abdullāh ibn 'Umar, Jābir ibn 'Abdullāh, Sa'd ibn Abī Waqqāṣ, Ḥudhayfah ibn al-Yamān, Anas ibn Mālik, Abū Qatāda, Abū Sa'īd al-Khudrī, Abū Hurayra, 'Ā'isha, Umm Salama, Muḥammad ibn Ka'b al-Quraẓī, Mujāhid, 'Aṭā', al-Qāsim, Sālim, Muḥammad ibn al-Munkadir, 'Urwa ibn az-Zubayr, Rabī'a ibn Abī 'Abd ar-Raḥmān, Makḥūl, al-Qa'qā' ibn Ḥakīm and others of the people of knowledge, all ordered that the *zakāt* be paid to the man in authority, and they used to pay it to them.[32]

Ibn Juzayy al-Kalbī confirmed this judgment saying: "If the Imām is just, then it is obligatory to pay the *zakāt* to him, and if he is not and it is not possible to avoid paying it to him, then it is valid; if it is possible to avoid paying it to him, then the person paying the *zakāt* is to pay it to those who are entitled to it, and it is recommended that he not hand it over himself lest he be influenced by the praise of those receiving it."[33]

In other words, the ordinary honest Muslim who is concerned to fulfil his religious obligation is trusted to know his own economic circumstances and to assess his own *zakāt* and to pay it to the *zakāt* collector, but he may not pay it to people whom he considers legally valid to receive it. It may well be that he will need the *zakāt* collector in order to understand and work out what he ought to pay. But if the collectors see someone of obvious wealth who has not come to them with any payments of *zakāt* or who has not brought something commensurate with the wealth they see, they have the authority to investigate his affairs and "take" what is due from him. However, when the Muslim "gives" his *zakāt* to the authorised collector, the latter has "taken" it.

The qualification of the Imām as "just" here has nothing to do with modern man's cynicism over the moral character of rulers, but rather over concern for the proper collection and distribution of *zakāt* to those worthy of it, and not using it even for praiseworthy initiatives such as building mosques, schools or hospitals, let alone flagrant misuse such as royal palaces. The man in authority has a legitimate right to make *ijtihād* judgments pertaining to many matters and indeed must perforce do that in many cases, and no one has a right to dispute that with him.

Although not about trade, it is essential to treat this topic here for two reasons: first, because the acts of worship and everyday transactions are inseparable, even though analytically it is useful to be able to separate them; and second because of the centrality of leadership in the *dīn*.

This topic epitomises much of the *dīn*. *Zakāt* is a societal act of worship, as is the *ṣalāt*, in which the whole integrates the acts of the worshippers and the community leader. Their part is, as per the numerous *āyat*s, to "*pay the zakāt*" and the leader's part is to *take* it and then distribute it. The whole is an act of worship, which is incomplete without either party. Similarly, with the *ṣalāt*, which, although acceptable when prayed alone with a valid excuse, is properly a societal act of worship intrinsic to which is the leadership of an *imām*. Even the Friday *jumu'a* is not a 'sermon' and a prayer, but rather the whole event is an act of worship in which the *imām*'s role is to deliver a *khuṭba* and the body of the gathered Muslims' role is to listen attentively. Together they become an *'ibāda*.

Importantly in empowering the leader, a significant consequence is that he has that much more authority to govern the market and commerce, for surely the crisis of the age is that commerce, in this case usurious finance and banking, is ungoverned and completely out of control, to the detriment of mankind and the planet.

### SŪRA 42 ASH-SHŪRĀ – *MĪZĀN* – SCALES & JUSTICE

Proceeding on in pursuing themes to do with trade and commerce we come to the issue of scales, the *mīzān,* weights and measures, and justice.

*Mīzān* means literally scales and metaphorically justice (*'adl*), as well as meaning the Scales used on the Last Day to weigh the deeds of the slaves. Al-Qurṭubī said about the *āyat*: *"It is Allah Who has sent down the Book with truth and the Just Balance"* (Sūra ash-Shūrā 42:17):

> *"And the Just Balance* (*mīzān*)*"*, i.e. justice. Ibn 'Abbās and most of the people of *tafsīr* say that *'adl* is called "scales" (*mīzān*) because the scales are the instrument of fairness and justice. It has been said that the *mīzān* is that which Allah made clear in the Books of that which it is obligatory for man to act upon. And Qatāda said, "The *mīzān* is justice in that which one is ordered to do and forbidden from doing." These statements are all very close in meaning. And it has been said that it is the recompense for obedience with reward, and for disobedience with punishment. And it is has been said that it is the actual scales with which one weighs. Allah sent it down from heaven and taught slaves how to weigh with it so that there would be no wronging each other among them or defrauding.... Mujāhid said, "It is the one that is weighed with. The meaning of 'He sent the *mīzān* down' is His inspiring people to employ it and use it."[34]

Ibn Juzayy al-Kalbī said: "The word *'Book'* here is in the generic sense i.e. *Books*, and *mīzān* is justice. It has been said that *mīzān* refers to the one which is used to weigh with, and it has been narrated that Jibrīl descended with the scales and gave them to Nūḥ and said to him, 'Tell your people to weigh with them.'"[35] He said that the occurrence of the word in the early *āyats* of the Makkan Sūra ar-Raḥmān where it is repeated several times is about physical scales.

The scales are the universal image of justice, indicating that must be a true equivalence in any transaction between two parties. Thus, the modern employment contract, for example, is not such a transaction since the terms and conditions of one party, the employer, are presented to the other party, the employee, who must either accept or reject them, the exception proving the rule. It is becoming more common now for some employees at higher levels in the hierarchy to be able to negotiate their contracts, which is a welcome development, but is not indicative of the situation in the employment market in general. The vast majority of employees in the world have absolutely no choice whatsoever, particularly since the concerted action of governments to effectively end the power of unions to negotiate, and so workers are actually slaves in all but name, and as Ernst Jünger pointed out in *Der Arbeiter*, the worker is a gestalt that includes far more than just manual labourers, but extends to almost everyone who enters the world to earn a living.

*Weights and measures*

Looking at weights and measures in general, it is important to bear in mind that the *dīnār* and *dirham* are also weights from the system of weights, which is where we find them in our primal sources, and about which the Messenger of Allah ﷺ said: "The weights are the weights of the people of Makka and the measures are the measures of the people of Madīna."[36]

These weights include the *mithqāl* – the weight of the gold *dīnār* – and the *ūqiyya* – the weight of forty silver *dirhams* – the *riṭl* and *qinṭār*. The measures include the *mudd*[37] and the *ṣā'*.[38] Speaking about weights and measures, Yaḥyā ibn 'Umar[39] said in his *Aḥkām as-Sūq*:[40]

> If the Muslims are in a situation in which the governor has neglected [the weights and measures] for the people in his care or they do not have a man in authority, then the best of them and the people of standing

and probity should get together to decide weights and measures for the people of their place similarly to what we have described.

Then when they have done that, they should show them to people and inform them of the weight that is in their weights and their *qinṭārs*, and that no one should alter them by increasing or decreasing them. If they discover anyone who has altered a weight or a measure, they should punish him and drive him out of the market until he has clearly turned in *tawba*, in the same way as the just man of authority would have done.[41]

The Prophet ﷺ himself defined the *ṣāʿ* and the *mudd*. Ibn Khaldūn said that ʿUmar ؓ investigated and determined the weights of *dīnār*s and *dirham*s which became the consensus in practice for all the Muslims from that time.

With the Prophetic weights and measures we are in a different conceptual space. Our contemporary perspective on weights and measures first emerged out of the French Revolution, even where older systems, such as the inch, foot, yard and mile, and the pound and ounce remain in place. Whereas such older measures were originally defined locally by the actual feet of monarchs, for example, the *mudd* and *ṣāʿ* were defined by the hands of the Messenger of Allah ﷺ. The people of Madīna had made vessels of those capacities and those were then transmitted. The people of Iraq held to very different measures but when the *khalīfa* Hārūn ar-Rashīd came to Madīna with his Chief Qāḍī Abū Yūsuf, one of the two main students of Imām Abū Ḥanīfa, they discussed this with Imām Mālik and Abū Yūsuf accepted Mālik's position.

[Abū Yūsuf] asked [Mālik] about the *ṣāʿ* and he said, "Five and a third *riṭl*."[42] So he said, "From where do you say that?" Mālik said to some of his companions, "Bring the *ṣāʿ* [measuring vessels] you have." The people of Madīna, or most of them, from the Muhājirūn and the Anṣār, came and with each of them was a *ṣāʿ*. They said, "This is the *ṣāʿ* which I inherited from my great grandfather who was a Companion

> of the Messenger of Allah ﷺ." Mālik said, "This information, which is widespread among us, is more reliable than *ḥadīth*." So Abū Yūsuf recanted and adopted his verdict.[43]

However, as with many other matters in respect of which Qāḍī Abū Yūsuf and Imām Muḥammad ibn al-Ḥasan ash-Shaybānī accepted Mālik's narrations and legal judgments, this was not re-absorbed back into the Ḥanafī *madhhab* except as something that can be useful in *fatwā* in certain circumstances. Instead Ḥanafīs adhere to the views of Imām Abū Ḥanīfa, even if his two main students differed with him. To some extent that might not have mattered, because in the main it was important for there to be local agreement and less important for there to be global agreement. However, there is little doubt that in the age of the global village, unity on weights and measures can be a distinctly important matter in commerce, and the Prophetic values as preserved in Madīna by large bodies of people are an obvious point of unity.

### *Currency*

As to the weights of the coins, Abdalhaqq Bewley had the following to say in his important essay on "The Prophet ﷺ as Ruler":

> Although he never minted any coins himself, the coinage in use in Madīna was precisely specified and defined by the Prophet ﷺ. The coin most commonly used was the silver *dirham*. An-Nawawī says in the commentary on *al-Muhadhdhib*, "The sound view on which one must rely and which one must accept is that the common *dirhams* in the time of the Prophet ﷺ had a known weight and known value. They were already understood, and *zakāt* was connected to them as well as other duties and values in the *Sharī'a*." The same applied to the gold *dīnār*. The precise weights of these coins were meticulously recorded and formed the basis of currency within the territories of Islam from then on, being used throughout history as the standard measure for the payment of *zakāt* and many other legal uses.[44]

Ibn Khaldūn said:

> Know that the consensus exists, since the very beginning of Islam and the age of the Companions and Followers, that the *dirham* of the *sharī'a* is such that ten of them weigh seven *mithqāls* of gold, and an *ūqiyya* of them consists of forty *dirhams*. Thus on this basis it [weighs] seven tenths of a *dīnār*. The weight of a *mithqāl* of gold is seventy-two grains of barley, so the *dirham* which [weighs] seven-tenths of it is fifty-five grains. These measures are all firmly established by consensus.[45]

He discusses the idea mooted by a couple of scholars that the *khalīfa* 'Abd al-Malik ibn Marwān was the first to establish these weights, and refutes it saying, "Scholars who investigate carefully and verify things (*muḥaqqiqūn*) deny that, since it would necessarily require that the *dīnār* and *dirham* of the *sharī'a* were unknown at the time of the Companions and after them, even though specific *sharī'a* rights were connected to them such as *zakāt*, marriages, legal parameters and the punishments for infringement of them (*ḥudūd*) etc. as we mentioned. The truth is that they were both known measures in that age because of judgments being carried out at that time in accordance with the rights connected to them both."[46]

Among the weights and measures, the weights of the *dīnār* and *dirham* are of concern. Umar Vadillo expended considerable thought and effort to bring about their use in the world today, about which Shaykh Dr. Abdalqadir as-Sufi says:

> This heroic and patient work over several decades was headed by Shaykh 'Umar Ibrahim Vadillo, author of the threshold text, 'The Esoteric Deviation in Islam'. After a tremendous battle he convinced the state government of Kelantan in Malaysia to produce these coins as legal currency. This was taken up from Jakarta to Europe. Yet its meaning lay in its application as an instrument of a Taken *Zakāt*. A Taken *Zakāt* is based on necessary primary givens. 1) An appointed Amīr. 2) That Amīr's appointment of *Zakāt* Collectors. 3) This resulting in a collected and assessed amount of *Zakāt*. 4) The gathering of the

*Zakāt* in a Bayt al-Maal. 5) The immediate distribution of the *Zakāt* to the legally worthy recipients.[47]

The core theme of these chapters is the indispensable link between acts of worship and ordinary transactions – *'ibādāt* and *mu'āmalāt* – in this case between the *zakāt* and the gold *dīnār* and silver *dirham*. However, the Shaykh notes:

> ... a newer and wider method must be adopted on a global scale PRIOR to the return of a local *ḥalāl* functioning community which restores Islam by the door of *Zakāt*.
>
> Men must begin to trade and exchange, hand to hand, and transfer across distance without recourse to the financial instruments and institutions of capitalism.
>
> Therefore, to that constructive future activity I call Muslims to begin a post-usury culture.[48]

This challenging passage reverses our previous thinking that the act of restoring *zakāt*, would in itself be a strategic move to counter capitalism. Rather, BEFORE the restoration of the *zakāt*, trading must be undertaken both locally and over distances. Of course the Shaykh is not suggesting that payment of *zakāt* can be delayed, but that *zakāt* is levied on wealth and for that purpose Muslims must be engaged in trade in the widest sense encompassing all meaningful activities on land, in manufacture, service and trading itself.

A danger in focussing on the use of the *dīnār* and *dirham* as the means of paying *zakāt*, is that it becomes ritualistic. It also necessitates a figure who both sells the coins to the *zakāt* payer and then redeems them from the recipient at a lower price, so that the latter can spend them on his needs. However, this is problematic in the *fiqh*. Although there is a separation of the two transactions, it can be argued that it is perilously close to two sales in one. Whereas formal *fiqh* merely looks at the apparent correctness of each step, it arguably licenses what is unacceptable if it conforms to the outward rules. As Ibn Juzayy notes: "...the *madhhab* of Mālik is to examine what leaves someone's hand and what it then receives, and the intermediary steps are nullified."⁴⁹ Indeed, the preferred explanation of the famous episode in the Gospels when Jesus 🌟 drove the money changers from the Temple was that "the money changers were there to convert various currencies into one standard coinage, the Tyrian shekel, that was used for the payment of the annual temple tax."⁵⁰

This issue was raised in Potsdam in a gathering of *'ulamā,* at which Dr. Asadullah Yate, then Imam of the Muslim community of Potsdam, presented an outline of many of the themes of this book:

"First, he spoke of the disaster inherent in the fact that the Muslims are using paper money for their transactions, since it is not small change in the classical sense of flous minted from copper or nickel for transactions less than the value of silver and gold coins; [it was] originally a debt, transacting with which is completely forbidden in the *fiqh*; and is at present a 'fiat' money of no worth at all.

Second, it is even more distressing that the Muslims pay their *zakāt* in paper money and as a personal charity, when the correct form is that *zakāt* must be collected by *zakāt* collectors appointed by an amir, and that it must be collected in gold and silver.

Third, he drew attention to the obligation upon amirs to establish markets in which no one may reserve a place, but in which anyone who shows up there after the dawn prayer may take any place that is free for the day. No one may charge rent on such a marketplace nor impose a tax on the trade done there.

Fourth, that we have forgotten the *awqāf*-endowments of Islam, one of whose essential preconditions is that they are properties dedicated to a purpose 'forever'. These endowments were responsible for a great deal of social welfare within the Muslim community.

In response to this, Muḥammad al-'Amrāwī spoke and said that there is no disagreement on these matters at all, and that they are all too well known in the *fiqh*. However, he said that this was the first time that he or any of the other assembled *'ulamā* have heard someone saying such things in this time. He added that all that is lacking is a practical way to implement them. Imām Abū Sayf Kharkhāsh and Muḥammad al-'Amrāwī both cautioned against putting the Muslims in the difficult position of telling them that the transactions they make using paper money are incorrect or that the mode in which they pay their *zakāt* is incorrect, without first creating ways for them to transact properly, e.g. by bringing about such markets for the Muslims to trade in, and minting *dīnār*s and *dirhams* with which they can pay their *zakāt*."

Muḥammad al-'Amrāwī "... cautioned against disheartening the Muslims," by telling them that *zakāt* is unacceptable when paid with fiat money, "and advised that as soon as possible practical steps need to be taken to make gold *dīnār*s and silver *dirham*s available to the Muslims to pay *zakāt*, and concomitantly the need for the creation of Islamic markets, as described above, in which the Muslims may use their *dīnār*s and *dirham*s, since there is little use in giving a poor and needy person a gold coin which he cannot spend."[51] With the implementation of the *dīnār* and *dirham* in Kelantan, Malaysia, under the direction of Umar Vadillo, the coins were widely adopted by traders, people paid their *zakāt* with them, and the recipients were able to use them for their needs without intermediaries.[52]

*Zakāt* is to be taken from actual held wealth. The fact that it ought to be paid *with* wealth taken *from* that held wealth – with livestock taken from livestock, grains and pulses, dates and raisins etc. taken from grains and pulses, dates and raisins, and with gold and silver taken from gold and silver – and not with promissory notes underscores the reality that very few people actually have wealth. An extreme view, which few hold, is that *zakāt* is thus not due on paper and digital currencies. *Zakāt* is the right of the poor and needy and other categories who may legitimately receive it, and it would be a gross error to excuse a wealthy person from paying it simply because his wealth is all in promissory notes. However, the thinking person, realising that he actually doesn't possess wealth, will begin to move from holding promissory notes to actual commodity wealth, and human beings have generally preferred gold and silver for that purpose.

Gold and silver have been tangible commodities and of value to people in all ages and climes. The *dīnār* and *dirham* are standardised weights which then obviate the need to weigh out and to verify the quality of the precious metals, thus allowing us the familiar capability of paying with numbers of coins. But the essence of the matter is the two precious metals.[53]

The importance of minting standard *dīnār*s and *dirham*s is undeniable, but there is no reason to prevent people buying and exchanging any gold or silver coins they might wish. This presents a problem in transactions, one which in fact is as old as the use of coinage: the exchange rates between coins of differing weights and dimensions and purities from various lands and countries. For gold exchanged for gold and silver exchanged for silver, the only things to attend to are that the weights are exactly equivalent, and that they are exchanged directly 'hand-to-hand'. Between gold and silver, there is no set exchange rate, but gold exchanged for silver and vice-versa, and indeed any two things treated as currencies, must be exchanged directly without delay.

### *The Ṣayrafī*

The first community, during the Prophetic era and after it, used the coins of the Romans and Persians for a considerable time. That is precedent. Thus, were some people to engage in selling well-established gold and silver coins in the market-places – they have to be sold hand to hand as otherwise it is a usurious transaction – and if people were to use them in trade in the markets there is nothing in the *sharīʿa* against that. In addition, there is very little against it in many national legal systems, although people ought to verify that in their own jurisdictions. An 'app' that translates the values of the coins and their exchange rates, including in terms of the gold *dīnār* and silver *dirham*, could be helpful to all concerned.

Although study of the *fiqh* largely focuses on the use of *dīnār*s, *dirhams* and *flous* in the markets, the picture was always more complex, not least because different cities and countries issued gold and silver coins to different standards and weights, among them coins from Europe and elsewhere. Thus, there grew to be a figure in the market called the *ṣayrafī* who was familiar with, and skilled in recognising, the different types and qualities of coins and their exchange rates. Lane defines this term thus: "... a skilful money-changer ... applied to him who knows and distinguishes the relative excellence, or superiority, of pieces of money."[54] Because there is no fixed exchange rate for them between gold and silver or with other currencies, there is room for him to earn on the transaction and thus have a profession. In an open market competition between such people will keep their charges down.

Although there is a fixed exchange rate of ten *dirham*s for one *dīnār* for the purposes of *zakāt* and other *sharīʿa* cases, the ordinary exchange rate depends on what the two parties agree to. The revival of the role of the *ṣayrafī* could be a dynamic matter in the renewal of trade between Muslims and with the growing numbers of non-Muslims who are increasingly aware of the issue of fiat currency and usury. None of the above detracts from the importance and urgency of minting gold *dīnār*s and silver *dirham*s according to the measures of the *Sunna*.

Once such coins are exchanged hand to hand and face to face, as is necessary to avoid the introduction of usury, then it is conceivable to use them for purchase of other goods at a distance.

The issue of a sound currency is one that the age more and more draws our attention to. One seriously misleading idea is that of a new global competitor to the dollar 'backed by gold'. Anyone with a sense of history will realise that the backing of gold is the means that banks and states use to inflate the money supply, the backing being used to promote confidence (remember how pivotal that word is in the history of banking and fiat currencies), confidence in a ballooning money supply, and that can only end in tears. Although such tactics can result in spectacular short term gains, the longer term outcomes are catastrophic. The insistence on regaining actual currencies of tangible commodities will be a distinct advantage to those farsighted souls who embrace this now.

### Sūra 65 aṭ-Ṭalāq – Provision

We come now to an important theme, which is the nub of the issue for the human being, about which the great have written much: provision. On this matter, Ibn Juzayy al-Kalbī said in *tafsīr* of Allah's words: "*Whoever has taqwā of Allah, He will make a way out for him and provide him from where he does not expect,*" (65: 2-3):

> One of the *'ulamā* said, "There are two types of provision: a provision that is guaranteed to every living thing throughout its life, and it is the nourishment that sustains life, which is indicated by His words: "*There is no creature but that its provision is the responsibility of Allah,*" and there is a provision that is promised to the people of *taqwā* in particular, and it is what is mentioned in this *āyat.*"[55]

This is important to include here since the topic we are looking at is fraught with the danger that we will scientise it according to the false parameters of economics. Allah is the Provider, and so how could *taqwā* not be a factor in our provision?

### Sūra 73 al-Muzzammil – Traders

Coming to Sūra al-Muzzammil, which was revealed first of all in

Makka about the night prayers, we come across the "trader" who is coupled with the person fighting in the way of Allah. The Messenger of Allah ﷺ is narrated to have said: "Nine-tenths of provision has been placed in trade, and one tenth in livestock."[56] This is not a value judgment on trade or any other economic activity, but merely relates to the amount of provision in it.

Allah, exalted is He, says:

> *He knows that some of you are ill and that others are travelling in the land seeking Allah's bounty, and that others are fighting in the Way of Allah.* (73:18)

This is a Madīnan *āyat* from Sūra al-Muzzammil, the first *āyat*s of which were revealed in Makka at the beginning of Islam about the obligation to stand in prayer at night, as Allah, exalted is He, says: "*...stay up at night, except a little, half of it, or a little less, or a little more.*" (73:1-3)

Then in Madīna, He, exalted is He, made exceptions from this obligation for three categories: first, the sick since their sickness is a valid excuse; lastly, the *mujāhidūn* because of the importance of *jihād*; and in between these two categories there are traders whom He, exalted is He, refers to as people "*travelling in the land seeking Allah's bounty*".

The noted scholar aṣ-Ṣāwī said in his gloss on the *tafsīr* of the Jalālayn:

> In this *āyat* Allah, exalted is He, regards *mujāhidūn* and those earning *ḥalāl* livelihoods in order to spend it on themselves and their dependants as equal, indicating that earning wealth is of the same rank as *jihād*, because of that which is transmitted in the *ḥadīth*, "Whoever conveys food from one city to another and sells it at its price on that day will have the rank of the martyrs with Allah." Then the Messenger of Allah ﷺ recited: "*others travelling in the land seeking Allah's bounty, and others fighting in the Way of Allah.*"[57]

> Ibn Mas'ūd ﷺ said, "Any man who conveys anything from one of the cities of Islam, patiently anticipating, and sells it at its price on that day, has a rank with Allah like that of the martyrs," and then he recited: "... *others travelling in the land seeking Allah's bounty.*"[58]

A trader, then, is someone *"travelling in the land"*, not someone sitting at a console buying and selling over the phone. Trade involves buying something in one market and then transporting it to another to sell it there with the intention of earning a profit, remembering that he "sells it at its price on that day". It is not to buy in a market and resell it in that same market, making a profit from no effort expended. Trade is serious work. How many farmers, craftsmen, artisans and manufacturers need the services of traders to get their goods to market! A trader may spend long periods of time away from home and family. Many of the other people in the market – producers and customers – depend to some extent on such traders. They take products to other markets that the producers themselves have not the time or the wherewithal to reach. From those markets they bring back things of benefit for the local community. This is the economic lifeblood of the planet, and always has been. From the earliest times we have records of civilisations far distant from each other trading, the Sumerians with India, Bronze Age Phoenicians with Cornwall for tin, where they probably would have met Bronze Age people from the Shetland and Orkney islands far to the north of Scotland.

### *Ṣidq – truthfulness & Amāna – trustworthiness*

The trader in an authentic sense has a number of qualities that are vitally important. The first is courage. He takes risks in a way that the craftsman or agriculturist doesn't. He must have a high degree of *amāna* – trustworthiness – which is one of the three core attributes of the Messengers along with *tablīgh* – transmission of the Message – and *ṣidq* – truthfulness and honesty. He needs these qualities because those possessing funds will advance him money, gold and silver, for him to trade with, trusting in his good judgment and relying on his trustworthiness. He will need *amāna* because when, not if, he engages in credit transactions, whether by taking on a debt, or engaging to pay later for goods delivered immediately, or engaging to deliver goods later that have been paid for in advance, he must fulfil his word. The *sharī'a* has no bankruptcy let-out clauses. A debt is a debt and must be repaid unless the creditor forgoes repayment, even though there is a strong recommendation for them to do that if the debtor is in difficulty.

The significance of truthfulness (*ṣidq*) or honesty in the life of trade and commerce is fairly obvious, and it might be thought that it does not need mention or even a textual proof. The Prophet ﷺ said to a trader who had hidden some defects in his goods, "Whoever deceives is not one of us."[59] Here, the person deceived is not specified, meaning that it is irrelevant whether it is a Muslim, Christian or Jew or anyone else. To say that someone who deceives is "not one of us" is perhaps one of the most terrible judgments possible.

Far from being merely a moral command, truthfulness is one of the three fundamental qualities of the Messengers along with trustworthiness (*amāna*) and transmission of the Message (*tablīgh*). Thus they are the core of what *Sunna* is.

Telling the truth, *ṣidq,* is a profound matter which is trivialised when truth is reduced to "facts" because facts themselves have been reduced to verifiable statements about physical reality, leaving out the greater part of Reality and thus human experience.

*Amāna* and *ṣidq* are united in the Prophet's description ﷺ of such traders.

> The trustworthy completely truthful trader is with the Prophets, the *ṣiddīqūn* (utterly truthful) and the *shuhadā'* (martyrs[60]).[61]

Al-Munāwī says:

> "The trustworthy completely truthful trader will be [gathered on the Day of Rising] with the Prophets, the utterly truthful and the martyrs/witnesses." The Ḥakīm said, "He only reaches their ranks because with his heart he has gained something of Prophethood, and the state of utter truthfulness and witnessing [to the truth], because Prophethood is drawing aside the veil, utter truthfulness is the conformity of the secret thoughts of the heart with the open reality of the limbs, and witnessing is a person anticipating in himself [a reward in the *ākhira*] so that he would be in His view at the furthest limit of trustworthiness in everything that is placed with him."[62]

Why such praise? Because, as we all know, it is in the market-place, in the everydayness of earning a living, that it is easiest to lie or prove untrustworthy, whereas maintaining an appearance of piety in the setting of worship is the simplest thing imaginable.

Trade is the one striking exception from the rule that you cannot "invest" in someone's business and just receive a share of their profit, because such investment is very carefully circumscribed. It is called *qirāḍ* in the language of Madīna and *muḍāraba* in the language of Iraq. It is a single investment in a trader not in a specific trade. The investor cannot tell the trader what to do with the money. When the trader returns to the investor – and no conditions can be placed on him as to when that is – he returns the capital and they divide the profits, if there are any, according to their pre-arranged scheme. If there was a loss, the investor carries it, and the trader has no responsibility for it, unless he was careless or at fault in some other way. The investor and trader do not "roll over" the capital. But having concluded the transaction, the investor may, of course, decide to engage in another transaction with the trader.

With these two core attributes of Prophethood, which lie at the core of the *dīn,* of the Sunna, we are not surprised then to find the bearer of them, the trader, also at the centre of the spread of Islam after the age of *jihād*. They joined *tablīgh* –transmission of the Message – to *ṣidq* – truthfulness and *amāna* – trustworthiness. It was merchants, most often Yemenis, who took Islam to Kerala in India, Indonesia, Bengal, Malaysia, and down the coast of East Africa. So it was these men who bore the mantle of the Message in the later generations, and whose astonishing beings transformed the people they met and drew them into Islam. It must be remembered that the Companions and their Followers removed the two great tyrannical empires that bestrode the ancient world. It fell to subsequent generations to welcome their peoples into Islam in the later years. But the merchants were standard bearers of the *dīn* and the Prophetic Message.

### SŪRA 83 AL-MUṬAFFIFĪN – THE STINTERS

We now reach in our study a *sūra* that is late in the sequence of the *sūras* but which pertains to the historical beginning of Islam. Contemplating this issue, when 'Umar ibn al-Khaṭṭāb was *khalīfa*, the assembled Companions posited three possible beginnings: the birth or the death of the Messenger of Allah ﷺ, or the beginning of the revelation, but it was when 'Alī ibn Abī Ṭālib ؓ proposed that the beginning was the *hijra* of the Messenger of Allah ﷺ from Makka to Madīna, that 'Umar and the Companions recognised the rightness of what he had said and began dating from that time. In other words, they counted that as the beginning of Islam. As-Suyūṭī has: "In the year 16 AH ... in Rabī' al-Awwal, dating was begun from the *hijra* on the advice of 'Alī."[63]

The *āyats* that were revealed at that moment of emigration from the city of Ibrāhīm ﷺ, Makka, to the new civic model for mankind in Madīna is of great significance. The first *āyats* of Sūra al-Muṭaffifīn are: "*In the name of Allah, All-Merciful, Most Merciful. Woe to the stinters! Those who, when they take a measure from people, exact full measure, but when they give them a measure or weight, hand over less than is due."* (Sūra al-Muṭaffifīn 1-3)

In his *tafsīr* al-Qurṭubī said: "There is also from Ibn 'Abbās that he said, 'It was the first *sūra* to be revealed to the Messenger of Allah ﷺ the very hour he alighted in Madīna, and it was about them. When they bought they would take full measure and more, but when they sold they diminished the measures and the scales. Then, when this *sūra* was revealed, they ceased doing that, and they are those who most fully measure out right up to this day.'"[64]

One consequence of this revelation that has reverberated down to our day in most of the lands of Islam is that Muslims are not just exact in measuring but that rather, when they have measured or weighed out carefully, they will give a bit more to be absolutely sure not to be stinters.

There is much in this. It was the very first revelation "at that very hour" after the Messenger of Allah ﷺ alighted in Madīna. Clearly the People of Madīna had hitherto considered there to be two zones: first the religious zone of prayer and worship, and second the "real world" of trade and the market-place. Suddenly they were disabused of this erroneous notion. So the beginning of the entire affair of the *dīn*, which begins in Madīna, is when the Madinans' attention was drawn to the fact that there are not two separate mosque and market realities, but one single reality, and this was before either mosque or market was established. In this revelation, *mu'āmalāt* are even prioritised over *'ibādāt*.

Although the division of *fiqh* into *'ibādāt* and *mu'āmalāt* is useful analytically, it introduces a distinction that in some respects is shallow. The *āyat* that opens this chapter, which is really the raison d'être of the chapters on *mu'āmalāt*, is: *"I have not created jinn and men but to worship Me."* (51:56) There is nothing outside of this. But the difference lies in the intention. *'Ibādāt* require the intention to be valid, whereas *mu'āmalāt* do not. However, the latter can be raised to the rank of the former by intention. Since all actions are according to their intentions, as in the noble hadith, it is worth reproducing what Ibn Juzayy al-Kalbī says: "Know that actions are of three types: commanded, forbidden and permitted.

> *Ikhlāṣ* – sincerity in those which are commanded denotes making the intention purely for the face of Allah by not mixing it with another intention. If it is done like that it is pure and acceptable. If the intention is not for the face of Allah, for example by seeking a worldly benefit or praise, etc., then the deed is pure *riyā'* – showing-off – and it is rejected. If the intention is mixed [for example, with a desire for the face of Allah and for praise or worldly benefit] then the situation is more complicated and people have different views on it and there are a number of possibilities.
>
> As for if one gives up what is prohibited without an intention then one has removed oneself from the threat of punishment but one has no reward for giving it up. If one gives up [what is prohibited] with the intention of the face of Allah, as well as removing oneself from the threat of punishment one obtains a reward.
>
> As for permitted things, such as eating, sleeping, sexual intercourse, etc., if one does them without an intention, one has no reward for them. If one does them with the intention of the face of Allah one has a reward for doing them. **Every permitted action can become a means of drawing nearer [to Allah]** if one intends by them the face of Allah, for example, if one intends to eat for the sake of having the strength for worship, or if one intends by sexual intercourse to enable oneself to abstain from what is forbidden to one."[65]

This passage is worth quoting in its entirety because it shows that all doing and leaving undone is potentially an act of worship. The only difference is that an ordinary action done without the intention of worship is valid even though it may have no reward for it.

# Chapter 17

## Trade and Commerce in the Sunna & Sīra

### Time and the age

We live within an evolutionary narrative that plots the development of the cosmos and then history in a linear fashion. Because of its roots in the Judaeo-Christian worldview, an event no longer generally believed lies at year zero, and from that point history is framed in a series of epochs the most recent of which are named tendentiously the Renaissance, Reformation, Enlightenment and so on. These are not so much careful scholarly delineations as polemical names. Modernity, another such term, is variously considered to have two stages, the most recent of which began with the French Revolution. From this perspective the beginnings of Islam are consigned to pre-modernity. A more useful perspective might be to reconsider this dominant narrative. We can say that the first group, the Children of Israel, were the Muslims of their age and had a mission to establish the *dīn*. For a variety of reasons, including their own recalcitrance, they were defeated twice by the great powers, the second time being the Romans. Henceforth, they would find a way to accommodate themselves to power. However, then there was the tremendous but little understood event of Jesus, peace be upon him, the last Messenger to them. For a variety of reasons, his actual teaching went into the deserts of Syria and Egypt after the Roman destruction of Jerusalem, and a heavily Hellenistic version with its problematic theology went into the metropolises of the Greco-Roman world and gave rise not only to what we call Christianity but to the epochs delineated above, which were in reality the attempts of Europe to work out the contradictions inherent in this strange marriage of Jerusalem and Greece, but quite unsuccessfully. Then there came the Messenger of Allah ﷺ.

Here was a new event outside of the confusions both of Judaism and Christianity and the permutations of the two, and outside of the Hellenic framing which, often precisely because it had been misunderstood by the Romans and subsequent generations, wreaked the havoc that it did on the West. The Muslims in their time also came to meet Greek thought, but filtered it – as Shaykh Dr. Abdalqadir as-Sufi says: Islam is not a culture; it is a filter for culture. So the Islam of the Messenger of Allah ﷺ represents a new beginning, a new epoch. Within the dominant narrative, whose knowledge of Islam is lamentably poor, it can only be understood in such prejudicial terms as 'pre-modern'. It, however, makes more sense when we see it as a new beginning.

Thus we are not as Muslims anachronistically trying to reach back to a more mythic pre-modern age, but have actually entered the epoch of that Last Messenger ﷺ. We are the people of the age.

### The New Inception

Wā'ila ibn al-Asqa' said: I heard the Messenger of Allah ﷺ say, "Allah chose Kināna from the children of Ismā'īl. He chose the Quraysh from Kināna and He chose from the Quraysh the Banū Hāshim. He chose me from the Banū Hāshim."[1]

Aṭ-Ṭabarī relates in his *Tārīkh*:

> Hishām ibn Muḥammad narrated from his father: 'Abd Manāf's sons were Hāshim, 'Abd Shams the eldest, and al-Muṭṭalib the youngest, the mother of these being 'Ātika bint Murra as-Sulamiyya, and Nawfal, whose mother was Wāqida. They succeeded jointly to their father's authority, and were called "those made mighty" (*al-Mujabbarūn*). Of them it was said:
>
> O man who is unfastening his saddle,
>
> Why do you not lodge with the sons of 'Abd Manāf?
>
> They were the first to obtain guarantees of immunity for Quraysh which allowed them to travel far and wide from the sacred precincts of Makka (*Ḥaram*). Hāshim obtained a treaty for them with the kings of Syria, Rome (Constantinople) and with Ghassān; 'Abd Shams obtained a treaty for them with the Great Negus, as a result of which they travelled regularly to Abyssinia; Nawfal obtained a treaty for them with the Persian emperors, as a result of which they travelled regularly to Iraq and Persia; and al-Muṭṭalib obtained a treaty for them with the kings of Ḥimyar, as a result of which they travelled regularly to the Yemen. By means of them Allah made Quraysh mighty, and they were called "those made mighty" (*al-Mujabbarūn*).

Aṭ-Ṭabarī also remarked: "It is also said that [Hāshim] was the first to institute the two yearly caravans – those of winter and summer – for Quraysh."[2] Hāshim's institution of the caravans was based on these prior treaties with the surrounding polities.

## The Ancient World, Usury, Debt and Slavery

Having arrived at the gates of the *sīra* it is time for us to stop for an overview that takes in Prophethood, revelation, the city and the *umma*. Throughout the Qur'ān, Allah, exalted is He, indicates to His Prophet ﷺ to return to the way of Ibrāhīm ﷺ, which He also indicates to us. All the traditional accounts place his origins in the first cities of mankind in which originated the writing that gives us a historical record, the cities that give us what we call civilisation. The innovation of cities is one of the definitive watersheds in mankind's story as is also writing.

However, neither of these two are quite what they seem to be. After a tribal- and clan-based society of extended brotherhood where the other, the stranger, ordinarily kept his distance or was incorporated through marriage and other types of tribal affiliation (for example as a *mawlā* in the case of the Arabs), the cities introduce the stranger into the midst of affairs, indeed whole tribes and clans.

Thus here we see, right at the origin of civilisation, something happens that is a confluence of the city and of writing. The presence of strangers allows something new: the charging of interest on a loan, something no one originally could do to family. Interest charging brings in its trail mathematics and, close behind that, writing to record the debt. The earliest writing, in Sumerian cuneiform for example, records debts and interest payments.

> Indeed, perhaps cuneiform writing was primarily invented with the purpose of facilitating the rising credit and trading activities. Most of the surviving Sumerian writings today are in the form of temple accounts (records of supplies and goods exchanged) and commercial transactions, amongst which some of the earliest recordings of interest-bearing loans are detailed.[3]

Here at the origins in Sumeria and in Babylonia, we find temples and priests intimately involved with debt and usury as they would be right up until the Catholic Church, which was to be gradually supplanted by banking in the late Middle Ages and then brutally in the French Revolution. That transformation is encapsulated in architecture, with banks from those epochs imitating the architectural style of cathedrals. Today of course, churches echo the architectural style of banks.

> The economic role played by Babylonian shrines is noteworthy. The temples were not only religious houses, schools and courts, but they were also centres of financial and monetary transactions similar to the national banks of today.[4]

Mounting debts that arose through the inexorable and exponential logic of compound interest led to bankruptcy and the enslavement of family members and finally of the debtor himself until, through their labour, the debt had been repaid.[5] Naturally enough such a system brings in its trail great social distress and resentment, and the despot has always been the societal recourse to keep the lid on a pot that could all too easily boil over. All the elements of subsequent history were there at the very beginning and we are still trying to work them out. The Greeks arguably tried to resolve the civil situation politically. The institution of the agora and the gathering of free men to decide affairs was their attempt, and the locus was the *polis*, the word for city and state that gives us our "politics". However, they did not do away with interest transactions and usury, for indeed their temples were a locus of them as they had been in Sumeria and Babylonia. Ammar Fairdous writes:

> During the following centuries, however, banking grew rapidly in Athens. Its functions were performed, in tandem with temples...[6]

He then comments in the footnotes: "Most notable are the shrines of Delphi and Delos. The latter was described as the greatest bank of the Greek world."

Participation in politics was limited to Greeks and excluded the stranger and women. Their civilisation went down before the Roman, which was based on Rome as a civic model and its elaborate republican apparatus balancing tribes, patricians and plebeians, and all the different voices in the society. In subsequent centuries they even included as citizens those strangers who were

Roman subjects. This is the foundation of the model that has come down to us in the West. Incorporating the stranger as a citizen was an advance, but the Empire was brutal in subjugating its foes, and seemed to find enemies with little difficulty. Moreover the strangers' citizenship came at the cost of the extinction of their authentic culture. Nevertheless, our modality has all the elements of the original Mesopotamian model, except that now, as in Professor Benjamin Nelson's insightful title, *Tribal Brotherhood* has been transformed into *Universal Otherhood*[7] through the ubiquity of usury. Modern people are strangers, even increasingly within the family.

### IBRĀHĪM ﷺ, THE *FIṬRA*, AND THE CITY

Right at the beginning of the great civilisations of Mesopotamia, the Prophet of the time, Ibrāhīm ﷺ, walked away from these despotically controlled, usury-ridden cities and laid the foundations of an entirely different order in the fastness of the desert where no empire was able to reach until comparatively recently. Allah, exalted is He, quotes Ibrāhīm ﷺ as saying one extraordinary thing, *"Allah created both you and what you do."* (Sūrat aṣ-Ṣāffāt 37:96). The artificial division between nature and civilisation that has plagued mankind, in which nature is thought of as God's creation and civilisation as man's, was over before it started. This insight is especially useful today when man's inventions, the technosphere, threaten to overwhelm us entirely, when we stand apparently helpless before what we think we ourselves are 'creating'[8].

There in Makka, in among the *ummiyyīn* – the unlettered Arabs in their tribal brotherhoods – who were unlettered particularly because they did not have a debt or interest-based economy that needed to be recorded, Allah was to raise up His Prophet ﷺ who was himself also unlettered. However, because his tribe

Quraysh had become a cosmopolitan trading body, engaging in commerce with the Romans, Persians, Yemenis, Egyptians and the Axum Empire, and arguably via the Yemenis with India and China, some of them had also taken to the practice of usury and enough writing to record debts. Thus the Messenger of Allah ﷺ was aware of this, along with all the other aspects of commerce he came to understand. Nevertheless a substantial part of their trade was also in the form of *qirāḍ/muḍāraba* profit-sharing trade investments, which were to endure into Islam and become a part of *sharīʿa*.

The civic model left to the human being in the West was largely the Roman republican model, which incorporated the stranger along with the original tribes as a citizen, and which, although it admitted usury, tried to limit it. This was the model to which the Greek model succumbed as did that of the Children of Israel, although the latter had already suffered defeat at the hands of the Babylonians. The Israelites had suffered an arguably more serious, self-inflicted defeat brought about by their recalcitrant resistance to their own Prophetic heritage, by, for example, frequently resorting to idolatry, marrying idolatresses and engaging in magic and usury, for which they are roundly condemned by Allah in the Noble Qur'ān, just as they had been by their Prophets as recounted in the Old Testament.

Then there was the astonishing event of Sayyidunā ʿĪsā ﷺ, who, along with Yaḥyā ﷺ, was the last of the Prophets and Messengers sent to the Children of Israel who rejected both of them.

It was in this situation, and after a gap (*fatra*) of six centuries or so during which there were no Prophetic voices, that the Last Messenger ﷺ appeared.

### The Messenger of Allah ﷺ, His Madīna and His Umma

When asked about the character of the Messenger of Allah ﷺ,

'Ā'isha ﷺ replied, "His character was the Qur'ān,"[9] later paraphrased pithily by Shaykh Dr. Abdalqadir as-Sufi, may Allah be merciful to him, as, "He was the Qur'ān walking."

There is absolute clarity in the narrations about the life of the Messenger of Allah ﷺ and on the way it was that the revelation came to him. The descriptions are very vivid and are clearly about actual events, and very far from the fantastical and mythical imaginations of easterners and the ancients. Equally clearly, the greater part of the time he ﷺ was not receiving revelation and had to live his life, his personal private life, his family life with his wives and children and his community, by his own lights, so to speak, and by the wisdom – *ḥikma* – that Allah had shown him. It is important to grasp this point. The revelation came but it was the Prophet ﷺ who translated it into human terms in his life, words and deeds. Being human there was the possibility of error, but being under Divine protection (*'iṣma*), there was a process that protected him ﷺ from error or righted it even if it came near to occurring.

Why is this important? Because had there merely been the revelation it might have been said, "That's all well and good, but who could do that? Who could live up to that?" In his humanness, Muḥammad ﷺ did do that. He was not a supernatural being but a human being, and he took the revelation and lived it, and made it the guidance for his own leadership and teaching of the community. The Companion Ḥassān ibn Thābit ﷺ wrote in his famous *qaṣīda*:

> Muḥammad is a human being, yet not like anyone else;
>
> no, he is a flawless ruby while other people are just stones.

This verse sets the parameters for approaching the Messenger of Allah ﷺ. A human being yes, but far greater than modernists admit. The Prophets and Messengers ﷺ were sent to the people of their times and their lands to demonstrate what a human being *is* and might be, and to guide them to becoming truly human. The Prophet ﷺ was sent for all of mankind of every race and colour, every language and culture from his time until the end of time. His way abrogates all the previous religions and ways. We are the species who need to be shown how to be what we are by revelation. So if the Messenger of Allah ﷺ is our model for what a human being is, how do we reconcile that with the age of humanism we now inhabit that somehow imagines that it already knows this? Humanism interprets human beings as individuals which in the aggregate make up a society. It deals with aggregates statistically.

The Prophet ﷺ under the eye of revelation, nurtured individuals, families and the society, with his *sunna fi'lī* demonstrated in action and in practice, his *sunna qawlī* – the words of instruction, counsel and wisdom that he uttered, and the *sunna iqrārī* – his endorsement, whether tacitly by his silence or explicitly, of what occurred in his presence or to which his attention was drawn. That society comprised ordinary people with families, children and their lives in the market, and some extraordinary people who were merchants, poets, scholars, great warriors or exceptional in other ways. They all went to make a society that would be a model for other societies to come.

He was the Prophet of Madīna, of the civic order revealed for mankind until the end of time. The Madīnan years were those in which the *Sharī'a* and the *Sunna* were revealed. Just as the Prophet ﷺ embodied the revelation in his behaviour and character, his family and Companions took it from him in practice, also under the tutelage of revelation. Mankind had experimented with city forms, civilisational forms right up until Rome, but now here was a city moulded by revelation. Most importantly, since the Prophet ﷺ no longer engaged in trade, Madīna is our source for how trade was conducted in his presence, under his guidance and in the presence of revelation. The Companions were said to have been fearful of what they said and how they behaved in their homes lest *āyats* of Qur'ān be revealed about them. That certainly applied in their behaviour in the world and in the market. But the Prophet ﷺ was to take us beyond even the Madīnan model that uniquely he was guided to. He brought about an *umma*.

> *Allāhumma ṣalli 'alā sayyidinā Muḥammadin 'abdika wa rasūlika-n-nabiyyi-l-ummiyyi...*
>
> O Allah send Your blessings upon our Master Muḥammad, Your slave and Your Messenger the Unlettered Prophet...

The word translated here as "unlettered" is *ummī*, an adjective derived from one of two nouns: *umm* (mother) or *umma*, or quite conceivably from both. Lexicographers say that, if it comes from the former, among its meanings are: "any one not knowing the art of writing nor that of reading: ... one who does not write;... because the art of writing is acquired; as though he were thus called in relation to the condition in which his mother (*umm*) brought him forth."[10] If it comes from the latter, it is said the meaning is: "one who is in the natural condition of the nation (*umma*) to which he belongs, ... in respect of not writing, ... or not having learned writing; thus remaining in his natural state."[11] The emphasis given in both senses to the "natural condition (*fiṭra*)" is striking. The people of knowledge say that Islam is the *dīn* of the natural condition (*fiṭra*). But I would like to propose that it relates also to what I want to delineate here, that he ﷺ was definitively the Prophet for whom his *umma* would have over-riding importance; not just the one from which he came but the one to which he would give rise.

But I do not advance this interpretation to undermine the correct translation of "unlettered", of his being ﷺ someone who did not read or write, and who had not studied either the earlier revelations or the sciences and philosophies of the Greeks and others. This meaning is important because Islam came into being, unencumbered by the ritualism and legalism of the Jews, the metaphysics of the Christians or the speculation of the Greeks. Moreover, the Noble Qur'ān was revealed to him, which, in addition to being a miracle in itself, proved to be, along with the *sunna,* the source of a world civilisation that easily filtered and absorbed the Greek learning and provided shelter for Jews, Christians and others under its capacious protection.

*Umma* is a type of global order that stands in contrast to empire. By this matter of *umma*, the Messenger of Allah ﷺ took us beyond the city/state-based order, which gave rise to the nation-state, and beyond empire. For the *umma* contains not only the urban city dwellers but the Bedouin who do not live in the city, whether nomads or settled or partially nomadic. Moreover, whereas the Romans had expanded their domains and granted the conquered peoples the right to become Roman citizens, in the process losing their original cultures and tribal relations, *umma* successfully grew allowing indigenous peoples the ability to retain their tribal relations and their original cultures, so that today a Chinese Muslim is authentically Chinese and authentically Muslim in the same way that an African Muslim is authentically African and authentically Muslim. That leads us to conclude that German, Italian and Irish Muslims will also similarly be authentically German, Italian and Irish and authentically Muslim.

He ﷺ was characterised particularly by his constant concern for his *umma*, so much so that at the very pinnacle of his own spiritual journey, during the Mi'rāj when in face to face meeting with the Lord of Existence, his prayer was for his *umma*:

> Jibrīl had indicated that the Prophet ﷺ should greet his Lord and so he said. "Greetings are for Allah and prayers and good words." Allah said, "Peace be upon you, O Prophet and the mercy of Allah and His blessings." The Prophet ﷺ desired that his Community should have a share of the greeting and so he said: "Peace be upon us and on the righteous slaves of Allah." Jibrīl and all the people of the heavens said, "I bear witness that there is no god except Allah alone without partner and I bear witness that Muḥammad is His slave and Messenger," and then Allah Almighty said: "*The Messenger believes...*", meaning that he is thankful and that the Messenger affirms "*what has been sent down to him from his Lord.*" The Prophet ﷺ wanted his Community to share in the honour and said: "*And so do the believers. Each one believes in Allah and His angels and His Books and His Messengers. We do not differentiate between any of His Messengers.*"[12]

The *du'ā* that follows was made by the Prophet ﷺ directly to Allah in His Presence for his *umma*: "*Our Lord, do not take us to task if we forget or make a mistake! Our Lord, do not place on us a load like the one You placed on those before us! Our Lord, do not place on us a load we have not the strength to bear! And pardon us; and forgive us; and have mercy on us. You are our Master, so help us against the people of the unbelievers.*"[13]

*Umma* comprises two senses: *umma ad-da'wa* the community comprising those who are invited to the *dīn*, and this includes Jews and Christians and others who are adjudged to fit the description of the People of the Book and who are permitted to live autonomously under Islamic governance provided they fulfil the contract of the *dhimma*; and the *umma al-ijāba* comprising those who have responded to the invitation (*da'wa*) and submitted in Islam. It is well to note that for most of the first century Muslims were a small minority of the wider *umma*.

### The Ruler

Abdalhaqq Bewley said:

> It is a commonplace that, for the Prophet ﷺ, the *dīn* was not limited to acts of worship but extended into the affairs of everyday life, and there is no doubt that this included, in detailed and practical terms, the governance and administration of the fledgling Muslim *umma*.[14]

"The affairs of everyday life" are of course the *mu'āmalāt,* including marriage and divorce, the issues of *ḥalāl* and *ḥarām* food and buying, selling and renting etc. Not only did the Messenger ﷺ rule and govern his *umma,* he also set the model for how that should be done, a model that has been followed by the best of his successors until our age. The centrality of leadership and rulership is stated clearly in the Noble Book: *"You who believe, obey Allah and obey the Messenger and those in command among you,"* (4:59) about which al-Qurṭubī said, "When Allah ﷻ had previously addressed himself to those in authority in the previous *āyah* and had begun with them and ordered them to discharge trusts and to judge justly between people, He then proceeded in this *āyah* to address Himself to their subjects, and He ordered obedience to Himself ﷻ first of all, which means obeying His commands and avoiding His prohibitions, and then secondly obedience to His Messenger in that which he ordered and forbade, and then thirdly obedience to the *amīrs,* according to the position of the dominant majority and Abū Hurayra, Ibn 'Abbās and others. Sahl ibn 'Abdullāh at-Tustarī said, 'Obey the person in authority in seven things: minting *dirhams* and *dīnārs,* measures and weights, judgments, *ḥajj, jumu'a,* the two *'Īds* and *jihād.*'"

Apart from specific matters, Allah, exalted is He, stresses the importance of leadership by placing obedience to the leaders after obedience to Him and obedience to His Messenger ﷺ. 'Umar ﷺ stressed this point too:

> Tamīm ad-Dārī said: At the time of 'Umar people went to great lengths in competing with each other in building, so 'Umar said, "Assembly of Arabs: the earth! the earth! There is no Islam without *jamā'a*/ community. There is no *jamā'a* without amirate. There is no amirate without obedience. Whoever's people choose him as their chief on the basis of *fiqh*, that will be life for him and for them. Whoever's people choose him as their chief on the basis of something other than *fiqh*, that will be destruction for him and for them."[15]

Another well-known saying – "Allah prevents by means of the man in authority that which He does not prevent by means of the Qur'ān," variously ascribed to the Prophet ﷺ, although without *isnād*, and more securely to 'Umar, 'Uthmān and 'Umar ibn 'Abd al-'Azīz – contains a profound truth. The man in authority may forcibly prevent usury in the market-place, whereas the individual left to himself is less able to do that. However, we can also extrapolate from this in a positive sense, for the man in authority has the ability to establish a free market and dedicate it as a *waqf*, and to mint a sound currency and other matters that the individual would struggle to do.

But rulership must be placed in a context, and ours is Madīna al-Munawwara – The Illuminated City.

### THE *MUWAṬṬA'* – THE BLUEPRINT FOR AN ILLUMINATED CITY

In looking at the *mu'āmalāt at-tijāriyya* – ordinary commercial transactions, we are looking at a part of the "blueprint for an illuminated city", which is Shaykh Dr. Abdalqadir as-Sufi's memorable description of the *Muwaṭṭa'* of Imām Mālik. And if that illuminated order subsequently fell into despotism or disorder occasionally, it also continually renewed itself and is likely to do so again before the Last Day.

With mention of the *Muwaṭṭa'*, we reach a point that is almost invisible even to great classical scholars, most of whom regard it correctly as the first *ṣaḥīḥ* work, but then discard it because, they think, the "*ṣaḥīḥ* books" supersede it. This perspective wrongly regards anything that is not a *ṣaḥīḥ ḥadīth* as extraneous. Two great *'ulamā* adhered to this perspective with regrettable effect: Imām Muḥammad ibn al-Ḥasan ash-Shaybānī, whose transmission of the *Muwaṭṭa'* as learned directly from Imām Mālik not only discards Imām Mālik's narrations of the *'amal* of the People of Madīna, which they and he regarded as sounder evidence of the *Sunna* than many of the *ḥadīth*,[16] but also discards almost everything apart from Prophetic *ḥadīth*. It then adds in Imām Muḥammad's commentaries on those *ḥadīth,* often undermining the way they had been understood in Madīna, as well as his own *ḥadīth* narrations, which are weaker than the originals in the *Muwaṭṭa'*;[17][18] the second was Shah Waliyullāh ad-Dahlawī who, confronted with the divisions among the *fuqahā* and *'ulamā* in India, tried to resolve them by resorting to the *ṣaḥīḥ ḥadīth* of the *Muwaṭṭa'*, but again ignoring the copious references to the *'amal* of the people of Madīna and the abundant accounts of the practice and views of the Companions and the Followers, and Followers of the Followers. These were two great *'ulamā* of the Muslims without doubt, but we only regret the opportunity they missed to grapple with the *Muwaṭṭa'* on its own terms, and thus with Madīna itself and the *'amal* of its people. So let us try to do that now.

We have been considering cities as such, but let us now consider, in a more focussed sense, social orders – the dynamic sets of transactions that make up city life – and particularly social orders formed and guided by revelation. Let the word 'city' stand as shorthand in place of such social orders. One of the earliest social orders schooled by the Divine that we know of was not a city but a ship, the Ark of Nūḥ which Allah commanded Nūḥ ﷺ to build:

*Build the Ark under Our supervision and as We reveal.* (11:37)

> Imām Mālik later connected that first social order to the one to whose safeguarding and furtherance he dedicated his life, the *Sunna*. Ibn Wahb narrated that Imām Mālik said: "The *Sunna* is the Ark of Nūḥ: whoever embarks on it is saved, but whoever hangs back from it is drowned."[19] With this pivotal insight, Imām Mālik named the complex of dynamic relations that make up a city "*Sunna*". Clearly, Imām Mālik is not talking about the *Sunna* as most of our contemporaries think of it as issues of dress code or the length of the beard, although we do not dismiss those issues lightly.[20]

The *Muwaṭṭa'* is a living picture of the Prophetic city over three generations. It can only be understood in the light of the chequered history of city itself over the millennia, a history that has inexorably fed into our contemporary cities and nation-states, with tragic consequences today. The significance of the *Muwaṭṭa'* still waits to be grasped and is ever more urgent in our time.

### Ibn Khaldūn, the Bedouin and *'Aṣabiyya*

Here we can go no further without Ibn Khaldūn whose vision of the cyclical nature of civilisation, and the vital role of the Bedouin in that cycle, is our key. But before proceeding, we must acknowledge his outline of the city, of civilisation and its arts, crafts, trade and commerce, of history and so much more, all of which he works through in chapter after chapter in the *Muqaddima*. Shaykh Abdalqadir writes in *The Time of the Bedouin:*

> It must be re-emphasised that Ibn Khaldūn's thinking projects a cyclical view of history that envisages human society curving in a pattern that moves with an evolutionary energy to a point of apogee and then fades down into a decay as in the cycle of seasons and of the human body. It is not a linear fantasy that envisages a utopian end with a society in a stasis of achieved goals. What is incumbent on thinking men is to recognise at what stage of the process they find themselves, and thus activate it and accomplish it, taking into account the different risks and dangers that their point in time imposes on them.[21]

So if we are in a period of decay, that is a part of the natural process, and it is incumbent on us to recognise it, not lament it, and to act with full consciousness of what is needed at such a time. Ibn Khaldūn sees the vital regenerative and renewing force as those whom he called the Bedouin. Shaykh Abdalqadir takes us further into discerning who they might be in our circumstances:

> Bedouinism is not, [Ibn Khaldūn] insists, nomadism. Nomadism implies a settled and organic community identified by its capacity and habit of movement from a place to a place for pasture or market. The Bedou is outside the urban system.
>
> The Bedou is cut off from the urban entity even if he is in it. In modern times, by application of his model this permits of the term being applied to Districtism or Townshipism.
>
> At a certain stage the Bedouin in their power of growth and expansion, and by a genetic vitalisation denied the passive urban community, begin to identify themselves as a new civic force. A natural need becomes wedded to a higher evaluation, an evaluation of themselves. There emerges among them the most powerful force that social man can experience. It is kinship, but not of blood. It transcends the tribal and the familial. This unification of the group takes them to the Second Stage. Stage Two is defined by Ibn Khaldūn with the term "Asabiyya". Asabiyya, normally "kinship", is here used to mark as distinctive the bond, the life and death unifying bond of a brotherhood without blood ties. In the excellent Pléiade edition of "The Muqaddima" its editor and translator calls it "esprit de corps", but it is much more than that, for it has in it also a moral evaluation as in the term "Futuwwa", chivalry or nobility of character. Asabiyya unites men to find the power to act and transform and command. If its motor power is high, its brotherhood is raised higher. If the binding factor (religio-to bind together) is there, that is Divine religion, it is, that being its highest possibility, assured a triumph.[22]

Few Arabs understood Ibn Khaldūn's thesis in his own time but the Osmanlı did. Professor Recep Şentürk[23] told me that, through their understanding of him, the Osmanlı's great achievement was to recognise the potential for revitalisation of the civilisation that the 'Bedouin' have. They did not wait to be swept away but invited those forces in and elevated them through their practice of *Devshirme* – the induction into the community of children of Jews and Christians, who often rose very high in the hierarchy of Osmanlı society. Thus they provided a continuous renewal of that society, that is until the suspension of the *khilāfa* and the Second Interregnum.

### The Messenger of Allah ﷺ, trade and the market

Returning to Madīna, before revelation the Messenger of Allah ﷺ himself engaged in trade:

> Ibn Isḥāq said: "Khadīja bint Khuwaylid was a merchant woman who possessed nobility and property. She would hire men to act for her in her property on the basis of *muḍāraba*. When that which reached her about the Messenger of Allah ﷺ did, of the truthfulness of his speech, how greatly trustworthy he was, and the noble generosity of his character, she sent for him and offered him to go out [trading] with her wealth as a trader to Shām, and she would give him more than what she gave other traders."[24]

However, I have come across no records of the Prophet ﷺ trading in the Madīnan period, that moment when the laws of *sharī'a*, and in particular those laws governing commerce, were revealed. How could he have engaged in trade when the revelation he brought contained rulings on it and he was the ruler[25] and the *qāḍī*, thus creating the possibility of a conflict of interest? Because the revelation required the regulation of trade and all matters pertaining to life in the world, he did speak and give guidance on it. But a complementary rich source of the *Sunna* is the market practice in Madīna. The Qur'ān cites people asking: "*What is the matter with this Messenger, that he eats food and walks in the market-place?*" (25:7) The implication here is that "*walks*" is a regular practice, and there are examples in the *ḥadīth* literature of the Messenger of Allah ﷺ doing that and also exercising the role of *muḥtasib* – market inspector. What is implicit is that when he did not find fault with something there was a tacit endorsement of it.

Market practice in Madīna, purified by the exclusion of those practices/matters that he ﷺ objected to, remained a rich source of the third form of *Sunna*,[26] and it is this that Mālik records in the section on buying and selling of his *Muwaṭṭa'*, along with his transmission of the *ḥadīth* concerning trade and many examples and traditions from *al-Khulafā' ar-Rāshidūn*, the Followers and the Followers of the Followers. Thus the *Muwaṭṭa'*, in its sections on commercial practice, joins together two forms of the *Sunna*: his instructions ﷺ and his confirmation of the practice of the people of Madīna whether implicitly or explicitly, and adds Imām Mālik's clarifications, just as in general the *Muwaṭṭa'* joins all three aspects of the *Sunna*.

Since the Companions, in their turn, took the *Sunna* and exemplified it, it became a societal phenomenon and then its name in Madīna became *'amal* – practice. We have also seen that *futuwwa* – the noble qualities of character, the *makārim al-akhlāq*, that the Messenger of Allah ﷺ defined as the very purpose of his having been sent when he said ﷺ, "I have only been sent to perfect the noble qualities of character,"[27] – is the essence of the *Sunna*, the *dīn* and thus of the *'amal*. Abdalhaqq Bewley said: "So according to this understanding, what *futuwwa* involves is simply following the *Sunna* of the Messenger of Allah ﷺ not in the usually understood sense of imitating his outward actions, but in taking on those noble qualities of character he so perfectly exemplified during the course of his life."[28]

*Makārim* derives from the root *karuma* meaning both to be noble and to be generous. In other words, nobility and generosity are at the very heart of the matter. As Anas ﵁ said, "He was the best of people, the most liberally generous of people, the bravest of people."[29] And it is this quality that is most significant in our discussion of the *mu'āmalāt māliyya* (financial transactions). Contrary to the grasping, mean and miserly character of capitalism, Muslims are not only generous in person but in the market when they trade.

In the practice of the people who modelled themselves on the people of Madīna, the *'amal* took on new judgments in response to new situations and took on the colour of the societal vessels it found itself in. One of the *uṣūl* principles allows one to utilise the customs of a land (*'urf/'āda*) unless they contravene known *sharī'a*. All of that became, in its turn, incorporated as part of the *'amal*, particular local variants of different countries and cities.

### Establishment of the market of Madīna

The Prophet ﷺ established the market of Madīna even though the city had other existing markets. We mean by establishment the dedication of land as a *waqf* for the purpose of trade and laying down the ground rules for its management (see below). He did so, after the establishment of the mosque, similarly by dedicating a piece of land as a *waqf* for that purpose. The foundation of a market is thus *Sunna*. Although in general such a market has been an open space, there is no particular reason why it should not be a covered and enclosed space in lands whose weather is inclement. He ﷺ laid down its ground rules. Those rules, established as *Sunna*, became the rules of all Muslim markets that were established thereafter.

> The Messenger of Allah ﷺ went to the market of Nabīṭ and examined it and said, "This is not a market for you," and then he went to another market and said, "This is not a market for you," and then he returned to this market – meaning the market of Madīna – and went around it and said, "This is your market. Let it not be diminished, and let no tax be imposed on it."[30]

A man came to the Prophet ﷺ and said, "May my father and my mother be your ransom! I have seen a place for the market; will you not then look at it?" He said, "Certainly." So he stood up and went with him until he came to the place for the market, and when he saw it he liked it and he stamped on it with his foot and said, "Your market is blessed, so let it not be broken up and let no tax be levied on it."[31]

'Aṭā' ibn Yasār said, "When the Messenger of Allah ﷺ wanted to make a market for Madīna he went to the market of Banī Qaynuqā' and then he came to the market of Madīna and struck it with his foot and said, "This is your market, so it should not be constricted nor should any tax be levied on it."[32]

Muḥammad ibn 'Abdullāh ibn Ḥasan said, "The Messenger of Allah ﷺ gave the Muslims their markets as a *ṣadaqa*." He meant that they are free and that no rent can be charged for them.

'Umar ibn 'Abd al-'Azīz, in conformity with this, ordered that no rents could be charged for space in the market-place.[33]

As for his usual practice ﷺ in the market: "He ﷺ used to mix with them in their markets and he would command them [to do right] and forbid them [to do wrong]."[34] As an example of this:

The Messenger of Allah ﷺ passed by a mound of food and he entered his hand into it and his fingers encountered dampness, so he said, "Owner of the food, what is this?" He said, "Messenger of Allah, some rain fell on it." He said, "Why did you not then put it on the top of the food so that people could see it." Then he said, "Whoever deceives is not one of us."[35]

In this, he ﷺ was demonstrating the action of the *muḥtasib* – market inspector – a figure of great importance in subsequent Muslim practice whose role could sometimes be equivalent to the mayor[36] of a Western city.

This conduct was again demonstrated by the second caliph 'Umar ibn al-Khaṭṭāb ؓ when walking in the market in Madīna:

> 'Umar ibn al-Khaṭṭāb passed by Ḥātib ibn Abī Balṭa'a who was selling some of his raisins in the market. 'Umar ibn al-Khaṭṭāb said to him, "Either increase the price or you will be ejected from our market."[37]

This has a number of points that are not immediately obvious: first, the reprehensible nature of undercutting, i.e. selling goods cheaper than other traders in order to take trade from them, which has become so much a part of the weaponry of modern trade as to be rarely questioned; second, that although it is not permissible for the leader or a cartel of traders to set prices in the market, the community leader or *muḥtasib* can demand that a trader sell at the regular price for his goods as acknowledged by the other traders in the market and, failing that, expel him from the market.

The Messenger of Allah ﷺ saw to it that markets had overseers. "The Messenger of Allah ﷺ put Sa'īd ibn Sa'īd ibn al-'Āṣ ibn Umayya in charge of the *sūq* of Makka when he opened [Makka to Islam], but then when the Prophet ﷺ wanted to go to Ṭā'if, Sa'īd ibn Sa'īd went with him and was martyred at Ṭā'if."[38]

The next step in our history, Caliphate (*khilāfa*), is often misunderstood, particularly by certain modernists, who have transformed it into a political institution. The word *khalīfa* means a successor who is in turn succeeded by another.[39] It is about a man. It is personal, not institutional. The initiative to restore 'the Caliphate' is a deeply flawed one. As Shaykh Dr. Abdalqadir says: "Now we don't have a ship, there's no use screaming for the captain. *Khilāfa* is a *farḍ* of our religion but it is a fantasy to ask for it now. You don't put on a roof until you have a house."[40] The house of Islam is of course sustained by its pillars underpinned by *ḥalāl* transactions in commerce and in the market.

### The *Khulafā' ar-Rāshidūn* and the Companions

The *Khulafā' ar-Rāshidūn* were the Prophet's heirs and their *Sunna* is the continuation of his *Sunna*.

Abū Najīḥ al-'Irbāḍ ibn Sāriya said, "The Messenger of Allah ﷺ admonished us with an admonition by which the hearts became frightened and the eyes flowed with tears, so we said, "Messenger of Allah, it is as if it were a farewell admonition, so advise us." He said, "I advise you to have *taqwā* of Allah, mighty is He and majestic, and to hear and obey even if a slave is given command over you. Whoever of you lives will see many disagreements, so you must take hold of my *Sunna* and the *Sunna* of the rightly guided *khulafā'* who take the right way. Bite on it with the molar teeth. Beware of newly introduced matters, for every newly introduced matter is an innovation, and every innovation is a going astray."[41]

This noble *ḥadīth* adds a dimension it is easy to overlook: the *Sunna* continued to be formed after the death of the Prophet ﷺ. *Al-Khulafā' ar-Rāshidūn* extended it and clarified much of it. In particular, in 'Umar's long caliphate, during which many of the Companions were still alive, he ordinarily took their counsel on matters and so his decisions often represent the consensus of the Companions, since they would not allow someone to get away with anything they knew to be false. This is why his *fiqh* represents a cornerstone of the *Muwaṭṭa'* whereas, in other collections, his views are often presented as if they were just those of one of the Companions.

Among the things he did was to make a *dīwān* [register of the Muslims] and appoint each Muslim a stipend from the funds that were beginning to flow into the *bayt al-māl*, a flow that would become a flood in the *khilāfa* of 'Uthmān ﷺ. 'Umar said, expressing the fundamental precondition of trade in the market: "No one sells in our market except for those who understand *fiqh*."[42]

'Umar put Sulaymān ibn Abī Ḥathma in overall charge of the market of Madīna. His mother was ash-Shifā' bint 'Abdallāh.[43] 'Umar used to "give preference to her view and pay close attention to her and honour her and often charge her with some of the affairs of the market."[44]

Reiterating and endorsing the words of 'Umar we saw earlier, 'Alī ibn Abī Ṭālib ﷺ said: "Whoever trades before gaining *fiqh* understanding will become inextricably enmeshed in *ribā*, then moreover he will become inextricably enmeshed, then moreover he will become inextricably enmeshed."[45]

As we have seen, responsibility for establishing a free market for the people devolves on the man in authority among the Muslims, at whatever scale of focus in terms of the fractal of Islamic governance we look. Something that is very immediately achievable for Muslims everywhere is to set up a local market on the grounds of the mosques where such exists. Naturally they will need the assent of the local authorities before doing this but many who have done so have experienced very favourable responses from people in local government.[46]

The benefits of doing this are enormous. Socially, it gives many non-Muslims access to the Muslim community who would otherwise understandably be too shy to enter a mosque, but it is also a way of reconnecting Muslims who might have found themselves for various reasons alienated from the wider Muslim community. It is my considered opinion that after the mis-named war on terror, we have entered what I would called a 'Hudaybiyya moment'. At that point in the *sīra*, which Allah characterised as a Clear Fatḥ (opening), conversations became possible between Muslims and non-Muslims and naturally enough trade, and as a consequence enormous numbers of people accepted Islam.

Most importantly, markets attached to mosques could be a first step towards creating a non-usurious economy and should not be despised for their apparently insignificant nature. Such markets could quite naturally be linked up by traders moving between them, whether locally, nationally or globally. As well, we should support existing markets, some of which are of great antiquity, and newer markets like the farmers' markets that have sprung up in recent years. These are actions that Muslim communities are well suited to undertake.

Arguably, for Muslims, the community is the nearest thing to a bank, with there being, alongside simple sales, purchases and barters, a complex web of credit and debt transactions. This was clearly the pattern in the Madīna of the Messenger of Allah ﷺ. Ibn 'Abbās narrated that the Messenger of Allah ﷺ died while his shield was pledged with a Jew for thirty *ṣā*'s of barley.[47] And there is this striking account of 'Umar ؓ on his death bed instructing his son 'Abdullāh to repay his debts:

> Then ['Umar] said to his son, "'Abdullāh, look and see what debts I have." They calculated them and found them to be eighty-six thousand[48] or thereabouts. He said, "If the wealth of the family of 'Umar is enough, then pay it. If it is not, then ask among Banī 'Adī, and if their wealth is not enough, then ask among Quraysh."[49]

When a number is mentioned without specification in *ḥadīth* like this it refers to *dirhams*.

The Companions often had substantial debts, as exemplified in the *ḥadīth* about Zubayr ibn al-'Awwām ؓ in *Ṣaḥīḥ al-Bukhārī*.

> 202. Abū Khubayb 'Abdullāh ibn az-Zubayr ibn al-'Awwām al-Qurashī al-Asadī ؓ who said: When az-Zubayr stood awaiting the Battle of the Camel, he called me over and I went to his side. He said, "Son, no one will be killed today except someone wrongdoing or someone wronged. I think that I will be killed today as one of the wronged. One of my greatest concerns is my debts. Do you think that any of our property will remain after our debts are settled?" Then he said, "O my son! Sell our property and pay my debts!" Then he bequeathed a third, and a third of it was for his sons, i.e. the sons of 'Abdullāh ibn az-Zubayr, a third of the third. He said, "If anything is left over of our property after paying the debts, then a third of it is for your children." (Hishām said, "Some of the sons of 'Abdullāh were the same age as the sons of az-Zubayr: Khubayb and 'Abbād. At

that time he had nine sons and nine daughters.") 'Abdullāh said, "My father began to order me concerning his debt and say, 'Son, if you are unable to settle any of it, then ask my Master for help in doing it.'" He said, "By Allah, I did not know what he meant so I said, 'Father, who is your Master?' He said, Allah.'"

He said, "By Allah! Whenever I ran into difficulty regarding his debt I said, 'O Master of az-Zubayr! Pay his debt for him!' and He would settle it." He said, "Az-Zubayr ﷺ was killed without leaving a *dīnār* or a *dirham*, but only pieces of land, one of which was al-Ghāba, and eleven houses in Madīna, two in Basra, one in Kufa, and one in Egypt."

He said: "The debt that he owed resulted from people bringing him money to leave in his keeping. Az-Zubayr would say, 'No, let it rather be a loan, for otherwise I fear that it might get lost.' He had never been appointed to a government post of any kind nor to the collection of land-tax (*kharāj*) nor anything else. What he had came only from expeditions with the Prophet ﷺ or with Abū Bakr, 'Umar and 'Uthmān ﷺ."

'Abdullāh ibn az-Zubayr said, "When I worked out the debt he owed, I found it to be two million and two hundred thousand." Ḥakīm ibn Ḥizām met 'Abdullāh ibn az-Zubayr and said, "Nephew, how large a debt does my brother have?" I concealed it and said, "A hundred thousand." Ḥakīm said, "By Allah, I do not think that your property will cover this amount." 'Abdullāh said, "What would you think if it were two million and two hundred thousand?" He said, "I do not think you will be able to pay this. If you are unable to cover any of it, then ask me for help."

He said: Az-Zubayr had purchased al-Ghāba for one hundred and seventy thousand, and 'Abdullāh sold it for one million and six hundred thousand. Then he stood up and said, "Anyone who is owed anything by az-Zubayr should come to us at al-Ghāba." 'Abdullāh ibn Ja'far came to him, and az-Zubayr owed him four hundred thousand. He said to 'Abdullāh, "If you like, I will forgo it." 'Abdullāh said, "No." He said, "If you like, you can delay payment if you want to." 'Abdullāh said, "No." He said, "So allocate me a piece of land." 'Abdullāh said, "You can have from here to there." 'Abdullāh sold some of it and paid his debts in full and there remained four and a half shares of the land. He went to Mu'āwiya while 'Amr ibn 'Uthmān, al-Mundhir ibn az-Zubayr and Ibn Zam'a were with him. Mu'āwiyah said, "How much have you valued al-Ghāba at?" He said, "Each share at a hundred thousand." He said, "How much remains?" He said, "Four and a half shares." Al-Mundhir ibn az-Zubayr said, "I will take a share for a hundred thousand." 'Amr ibn 'Uthmān said, "I will take a share for a hundred thousand." Ibn Zam'a said, "I will take a share for a hundred thousand." Mu'āwiya said, "How much remains?" He said, "A share and a half." He said, "I will take it for one hundred and fifty thousand."

He said: 'Abdullāh ibn Ja'far later sold his share to Mu'āwiya for six-hundred thousand. When Ibn az-Zubayr finishing settling his debts, the sons of az-Zubayr said, "Distribute our inheritance between us." He said, "No, by Allah, I will not distribute it until I have made this announcement for four years during the *ḥajj* festival: 'Anyone who has a debt owed him by az-Zubayr should come to us and we will settle it.'" He announced that every year at the festival and when the four years were up, he distributed it between them and paid over the third. Az-Zubayr had four wives and after the prescribed third was removed, each wife got a million and two hundred thousand. So the total amount of his property was fifty million and two hundred thousand.[50] [51]

This also reflects accurately what is clear in the history of the Companions: their extensive interconnectedness financially through loans, credit and debt, both commercial and personal, and it is cited not to encourage reckless indebtedness but to show that prior to banks Muslims borrowed from and lent to each other. We have already seen the *ḥadīth* of 'Abdullāh ibn Ja'far who said: "The Messenger of Allah ﷺ said, 'Allah is *with* the debtor until he settles his debt as long as it is not for something which Allah dislikes.'" This of course is conditional on the debtor taking his debt seriously and being determined to repay it.

We conclude this section on trade and commerce in the *Sunna* and *Sīra* with one warning note from 'Umar ibn al-Khaṭṭāb ؓ.

Shaykh 'Abd al-Ḥayy al-Kattānī has a very full section amplifying the issue of the importance of *fiqh* for traders in his *at-Tarātīb al-Idāriyya* with much supporting material from 'Umar ﷺ, from Imām Mālik and from a number of Ḥanafī *'ulamā*. After that he writes about 'Umar's exhorting the Companions not to abandon trade even though they had become free of need to do so because of the stipends he had given them and the very substantial booty that the *mujāhidūn* had gained in *jihād*:

> Mālik said in *al-'Utbiyya* that 'Umar ibn al-Khaṭṭāb said, "You must trade. Do not let the 'red ones' cause you tribulations in your worldly affairs." Ashhab said, "Quraysh used to trade but the Arabs despised commerce," and the "red ones" are the *mawlās*.[52] (From *al-Bayān wa at-taḥṣīl* [by Qāḍī Ibn Rushd al-Jadd]). In the *Madkhal* by Ibn al-Ḥājj, it is related that 'Umar ibn al-Khaṭṭāb entered the market during his caliphate and for the most part only saw Nabateans. He was grieved by that. When the people were gathered together, he told them about that and rebuked them for abandoning the market. They said, "Allah has freed us from needing the market by the victories which He has opened up to us."
>
> He said ﷺ, "By Allah, if you do it (abandon the market), then your men will need their men and your women will need their women." When one of the right-acting first generations (*salaf*) saw the Nabateans studying knowledge he wept. That is only because when knowledge falls to people other than its own, corruptions will enter into it, as you see.[53]

The Nabateans were Arab tribes from the north of Arabia and the south of Shām. Before Islam they had become christianised. Sufyān (one of the right-acting first generations (*salaf*)) saw that merely recording *ḥadīth* was simply not enough to secure their trade from injurious practices, i.e. usury. Contrast this with the advice of Imām Mālik to the man who wanted to learn *fiqh*, when he said, "If you want knowledge take up residence. The Qur'ān was not revealed on the Euphrates."[54] He meant he should take up residence in Madīna in order to study both *fiqh* and *ḥadīth* with him and in order to imbibe the ethos and the practice of the People of Madīna in their homes, their streets, their mosque and their market-place.

> I ['Abd al-Ḥayy al-Kattānī] say:[55] The insight of 'Umar about this community proved true. When they abandoned trade by the prescribed, desired methods and successful forms, others took it over and the community became dependent on others – our men dependent on their men and our women on their women in everything – from needle and thread to the highest and most expensive things.[56]

The author is speaking from his vantage point of the 20th century; he knew the world of his time and history widely. He continued:

> What Ibn al-Ḥājj mentioned about one of the right-acting first generations (*salaf*) without naming him, was referring to Sufyān. Al-Khaṭīb narrated that Muḥammad ibn 'Abd al-Wahhāb al-Baskarī said, "When Sufyān saw these Nabateans recording *ḥadīth* in an inappropriate way it was very hard for him, so I said to him, 'Abū 'Abdullāh, we noticed that when you saw these people recording knowledge, it was hard for you.' He said, 'Knowledge used to be among the Arabs and the lords of people. Then when it left them and went to these people, meaning the Nabateans and lower types of people, 'they altered the *dīn*.'"[57]

So this is where we are and and a significant part of how we got here. The progressive abandonment of trade by Muslims and our leaving it to others, who have no scruples about usury, has brought us to the situation we are in. Conversely that tells us exactly what is needed for restoration of the *dīn*. If that task seems gargantuan, Shaykh Abdalqadir says about the nature of the *dīn*:

> This pattern can go from a city, from a country – it can shrink down to a group. It can be nomadic, it can be a civilisation. It is a totally functional, social reality the minute two people are there and not one – which is what Islam is.[58]

It is fractal "in which similar patterns recur at progressively smaller scales."[59] Governance partakes of this nature and pertains at whatever scale we are.

Returning to the theme with which we began this chapter, we know that we are not beleaguered people trying desperately to cling to some remnant of a pre-modern teaching, nor, as in the perennialist[60] telling, trying to go back to a 'tradition', a highly problematic matter, but that we are in tune with the true nature of the epoch that began with the Messenger of Allah ﷺ. This epoch began after the collapse of both prior branches of the Prophetic way, the Judaic and the Christian, whose failure becomes ever more obvious in the global crises that assail us from all sides. If the claim to be of the age sounds exclusivist and not a little triumphalist, one must counterbalance it by the sobering thought that, whereas large numbers of Westerners are reaching out to the post-modern post-Judaeo Christian synthesis, many Muslims in their individual and commercial lives and lives as citizens in their nation-states are not only embroiled in usury but arguably believe in it and the technical world order more fervently than others. And from this criticism we exempt those huge numbers compelled to comply under the force of circumstances.

Let us retrace our steps to understand the technical age. The Greeks inherited from the depths of the mythopoeic age a plethora of gods, which in the dawning of the metaphysical era began to embarrass the thinkers who tried to formulate explanations for existence that did not rely upon the supernatural. They began to talk about *physis* (pronounced *phusis*), the processes in which things come about without human agency, contrary to *techne* and *poeisis*. This led on to the Roman misunderstanding which we have inherited couched in terms of *nature*, and then in early modernity to the ascendancy of physics, upon which the other sciences modelled themselves because of the astounding success of Galilean-Newtonian theories. Although, these early scientists were Christians, the inherent character of their disciplines asserted itself in the often unspoken thesis that material reality is all that there is. Subsequent history is the working out of this thesis and its articulation, and the materialist world is its consequence. In the larger scale it is the result of Greek thinking and of the ways it had been misunderstood. Heidegger characterises it as forgetfulness of be-ing and the endless remembrance of and thought about beings. *Techne* gave us the technique/technology whose essence, as Heidegger said, is nothing technological but the enframing that forces reality to reveal itself as standing reserve, as resources to be used. That this includes the human being, 'human resources', has organised crime as its most extreme manifestation and the sale of women and children on an industrial scale globally. One doesn't know if that horrific fact is worse or the reduction of the planet to a 'workforce' for global capitalism.

It is no accident that after the debacle of Judaeo-Christian usury capitalism and its subjection of the world to the perilous state that everyone understands it to be in now, that Allah had already revealed the *dīn* of Islam equipped with what is necessary for resolving the metaphysical issues of modernity but also the bases for a functioning non-usurious mode of commerce, which is the subject of our next chapter.

# Chapter 18

## Transactions – Mu'āmalāt

*In order that man's knowledge should be balanced and integrated, information ought to be derived from both the revelation and existence together; it is a matter of how we understand the revelation and how we put it into effect in our actual situation; of how we transact with existence on the basis of the Divine commands and prohibitions.*[1]

Perhaps the significance of the statement "Islam is the *dīn al-fiṭra* – the natural condition" can be measured by the fact that it is often mistaken for a Prophetic hadith, which it is not. Thus it is neither a point of *'aqīda* nor has it any legislative force. Its benefit is something else. It is an indicator.

The emergence of the *madhhab*s was in the years when first the Muslims were governing East and West, and then, in the century that followed, were engaged with the establishment of Islam, which included teaching the vast influx of new Muslims. This is the context for that early epoch's intellectual endeavours. The need was extremely real and practical. The three early generations absorbed what had been transmitted, and applied their intellects to it to try and resolve apparent contradictions. In the process there took shape a number of bodies of practice and precedent from which emerged theoretical articulations that, however, were always closely integrated into practice – the *uṣūl al-fiqh* – principles of *fiqh*. In a mid-historical point a part of the theoretical articulation involved a deeper study of what are called *maqāṣid* – the purposes of the *sharī'a*, which were meant to aid the thinker in exposition of the practice and precedent, and possibly also in reaching new judgments, but were never considered separate sources of legislation. One of their most famous exponents, the Mālikī scholar ash-Shāṭibī in his book *al-Muwāfaqāt*, held tenaciously to practice and precedent refusing new introductions. We mention this because in the 19th and the 20th centuries, *maqāṣid* and the *uṣūl al-fiqh*, which had emerged from the practice to explain and elaborate it, were used as separate 'principles' of legislation that were utilised to introduce new matters contrary to Sunna and actual practice. Ironically, this highly theoretical approach, which is reminiscent in character of Napoleonic law, happened under British colonial rule whose law, the Common Law, is also based on precedent and custom. But suffice it to say that a theoretical law of principles has relinquished any connection to the *dīn al-fiṭra*, has severed the connection with Sunna and practice, thus taking it into the hands of an intellectual elite who can drive it in whatever direction they wish, and our problem is that in the zone that is the topic of these chapters that elite are beholden to power and economic forces and committed to usury.

What follows is based on the practice informed by *uṣūl*. It is of the texture of the *dīn al-fiṭra*.

## Context

The Muslim world and the khalifate were conquered not by military powers but by usury capitalism, not from outside but from within by the admission of the very view of existence into Muslim hearts, families and communities.

Today, every single Muslim country and land is dominated by banks, our countries are enslaved to national debts, using paper and digital currencies, with students earnestly studying economics, banking and business administration, and going on to work for Deutsche Bank, Goldman Sachs and and Blackrock, without thinking twice about the incongruity, and often with their personal piety apparently unimpaired.

Nevertheless, along with that there has been a parallel development of interest in learning the *dīn* again, not necessarily by following the route of the madrasa and traditional studies. Therefore, increasingly there is an awareness of the issues addressed in this chapter in particular. However, something whose roots lie deep in the two or more centuries of defeat we have suffered, has emerged from Islamic modernism, embracing the very thesis that sank the khalifate: we should make modernity ours entirely at whatever cost. This has proceeded by the idea of Islamisation: let us make capitalism Islamic. The most pronounced element here has been Islamic banking. Almost the entire literature on this area is developed to this thesis and the application of this thesis. Our examination thus has to deal with the *aḥkām* rulings of the *mu'āmalāt at-tijāriyya* and their misuse by Islamic banking. In the end, after this dismal subject matter we will come to Shaykh Umar Vadillo's interesting proposals for a way forward for that industry and for the umma.

## The Heart

The Messenger of Allah ﷺ said, "Everything has a heart and the heart of Qur'ān is Yā Sīn."[2] This twofold statement attracts our attention to the merits of Sūra Yā Sīn, but its opening is important too: "everything has a heart", or we might say a core or an essence. The number of words that indicate the essence of something in Arabic are numerous and are given great stress in our tradition, for example, *dhāt* – essence, *lubb* – core, *ma'nā* – meaning, *nafs* – self, *fu'ād* and *qalb* – heart, and others.

The *mu'āmalāt* are about the interactions between brothers, and between others and brothers. However, others and strangers can all too quickly become enemies and truly 'others'.[3] The mode of being that lies behind usury was identified by Heidegger as *gestell*, translated as 'enframing' although he himself did not equate the two. That connection was made by Ibrahim Lawson:

> What follows is closely based on Heidegger's well-known essay 'The Question Concerning Technology' whose argument it repeats. In this sense, the paper may be read as a commentary on Heidegger's work. However, another aim is to uncover the parallels between technik[4] and usury/riba and to show that they are essentially the same.[5]

Enframing is a mode of being through which reality, including human beings, is forced to reveal itself as a standing reserve. This results in our entering the world and the market-place prepared for combat with enemies. Earnest businessmen in this mould study Clausewitz and Sun Tzu seeking clues to victory in the market-place, which they regard as a zero-sum game: we win you lose, or you win we lose. The opposite mentality sees others as actual or potential brothers, but not in such a naïve way as to miss the enmity of those who think in the former way.

The term *mu'āmalāt* is the plural of *mu'āmala* which ordinarily means behaviour. Shaykh Dr. Abdalqadir as-Sufi says:

> The Deen is Mu'amala, the Deen is Behaviour. "Behaviour" is not the best word, but it will do for the moment.
>
> If the Deen is nothing but correct manners and correct behaviour, it is therefore the responsibility of every Muslim to know what that is and what is expected of him.[6]

Thus *mu'āmalāt* are in fact 'behaviours'. The word derives from the root *'amal*, which means work, deed, action and indeed practice. It derives from the 3rd form of the verb, *'āmala,* which means action towards, and treatment of, another.

It is common to set up an opposition between *'ilm* and *'amal* – knowledge and action – but intriguingly both Arabic words share the same letters. Moreover, the Messenger of Allah ﷺ is reported to have said, "Whoever acts (*'amila*) according to what he knows (*'alima*), Allah will cause him to inherit a knowledge he did not know," or, "knowledge of what he did not know."[7]

A transaction is both give and take. The giving and the taking can have different intentions and different qualities. Transactions can be immediate and hand to hand or deferred, whether in payment or delivery. Deferred transactions are the ones that the *āyat* in Sūra al-Baqara (2:282) recommends[8] should be both witnessed and recorded.

The witness required in the *sharī'a* is qualified as *'adl* (plural *'udūl*) literally "just", which in Mālikī *fiqh* is someone with unquestioned integrity as well as knowledge of *fiqh*. Moroccan Mālikī *fuqahā* systematised this, producing office-bearers whose functions sometimes resemble those of notary publics in Anglo-Saxon Common Law. If people of such integrity and knowledge are lacking, Mālikī *fuqahā* make an allowance for a larger number of people of lesser standing to act as witnesses. They are called a *lafīf*, a concept which John Makdisi considers as having contributed to the establishment of the the jury system in Common Law. Although a jury is not exactly the same as a *lafīf* he makes a very good case for it having made this journey to English Common Law along with other elements of *fiqh*.[9]

But before proceeding to transactions, one must certainly pay some attention to that which is most often transacted with: money.

## Gold Dinars and Silver Dirhams

In this section the issue of the value of a currency comes to the fore, but it is well to remember the various meanings of that word 'value', and that its reduction to a merely economic sense is clearly reflective of our values in the age of nihilism.

One of the first matters in the *mu'āmalāt* of trade and commerce is the nature of the currency, because by and large we use money,[10] whether immediately as cash, payment in advance, or deferred payment i.e. credit, to buy and sell. A lack of clarity about the currency according to the *fiqh* of *mu'āmalāt* would be as if one did *wuḍū'* correctly in every detail but instead of water using milk, wine or even urine. The first chapter in the *fiqh* of purification is often on the nature of the water itself and its purity. Because of something our predecessors, the right-acting first generations (*salaf*), could not have foreseen – the introduction of currencies that they could not have imagined – we need similarly to precede our chapter on the *fiqh* of *mu'āmalāt* with a section on the nature of currency itself.

The *fuqahā*s maxim that *al-ḥukm far' at-taṣawwur* means that judgment is merely a derivative of having visualised or conceptualised the subject. In what follows, although I examine the case of gold and silver, whatever commodity is acceptable without coercion as a means of exchange is legitimate, provided that it does not contravene the *sharī'a*. If we bring the various types of currency before our mind's eye, we realise that gold and silver are actually in themselves intrinsically attractive to the human being. It is not about any utility they might have, it is just that they in themselves possess beauty. Allah says, exalted is He, in His Noble Book:

> *To mankind the love of worldly appetites is painted in glowing colours: women and children, and heaped-up mounds of gold and silver, and horses with fine markings, and livestock and fertile farmland.* (3:14)

In other words, it is part of the natural pattern (*fiṭra*) upon which Allah has created us that we find gold and silver attractive, just as it is a part of men's nature to love women and vice versa. At another level it is *shayṭān* who adorns these appetites and misleads us by them, and thus there are the traditional warnings against the appetites. But our purpose here is first of all to look at this basic attractiveness that we find in our natural patterning. Ordinarily, discussion of a currency starts with concepts such as its being a store of value and its acting as a medium of exchange, but first of all we wish to get 'underneath' these concepts to that very immediate experience.

Hülsmann of the Austrian School of Economics has this to say:

> When a medium of exchange is generally accepted in society, it is called "money." How does a commodity such as gold or silver turn into money? This happens through a gradual process, in the course of which more and more market participants, each for himself, decide to use gold and silver rather than other commodities in their indirect exchanges. Thus the historical selection of gold, silver, and copper was not made through some sort of a social contract or convention. Rather, it resulted from the spontaneous convergence of many individual choices, a convergence that was prompted through the objective physical characteristics of the precious metals. To be spontaneously adopted as a medium of exchange, a commodity must be desired for its nonmonetary services (for its own sake) and be marketable, that is, it must be widely bought and sold. The prices that are initially being paid for its nonmonetary services enable prospective buyers to estimate the future prices at which one can reasonably expect to resell it. The prices paid for its nonmonetary use are, so to speak, the empirical basis for its use in indirect exchange.[11]

Furthermore, he adds:

> The medieval scholastics called money a *res fungibilis et primo usu consumptibilis* (a thing that is fungible and primarily used in consumption). It was in the very nature of money to be a marketable thing that had its primary use in consumption.[12]

Paper money also has a lust associated with it, as is evident from popular culture and from life. People will do a great deal to gain as much of it, or of its digital equivalents, as they possibly can. But if we examine that first experience of a paper banknote, we will find that it has in itself no existential attractiveness or usefulness, but rather that our lust for it is a learned reaction because of what we have been taught to think that it 'represents'; it is a Pavlovian response. Gold and silver, in the first instance, do not represent anything else other than themselves. Even when they have not been currency, people have acquired them and adorned themselves and their loved ones with them, adorned their temples and ritual objects with them too. That was not because they *represented* something else, but for what they *are*. I am not talking here about the idea of intrinsic value, which again is an *idea* of how they might 'represent' something called value. The value of gold and silver is that originally they have no value in monetary terms. They have value because they are attractive for what they are, gold to a greater degree than silver.

This existential attractiveness is what leads to their being currencies, leads to their being units of account, stores of value, and media of exchange. Gold and silver excite in the person who comes across them a love for them and a wish to possess them. This love can of course lead to excess and matters that are reprehensible, but in itself it is the very basis of their being currency. The one who comes upon them wishes to own them. Perceiving their beauty, he wishes to have that beauty in his possession. The worst aspect of this is acquisitiveness and miserliness. However, the love of man for woman is a higher love and outweighs the love of gold and silver, and so, in giving gold to her in a marriage settlement or as a gift, he is demonstrating that the measure of his love for her is greater than his love for the metal.

Similarly, on a higher level, when someone wishes to help another, his love for helping that person becomes stronger than his acquisitiveness and leads, among other things, to him giving them gold and silver. This is as much a part of human character as the simpler acquisitiveness we have described. When such people rise to being among those who love their Lord, then they are delighted to give away many things they love, among them gold and silver. So the love of gold and silver can be expressed merely in an acquisitive way or in a whole spectrum of other ways the highest of which are *zakāt* and *ṣadaqa*.

Returning to the base level, our foundational level of the desire to own these beautiful materials, that response was also one of the matters that ostensibly prevented the Gold Dinar Movement's[13] success, because in spite of rational reasons that were advanced in favour of making them currency, people bought *dīnār*s to save and did not use them as currency. They used them for savings, dowries and other matters, but they did not become currencies to the degree that would have made a significant impact, since the rational arguments for their use as currencies was not strong enough to overcome the acquisitive desire to possess and keep them.

Nevertheless that acquisitive possessiveness is actually the basis of their use as currency. Entering the market with gold and silver actually makes man and woman conservative about their acquisitions. A purchase with their valued coins represents a gain of the object purchased but, at the same time, a loss of those coins. Balancing these two aspects is the pricing mechanism. It is entirely subjective. Things do not have set prices. The seller knows what costs were involved in his goods, and he knows the markup he would like to achieve. The buyer knows what funds he has and what he thinks he can afford to pay. The price is what happens when the buyer and seller reach that balance point in which both are pleased with what they have received for what they have given. Allah, exalted is He, characterises that as: "*'an tarāḍin minkum – by means of mutually agreed trade*" (4:29), in which *tarāḍin* means 'mutually pleasing' or 'mutually satisfactory', something almost entirely missing from contemporary financial dealings, in which, by and large, one side dictates and the other must accept the price or forgo the trade. Try to bargain in any shop today and you will not get very far. When I heard that Imām ash-Shāfi'ī regarded transactions in which there is no talk as being invalid, I mistakenly thought that it meant one should talk to shopkeepers and people at the till, in itself not a bad thing to do, but of course he meant reaching a mutually agreed price.

So entering the market-place, we are tugged in two directions: first, we are very much drawn to keeping our beautiful gold and silver coins, a desire which, in extremis, is miserliness and meanness. On the other hand, we are drawn to acquiring the things on sale, whether they be basics such as meat, fruit and vegetables, or clothing or fine luxury items. Their prices and values are established by that subjective evaluation we make of the balance between keeping our coins or acquiring the desired object and the salesperson's counterbalancing evaluation. By and large, everyday items such as meat, staples, fruit and vegetables have their known prices and we are unlikely to bargain for them, but in higher price items such as clothing, it is not uncommon, in the natural setting, for there to be some negotiation of the price. Thus it is clear that the very attractiveness of gold and silver leads to the subjective evaluation and pricing that each person makes when faced with something they are considering purchasing.

Of course, there is also the case of flous (*fulūs* singular *fals*) – the small copper coins whose value was pegged at a forty-eighth part of a silver *dirham* – and whose value was not based on the value of their copper content but set conventionally, and which were used as small change. Here we do have something that 'represents' a value, a value based on the prior value of silver. But since flous by its nature is a very small part of the money supply, we will not deal with it in great detail here, except to note that ironically the worth of their copper today is not negligible.

Debt and credit, in addition to the far from entirely moribund cash transactions that still take place, are a substantial part of modern economy. Although the *sharī'a* takes account of debt and credit and regulates them, transactions in *'ayn* (cash) weigh heavily too. When one reads the *Muwaṭṭa*'s section on buying and selling, one is at first somewhat surprised to discover a great deal of attention devoted to transactions involving delay in payment or delay in delivery of the goods, and more complex transactions some of which amount, in Imām Mālik's judgment, to loans at interest. We are here dealing with a sophisticated regulation of credit transactions since it is through them that *ribā* often enters into the picture, whereas in our time it is thought that it is only interest charges that bring that about. Although such charges are indisputably usurious, they are by no means the entirety of the matter. In other words, Imām Mālik turns his attention to the very root of the capitalist modality and he does so, moreover, from the vantage point of a civilisation that embraced commerce and had a sophisticated trade model involving debt and credit that extended across much of the earth.

Gold may only be exchanged for gold, silver for silver, wheat for wheat, and so on with all the foodstuffs that are sold by weight and measure, provided it is done like for like and hand to hand, meaning they must be exactly the same weight or measure and exchanged immediately without delay. The exception is a personal loan (*qarḍ*) which must be repaid in the exact same amount, weight or measure that was borrowed but at a different time. Gold may be exchanged for silver and vice versa, and wheat for barley etc. according to whatever exchange rate is agreed, but again it must be done hand to hand without delay. Included in that is the exchange of flous for gold or silver, and anything else that people accept as a currency, on the basis of an explicit text from Imām Mālik. The transaction must be done hand to hand, immediately without delay. This affects other things, such as the sale of jewellery online, for example. Things that are neither precious metals nor foodstuffs, such as gravel, may be exchanged in unequal amounts hand to hand, but not if there is a delay.

There are disparities and deferrals that are permitted without question: for example, in trading horses it is acceptable to trade one superb horse for a number of mediocre or lesser quality horses and for the exchange to be delayed, with one party advancing the delivery of their horse or horses and the other delivering them later at an agreed date. This is because the issue at stake is not the weight or the volume of the horse but immeasurables such as speed, strength and spirit that together go to make horsiness.

This prelude on cash and money was necessary before advancing to the details of transactions, because, as we will see, many people have overlooked this step and have erected the false edifice of 'Islamic banking' on a mistaken premise. In what follows let us explore some of the standard topics of the *mu'āmalāt* as they are presented in the works of *fiqh*, beginning with prohibitions.

### The Prohibition of Going Out to Meet the Caravans – Forestalling

Although it is too late to prevent this happening, since we neither have caravans nor markets, it is, nevertheless, something worth reflecting on and learning from. Mālik related from Abū az-Zinād from al-A'raj from Abū Hurayra that the Messenger of Allah ﷺ said, "Do not go out to meet the caravans for trade ..."[14] This happens when a trader in a market does not wait for the goods to arrive in the public area of the market-place where all the traders and the public would be on an equal footing. In our time, the goods are never brought to a market where people, both traders and customers, may bid for them but are bought at source. There are rarely any traders bringing them to market; rather there are distribution channels that bring them to shops, whether called supermarkets or hypermarkets. In other words, it is hard for us to see the significance of this prohibition since we are completely within a paradigm that is diametrically opposed to it.

And yet, not so long ago in Europe there was an identical prohibition of this practice which was known as forestalling: "The offense of forestalling the market is also an offence against public trade. This, which is also an offense at common law, is described ... to be the buying or contracting for any merchandise or victual **coming in the way to market**; or dissuading people from bringing their goods or provisions there; or persuading them to enhance the price, when there; any of which practices make the market dearer to the fair trader."[15] The concurrence between Islam, Judaism and Christianity on the ways their followers evaded the prohibitions of usury is very striking; and the original outline of acceptable trade and commerce and the prohibition of what would work against them are also almost identical.

### Hoarding or engrossing – Monopoly

The prohibition of hoarding must be distinguished from perfectly natural rhythms of nature and society such as buying enough grain at harvest time for the year. That is called *iddikhār* and is not considered to be hoarding. What is prohibited is the hoarding that is called *iḥtikār* as in the *ḥadīth* of 'Alī ﷺ, "Hoarding in a region was prohibited,"[16] which al-Munāwī explains as "buying food and keeping it so that it becomes scarce and expensive."[17] Mālik related in the *Muwaṭṭa'* that he had heard that 'Umar ibn al-Khaṭṭāb said, "There is [to be] no hoarding in our market, and men who have excess gold in their hands should not buy up one of Allah's provisions which He has sent to our courtyard and then hoard it up against us. Someone who brings imported goods through great fatigue to himself in the summer and winter, that person is the guest of 'Umar. Let him sell what Allah wills and retain what Allah wills."[18]

The reasons for the prohibition of hoarding things such as foodstuffs are fairly obvious to most people, but one of the types of hoarding is perhaps not so clear: hoarding money. Because money is meant to circulate as a medium of exchange for everyone, individuals or institutions that hoard it do cause harm to others. Among other things it will be a cause of inflation, in other words the rise in prices. One of the beneficial effects of *zakāt* is that, since it is charged on saved and hoarded wealth, *zakāt* encourages people to put their money to use, thus making it available as a medium of exchange for others. Articulating the encouragement to try and avoid having to pay *zakāt* on wealth, in this case the property of orphans under one's care, 'Umar ibn al-Khaṭṭāb said, "Trade with the property of orphans and then it will not be eaten away by *zakāt*."[19]

Hoarding money is shortsighted and harms those who do so as much as the wider society. It is important to emphasise that this benefit of *zakāt* in preventing the hoarding of gold and silver is not considered to be the reason for paying *zakāt* in the *sharī'a*. The reason is solely as a means of obeying and worshipping Allah and fulfilling the rights of those who may lawfully accept *zakāt,* such as the needy and the poor. But inarguably, the payment of it in a society does have this beneficial effect.

*Caravanserai*

The last remark of 'Umar ﵁, "Someone who brings imported goods through great fatigue to himself in the summer and winter, that person is the guest of 'Umar," reflects what was to become institutionalised in later Muslim society as the caravanserai or the *funduq* (in modern Arabic a hotel) where, because the work of traders in bringing provision from afar and, similarly, in taking local goods to other lands was considered so important, they were granted three days free hospitality and a number of other services. About this institution Humaira Shahid[20] writes:

> · A unique characteristic of the public markets is the reservation of a space for the foreign traders. In Arabic the original word for that institution is *funduq*, which today is translated as hotel, but originally it was a place to accommodate caravans.
>
> · The hospitality offered to caravans coming from other markets was expected to be reciprocated when the local caravan visited that other market. This relationship was therefore reciprocal in terms of all trading conditions including taxes (if they existed in other markets).
>
> · The caravanserais are the basis of the trading routes. From caravanserai to caravanserai, traders established routes, such as the Silk Road.
>
> · The caravanserais were established in cities and also in the countryside along the route. Many of those outposts were transformed into new settlements and eventually became cities. The caravanserais have the capacity to generate new cities.[21]

The caravanserais/*funduq*s are part of a nexus of social/economic institutions including guilds and caravans that lift the *mu'āmalāt* from the realm of the individual to the societal level.

### Engrossing

Returning to the point about hoarding, the identical practice was widely prohibited in Christendom and was known as engrossing. "By the same statute, engrossing is the getting into one's possession, or buying up, of corn or other dead victuals, with intent to sell them again. This must of course be injurious to the public, by putting it in the power of one or two rich men to raise the price of provisions at their own discretion. And the penalty for these three offenses by this statute (which is the last that has been made concerning them) is the forfeiture of the goods or their value, and two months imprisonment for the first offense; double value and six months imprisonment for the second; and, for the third, the offender shall forfeit all his goods, be set in the pillory, and imprisoned at the king's pleasure."[22]

Of course, the most striking example of hoarding, apart from the edifice of supermarkets and their monopolistic distribution channels, is the one on which the entire economic system is now built: central banks and others hoard gold and silver in order to force the use of their fiat currencies; but they also do this because they have simply been overcome with the lust the precious metals induce. It illustrates their very real benefit as 'storage of value' since both bankers and the very wealthy insist on owning them.

### *Gharar* – Uncertain and Risky Transactions

Sales are considered to contain *gharar* – uncertainty and risk – if they are not clearly defined, such as not making clear what is being bought, or how much of it, or the time of delivery etc. Such sales are prohibited by the Messenger of Allah ﷺ. Mālik said about one such case, "That is not a sale. It is taking risks and it is an uncertain transaction. It falls into the category of gambling because he is not buying something from him for something definite which he pays. Everything which resembles this is also forbidden."[23]

### Price fixing, whether by the state or a cartel

Yaḥyā ibn 'Umar said: "From Anas ibn Mālik there is that some people came to the Messenger of Allah ﷺ and said, 'Messenger of Allah, set our prices for us.' So he said, 'People, your high prices and your low prices are in the hand of Allah, glorious is He, and I hope from Allah that I meet Him without having wronged anyone in terms of wealth or in terms of blood.'"[24] The occasion is said to have been at a time of dearth and famine in Madīna.

Certainly if it is not acceptable for the authorities to set prices at times of great public need, it would be far more reprehensible for commercial cartels to do so in order to enrich themselves in ordinary times and even more so in times of scarcity.

An unexpected consequence of this is that the prices of *dīnār*s and *dirham*s may not be fixed, neither in terms of each other nor in their exchange rates with other currencies. Fixing their exchange rates was the basis of the gold standard, which many mistakenly imagine to be something praiseworthy rather than a key step towards the system that we have today.

### Undercutting and overpricing

One must necessarily follow up the above with a note about traders taking advantage of the authorities' hands being tied in terms of price setting by overpricing their goods or undercutting. Following on from the previous quote from him, Yaḥyā ibn 'Umar said: "Similarly, those of my shaykhs I named to you narrated to me from Ibn Wahb who said: 'I heard Mālik ibn Anas saying, "Do not set the price for anyone of the market people because that would be injurious wrongdoing. However, if there are ten *ṣā'*s in the market, and such a one lowers [the price] by a *ṣā'* then he must leave the market."'" Yaḥyā ibn 'Umar then said: "This is what I take and choose for myself. The price is not to be imposed on anyone, but anyone who lowers the market price must leave. 'Umar ibn al-Khaṭṭāb ﷺ did that. He said to a man selling raisins, 'Either you increase the price or you get out of our market.'"[25]

He continued on the subject of price-fixing by cartels:

> Even if the market people were to agree unanimously that they would only sell for that which they want, which they are mutually pleased with, but in which there is some harm for people, and they make a disorder in the market, then it is the duty of the man in authority to drive them out of the market. On behalf of the Muslims he should investigate that which will put them right and whose benefit will encompass them generally. He should make others go into the market; if he does that to them they will return from that which their lower selves had aspired to, such as much profit, and they will be contented with that amount of profit whose benefit they would receive, and through which they will not become involved in harming the public.[26]

So although the man in authority cannot set the price, he has a very effective measure for disciplining those who depart from the real values of the items they trade in, whether by undercutting or overpricing, by removing them from the market. Undercutting is a standard weapon in the hands of corporations to unjustly drive their competitors out of the market, in particular smaller companies who don't have the margins to compete with them.

*Supply and Demand*

Someone might ask how traders and artisans should price their goods? This brings in an important issue: supply and demand. Ivan Illich said:

> Aristotle [in the *Politics*] observed something new and unheard-of in Athens. Some citizen merchants were using a previously unknown technique when they offered their goods in the market. Instead of selling these goods at cost plus profit, or keeping to the values established by treaty with a foreign supplier, these innovators let the price vary according to offer and demand. Aristotle was fascinated

that such a transaction could take place and wondered how it worked. Polanyi was the first to recognise this.

> He assembled a team of historians at Columbia University. Each studied a different society, trying to discover when prices first began to move according to supply and demand in ordinary times. All of them reported the same finding. The replacement of simple trade by this marketing technique, though practised occasionally while being generally legally proscribed, was not part of the ordinary social life in any ancient society. Further, such an arrangement only became the form of common behavior at the time of Aristotle and after. Here I began to see the first lineaments of what is today called the economy – a system resting on scarcity.[27]

What Aristotle had observed originally – that traders sold goods 'at cost plus profit' – is the basis of pricing. This is the original nature of *murābaḥa* which Islamic bankers have appropriated as a term and altered beyond recognition. It consists simply in a trader making clear how much he paid for something and how much he would like to earn on it, it being understood that there are limits to that. One only needs to look at the extremes to understand the evil of supply and demand: during a famine, food is scarce and thus its price could conceivably rise according to this 'law' and the restricted supply and inflated demand, whether people are starving or not. Across the world today when relatively prosperous people would like to live in a beautiful scenic setting their move there affects the property prices for local residents, making life there unlivable for them because of the rise in prices. However, this is not their fault directly, but the fault of the residents of that country who see a chance to get more for their property.

### Positive aspects of *mu'āmalāt*

So far we have focused on negative issues such as *ribā,* but now we must turn to recommended and approved practices of actual Muslim commerce. The reason for proceeding in this way is the *ḥadīth* of the

Messenger of Allah ﷺ: Abū Hurayra 'Abd ar-Raḥmān ibn Ṣakhr ؓ said, "I heard the Messenger of Allah ﷺ saying, 'That which I forbid you, avoid it, and that which I command you, do of it what you are able, for the only thing that destroyed the ones who were before you was their great numbers of questions and their disagreements with their Prophets.'" Al-Bukhārī and Muslim narrated it.[28]

Avoiding what is prohibited is unqualified, but engagement with the positive commands is commensurate with one's abilities.

### *Qirāḍ/Muḍāraba* and Trust (*Īmān*)

This is a one-time loan of cash by an investor to an agent – cash being defined by Ibn Juzayy al-Kalbī as gold *dīnār*s and silver *dirhams*[29]. Note here that the investor, unlike in parasitic capitalism, does not require collateral from the agent. In not doing that he is exemplifying the trust corresponding to the agent's necessary embodiment of *amāna* – trustworthiness. Among the meanings of *īmān* are "trusting, or confiding, or having trust or confidence,"[30] and "becoming true to the trust (*amāna*)" is "the primary meaning" of *īmān*.[31] A Madīnan order is a society based on trust, both in the Divine and in His slaves. Nevertheless, in the *sharī'a* the investor has legal recourse if the agent is cavalier or careless or if he embezzles.

The investor cannot set the object of trade for the agent, or the time when he expects his money back. When the agent returns and sells what he was trading in, he returns the capital and they divide up the profits according to the previously agreed proportions. If there is a loss, the investor must bear it unless it was due to the agent's wrongdoing or proven incompetence. Depending on the scale of the transaction, the agent may support himself from the capital during his travels.

A university study for the American recording industry said that if they control distribution they control the industry. In other words, worried about black American recording artists showing some independence and wishing to start their own record labels or re-negotiate their contracts, the academics advised the recording industry not to be concerned about that, because if they controlled the distribution of recordings they would control the record industry. Distribution is the key to an aspect of capitalism, and thus conversely to the work of the trader.

The genuine trader opens up what has been monopolised by distribution channels. He is not made redundant by their existing. Indeed they make his presence and work even more urgent. Today's distribution channels bring English people tasteless apples from Canada and South Africa, which were probably delicious in their homelands, while at the same time English apple-growers cannot sell their delicious apples, in all their extraordinary varieties, in England. A trader could take those apples from orchards in Suffolk to markets in Norfolk – he would not need to go to Canada or China for his goods. But this of course is interrelated with the establishment of free markets. Indeed, all the aspects of genuine open trade are interrelated.

### Caravans versus distribution

Humaira Shahid expands the work of the single agent who undertakes *qirāḍ* and connects it to the activities of the caravan:

> A caravan is a guild of traders. Members shared logistic infrastructure like warehouses, trading licences, security and means of transport. They also vouched for each other, creating a common liability. If a member leaves a payment unpaid, all other members will undertake the responsibility for the payment. Caravans are inclusive, allowing small traders to participate in export trading. They are financed by *qirāḍ*.[32]

Along with the guilds, caravans are what lift *mu'āmalāt* from the individual level to the societal. Indeed, according to Humaira Shahid the caravan itself was the first guild. But distribution is the opposite of the caravan. That is when a company or corporation themselves get their products, not to market, but to outlets owned by themselves or other corporations. A market, on the other hand, is where there is free trade.

### *Mushāraka* – Partnership

It is well known that when the Messenger of Allah ﷺ emigrated to Madīna along with the *muhājirūn* of Quraysh, he established a bond of brotherhood between them and the Muslims of Madīna. About that brotherhood Imām al-Ghazālī wrote:

> Know that the contract of brotherhood is a bond between two persons, like the contract of marriage between two spouses. For just as marriage gives rise to certain duties which must be fulfilled when it is entered into, so does the contract of brotherhood confer upon your brother a certain right touching your property, your person, your tongue and your heart – by way of forgiveness, prayer, sincerity, loyalty, relief and considerateness.[33]

It is often said that marriage is the core of society, but one cannot neglect the ways in which men are bonded to each other. Although not as elevated as pure brotherhood for the sake of Allah, the commercial relationship of partnership shares many of its attributes. Like all of the *mu'āmalāt* it is infused with the noble qualities of *futuwwa*. Specifically it is definitely not a legal device that allows the 'Islamic bank' to enter into a 'partnership' with you and charge you what is usury in all-but-name.

Partnership sub-divides into two: *māliyya* and *badaniyya*. The first is a financial partnership, in which the partners put their *dīnār*s and *dirham*s together. This has two alternatives: that either partner may dispose freely of the common fund without consulting the other; or that the partners may only do so after consulting together. An example of such a partnership would be where partners put their funds together to buy equipment and materials, and employ craftsmen and workers to produce items for sale. A partnership that is *badaniyya* is a physical partnership, usually in terms of some skills the partners have in common, for example C++ programming or web-design. Properly speaking a graphic designer cannot form a partnership with a programmer. Partnership should be between people with the same skill. Mālikīs stipulate that they work in the same workshop.

In contrast to partnerships one might consider stocks and shares, which are thought of by many as fulfilling the requirements of the *sharī'a* because risk is shared and there is no fixed return. But in essence what is at issue here is the different understanding of contracts. In *sharī'a* a contract is something that persons make verbally with each other, which is witnessed and recorded. In other words it takes place between some people and is an actual agreement to cooperate and work together. A written record is not a contract. It cannot be bought or sold, which is what is essentially happening with stocks and shares. But more fundamentally, there is no *ḥalāl* way to earn passively on invested funds apart from *qirāḍ/muḍāraba*, which is only for actual trading. Partnership involves joint ownership and participating and working together.

### GUILDS

The larger organisation of Muslim professional life takes place through the guilds, the first of which was the caravan. The Muslims adapted Persian and Roman models, filtering them through the *sharī'a.* Humaira Shahid writes: "Muslims adapted the existing Roman and Persian model of guild and – as they did with the markets and the caravans – refined it and improved it by adding the wisdom of Islamic Law.

> AL ANDALUS: They took the *'amal* of the ahl al-Madīna to the West (Mālikī *fiqh*). From the early days, Andalusian guilds became a feature of Andalusian culture. They emerged from the commons of the *sūq*

and cooperation culture of the caravans. They became the seed of the medieval revival of guild culture in Europe.

OTTOMAN EMPIRE: The Ottoman Turks embraced the guilds. The guild system of the *ahilik* rose in Anatolia from the 13th century onwards. By the 19th century practically all of the work force in Istanbul belonged to a guild."[34]

Doubtless there are those who will say that if the Muslims adapted existing societal and commercial structures such as guilds to *ḥalāl* purposes, we should do the same with banks and stock exchanges. There are, however, insuperable obstacles to that: the nature of the currency, which we have looked at in detail, and the reality that there is a fundamental contradiction between accepting deposits that depositors can reclaim whenever they wish, and taking money to invest and providing a return (and we don't even need to talk about the prohibition of interest), in which case the depositor cannot simply withdraw his funds whenever he wishes. Then we could also note the regulatory obligation for the bank to lodge funds in the central bank, at interest, and we are adding insuperable obstacle to obstacle. There may be elements of modern banking that we have to look at, such as the transfer of funds over distances, but the institution itself is irredeemable.

### *Murabāḥa*

This is a sale in which the person selling discloses how much the item cost him and how much markup he wants, whether as an actual figure or a percentage. Of course, 'Islamic bankers' have appropriated the term for quite different ends. But, as we noted already, this shows a completely different approach to pricing from that embodied in the concept of "supply and demand", which simply authorises greed allowing people to price things according to what they can get rather than from an actual evaluation of what their products are worth and the markup they would like to receive.[35]

### A digression on terminologies

We have seen how 'Islamic finance' and 'Islamic banking' appropriate terms from the *mu'āmalāt* and reuse them in ways they were never intended for and in ways that are quite inappropriate. The following illustrates the mentality behind this approach. A group of us attended the inaugural BRAIS – British Association of Islamic Studies – conference in Edinburgh in 2014.[36] In one presentation, two gentlemen introduced a new *ṣukūk* instrument they had devised. When it came time for Q & A, I asked in a very neutral manner, and genuinely wanting to know, what the relationship was between the *ṣukūk* mentioned in the *Muwaṭṭa'*, which were chits for food to be taken from the market the sale of which before taking possession of the food is considered usury, the *ṣukūk* that some have said were used by the Muslims and are said to be the origin of our cheques, and the *ṣukūk* that they had just presented. For some reason, the question threw them into disarray and they conferred together before admitting that there was no relationship between their usage of the term and the historical usages, but it was just an Arabic term they liked. The 'Islamic finance industry' is usually this cavalier with its use of terms.

Returning to our examination of prohibited as well as recommended and endorsed types of trade and economic activity, we will look at land usage, first prefacing that with some general remarks on land and its importance.

### Land usage

A city is part of a region, which includes the arable and pastoral land around a city and often within it, as well as the hinterland around that. Madīna appears to have been very much what we would call a 'garden city' with orchards and other agricultural areas within it. Some of the land within and around a city would have been common land and there were also *awqāf*, which later would comprise a great part of Anatolian Osmanlı land. While a sane balance in land ownership has always included a great number of commons and public spaces, it is certainly not, in the *sharī'a*, prohibited to own land, nor is it prohibited to rent it out. What is prohibited is to rent it out in return for produce from that land, a practice which is probably as old as the first cities in Mesopotamia and inevitably resulted not just in the indebtedness and then slavery of the debtors, but, in the end, in the collapse of the society, which some have said may not have been a bad outcome.[37]

### RENTING LAND FOR CROPS – *MUḤĀQALA*

We have from the *Muwaṭṭa'*: "Yaḥyā related to me from Mālik from Dāwūd ibn al-Ḥusayn from Abū Sufyān, the *mawlā* of Ibn Abī Aḥmad, from Abū Sa'īd al-Khudrī that the Messenger of Allah ﷺ forbade *muzābana* and *muḥāqala*. *Muzābana* is selling fresh dates for dried dates while they were still on the trees. *Muḥāqala* is renting land in exchange for wheat."[38] Although renting land for wheat to be paid at harvest time is prohibited, to rent it for gold or silver is not, and cropsharing agreements between a landowner and someone who works the land are permissible.

*Musāqā* (cropsharing) means literally "watering" or "irrigation" and can consist, for example, in tending date-palms. It is better not to translate it as "share-cropping", because that was a usurious scheme used in the US to trap newly freed slaves in usurious debt that was often worse than the slavery they had just been released from. They worked a piece of land in exchange for so many bags of the crop to be paid at harvest, bought tools and seed in exchange for so many bags of the crop to be paid at harvest time, and bought food for their family in exchange for so many bags of the crop to be paid at harvest time.

> African Americans had been promised forty acres and a mule when the War was over; they didn't get them but the plantations were broken up into small farms. Those who couldn't purchase farms could rent them, or they could work a 'share': in return for their 'furnishings' of a mule, equipment, a hut and basic foods, they could work a plot of land, paying off their debt with their labour and giving half their produce to the landowner. A new system of slavery, share-cropping peonage, came into being.[39]

Burdened with crushing unpayable debts they were forced to migrate to the industrial centres of the north where they were equally exploited. The whole affair was merely the transfer of slaves from an agrarian economy to work in an industrial one under conditions no better than the slavery from which they had just escaped, and in some cases worse. On the other hand, in the case of Islam, cropsharing was a known Madīnan agreement which is carefully regulated in the *fiqh*. [Mālik said]: "Cropsharing is contracted on the basis that all the care and expense is outlayed by the cropsharer, and the owner of the property is not obliged to do anything. This is the accepted method of cropsharing."

After the Conquest of Khaybar, the Prophet ﷺ left the inhabitants in possession of their lands in exchange for a share of their crops. This is the first example of cropsharing cited in the *Muwaṭṭa'*. Later, after the conquest of Iraq with its vast date-palm groves, the Companions might have expected the land to be distributed among them as *ghanīma* – spoils. 'Umar ؓ took the unusual decision to confirm the people of Iraq on their land in return for their payment of *kharāj* – a share of the crops – or, in lieu of it, *dīnārs* or *dirhams*. This wasn't precisely cropsharing but certainly bears some resemblance to it.

For thoroughness, we could not leave this chapter without considering one issue of our age: cryptocurrencies.

## Bitcoin and cryptocurrencies

A cryptocurrency is a mathematical entity. Mathematical entities are objects of the mind but they don't *exist*, since existence is "from *ex-* 'out' + *sistere* 'take a stand". You can show me two sheep, three apples or four politicians, but you can never show me 2, 3 or 4. You can buy 2 sheep, 3 apples or 4 politicians but you cannot buy the numbers 2, 3, or 4. Historically, in the period before cryptocurrencies emerged, many people who were disillusioned with the economic system of capitalism promoted gold and silver. However capitalists were able to manipulate those markets, so those people quite suddenly gave up on gold and silver and began promoting cryptocurrencies.

The argument of cryptocurrency advocates is that fiat currency is much worse than cryptocurrency and that a cryptocurrency is a way of using an alternative currency that is not under the control of the banks. That may certainly have been thought to be their potential in the early days but many of the major institutions, banks and hedge funds piled into the cryptocurrency market and contributed to their meteoric rise in value. Of course, if they similarly get out of the market, they will contribute to a catastrophic collapse in value, and they are not above doing that quite deliberately.

There is little doubt that for a great many people who buy cryptocurrencies – both private individuals and institutional investors – their attraction is the possibility of their steep rise in value. Perversely, for others, whom the first group rarely understand, their attraction is precisely the opposite: their potential for precipitous loss in value, which people who short stocks and shares love in the way other people love cocaine. In either case it has exactly the same profile as gambling.

I consulted two studies by Muslims on the issue of Bitcoin.[40] Both are clearly written, earnestly looking for ways for Muslims to become free of *ribā*. What they overlook is the way that huge entities such as hedge funds bought into cryptocurrencies and the ease with which such entities can destroy them by dumping their stock. Thus in 2022 cryptocurrency exchanges were racked by scandals, crashes and bankruptcies.

### Blockchain

Blockchain is the underlying technology of cryptocurrencies. Theoretically it could be a means of expediting and recording transactions particularly over distances, and thus there is little doubt that it could be used to record transactions using gold and silver, the *dīnār* and the *dirham*. The issues involved in this are beyond the scope of this work without further research, but they certainly demand further study.

Some are hoping to utilise blockchain as a register of transactions because it is intrinsically *public and open to inspection* but an issue here is that although registered, the transaction is not *witnessed* by humans, let alone by *'udūl* witnesses of integrity, knowledge and competence, or even a *lafīf* of lesser witnesses. The second issue is whether one wants a permanent record of all transactions. Clearly, were the state, or indeed other actors such as the burgeoning surveillance capitalist techno-elite that Shoshana Zuboff has written about,[41] to come into possession of this data – and both parties are intent on doing that – then the negative possibilities are innumerable. Aisha Bewley writes: "And the surveillance capitalists have indeed declared our private transactions and experience to be theirs once they have been rendered into the form of data. They exploit us as a resource. You aren't even the consumers anymore, but the consumed."[42]

But the issue is more profound than even a dystopian Orwellian future, forbidding though such a future would be. It is about the way that systems undermine and then replace trust. Underscoring the concerns expressed by Zuboff and Aisha Bewley above, the former writes: "Information scholars Primavera De Filippi and Benjamin Loveluck conclude that contrary to popular belief, 'Bitcoin is neither anonymous nor privacy-friendly... anyone with a copy of the blockchain can see the history of all Bitcoin transactions... every transaction ever done on the Bitcoin network can be traced back to its origin.'" Then she continues: "Such systems rely on 'perfect information,' but the kinds of coordination processes that build open democratic societies, such as 'social trust' or 'loyalty,' are 'expunged' in favor of 'a profoundly market-driven approach.'"[43]

What are De Filippi and Loveluck saying? Systems such as blockchain are designed to circumvent the need for 'trust' and so, in the process, they undermine it. Whereas everything we have looked at is based on trust and hinges on restoring and rebuilding it – individually, in the family, and socially – blockchain is designed to contribute to an automated future in which trust will simply be unnecessary. But trust is one of the meanings of *īmān*.

Foremost among those who are actively embracing new technologies such as blockchain and AI is Umar Vadillo. I came across his most recent work[44] on this area shortly before going to publication and have not been able to digest its implications in time for this book, but unhesitatingly recommend study of it for those who would welcome a genuinely radical – in the sense of getting to the real roots of things – and challenging approach.

### *Awqāf* endowments & the Commons

The *mu'āmalāt* are predicated on a view of existence in which *īmān* and trust are paramount, and *awqāf* endowments and the commons are perfect illustrations of that.

Two concepts and practices – *awqāf* endowments and the commons – come together fruitfully here. A *waqf* (sing. of *awqāf*) is an endowment established for the sake of some noble purpose whose ownership is relinquished by the founder in perpetuity and a legal document with its terms lodged with the *qāḍī*. The *waqf* belongs to Allah and may not be expropriated, neither by local or national government nor by private or commercial interests, although the history of the 20th century was precisely one of that expropriation, whether outright or through the intermediary of Ministries of *Awqāf*, that in essence placed *awqāf* under governmental control, such as Egypt's control of the Azhar by means of its *awqāf*.

The commons denote those matters that are of common concern to the society and thus the property of no single entity. One example was grazing land on which people could pasture their flocks and herds, or gather firewood. *Awqāf* are properties of some public utility including those which yield an income devoted to a good purpose. They also include mosques and market-places neither of which yields income. When we evoke the idea of the commons, we acknowledge that we are in an era in which local and national government and commercial interests have expropriated them much as they did the *awqāf*, so that the concept hardly exists. Socialism stepped into the gap and thus created and posited national ownership of such commons, including, in the UK, the railways, the original telephone company, water utilities and so on. However, that is located within the Western worldview that assigns sovereignty to "the people". In the sleight of hand that is parliamentary democracy, sovereignty was transferred to the banking and corporate classes through their acolytes the political class in the name of "the people". Moreover it fell as a casualty to the dialectic of "freedom" versus a controlling state, freedom having been re-interpreted as freedom from control and regulation, which is an absurd position when that very freedom is legislated, and its advocates obey a thousand controls and regulations without demur. Of course, it is understandable to wish to be outside the despotism of the state. So it is necessary to step outside of the dialectic of personal freedom versus the state, and we don't wish to admit the latter via the backdoor of "the common good".

*Awqāf* provide an intermediate step: they are neither privately owned nor controlled by the state. Regrettably, with the adoption of the nation-state model by Muslims, the *awqāf* were seized, and at best we saw Ministries of *Awqāf* emerge. Thus, the independence of the Azhar, which had been sustained by its *awqāf* for centuries, was finished, and its *fatwās* consequently became more and more problematic. For example, a correspondent recently told me that when faced with the choice between taking a banking job or going abroad for work, he had contacted the Azhar for a *fatwā* and had been told that he should take the banking job, which they thought unproblematic.

In terms of *awqāf*, an example is medicine, which was often made available to people in Muslim societies through *awqāf*, particularly in the long history of the Osmanlı who established public medicine for Muslims and non-Muslims based on *awqāf*. There is no particular problem with private practice in medicine except that there must be clarity about what the patient is paying for and how much and when. For example, if he is paying for a cure, then the doctor should only be paid when he gets better, but not if he doesn't. There is also the issue of liability for mistakes and errors of judgment. So, as in all transactions, there needs to be clarity about what is being paid for and how much and when it is due. The provision of medical treatment is particularly suitable for the *awqāf* model, as the very basis of medical studies is doing something to alleviate people's suffering. Similarly, with education. In its essence it is quite different from providing a product. It is questionable, and a matter over which people of knowledge differ, whether it is permissible to charge for knowledge. Leaving that aside, education is clearly a matter very suited to the *awqāf* model, as evidenced throughout Muslim history.

As Professor Mehmet Maksudoğlu shows, the *waqf* was at the very centre of Muslim society right through the time of the Osmanlı, a great part of whose commercial property and agricultural land was *waqf* property devoted to the general welfare of society as a whole. There is perhaps no other institution as emblematic of Muslim civilisation as that of the *waqf*. Prof. Maksudoğlu writes:

> In short, as Ibrāhīm Hakki states, "The Muslim Turks dedicated *waqf*s for all sorts of human needs; it would take a long time to mention all of them and would fill an enormous number of books." They dedicated *waqf*s for widows, for poor girls to purchase brides' trousseau, for travellers, for arranging the funerals of the poor and destitute without relations, for the slaves, for feeding birds in winter when they could not find anything under the snow, for providing nurses to look after the children of working women, for looking after poor and orphaned children, for their education as well, for providing replacements for pitchers broken by children and servants, and for covering mucus on roads with ashes. Men were paid by the *kül vakfi* (*waqf* of ash) to patrol streets, roads, lanes in the cities and towns, according to their assignments. When they saw anyone spitting saliva or phlegm, without saying anything to him they would simply cover it with ash taken with a wooden spoon from a saddle-bag carried on the shoulder.
>
> *Wāqif*s would build nice looking places for birds on the walls of their mosques and other buildings. A certain Mürseli Aga dedicated a *waqf* in Ödemish, western Anatolia, to storks that remained behind the flock because of illness, etc. He dedicated the revenue of his *waqf* to feed the birds on liver, lung and tripe. Another *wāqif* dedicated the revenue of his *waqf* to the birds that came into the towns and cities in winter looking for something to eat. Many people had small basins made on their tombs to provide water for birds.[45]

To complete this topic let us mention *sadaka tashlari* (stones/pillars for the poor). A *sadaka tasi* was a one and half metre high stone or pillar with a smooth or concave surface on top. For *ṣadaqa*, charitable people would put some money on top of it. Then, after 'Ishā when everyone went home, those who needed money would go and take it, saving their honour, without coming together, not knowing one another. Some of the *ṣadaqa tasi* had lids or covers so that people could not see whether a person was putting money in or taking it out.[46]

### Islamic Banking – the Trojan Horse in the Heart of the Sharī'a, or, If the wolf pays the shepherd what hope is there for the sheep?

Why should we consider Islamic banking and Islamic finance to be worse than usury, which we have already established to be of the utmost seriousness? That is because it is introducing something *ḥarām* into the heart of the *sharī'a*, and making it a part of Islam itself, which is much worse than simply doing something that is *ḥarām*. We Muslims take the issue of innovation very seriously even when it involves something which in itself seems quite innocent, but when it is something utterly unacceptable it is a terrible matter. The *'ulamā* who enable this are criminals of the highest order who are changing the *sharī'a* for their own worldly gain. Those who have introduced usury into the *sharī'a* itself have done so in order to make money. The Messenger of Allah ﷺ said:

> "Woe to my *umma* from the *'ulamā as-sū'* – the scholars of evil."[47]

And in another narration:

> "Woe to my *umma* from the *'ulamā as-sū'* – the scholars of evil who take this knowledge as a trade which they sell to the people in command in their time for a profit for themselves, may Allah not give any profit to their trade."[48]

When we realise that the people who are 'in command' in this age are not the political class, neither here in the West nor in the East, but bankers, financiers and corporatists, then it becomes clear who the *'ulamā as-sū'* of today are: the scholars of Islamic finance and banking.

A study of the scholars working in the field of so-called 'Islamic Finance' has shown:

> There are over 400 sharia scholars (sic)[49] worldwide but only around 15 to 20 prominent and experienced ones, which creates demand for scholars to sit on multiple boards. The top 20 scholars hold 14 to 85 positions each, occupying a total of around 620 board positions or 55 percent of the industry.
>
> And this leads to sky-high fees paid to the top scholars. A senior banker at an Islamic lender said some scholars could be paid $1,000 to $1,500 per hour of consultation -- in addition to an annual bonus of between $10,000 and $20,000 per board seat.[50]

This is unacceptable not simply because of the scale of the self-enrichment, but because to take even one rupee in payment for a *fatwā* that empowers banking is utterly intolerable. The disaster of Islamic banking and Islamic finance, which are merely means by which the super banking entities and corporations get access to the wealth of the Muslims, has been facilitated by scholars who help them in this process.

The banks, including 'Islamic' ones, take collateral for lending money that they created from nothing at the point of lending it. If and when the loan fails they take the collateral. In this way, vast swathes of Muslim wealth are being swallowed up by the banking system. These 'scholars' are serving super-*kāfir* entities such as HSBC[51] and Goldman Sachs[52] who are determined to plunder Islam and its people as they have plundered the world.[53] Some of the transactions used by Islamic banking are as follows:

*Bay' al-'īna*

Ibn Juzayy al-Kalbī says: "Regarding the sale [known as] *'īna*, which is that two parties do something which appears to be permitted in order to arrive at something that is not permitted, in which case it is prohibited on account of the suspicion [attached to it] on the basis of *sadd adh-dharā'i'* – blocking the means to arrive at something illegal...." Ibn Juzayy gives an example: "That one man says to the other: 'buy a commodity for me for such-and-such and I will allow you such-and-such a profit on it', or he says: 'buy it for ten and I will give you fifteen for it later' for this may be understood as *ribā* ..."[54]

Most of the transactions of Islamic banking consist of exactly this transaction, although sometimes given a bewildering variety of Arabic names. The commodity could, in our contemporary situation, be a house or a car or just some basic commodity for trade. A very key matter in some of these deplorable approaches to *fiqh* is to accept formalities at their face value even if the intention behind them is to circumvent the law and achieve something reprehensible. Ibn Juzayy continues: "...because the *madhhab* of Mālik is to examine what leaves someone's hand and what it then receives, and the intermediary steps are nullified – for it is as if this man gave someone ten *dīnār*s and took fifteen from him with delay, the commodity being the invalid means."[55] In other words, intention does matter and using some combination of transactions to achieve something reprehensible is itself reprehensible. In the case Ibn Juzayy outlines, no goods change hands. The whole thing was a subterfuge to get a loan and to pay interest for it. Sometimes the bank's client does actually want to buy a commodity of some sort, but for the bank the transaction is simply a means to lend the client money and take interest from them, although calling it something different.

*Two Sales in One*

Mālik [said] that he had heard that the Messenger of Allah ﷺ forbade two sales in one sale.[56] There is unanimity (*ijmā'*) among the people of *fiqh* regarding this prohibition. Mālik illustrates this prohibition with the following example: "Yaḥyā related to me from Mālik that he had heard that a man said to another, 'Buy this camel for me immediately so that I can buy it from you on credit.' 'Abdullāh ibn 'Umar was asked about that and he disapproved of it and forbade it."[57] Again, the point here is that the camel doesn't change hands, but someone receives money and promises to repay it with extra. This is exemplified on a gargantuan scale by the repo agreement.[58]

*Tawarruq*

This transaction simply compounds the two sales in one by making it three or more sales in one, as if by this piece of footwork the result would become acceptable. If two sales in one is unanimously agreed to be prohibited, adding a third is simply doubling down on the wrongdoing. The intention is only for someone to gain some funds and pay interest for the use of the funds. If it was not defiance of the Divine prohibition of usury, it would almost be comic that someone could imagine that by this devious trick of bringing in a third party, the act of paying money for the use of money would become legal. Remember that originally the term 'usury' was a euphemism indicating paying for the 'use' of money. It was a rationalisation of something abominable, but the abomination then became attached to the word itself.

*Murābaḥa*

This was originally a simple sale, but it was changed into a 'mode of financing' by Mufti Taqi Usmani.[59] Originally, as he makes clear in his book *an Introduction to Islamic Finance, murābaḥa* is that someone sells something that he possesses, declaring his costs *and* the profit he wishes to make, whether a lump sum or a percentage of the costs. Mufti Taqi says about sale in general, for example:

> Rule 2. The subject of sale must be in the ownership of the seller at the time of sale.[60]

This is one of the rulings supported by the hadith from multiple sources: "do not sell what you do not possess."[61] In more detail, an account is narrated by Imam Mālik in the *Muwaṭṭa'* about 'Abdullāh ibn 'Umar ﷺ:

> 45 Yaḥyā related to me from Mālik that he had heard that a man wanted to buy food from a man in advance. The man who wanted to sell the food to him went with him to the market and he began to show him heaps, saying, "Which one would you like me to buy for you?" The buyer said to him, "Are you selling me what you do not have?" So they went to 'Abdullāh ibn 'Umar and mentioned that to him. 'Abdullāh ibn 'Umar said to the buyer, "Do not buy from him what he does not have." He said to the seller, "Do not sell what you do not have."[62]

Clearly here 'Abdullāh ibn 'Umar is giving judgment according to the former Prophetic hadith without citing it although using the identical wording, a practice that was very common among the Companions. But what is equally clear is that this prohibition is related particularly to foodstuffs that are bought and sold by weight or measure, and is not a general prohibition. What underscores that connection is that the considerable section of hadith gathering together here in the *Muwaṭṭa'* are on the subject of the prohibition of selling food before having it in one's possession.

The Prophet ﷺ forbade selling food before taking possession of it. (A result of that is that futures markets in foodstuffs are also prohibited.) This prohibition was the reason the Companions objected to the sale of chits (*ṣukūk*) at the time when Marwān was governor of Madīna.[63] The chits were issued representing foodstuffs that the Muslims could collect from the market. Selling the chits, therefore, was selling foodstuffs before actually having received them.

The prohibition of futures markets in foodstuffs if enacted today would have great benefits for many people on the earth. For example, studies on the cocoa market showed that while chocolate prices were steadily rising, the producers were receiving less and less, pitching workers into conditions akin to slavery. The producers had been persuaded in some countries to abandon their collective bargaining power and adopt an every-man-for-himself approach, but then they found themselves competing with each other and being forced to accept less and less for their cocoa beans. Where was the money going? In between them and the chocolate market was the futures market which was selling cocoa crops years in advance and speculating in them numerous times before the beans were even close to harvest, with a small group of speculators sucking up the great majority of the wealth without doing any work for it whatsoever. Of course, this process is now governed by algorithms and can happen multiple times a minute.

Similarly, in the signal events of 2022 and the rising prices of energy and wheat etc., futures markets in many commodities were busily adding to the chaos. In addition, a great part of the inflation was a consequence of the vast amounts of fiat money created during the Covid pandemic and pumped into the system.

Thus, foodstuffs of this description which are not owned by the seller cannot be sold before receiving them in full. If he sells them before acquiring their ownership the sale is void.

Writing in a general sense, Mufti Taqi Usmani transformed *murābaḥa* into a mode of financing in which the purchaser who wants to buy a commodity, offers to buy the aforesaid items and allows the seller a profit. He says, for example:

> 6. The best way for murabahah, according to Shari'ah, is that the financier himself purchases the commodity and keeps it in his own possession, or purchases the commodity through a third person appointed by him as agent, before he sells it to the customer.

Because different things might fulfil the category of 'commodity' there is an ambiguity here, for commodities do not all have the same ruling. But because foodstuffs comprise a tremendous amount of world trade, the unspecificity of the wording is problematic. If he refers to weighable and measurable foodstuffs, then this is an unacceptable transaction. This, however, would be a genuine *murābaḥa* sale if 'the financier' had acted as an entrepreneur and gone out and bought the commodity, and then sold it, declaring the costs and adding a markup. What has really happened is that the customer has suggested that he would like to buy that specific commodity if the financier purchases it. This is a clear example of selling something before having it one's possession: "you buy that commodity and I will purchase it from you," which in the case of weighable and measurable foodstuffs is not permitted.

It is important to note that this is only one objection to this transaction, although this objection is fatal. For example, in reality 'the financier' is often a bank, a fractional reserve entity that is deeply usurious on every level.[64] Banks also accept 'deposits' from customers, in which case it would only be permissible to store those deposits and charge something for doing so. However, then it 'invests' them and shares the proceeds with the customer. So which is it doing? Is it holding the deposits safely for the customer who may withdraw them whenever they need, or investing them, in which case he may not withdraw them until the 'investment' reaches its term and the funds are divided between them?[65]

*The unilateral promise*

Ammar Fairdous writes about Islamic banks trying to circumvent the prohibition in the hadith: "do not sell what you do not possess."

> This state of affairs left the moneylenders with the problem of how to continue to secure the guarantee of a fixed return from such sale arrangements whilst meeting the legal requirement of not selling what is not in one's possession – a requirement that all Muslim jurists are agreed upon. Interestingly, the IFIs with the help of their Sharia boards

> have managed to achieve this in modern times by requiring the would-be purchaser to make a legally binding 'promise' (instead of concluding a prohibited future-sale contract) that he will buy the commodity in question once it is owned by them. Otherwise, if the promise is not fulfilled, he will be forced to pay all the relevant costs incurred.[66]

Because there is unanimity that one may not contract to sell what one does not possess in the case of weighable and measurable foodstuffs, Islamic bankers take a unilateral promise from the client to purchase such a commodity, if and when the bank buy it. Thus the client of the bank makes a unilateral promise that if the bank purchases such-and-such a commodity, for example, he will buy it from them with such-and-such a markup. The promise allows the bank to sell what it does not yet own, which in the case of weighable and measurable foodstuffs is forbidden. They insist on this promise because otherwise, they would be at risk in buying the commodity, as the client might change his mind and refuse to buy it.

The unilateral promise is utilised as a *ḥīla* device to circumvent the prohibition of the financier or bank selling a weighable or measurable foodstuff it does not own, which the Messenger of Allah ﷺ forbade.

*The core issue: the legitimation of paper and fiat money*

But there is an even more fundamental contribution to the issue of introducing usury into the heart of the *sharī'a*. As we have seen, currency is the very core of the matter. While people worry nervously about interest payments on money, they overlook the fact that the money itself is such a monstrous example of usury as to make interest look comparatively innocent.

If we examine the existential encounter with paper currencies, what is the nature of that experience? What is a bit of paper? First, it is something which in itself is worth very little indeed, if anything at all. It becomes dirty and grubby. It burns. Its worth consists entirely in being able to write on it, but if it is already written upon, even that worth has gone. What difference does it make to write something on it? The writing represents in the circumstances we are looking at some form of contractual arrangement. However, in our *sharīʿa* a contract is between two parties, and is a witnessed transaction and agreement between them, which, for thoroughness, is recorded in writing. As there have not been two parties at the issuance of paper money, the writing on it represents a unilateral promise on the part of one of the parties. Nevertheless, even that paper promise means nothing at all in the *sharīʿa* since it is the witnessed agreement that matters, not a piece of paper. At one time, the promise was "I promise to pay the bearer on demand the sum of £x" as in the case of the British currency, a declaration that it still carries even though that promise will no longer be honoured.

Fiat currencies that do promise to pay the bearer a sum of real money on demand are making a promise that is not legally enforceable according to the majority of the *fuqahā*, but in any case, writing it on a piece of paper is not in itself a contract. A true contract is between the two parties and is witnessed and then recorded in writing.

In a research paper, ʻAbdullāh ibn Sulaymān ibn Manīʻ writes:

> There is a wisdom particularly for the occurrence of *ribā* in the two coins, which Ibn al-Qayyim, may Allah be merciful to him, pointed out in *Iʻlām al-mūqiʻīn* when he said: "Because dirhams and dinars are the prices of things sold. The price is the standard by which the values of properties are recognised. Thus it is necessary that it should be defined exactly, neither rising nor falling, since if the price were to rise and fall like goods, we would not have a price with which to reckon items for sale, but on the contrary everything would become goods, whereas the need people have for a price with which to evaluate items bought and sold is a universal imperative need. That is only possible with a price by means of which the value is known, and that only exists with a price by

means of which things are valued and which remains in a single state, and which is not valued by something else."[67]

Gold and silver coins over many centuries do retain their value, but not because they have been fixed or set by an external authority. Thus, even in Muslim societies, there have been times when the coins' values temporarily fluctuated against each other and against the values in the market place, and this is as it should be, for as we have seen prices "are in the hand of Allah,"[68] and that includes the prices of money itself. Money does not represent an objective and invariable pricing mechanism and never has. Nevertheless, there has been nothing more stable than gold and silver in this respect.

Mufti Taqi Usmani, in his paper delivered at the World Economic Forum in Davos, Switzerland, in 2010, says about gold and silver: "They are stones having no intrinsic usufruct or utility" and "...their being the measure of value of all commodities is based on the fact that they are not an objective (*gharaḍ*) in themselves." This means something problematic indeed in the age of ubiquitous usury when delivered as a speech in Davos at the World Economic Forum, the club of bankers, plutocrats and oligarchs. It could be understood to imply, "Because they are not an objective in themselves and have no utility, anything that is without utility and has no objective in itself can serve equally well as money, and thus paper or even digital signals can serve." This is precisely the mischievous use made of this argument. The Mufti adds:

> (a) Money has no intrinsic utility; it cannot be utilized in direct fulfillment of human needs. It can only be used for acquiring some goods or services. A commodity, on the other hand, has intrinsic utility and can be utilized directly without exchanging it for some other thing.

In fact this argument does not accord with the usage of the English word commodity, which is: "a raw material or primary agricultural product that can be bought and sold, such as copper or coffee."[69] Clearly gold and silver are commodities in this sense of the term, at least as much as copper is, and have many uses in industry, medicine, computers, and electronics etc.

> (b) The commodities can be of different qualities while money has no quality except that it is a measure of value or a medium of exchange. Therefore, all the units of money of the same denomination, are hundred percent equal to each other. An old and dirty note of Rs.1000/= has the same value as a brand new note of Rs.1000/=.[70]

Here by starting with an abstraction, 'money', he establishes what he has set out to do, which is to establish it as an abstract concept so that a piece of paper or a digital signal in a computer system, in his mind, is certainly the equal of a gold or silver coin.

Contrary to his argument, gold and silver are commodities and do have many objectives in themselves. They have served for beautification of buildings, temples and other places of worship, and of objects for sacred and other purposes for millennia, they have been used to embellish *muṣḥaf* copies of the Qur'ān and swords, they are given as dowries to brides, and as jewellery to wives and daughters, mothers and sisters. In themselves they have value in the eyes of human beings which is the basis for their acting as stores of value and media of exchange. It is the very fact that they have such value, that they are indeed commodities, that makes them work so well as media of exchange.

This pivotal passage licences the foundation of Islamic finance and banking, by ignoring the very usury in money created from nothing, which far outweighs the undoubted usury involved when people charge interest for lending money. The purpose in the argument is to skip over a deeply problematic issue, and thus be able to apply the *fiqh* to ordinary transactions using paper and digital money.

The consequences of the *ribā* intrinsic to fiat money are immense.

If something has no value and is assigned an arbitrary value and interest is charged on it, the real interest becomes enormous and approaches infinity. For example, someone borrows £75 and agrees to repay £78 after a year. £78 – £75 is equal to £3 which is the amount of 'profit' the lender makes. The interest can be shown by dividing the £3 by the original sum of £75 and then multiplying by 100 to get a percentage. In this case it results in Calvin's *reasonable* usury whose interest rate here is 4%.

However, if that £75 were a banknote, which costs 4p to print, then the borrower would be paying £3 for the loan of this 4p. In this case the bank's 'profit' is £78 – 4p, i.e. £77.96 which we then divide by the original sum of 4p and then multiply by 100 to get a percentage, which gives an interest rate of 194,900%. The bank can then afford to 'repay' the original £75 which it created out of nothing at a cost of 4p. Note that paper money and ordinary coins represent only 4% of the money supply, the rest being created by banks whenever they make a deposit, and thus not involving the cost of making a banknote or minting a coin. Increasingly, this activity takes place algorithmically at speeds that bewilder the mind. If the money costs nothing at all, and is lent out at interest, the real interest rate becomes infinite. This is the core of the modern usurious project compared to which even extortionate interest rates such as 250% or 2500% look insignificant. The problem for Islamic banking is that however they try to present it they are actually charging interest for loans.

It is important to understand the significance of this apparently abstruse argument about the abstract nature of money that has been made *in order just to get on* with the business of applying the *fiqh* of the *mu'āmalāt* to our debased monetary and banking system without having to consider the usury inescapably wed to the creation of money from nothing.

The 'Islamisation' of capitalism is in reality the reverse: the transformation of the *sharī'a* governing trade and commerce into a form of usury capitalism.

*Transforming Islamic Banking*

After a trenchant criticism of all these matters in a series of podcasts, Umar Vadillo makes a challenging and important proposal. It is based on two understandings: first, that many Muslims have engaged with Islamic banking genuinely believing that it is something wholesome and a way forward for us, and among people in Islamic banking there are a large number who are disquieted to find that it does not live up to their high ideals and they want change; second, there is the well known position on *ḍarūra* – circumstances that compel one to undertake things one would not ordinarily do, such as eating what is not *ḥalāl* because of the threat of starvation.

### *ḌARŪRA – EXCEPTIONAL NEED*

Because of the importance of this matter, let us take a look at a careful summary of the issue of exceptional need. This applies particularly to food, but its analogical application to other situations is what most concerns us here, and Allah in particular says not to consume usury (*akl* – means eating) usury. Ibn Juzayy summarises the issue thus:

> It is quite evident that carrion is licit when an exceptional need arises. Then one examines the degree of need and the kind of sustenance that would become licit in this case and the amount in question.
>
> *As for need*
>
> This refers to the situation in which one fears death, but it is not stipulated that one wait patiently until one is close to death.
>
> *The kind of sustenance that would become licit*

This could be anything which would ward off hunger or thirst, like carrion from any animal except that of the son of Adam, and like blood, pig, food which are *najas* or liquids which are *najas* , except wine as this is only *ḥalāl* to clear something on which someone is choking, although there is a difference of opinion here. It does not become licit, neither in the case of hunger or thirst as it does not remove them, although it has also been said that it is licit. It is not licit for using as medicine, according to the well-known judgment (*mashhūr*), although it has also been said that it is permitted, in agreement with ash-Shāfi'ī.

*The amount permitted*

It is that he eats his fill, and if he fears that he shall want in the future, then he may take some as provision, but if he no longer is in need he must discard it....[71]

Availing of this license is predicated on making strenuous efforts to get out of the situation that has precipitated the severe need and to get back again to the circumstances where one may eat food that is permissible. No one would permit setting up shop selling what is not permissible.

Thus, if someone makes the case that it is unavoidable in our circumstances to transact with what is not permissible, and if one concedes that, one would add that this must be done in such a way as to aid us in returning to a situation that is entirely *ḥalāl*.

Now one ought not to call banking 'Islamic' because that is, as we saw, to introduce something deeply unacceptable into the *sharī'a*. Accepting that it is neither Islamic nor *ḥalāl*, and the need of the starving person to eat of what is not *ḥalāl* and take provision from it until he may return to the *ḥalāl*, Umar Vadillo makes a series of proposals that proceed first to uniting existing Islamic banks to form a sizeable consortium, transforming their practice by phasing out the contracts that are so clearly unacceptable and replacing them with genuine *qirāḍ/muḍāraba* and *ijāra* contracts, moving over to transacting in gold since with the demise of the dollar and the reluctance to grant the cloak of hegemon to China many are already moving towards transacting in gold and silver, culminating in transforming a united Islamic banking industry into the generator of a sovereign fund dedicated to bringing about the *mu'āmalāt* on a truly substantial scale as a step towards the *ḥalāl*.

Note, that this approach towards *ḍarūra* is much more profound than a private individual concession, but this is to approach it as an *umma*, as a world community with a common problem that must be solved.[72]

## Dismantling the machine

Where Heidegger speaks about the essence of technique/technology as something that makes the real reveal itself as standing reserve, and we might well posit that this is exactly the essence of usury too, others such as Mumford speak about 'the machine'. Riyad Asvat has painted a picture of the machine of usury capitalism as one plundering the human and the planet on every level. If we take the position that no one should ever build a nuclear power plant, contrary to those greens now opting for it, nevertheless it is when one comes to dismantle a nuclear power plant that nuclear scientists, engineers and physicists become necessary, because one could not leave the task to poets, philosophers and organic gardeners.

Arguably, the situation with the global reach of usury capitalism is much more serious than that example, and similarly it will take people with expert knowledge and substantial resources to dismantle it. Most importantly, the dismantling takes place by bringing into being something healthy and wholesome just as is the case with authentic healing, which, rather than fighting the disease, reinforces the wellbeing of the patient – although fighting the disease may very well be necessary sometimes. The expertise of Islamic bankers and their resources could be channelled into bringing about something quite different, a restoration of the *mu'amalat* on a world level.

These three chapters have been an exploration of the thesis that the *'ibādāt* and *mu'āmalāt* are inextricably joined together. How could this not be when *zakāt* is an act of worship performed with one's wealth, and the purity of that wealth is a fundamental consideration? The victory of usurious capitalism over the Muslim *umma* in our time is to some extent attributable to the division between *'ibādāt* and *mu'āmalāt* that was artificially introduced in the colonial era.

A mistaken perspective was also adopted that discarded much of the practice of the people of Madīna of the first generations because it was supposedly unsupported by *ṣaḥīḥ ḥadīth*. However, there is no disagreement that Allah has announced war from Himself and from His Messenger on those *mūminīn* who do not give up usury. It was for that reason that the people of Madīna were particularly zealous in weeding it out of their transactions and not even approaching those transactions about which they had any doubts, and their practice is an invaluable resource for our time, just as is their ethos.

This twofold mistake led to great misfortune for the Muslim *umma*, and the time has come to put that right in sha'Allāh. There is no better beginning to this than restoration of *zakāt* collected and distributed locally by community leaders and their delegated collectors,[73] thus restoring the pillar in which the *'ibādāt* and *mu'āmalāt* are most directly linked, enfolded within the threefold *dīn* of Islam, Iman and Ihsan expounded in the *ḥadīth* of Jibrīl ﷺ a unity that is so integrally preserved in the practice of the People of Madīna.

## Afterword

Yaḥyā ibn 'Umar said: "What is obligatory on all Muslims is to hold fast to the *Sunna* and to follow the commands of our Prophet ﷺ for when they do that and are in accordance with it, everything they desire will come to them from their Generous Lord. Our Lord, majestic is His remembrance and pure are His Names, made that clear to us in the decisive and unambiguous parts of His Book, when He says, blessed and greatly exalted is He over that which the wrongdoers say: '*If only the people of the cities had believed and been godfearing, We would have opened up to them blessings from heaven and earth. But they denied the truth so We seized them for what they earned.*' (7:96).

"And He, majestic is His remembrance, says: '*If only they had implemented the Torah and the Gospel and what was sent down to them from their Lord, they would have been fed from above their heads and beneath their feet. Among them there is a moderate group but what most of them do is evil.*' (5:66) He meant – and Allah knows best – if only they had acted upon that which was revealed in the Torah and the Gospel and in this Qur'ān they would have eaten from above their heads and beneath their feet, meaning – and Allah knows best – He would have bestowed the world upon them fully."[74]

# PART 4

# Conclusion

The two billion strong Muslim *umma* (world community) and the rest of humanity is unequivocally paralysed. Not able to unbind the noose of capitalist oppression and exploitation from around its neck. Shaykh Abdalqadir says with regards to this paralysis: "The horror of this modern age is not the annihilation of millions in Nazi Death Camps and Stalin's Gulags, nor is it the obliteration of a whole society in Iraq and Afghanistan. It is not the slaughter and torture of the innocents. The horror of this age is the somnambulistic helplessness of the masses to ACT[1] in order to stop the global holocaust. It is this unarguable condition of mankind which permits us to define the technique society as a psychosis. In Darwinian terms it means the species is in devolution."[2] Psychosis means to lose touch with reality, that is, to perceive the world and how it works in a way that is false. Mediating between ourselves and the reality of the world around us is our brain, that is, our intellect. The intellect creates a series of structured pictures by which we understand the world around us. Today we perceive ourselves and the world around us through the prism of capitalism. The prism of capitalism is ideology. This ideology is propagated through economics, politics, the corporate state, scientific materialism, public relations, the nuclear family, education and media. Belief in this ideology is the psychosis of capitalism. The nature of human beings has changed, we have devolved from being *homo sapiens* to become *homo economicus*.

This devolution began with the arrival of modernity. Prior to the modern period it was generally understood that Allah has created the world as a stable and secure home with ample provision for all human beings. Allah has also imbued human beings with *fiṭra*, which is an inborn natural predisposition to fulfil their destinies that are predetermined by their life-forms. In Qur'ānic terminology to act in harmony with one's *fiṭra* is called service or worship.[3] All belief and behaviour existed within this context or framework of understanding. In pre-modern Islamic society this "background" understanding allowed the believers to function in a way in which there was no distinction between experience and its construed meaning. The presence of Allah was undeniable. The natural world displayed order, design, Divine purpose and action. Caliphs ruled in the name of Allah and society was ordered in accordance with the guidance of the Qur'ān and *Sunna*. It was taken for granted that the mercy and compassion of Allah would repel the forces of evil. Atheism was almost inconceivable in a world which had these features as its background understanding.

## The Modern Worldview

It was in Europe that the dominant modern worldview, which now pervades the entire world including Muslim society, developed. Modernist epistemology (sources of knowledge that formed the basis of its worldview) took the form of mechanism, materialism and structuralism. The assumptions that underpinned modernisation were secularism, individualism and a commitment to progress through science and technology. From this framework was born the Cartesian body-mind dualism that so dominates scientific thinking today.

Development was defined as the control of nature for the benefit of human beings, according to the principle of liberal market forces. Modernity led to the establishment of nationalism, capitalism and democracy and the end of the age of faith. The religious worldview was supplanted by the modern worldview over a period of time, the chronology of which is disputed by historians. The transition from the medieval to modern modes of thought and practices was supported by rational methods in all fields of inquiry. Empiricism and rationalism became the primary sources for the acquisition of knowledge. Rationalism is the belief that phenomena are best understood through logic and reason, and empiricism is the belief that knowledge is based on sense experience i.e. observation, hypothesis and experimentation. Much of the modernisation process outlined above was made possible through the development of the scientific worldview.

The worldview fostered by science came into direct conflict with that of religion and in order to make science possible, religion's hegemony over the mind had to be broken. The triumph of the scientific attitude over religious belief as the final arbiter over thought and action was a victory of atheism over religion. The social sciences adopted the paradigm of mechanical science (i.e. structuralism with its belief in the objectivity and universality of scientific knowledge and method) as the model for morality, law and government. Once the power of the Divine over individual thought and social action is denied, religion ceases to be a vital factor in human life, even though belief in God may subsist. In other words, as expressed in the philosophy of Nietzsche, God dies. It is in this sense that Shaykh Abdalqadir argues: "At the centre of this ruined world is the lack of recognition of the Divine. The age is both atheist and bankrupt. Man has been reduced to being a debtor when the world is rich and full. The atheist is at the core of the disaster, having mistaken the idea of god for Divinity. Rightly he rejects theism. So too, do the Muslims. The reality of man is that he has a dynamic opening to the Divine."[4]

Modern science and philosophy have failed to provide the answers to life's two most important questions: (1) what is a human being? and (2) how to establish a harmonious society? Modernity has in fact covered over the truth (the literal meaning of the word *kufr* (unbelief) is "covering over") relating to these questions. What we have been given instead is capitalism.

### Capitalism – the religion of modernity

At the time of the Reformation Christianity changed itself into capitalism and, far from being an agent of disenchantment, capitalism has been a technique of enchantment and a rebranding of our intrinsic longing for the Divine. The animating spirit of capitalism is money, its theology, philosophy and cosmology is economics and its sacraments are the material culture of production and consumption of commodities and technologies. Its moral codes are contained in management theory and business journalism, and its priests are the corporate intelligentsia made up of economists, executives, managers and business writers. Its icons consist of advertising, public relations, marketing and product design. Under capitalism, money occupies the throne from which God has been evicted. In other words for capitalists money is god and ecstasy can be bought with it, in spite of the fact that capitalism sanctions the printing of counterfeit paper money by banks.

We live in a corporatocracy, that is, in a society which is controlled by corporations made up of the financial, commodity, media and information technology sectors. The finance sector dominates all the major corporations and without it none of the others could exist. Shaykh Abdalqadir says: "The banking entity is a pharaonic tower reaching to the heavens in its ambitious unified structure."[5] The core activity of banks is the creation of the money supply *ex nihilo* through fractional reserve banking and lending money at interest – both of which are *ribā*[6] and prohibited in Islamic law. As Shaykh Abdalqadir says: "The banking system is, in detail and in general, a usury edifice with a usurious central principle and with usury its necessary condition."[7] Allah and His Messenger are uncompromisingly at war against *ribā*: "*You who have īmān (belief)! Have taqwā (fearful awareness of Allah) and forgo any remaining ribā if you are mu'minūn (believers). If you do not, know that it means war from Allah and His Messenger (bi ḥarbim minallāhi wa rasūlihi). But if you make tawba (repent) you may have your capital, without wronging and without being wronged.*"[8] Commenting on these verses Shaykh Abdalqadir says: "This is a clear declaration of war by Allah and His Messenger. That is, by Divine Decree and the laws of Islam, where usury is practised is *dār al-ḥarb* and a zone for *jihād* under Divine and Prophetic authorisation."[9] Shaykh Abdalqadir cautions us by saying that it is vital that the Muslims "do not mistake the enemy and think this is a war against a nation or leader. Although the struggle may present leaders and nations to distract and ensnare the Islamic forces ... it is a *jihād* [war] against the usurious banking entity. The enemy is not merely a personnel but a method, a *dīn*, with its Temples – the banks; with its holy places – the Stock Exchanges of the world; and its false scriptures – the data-banks of figures, these magical millions and billions that hold the world's poor to ransom for the sake of a small elite of *kāfir* [disbelieving] power brokers. It is with these that war must be waged."[10]

### Allah's war on ribā

Allah tells us: "*That is Allah's pattern* (*sunnat Allah*) *which has passed away before. You will not find any changing in the pattern of Allah.*"[11] *Tafsīr al-Jalālayn* says that the meaning of "*which has passed away before*" is "defeat for the unbelievers and victory for the believers."[12] Allah has destroyed many societies that were not in harmony with His *rubūbiyya* (ordering and commanding of the universe). This is indicated in the following verses of the Qur'ān: "*Not one of their Lord's Signs comes to them without their turning away from it. They deny the truth each time it comes to them but news of what they were mocking will certainly reach them. Have they not seen how many generations We destroyed before them which We had established on the earth far more firmly than We established you? We sent down heaven upon them in abundant rain and made rivers flow under them. But We destroyed them for their wrong actions* (*fa ahlaknāhum bi dhunūbihim*) *and raised up further generations after them.*" (Q. 6: 5-7) The phrase *fa ahlaknāhum* (We destroyed them) indicates that Allah has destroyed many societies that were not in harmony with His ordering and commanding of the universe, that is, for their wrong actions (*bi dhunūbihim*).

The cancer stage of capitalism is an example of Allah's *Sunna* in action. Allah is destroying capitalist society as a consequence of its foundation on *ribā*. Capitalism has had disastrous consequences for the world at large and for the USA, the citadel of capitalism, in particular.

### Consequences for the world

Shaykh Abdalqadir categorically states that "the monetarist system has in effect collapsed, its theoretical foundations cannot sustain rational critique, cannot pretend that 'business' can continue using these instruments, institutions and protocols."[13]

Capitalism is a life-threatening disease that is a danger to the human species and capitalist ideology is complicit in perpetuating it. So pervasive is its psychotic nature that civic resistance to capitalist modalities has been virtually non-existent.

Global capitalism is the reason that nearly ½ of the world's population – more than three billion people – live on less than USD $2.50 a day. More than 1.3 billion live in extreme poverty – less than $1.25 a day. 22,000 children die each day due to poverty, and hunger is the number one cause of death in the world, killing more than HIV/AIDS, malaria, and tuberculosis combined.

On the other hand, according to a Credit Suisse report, the wealthiest 1 percent of the world's population now owns more than half of the world's wealth. The total wealth in the world has grown by 6 percent over the post-COVID pandemic period to $280 trillion, marking this as the fastest wealth creation since 2012. More than half of the $16.7 trillion in new wealth was in the US, which grew $8.5 trillion richer. The world's millionaires are expected to do best in the coming years. There are now 47 million millionaires in the world, and their numbers are expected to grow to 87.5 million by 2026.

### Consequences for the USA

The American empire is coming to an end and has lost the power and respect needed to induce allies in Europe, Latin America, Asia, and Africa to do its bidding. The empire will limp along while continuing to lose influence until the dollar is dropped as the world's reserve currency. As this happens the United States will plunge into a crippling depression forcing a massive contraction of its military machine. One of America's leading intellectuals, Chris Hedges, says: "Short of a sudden and widespread popular revolt, the death spiral appears unstoppable, meaning the United States as we know it will no longer exist within a decade or, at most, two.

The global vacuum we leave behind will be filled by China, already establishing itself as an economic and military juggernaut, or perhaps there will be a multipolar world carved up among Russia, China, India, Brazil, Turkey, South Africa, and a few other states."[14] A coalition of transnational corporations is emerging that is forging a supranational nexus to supersede any nation or empire. At the United Nations General Assembly on September 20, 2021, UN Secretary General Antonio Guterres called for a total overhaul of all human collective behaviour, thinking and traditions. This is what is called the Great Reset of capitalism and formed the basis of a strategic partnership between the UN and the World Economic Forum (WEF) which was signed in a meeting held at United Nations headquarters between Guterres and World Economic Forum founder and executive chairman Klaus Schwab. The WEF represents the world's largest corporations. The Great Reset is in fact a *coup d'état*, a corporate takeover of global governance. The WEF is promoting the idea that global capitalism should be transformed so that corporations no longer focus solely on serving shareholders but become custodians of society by creating good outcomes for customers, suppliers, employees, communities and other 'stakeholders'. There are now over one hundred global standard-setting, multistakeholder initiatives (MSIs) establishing guidelines and rules for a wide range of products and processes such as health care, cyber security, climate change etc. We are witnessing the emergence of global corporate totalitarianism, and the US, like all other countries, will be used to further the goals of capitalism.

In the meantime American society is tragically disintegrating. Exploitation and oppression are justified by the "permanent lie". The permanent lie is different from the falsehoods and half-truths uttered by politicians such as Bill Clinton, George W. Bush, and

Barack Obama. The permanent lie is not limited by reality. It is perpetuated even in the face of overwhelming evidence against it. It is irrational. Those who speak the truth and state facts are attacked as liars, traitors and purveyors of 'fake news'. "The iron refusal by those who engage in the permanent lie to acknowledge reality, no matter how transparent reality becomes, creates a collective psychosis."[15] Society has become fractured and atomised rendering real relationships almost impossible. Capitalism has shattered the communal and the sacred leaving in its wake addiction to drugs, alcohol, pornography, and gambling. Violence is tearing apart the fabric of society and no one is safe from it. The corporate state uses coercion, fear, police terror and mass incarceration as forms of social control while it devours the nation and the globe in its greed for profits. On average 44,000 Americans commit suicide every year and another 1.1 million attempt suicide annually.

This horrendous state of affairs is a consequence of disobedience to Allah. Allah's *Sunna* never changes and societies that are not in harmony with His *rubūbiyya* are destroyed. The American experience is global as is capitalism and *ribā*.

### THE MESSENGER'S WAR ON *RIBĀ*

Shaykh Abdalqadir says: "It is time to identify the enemy and declare the *jihād*. It is time to finish with an emasculated Islam voided of its *farā'iḍ* (obligations) and the necessary conditions without which it cannot win and it cannot survive. It is time to restore the Book and the *Sunna* to their sublime position of uncompromising success and take the promised victory assured to us by Allah. Identify the enemy. Declare the *jihād*. Define its parameters. Indicate its opening stages. Delineate its outcome and indicate its end."[16]

Shaykh Abdalqadir outlines the steps that we need to take, as follows: "Firstly, the *jamā'at* must form itself into a legal entity like the rebel humans did with trade unions, but this is step one to a new life. Secondly, the local leaders, by their wealth and influence in the land, have to be taken, enjoining them to right action. Islam has no priesthood, imams take prayer, governance is a social capacity. Thirdly, move constructively from capitalist modalities – currency, banking, taxation – to free exchanges between men and groups. Fourthly, remember physical and military opposition are the lifeblood of capitalist atheism. The revival of Islam is dependent on step by step turning away from *kufr* and finally, submitting to the natural religion. Fifthly, this program of life will be founded on the movement from money as pure electronic stored units of numbers to real wealth – gold, silver and commodities. This will lead to the abolition of capitalist supermarket distribution, that is, of goods and paper money and the restoration of hand to hand trade locally and usury-free container caravans around the world. The abolition of value added tax – of sales tax – would be the first indication of the *kuffār* abandoning their hypocrisy. The gold Islamic *dīnār* and the silver Islamic *dirham* are the signs of our emergence."[17]

## Basis for Revival

The five steps of Islamic revival outlined by Shaykh Abdalqadir are derived from his profound understanding of the *Muwaṭṭa'*[18] of Imām Mālik ﷺ. Shaykh Abdalqadir's explanation of the significance of the *Muwaṭṭa'* is perhaps his greatest contribution to the Muslims in particular and to mankind in general. The issue of our time is reinstating the superstructure of Islam, that is, the Islamic socio-political and economic order. As long as the superstructure of Islam, that is Caliphate, the *dawla*, wazirate, *kuttāb*, guilds, *awqāf*, the mint, the market, *ḥisba* and the courts was functioning the four *madhhab*s historically functioned successfully. Shaykh Abdalqadir argues, however, that it is only through Imām Mālik that one can have access to the very source of Islam in order to be able to reinstate it again. The Ottomans and Moghuls, both Ḥanafī dynasties, established their *dawlas* through a dynamic motivation and determination which modern human beings lack. Modern men and women are entrapped within a "somnambulistic helplessness" of capitalist psychosis which they have to break out of. The *'amal ahl al-Madīna*, that is, the practice of the people of Madīna during the first three generations of Muslims, is the antidote to the modern malaise. In order to understand this proposition we need to look at the sources of Islamic law, the *uṣūl al-fiqh*.

Allah has commanded that: "*You who have īmān (belief)! obey Allah and obey the Messenger and those in command among you.*"[19] The Prophet ﷺ said: "I have left two matters with you. As long as you hold to them you will not go the wrong way. They are the Book of Allah and the *Sunna* of His Prophet."[20] The Qur'ān and the *Sunna* are the primary sources of Islamic Law. *Ijmā'* (consensus), *qiyās* (analogical deduction), *istiḥsān* (juristic preference) and *al-maṣāliḥ al-mursalah* (public interest) are among the secondary sources of Islamic law.

With regards to the Book of Allah we know that the Prophet Muḥammad ﷺ was unlettered and retained the Qur'ān in his memory as it was revealed to him. He in turn recited it to his Companions ﷺ who memorised it in part or in full. The Qur'ān was transmitted orally in the time of the Prophet ﷺ and, by the practice of its precepts, he taught it to his Companions. The Prophet ﷺ also dictated it to scribes who wrote it on paper, papyrus, leather, shoulder blades of animals and leaf stalks of date palms. Whilst we can say that the writing down of the revelation was a structuralist process it had many benefits. The most important benefit was that one single copy of the Qur'ān was compiled from all these materials and also from the oral reports by the first caliph Abū Bakr ﷺ. This copy was later kept by the second caliph 'Umar ﷺ and then his daughter Ḥafṣa ﷺ. 'Uthmān ﷺ, the third caliph, had many copies made using this initial copy and sent them to various places around the Muslim world. It is this version, known as the *Muṣḥaf 'Uthmānī* that has become the standard text today. As such there is no doubt as to the authenticity of the Qur'ān.

The problem facing the *umma* is authentication of the *Sunna*, that is, the normative practice of the Prophet ﷺ. Amongst Muslims there are two views with regards to the definition of the *Sunna*, that of Mālik and that of post-Shāfi'ī scholars. For the latter, knowledge of Islam and Islamic law is restricted to the knowledge of texts. Firstly the text of the Qur'ān and secondly those of *ḥadīth* particularly the collections of al-Bukhārī and Muslim and to a lesser degree the collections of at-Tirmidhī, Abū Dāwūd, an-Nasā'ī and Ibn Mājah.[21] The major area of structuralism in Islam was the collation of *ḥadīth*. Shaykh Abdalqadir tells us that after the time of Imām Mālik there "began the ossification, complexification, and structuralisation of the method by which *ḥadīth* were collected, by which *ḥadīth* were narrated and by which *ḥadīth* were transmitted."[22]

From the perspective of Mālik ibn Anas a *ḥadīth* is a report of what the Prophet ﷺ said, although in its early usage it included reports of what he did also. Studies of *ḥadīth* were aimed at determining the *Sunna* of the Prophet ﷺ. Imām Mālik's view as expressed in the *Muwaṭṭa'* regards Islamic law as based on the Qur'ān and *Sunna* but it differs from the post-Shāfi'ī definition of *Sunna*. *Sunna* for the post-Shāfi'ī scholars refers almost invariably to *ḥadīth*, whilst in its Muwaṭṭan sense it is not coterminous with *ḥadīth* but is, rather, intimately linked with the idea of *'amal*, or 'practice'. *Ḥadīth*, in its Muwaṭṭan connotation therefore refers to texts whereas *Sunna* refers to actions. However, not only must *Sunna* be distinguished from *ḥadīth*, but *Sunna* must also be distinguished from *'amal*. Yasin Dutton explains that: "*sunna* in the Muwaṭṭan sense refers to a practice originating in the practice, or *sunna*, of the Prophet, *'amal* is a broader concept which includes not only the *sunna* established by the Prophet but also the *ijtihād* [independent reasoning] of later authorities. Thus all *sunna* is *'amal*, but not all *'amal* is *sunna*; indeed, as we shall see, Mālik typically differentiates those parts of *'amal* that contain elements of later *ijtihād* in addition to a base in Qur'ān and/or *sunna* by using the word *amr* rather than *sunna*."[23]

Imām Mālik regarded the Qur'ān, *Sunna* and *ijtihād* as bound together in one whole, namely the *'amal ahl al-Madīna* (the practice of the people of Madīna). The *Muwaṭṭa'* provides a composite picture including the judgements of the caliphs, governors and scholars up until the time of its compilation in the middle of the second century AH. Although Imām Mālik presents the *Muwaṭṭa'* in the textual form of a book it is about action (*'amal*) and as Yasin Dutton says it "allows us a fundamentally different perspective on Islamic legal history where the true expression of the law is seen as being preserved not in a corpus of texts but in the actions, or *'amal*, of men."[24]

Imām Mālik was aware of the problems associated with the codification of *ḥadīth*. It was with this in mind that he provided, in the *Muwaṭṭa'*, the methodology by which the *fiqh* could be extrapolated from the Qur'ān and the *Sunna*. This methodology of Islamic law, which we can call the *madhhab* (legal school) of Madīna, is the "*umm al-madhāhib*" or "mother/core of the *madhhabs*" due to the fact that all *madhabs* derive from it. Once the Islamic socio-political and economic order are in place, all the *madhāhib* (plural of *madhhab*) work well in the implementation of the Qur'ān and the *Sunna*. The crucial point is that the *madhāhib* (Ḥanafī, Shāfi'ī, Mālikī[25] and Ḥanbalī) did not establish the Islamic socio-political and economic order in the first place. They were only developed in the second and third centuries after the *Hijra* (the Prophet's ﷺ migration to Madīna) when the Islamic socio-political and economic order was already in place. The methodology of codification upon which the *madhāhib* are based was not present in the original *madhhab* of Madīna, which is also known as *'amal ahl al-Madīna*. The *'amal ahl al-Madīna* was based on the actions of men and women, but the *madhhab*s that developed out of it were based on texts with the added application of rationalism as in the case of the Ḥanafīs. The methodology of Imām Mālik ibn Anas is based on *fiṭra,* which is unstructured, natural and organic. Imām Mālik was aware that it was the methodology outlined by him that would have to be resorted to if the integrity of the Muslim world community was shattered and thus in need of restoration. This viewpoint is reflected in his statement that: "Nothing will put the last of this *umma* in good order except that which put the first of it in good order."[26]

Elaborating on this statement, Shaykh Abdalqadir argues that it is only through Imām Mālik that one can have access to the very source of Islam in order to be able to reinstate it again. This is affirmed by the following *ḥadīth* of the Prophet ﷺ: "The world will not come to an end until an *'ālim* appears in Madīna, and people will beat the livers of their camels to come to him. There will never appear on the face of the earth a man with more knowledge than him."[27] Shaykh Abdalqadir commenting on this *ḥadīth* says: "Now this great *ḥadīth,* every single person is in agreement, refers to Imām Mālik. Nobody has assigned it to anybody else, and this is in itself a kind of seal on the whole matter."[28] The *'amal ahl al-Madīna* otherwise known as *madhhab 'Umarī* (the *madhhab* of 'Umar ؓ) was the *madhhab* followed by Imām Mālik and his generation (*tābi'i-t-tābi'īn* – the Followers of the Followers) and the generation before his (*tābi'ūn* – the Followers) and the generation before that (the Companions of the Prophet ﷺ) in Madīna.

Let me illustrate the difference between the *'amal ahl al-Madīna* and the *madhhabs* by using the example of leadership. *Ḥadīth* texts relating to leadership exist in abundance. For example the following famous *ḥadīth*: "'Abdullāh ibn 'Umar reported: I heard the Messenger of Allah ﷺ say, 'Whoever takes off his hand from allegiance, will meet Allah on the Day of Resurrection without having any proof for him; and whoever dies while there is no allegiance on his neck dies a death of the Days of *Jāhiliyya* [Days of Ignorance prior to Islam]."[29] Ninety-nine years have elapsed since the caliphate was abolished and despite the widespread following of the four *madhhabs* (Ḥanafī, Mālikī, Shāfi'ī and Ḥanbalī) it has not been re-established. Yet the five obligatory practices of Islam (*shahāda*, *ṣalāt*, *zakāt*, fasting and pilgrimage) all require leadership and authorisation to be implemented properly. Without leadership and authorisation one dies a death of the Days of Ignorance. It does not mean one dies a disbeliever, it means one dies with an incomplete Islam. The obligatory acts of worship have both an individual and a social aspect. When one takes the *shahāda*, through the oath of allegiance one enters a community with an *amīr* (leader) who governs over a specific region. He in turn is under the authority of a caliph, sultan or *amīr al-mu'minīn*. The *ṣalāt* is led by the *amīr* or one appointed by the *amīr*. The *amīr* announces the beginning and end of the fast of Ramadan and the dates of the *ḥajj*. Allah's command with regards to *zakāt* is unambiguous. It is directed to the leader, to collect the *zakāt* and distribute it.

For the four *madhhabs* the above *ḥadīth* has become merely a text and texts are subject to structuralism, reductionism and materialism. In other words the theory and the practice become separated and whilst accepting the guidance contained in the *ḥadīth* its practice can be ignored. However, when the *ḥadīth* is taken to be the indication of *'amal*/practice no such separation is possible. For Imām Mālik, practice or behaviour is evidence of knowledge, or to put it differently, the *'amal ahl al-Madīna* guarantees that theory and practice are inseparable. The *dīn* of Islam in Imām Mālik's view was not something people thought but something they did and the truth of the *dīn* was acquired through practical action, which in turn led to the knowledge of deeper levels of being (*ma'rifa*). This brings us to the relationship between the *Sharī'a* and *Taṣawwuf*.

The *Sharī'a* and *Taṣawwuf* are inextricably connected, thereby eliminating the split between the inner and outer aspects of human personality.

The political teachings of Shaykh Abdalqadir are encapsulated in his statement that the *Ḥaqīqa*[30] has to be firmly established on the *Sharī'a*. Shaykh Abdalqadir argues that the prime example of a society in which the inward and outward sciences had been unified, was Madīna, the city in which the social contract was "at its healthiest and most balanced."[31] As we have observed this phenomenon was recorded by Imām Mālik in his book *al-Muwaṭṭa'*. Madīna was a nomocracy (law-governed society) governed by the Prophet Muḥammad ﷺ, Allah's caliph (representative) on earth, in accordance with His revelation, the Qur'ān.

Shaykh Abdalqadir points out that correct outward behaviour should not cause one to wither inwardly. He has repeatedly brought to attention Imām Mālik's statement about combining the practice of Sufism and obeying the law: "He who practises *Taṣawwuf* without learning *fiqh* corrupts his faith, while he who learns *fiqh* without practising *Taṣawwuf* corrupts himself. Only he who combines the two proves true."[32] In *Root Islamic Education*

Shaykh Abdalqadir describes three jurists who had followed the *'amal ahl al-Madīna*. Being jurists they were knowledgeable of the outward sciences and how their legal decisions impacted on society and governance. Their *'amal* (actions) elevated them spiritually and precipitated for them the opening of inner knowledge. One of these jurists was Imām Abū Sa'īd Saḥnūn. Shaykh Abdalqadir described Saḥnūn as a man of the highest integrity and reliability. He was *ḥāfiẓ* (knowing by heart) in knowledge and a thoroughly accomplished *faqīh* (jurist). He was scrupulous and utterly uncompromising in his defence of the truth. He was *zāhid* (doing-without) with regards to things of this world. He wore rough garments and ate coarse food but was generous in times of hardship as well as in times of ease. He never accepted gifts from the sultans but would give his companions large sums of money. Despite these outward qualities Saḥnūn was a man with a very soft heart. He wept very much out of his fear of Allah. He was modest, humble, noble in his conduct and had excellent manners. "His heart was sound. It did not have the least enmity toward other people. ... When Saḥnūn remained silent it was for the sake of Allah. And when he spoke it was for the sake of Allah. When he had the desire to speak he would remain silent and when he had the desire to remain silent he would speak."[33] The behaviour and character of Saḥnūn is the same as that espoused by the Sufis except that in Shaykh Abdalqadir's words: "This is a protected *tasawwuf* because it is not accessible, touchable, visible or speakable. It is buried in the hearts of great men of knowledge of *Kitāb wa Sunna*. And if we take this path, there is no need for anything visible on the face of the earth that you can call Sufism."[34] Shaykh Abdalqadir describes this as "the pure *salafī* phenomenon"[35] meaning that it was the behaviour of the Prophet ﷺ, his Companions, the generation after them (*tabi'īn*) and the generation after them (*tābi'i-t-tabi'īn*) in Madīna. This is the *'amal ahl al-Madīna* and Imām Mālik ibn Anas lived it and recorded it.

Shaykh Abdalqadir found the antidote for structuralism in the teachings of Imām Mālik, specifically in Imām Mālik's proposition that the *Sunna* is the *'amal ahl al-Madīna* and secondly, in his insistence on the fact the *Sharī'a* and *Taṣawwuf* are inseparable. Unlike the modern world, in which the epistemological foundations for understanding and interpreting the meaning of reality are rationalism and empiricism, in Islam there are in addition to these, other epistemic sources which we may call spiritual and religious. Religion was something that was related to action rather than thought. It was action/behaviour that enabled one to deepen the perception of the heart. This, it was understood, could not be acquired through reason. Knowledge of Allah comes only through dedicated practice and lies beyond thoughts and concepts. Knowing *about* Allah is different from knowing Allah. Knowing *about* Allah is the subject of *'ilm al-kalām* or *'aqīda*, that is "theology", whereas knowing Allah is the subject of Sufism, because the experience of Allah's Presence cannot be contained within the dogmas of theologians or the hypotheses of scientists or the speculation of philosophers. Allah is beyond space and time and human imaginings.

What are these other epistemic sources which we may call spiritual and religious? For human beings there are three realms in Islamic cosmology, *mulk*, *malakūt* and *jabarūt*, and three corresponding dimensions of human personality, *nafs*, *rūḥ* and *sirr*, and the sciences appropriate to each dimension are *'ilm al-'aql*, *'ilm al-aḥwāl* and *'ilm al-asrār*. The *nafs* (the body and psyche of the human being) inhabits the *mulk* (the kingdom of forms) and the means by which it perceives its realm of existence is through *'ilm al-'aql* (the science of the intellect). The *rūḥ* (soul) inhabits the *malakūt* (the kingdom of unseen forms) and the means of perceiving its realm is *'ilm al-aḥwāl* (science of states). The *sirr* (innermost consciousness) inhabits the *jabarūt* (kingdom of power or lights) and perceives its realm by means of *'ilm al-asrār* (the science of the innermost consciousness). The science of the intellect relates to rationalism and empiricism but the sciences of states and innermost consciousness are inaccessible to modern people due to their being restricted to rationalist and empiricist methodologies.

Allah is beyond the three worlds of Islamic cosmology *mulk*, *malakūt* and *jabarūt*, that is, beyond space, time and phenomena. Allah cannot be contained within space, time and phenomena, He created them. Allah was not diminished by His creation nor was anything added to Him. He is as He was before He created the universe. The goal of the human being, as explained by Shaykh Abdalqadir, is to reach Allah. The archetypal experience of the Divine Presence is the *Mi'rāj* of the Prophet Muḥammad ﷺ. The Prophet ﷺ was taken from Makka to Jerusalem for the Night Journey on the 27th of Rajab in 621CE. This part of the journey is known as *Isrā*. From there he ascended through the seven heavens and then entered into the Divine Presence. This part of the journey is known as the *Mi'rāj*. This was unique to the Prophet ﷺ because his experience was physical as well as spiritual. Descriptions of his experiences are to be found in the Qur'ān and *ḥadīth* literature. This was a gift to the Prophet ﷺ from his Lord. As a gift to mankind Allah ﷻ enabled human beings to have a spiritual *Mi'rāj* in the the *ṣalāt* (prayer) as is indicated in the saying: "*Aṣ-ṣalātu mi'rāj al-mu'minīn*" (*Ṣalāt* is the *mi'rāj* of the believers).[36]

To supplement the practices of the *Sharī'a* the Sufi *ṭarīqas* (Orders) have devised practices to enable people to experience the Divine Presence. The practices that Shaykh Abdalqadir adopted in his *ṭarīqa* are those outlined by Imām Abū al-Qāsim al-Junayd. They are:

1. Conformity to the *Sharīʿa* as revealed by Allah in the Qur'ān and as practised by the Prophet Muḥammad ﷺ.
2. Taking a shaykh (master) of instruction (*tarbiya*).
3. Engaging in *dhikr* (invocation and remembrance of Allah).
4. The transformation of states (*aḥwāl*) into stations (*maqāmāt*).
5. *Khalwa* i.e. withdrawal from the world in the concentration of invocation of the *ism al-aʿẓam* (the Supreme Name i.e. Allah) under the supervision of a shaykh.

Access to direct knowledge of Allah is dependent on the annihilation (*fanā*) of the *nafs*, *rūḥ* and *sirr* and their capacities. After their annihilation all that remains is consciousness of Allah. *Fanā* means 'annihilation' and in the context of *Taṣawwuf* it is understood to be annihilation in Allah, the cessation of personal actions, attributes and essence. Imām al-Junayd explained that belief in Allah implies obedience to His commands and obedience leads to ascent toward Him and ultimately to reaching Him. When annihilation is attained, His manifestation is so overwhelming that the elect worshipper, whilst unable to describe Allah, discovers the meaning of his own existence. From this comes the vision of Allah and the loss of his individual identity.[37] Shaykh Ibn 'Ajība points out that *fanā* can only be grasped by the people of taste (*dhawq*) and penetrating inner sight; it is beyond the grasp of the intellect and the written records of it.[38] The Self-disclosure of Allah does not alter His immutability in any way. He is not subject to change, multiplicity, incarnation (*ḥulūl*), union (*ittiḥād*) or division.

*Baqā* pertains to subsistence in Allah after the Sufi has returned, so to speak, from the experience of *fanā*. Imām al-Junayd explains that after *fanā* Allah restores personal attributes and actions to the Sufi. When the Sufi returns to this world after having "reached the zenith of spiritual achievement vouchsafed by Allah, he becomes a pattern for his fellow men."[39] Al-Kalabādhī said that *baqā* "is the station of the Prophets."[40] Shaykh al-Akbar Ibn al-'Arabī said that like the Prophets, the friends of Allah (*awliyā-Allah*, commonly known as saints) also take great benefit from the Divine Presence. He said that the friend of Allah (*walī-Allah*) before Divine Self-disclosure did not dare to describe Allah except according to what the revealed Books speak about and according to the reports related by Allah's Messengers ﷺ. After *fanā* he speaks about Allah with firm knowledge which was granted to him through Divine Self-disclosure.[41] Shaykh Abdalqadir summarises the matter very succinctly by describing the man of *baqā* as: "outwardly slave, inwardly free, outwardly dark, inwardly illuminated, outwardly sober, inwardly drunk. He is the *barzakh* (interspace) of the two oceans – the *Sharī'a* and the *Ḥaqīqa*. Separation does not veil him from gatheredness and gatheredness does not veil him from separation."[42] When expressed this way sobriety is not viewed in contradistinction to ecstasy. The way of ecstasy is the way of sobriety and the accomplished Sufi is fully aware of his or her ecstasy and can conceal it. *Fanā* must proceed to *baqā* if the Sufi's light is to be shared and transmitted to illuminate the people.

### Mu'āmalāt

There is a common misunderstanding that *ruḥānī* (spiritual) openings/illuminations result from the practices of *Taṣawwuf*, that is, the *Ṭarīqa*. *Ruḥānī* openings are a result of one's struggle in the establishment of the *Sharī'a*, and *Taṣawwuf* provides the knowledge and guidance required for the *ruḥānī* journey. We noted in the last section that Imām al-Junayd said that belief in Allah implies obedience to His commands and obedience leads to ascent toward Him and ultimately to reaching Him. We also noted that the political teachings of Shaykh Abdalqadir are encapsulated in his statement that the *Ḥaqīqa*[43] has to be firmly established on the *Sharī'a*. Everything happens in the here and now, as Shaykh Abdalqadir says, "what happens in life occurs simultaneously at three levels: the outward, the inward and the hidden."[44] We get a clearer understanding from the following words of Shaykh Abdalqadir: "There are times in *Taṣawwuf* when the *tarbiya* of the Sufis is *'ilm an-nafs*, which entails struggle against the *nafs*, *hawā*, *shayṭān*, to clean the heart. The purification of this age is not interior. The purification of this age is everything exterior, to make it clean. To make the behaviour clean. To separate the enemy from the friend. This is the *tarbiya* of this age. This is the *jihād an-nafs* of this age. It is that the market is not *ḥarām*, that the money is *ḥalāl*. How can we make the *ḥaḍra* if we are in a dirty place. Everything about Islam is clean, before *ṣalāt* there must be the *wuḍū*. Before *ḥaḍrat ar-Rabbānī*[45] there must be *Sharī'a* of Islam."[46] Shaykh Abdalqadir, explaining the primacy of the *Sharī'a* quotes Shaykh al-Faytūrī's statement: "*Ṭarīqa* is not *wird*, or *waẓīfa*, or *bay'a* or *silsila*, but *Ṭarīqa* is *ma'rifatullāh. Ma'rifatullāh*."[47] We have noted earlier that *ma'rifatullāh*, that is *'ilm al-aḥwāl* and *'ilm al-asrār*, in Imām Mālik's understanding, results from the establishment of the *Sharī'a*. Expressing it in another way Shaykh Abdalqadir says: "To sum up I would say that *Taṣawwuf* is *Futuwwa*. It is the building and creating of excellence of character in the *Jamā'at*. That is *Taṣawwuf*. Hidden in that is the secret of *Ma'rifa* and only Allah knows where it goes among the *Fuqarā*. That is the fundamental position I have: *Taṣawwuf* is *Futuwwa* and its secret is *Ma'rifa* – not the opposite way around like you now get in the subcontinent and North Africa."[48] Shaykh Abdalqadir continues on this theme by saying: "In the matter of *Taṣawwuf* it is axiomatic and everyone agrees that there is no Sufism without the *Sharī'a* of Islam. But the truth of the matter is that Islam has been abandoned.

You cannot have *Taṣawwuf* in its fullness unless you have Islamic fundamentals established. Now, the pillar of *zakāt* has fallen, since there is nowhere today that *zakāt* is taken by *zakāt* collectors. *Zakāt* is not a given *ṣadaqa*, it has to be taken. It is the foundation of the state of the Muslims. In the Qur'ān we find that it says: Purify yourself with the *zakāt*. In as much as *Taṣawwuf* is purification of the self, this means you cannot have it unless you have *zakāt*. So you cannot talk about 'states' and 'stations', you cannot talk about *dhawq*, you cannot even dare to talk about *fanā* and *baqā* when you do not have the fundamentals of the *zakāt*. You cannot have Sufism in a bordello. That is really the point."[49]

Shaykh Abdalqadir explains that Islam is transactional. "The *dīn*, as is declared in a renowned *ḥadīth*, is *mu'āmala*. In other words Islam while advocating supreme governance *khilāfa*[50], as categorically insisted on by Imām al-Qurṭubī, leaves the issue of local governance an open matter. What is non-negotiable is the *dīn* itself. And the *dīn* is *mu'āmalāt*."[51] The *dīn* is comprised of *'ibādāt* (worship) and *mu'āmalāt* (social transactions) and what this *ḥadīth* is emphasising is that the *dīn* is not only *'ibādāt*. If it were so, that will be secularism which is alien to Islam. *Mu'āmalāt* is an integral part of the *dīn* and has to be conducted according to the *fiqh*.[52] Shaykh Abdalqadir explains that: "All *'ibāda*, the first half of the *dīn*, is expressed in fiduciary metaphor, debt, profit, gain, loss – all these indicate the spiritual transaction. All *fiqh* regulates every single fiduciary event as a spiritual metaphor. It is in its totality a socio-financial system devoid of usury, abhorring stored wealth, inviting expenditure, and looking on debt as dreadful."[53] On this basis, Shaykh Abdalqadir comes to the profound conclusion that: "Islam is not a political movement, but it IS a market movement."[54]

The battles in the war against capitalism will be fought and won in the market place, both physical and virtual. Shaykh Abdalqadir brings to our attention that the current world crisis of society and environment is nothing other than the collapse of capitalism and its fundamental principle – usury. The message from Allah is that wealth should "*not become something that merely revolves between the rich among you.*"[55] This injunction is intended to eradicate oligarchy, which was predominant in Arabia at the time of the revelation. The circulation of wealth is guaranteed by the *Sharī'a*. It must be emphasised that Islamic law promotes the circulation of wealth and inhibits its stagnation. Facilitating the circulation of wealth is the obligation to pay the *zakāt* and of particular significance to the stagnation of wealth is the prohibition of hoarding. Other legal stipulations that inhibit the development of capitalism are:

1. Islamic law only recognises natural persons, it does not grant legal standing to corporations;
2. The prohibition of *ribā* eradicates banking and fractional reserve generation of money supply;
3. The laws of inheritance prevent the accumulation of wealth and the rise of corporatisation;
4. Trading practices and contracts prohibit inequity in transactions;
5. The physical market should be a *waqf* or *ṣadaqa*, and no rent is to be levied on the merchants;
6. Islamic society should be financed through the *waqf* system. Public or municipal services e.g., welfare, education, religious services, construction and maintenance of the water system, hospitals, etc. should be set up, financed and maintained by *awqāf*. The need for political authorities to borrow money is significantly reduced because of this arrangement;
7. The economic functions performed by the guilds include: inhibiting monopoly capitalism; providing social security; and protecting the integrity of the bi-metallic currency;
8. Historically gold and silver were used as general equivalents

in which the value of other goods would be expressed. The Revelation mentions them and attaches many judgments to them, for example, *zakāt*, marriage, and *ḥudūd*, etc. Gold and silver have tangible realities unlike virtual currencies such as paper-, digital- and crypto-currencies. The internet and blockchain technology, however, can be used to provide efficiency, transparency and tracking transactions in real time.

All of the above are part of a new nomos, a new legal order.

## The New Nomos

Shaykh Abdalqadir is of the view that this is clearly that moment when a new nomos must arise in response to "the identified nihilism which is the immediate present."[56] In a world that has lost its moral and Divine imperatives he sees the Muslims as people who can replace materialism, consumerism and nihilism with the natural *nomos* (*dīn al-fiṭra*), with respect for women, safety for children, protection of human beings by the rule of law, and defending the ecosphere from destruction, pollution and over-exploitation. Shaykh Abdalqadir says: "The new nomos has not vanished from the earth. It has survived, now it is ready, yet again, to emerge into the wider arena of civic revival."[57]

For Shaykh Abdalqadir the new *nomos* is none other than the *'amal ahl al-madīna*, the Mālikī existential methodology. The Madīnan model is nomocratic, that is, it is a law-governed society. Since the act of governing is primarily associated with the production, distribution and consumption of resources, the Islamic *dawla* has to guarantee justice and equity in the financial affairs of its citizens. These matters cannot be overemphasised. The central function of governance in the *dawla* is to facilitate the movement of wealth to all sections of the community and this circulation of wealth is guaranteed by the *Sharī'a*. In economic terms Islam demands equity, freedom and justice in trade and commerce. Islamic law inhibits the development of capitalism and oligarchy.[58] The application of the *Sharīʿa* should therefore result in prosperity for society. The institutions that developed from the Madīnan model in subsequent Islamic history were the caliphate, the *wazirate* (vizierate), the judiciary, the *bayt al-māl* (the treasury), *ḥisba* (administration of the city), the mint, the *sūq* (market), the *awqāf* (charitable endowments) and the *aṣnāf* (guilds). These institutions, regulated by Islamic law, provide the means by which Muslim societies function.

Shaykh Abdalqadir says: "The first pillar of Islam is the double *shahāda*, 'I confirm that there is no god but Allah, and I confirm that Muḥammad is the Messenger of Allah.' May Allah bless him and grant him peace. ... Confirmation of the second *shahāda* is confirmation of the *Sharīʿa* itself so if it disappears from a society and its *ʿamal* then it is gone. The *kāfir* will accept one who believes in God, even His Oneness, but they cannot and will not accept the full splendour of the second *shahāda* which is by definition, *ʿamal*, living within the *ḥudūd* and *jihād fī sabīlillāh* (war in the way of Allah)."[59]

### The cyclical nature of political power

The earthly consequences of deviating from governing by Allah's just laws are either the destruction of the society or the replacement of one government by another. Allah destroys the oppressive and disbelieving dynasties and replaces them with the believers. This is indicated in the following verses of the Qur'ān:

> *"Whole societies have passed away before your time, so travel about the earth and see the final fate of the deniers. This is a clear explanation for all mankind, and guidance and admonition for those who have taqwa (fearful awareness of Allah). Do not give up and do not be downhearted. You shall be uppermost if you are believers (wa antumu-l-ʿalawna in*

*kuntum mūminīn). If you have received a wound, they have already received a similar wound. We deal out (nudāwiluhā) such days to people turn by turn, so that Allah will know those who have īmān (believe) and can gather martyrs from among you – Allah does not love wrongdoers (ẓālimūn) – and so that Allah can purge those who have īmān (belief) and wipe out the kāfirūn (unbelievers)."* (Q. 3: 137-140)

The etymological root of *nudāwiluhā, d-w-l,* means to rotate, to take turns, to alternate, and to circulate. The political implications of "*We deal out (nudāwiluhā) such days to people turn by turn*" is expressed by the term *dawla*, which is derived from the same root. *Dawla* means rotation, turn of fortune, and dynasty. In this verse and subsequent Islamic political history *dawla* is taken to mean the divinely granted turn in power. Allah destroys the oppressive (*ẓālimūn*) and disbelieving (*kāfirūn*) dynasties and replaces them with the believers (*wa antumu-l-'alawna in kuntum mūminīn*).

Societies (like human beings) are like trees, they have a life-cycle: from conception (seed), to infancy (seedling), to juvenile (sapling), to adult (mature), to elderly (decline) and finally to death. Shaykh Abdalqadir sees society in a similar way to biological phenomena which are entities moving through time and taking their meaning from their full realisation in nature, from seed to decay. As Allah says: "*Do you not see how Allah makes a metaphor of a good word: a good tree whose roots are firm and whose branches are in heaven? It bears fruit regularly by its Lord's permission. Allah makes metaphors for people so that hopefully they will pay heed. The metaphor of a corrupt word is that of a rotten tree, uprooted on the surface of the earth. It has no staying power. Allah makes those who have īmān firm with a Firm Word in the life of the dunyā and the ākhira. But Allah misguides the wrongdoers. Allah does whatever He wills. Do you not see those who have exchanged Allah's blessings for kufr, and moved their people to the abode of ruin: Hell where they will roast? What an evil place to stay!*"[60]

It was the once powerful tribe of Quraysh that went "*to the abode of ruin*" at the hands of the Prophet ﷺ and the Muslims. The Quraysh, under the political control of its merchant oligarchy, succeeded in creating a network of markets that extended throughout Byzantium, Abyssinia, Yemen, and Persia with Makka as the centre of that commercial network. From the level of institutional complexity, the ability to collect taxes and the monopoly of power held by the Quraysh to make and enforce the law, Makka was a powerful state. From the beginning of his prophethood the Prophet ﷺ delivered the Qur'ānic message, which was that Allah is the Sovereign; He is the Creator of the world and He has made laws by which human societies can function harmoniously and in peace. These laws also enable humans to coexist with their environment. He taught that the aim of leadership is to preserve social order and assure the prosperity of Allah's servants. He insisted that the legitimacy of a government is dependent on its execution of justice and that the motivating factor for maintaining justice is accountability to Allah on the Day of Reckoning. He maintained that the circulation of wealth must be guaranteed by the law (*Sharī'a*). As expected, the Makkans reacted to the Prophet ﷺ with extreme violence. They felt that all their values and institutions were threatened. This conflict eventually led the Makkan state "*to the abode of ruin*" and saw the rise of the Muslims.

The Madīna of the Prophet Muḥammad ﷺ was established as the primary model of governance for humankind. This is clearly stated in this verse: "*You are the best community (umma) that has been raised up for mankind. You enjoin right conduct and forbid indecency and you believe in Allah.*"[61] Allah also says: "*In this way We have made you a middlemost community (umma), so that you may act as witnesses against mankind and the Messenger as a witness against you.*"[62] The *umma* is the body of Muslims as one distinct community. In this context it means the Muslim *umma* is a justly balanced society setting the standard for mankind. This, of course, is made possible through the Prophet ﷺ being the standard (*uswatun ḥasana*) for the society. As Allah says: "*You have an excellent model* (*uswatun ḥasan*) *in the Messenger of Allah.*"[63] Let us repeat Shaykh Abdalqadir's explanation of the Madīnan phenomenon: "The Madīna of the Salafī community [the first three generations of Muslims] was neither a primitive nor a formative society but a complete blueprint pattern for Islamic societies from then on. It is clear that in Madīna at the time of the Salafī communities man was at his greatest and the social contract at its healthiest and most balanced."[64]

Reflecting on dynastic change we find in Ibn Khaldūn's philosophy of history that the first stage of social change is Bedouinism (people becoming estranged from mainstream society). The Bedouin (persons estranged from mainstream society) are cut off from the project of society and they do not identify with the social system within which they live. They are the oppressed, exploited, stateless, homeless and poverty-stricken people of the world. The second stage is when the Bedouin coalesce into a group, united by kinship (*'aṣabiyya*). The third stage is when the Bedouin adopt Kingship by swearing allegiance to a leader. This new force then overthrows the old dynasty and establishes itself in power.

Shaykh Abdalqadir instructs us to be aware of the moment we are in, to know the phase of the political cycle that we are in. To explicate the phase of the political cycle that we are in, Shaykh Abdalqadir gives us another illustration of the dynastic change paradigm, that of the Greek historian Polybius (200-118 BC). He outlined six stages, the first of which is monarchy which emerges from primitive leadership. Monarchy then degenerates into tyranny which in turn gives way to aristocracy. The rule of the few becomes corrupted into oligarchy. The resistance of the masses against injustice gives rise to democracy. Democracy abandons its values and moral clarity leading ultimately to the breaking of laws and mob-rule, bringing the cycle to an end. We are in the period of mob-rule (ochlocracy), that is, corporatocracy, the rule of corporations. Some of these mobs (corporations) are wealthier and more powerful than many countries. Shaykh Abdalqadir says: "Since we cannot choose which zone is to be preferred or even which kind of man we should be, fated to a particular time and a particular parenthood we then must fulfil or go beyond the lived moment of the cycle."[65]

### Living in the moment

Existence is a journey. Everything in existence is alive, dynamic, moving and in action, including the movement of the actual atoms themselves.[66] The name by which Shaykh Abdalqadir calls physical time (such as year, day, hour etc.) is natural time and the name he gives to spiritual time is time of destiny. The movement of a thing or the journeying of a person is called its/his/her destiny. Natural time is fixed by Allah as part of His governance of the universe (*rubūbiyya*), for example planetary movements, weather changes and the DNA in biological entities. They are subject to the decree of Allah (*qadr*). The time of destiny is when Allah executes His decree (*qaḍā*). The human being is the locus for the intersection or meeting of natural time and the time of destiny. In the moments when physical time and the time of destiny intersect, Allah, without interfering with the universal laws, manifests the *tajalliyāt*[67] of His light.[68]

This event is made possible by wayfaring. Shaykh Abdalqadir points out that the root verb from which the word wayfaring (*safar*) is derived is *yusfiru* (he unveils). In the context of Sufism therefore wayfaring is Divine Self-unveiling to the one who has submitted to his or her destiny, which in turn is the literal meaning of *muslim*. The Muslim then is one who has annihilated his or her *nafs* (ego) in Allah and this is what all human beings naturally aspire to do consciously or unconsciously due to their *fiṭra*. This is the first of Imām al-Junayd's five rules by which Sufis acquire unveiling.[69] In his description of this phenomenon Shaykh Abdalqadir has elaborately woven together Ash'arī theology, Mālikī legal methodology and Junaydī Sufism, all of which are incorporated in the dictum: "Allah is One in His Essence, attributes and actions."[70] The acts and attributes of Allah can be contemplated but whilst His Essence is unthinkable it can yet be known through *fanā*.

Shaykh Abdalqadir says that for the "unveiling of Allah ﷻ the *mūmin* [believer] has to be prepared. His preparation is to recognise that that moment comes into the in-time when he has submitted to the realities of the in-time. He is not rushing forward any more than he is pulling back. This allows us to deduce from this that if a man ignores his *ḥāl* – if a man is ignorant of the states he is passing through – he ignores his *waqt*, he is also ignorant of the time that he is living in. If he does not know his state he does not know the moment he is living in. If a man ignores his *waqt*, he ignores his *nafs*. If a man ignores his *nafs*, he ignores his *Rabb* [Lord]. While it is not a *ḥadīth*, the great Sufis repeat and the great *'ālim* ar-Rāzī, who was almost a rationalist, quoted it often – the famous saying: 'He who knows his self, knows his Lord.'"[71]

Allah tells us : *"O you who believe! enter Islam totally. Do not follow in the footsteps of Shayṭān. He is an outright enemy to you."*[72] In the *Tafsīr al-Jalālayn* the author says that *"enter Islam totally"* means "follow all its laws." Shaykh Abdalqadir's advice to his *fuqarā* was as follows: "Everything that is *ḥalāl* [permitted] has a blessing and everything that is *ḥarām* [prohibited] has a punishment. So you must fulfil the *ḥalāl*, and what is *ḥalāl* is in commerce, is in the money, is in the trade, is in the way you live and is in your refusing to submit to the *kuffār* [disbelievers]. By that I mean the state! Sayyidinā Muḥammad ﷺ did not come to sweep aside Caesar in order to be a new kind of Caesar; he finished with the whole need for Caesar. He abolished the state and what he created was Madīna; what he created was *fiqh*, justice from men of nobility, modesty and poverty who were judges supervised by an Amir. What he left was *amr* [command/authority]; what he left in Madīna was *amr*. This is your responsibility and I cannot emphasise it enough. The ones who will give themselves to it one hundred percent, twenty-four hours a day, everything will come and support them and carry them. Their food will be provided for them, their clothes will be provided for them, their houses will be provided for them, their wives will be provided for them, women who believe. *Muslimūn wa-l-muslimāt* [muslims male and female], *mūminūn wa-l-mūmināt* [believers male and female], *sābiqūn wa-s-sābiqāt* [those who outstrip each other in drawing near to Allah, male and female], *ṣādiqūn wa-ṣ-ṣādiqāt* [those who are sincere, male and female]. You will get to the level of yourselves, your partners and the *dunyā* [world] will run after you."[73]

This is how Shaykh Abdalqadir was. He had devoted his life to Allah and service to Him, may Allah be pleased with him, and he paid the price for it. As an *'ālim* and academic, whilst having some support from his peers and society in general, his influence was deliberately kept to a minimum. The media has been hostile to him. Refer to articles that appeared in Australian newspapers as examples.[74] Nevertheless Shaykh Abdalqadir's successes have been spectacular. He revived the *dīn* of Islam.

Shaykh Abdalqadir is the light that was sent by Almighty Allah to illuminate the darkness of this age of modern capitalist dystopia. Every Islamic century was blessed with revivers of the *dīn* of Islam and he, may Allah be pleased with him, has revived it for us in ours. The Muslim world has kings, amirs and sultans all of whom are beholden to their capitalist overlords. In contrast to them Shaykh Abdalqadir has revived the institution of Islamic governance, that is *amirate,* by founding the Murabitun World Movement. The name and size of this movement is not important. As Shaykh Abdalqadir reminds us, Islam is a totally functional, social reality the minute two people decide to take it on. The social pattern, as at its very beginning, can go from a city to a country and it can shrink down to a group. It can be nomadic and it can be a great civilisation.

The enemies of Allah have done an efficient job in turning people away from Islamic governance by creating deviant groups such as al-Qaida, the so-called Islamic State, and the Islamic Republic of Iran. None of these groups or any of the existing Muslim nation states are effectively challenging the important systems and techniques that are keeping them subservient. These systems and techniques include *ribā*, the US dollar – the world's reserve currency, inflation and US hegemony. China, due to its rise in the capitalist world order and US opposition to it, is being forced to create an alternate empire. Part of the Chinese strategy is to co-opt Muslims e.g. Saudi Arabia, Iran and other developing countries, into its sphere of influence. This new alliance is no less toxic since Chinese capitalism is infected by the same disease of fractional reserve banking. These geopolitical alliances simply mean that Saudi Arabia, Iran and other developing countries are junior partners in the political system of corporatocracy. Muslim countries have little economic, political and military strength, their geopolitical value lies in the extraction of their natural resources by multinational corporations.

Shaykh Abdalqadir is the most important Islamic scholar of the last hundred years as well as the most important Western intellectual of this period and he was a prolific writer whose literary output spanned well over sixty years. He was able to simultaneously unify the outward (physical), the inward (psychological) and hidden (spiritual) dimensions of reality whilst our education has trained us to do the opposite, that is, to divide, compartmentalise and analyse. Shaykh Abdalqadir's greatest contributions to humanity have been: (1) his analysis of contemporary society; (2) his description of the original Islamic phenomenon; and (3) the steps he outlined for Islamic revival. Through his analysis Shaykh Abdalqadir left us with an understanding of the primary sources, coupled with an analytical framework which translates into a coherent existential methodology, inwardly and outwardly, to activate Islam, and by so doing displace the value system of the current world order. He did not put a time frame for the Islamic revival. It might well take a hundred years. After all, the capitalists abolished the caliphate in 1924 through a process of modernisation that began in 1789. Success, however, is by Allah. *"Allah created both you and what you do."*[75] Shaykh Abdalqadir says: "*Safar* on the *bismillah*, [be a wayfarer in the Name Of Allah]."[76]

There is no god except Allah and Muḥammad is the Messenger of Allah, may Allah bless him and grant him peace and may Allah bless his family, his Companions and all the believing servants of Allah.

# Endnotes

## PART 1

### Chapter 1: Governance is a Divine Contract

1 https://www.youtube.com/watch?v=XO70G3zrR3g

2 Shaykh Abdalqadir as-Sufi, *Sultaniyya*, Madina Press, Cape Town, 2002, pp. 137, 138

3 Shaykh Abdalqadir as-Sufi, *Sultaniyya*, pp. 129, 130

4 Abū'l Ḥasan al-Mawardī, *Al-Aḥkām as-Sulṭāniyyah*, Ta-Ha Publishers, London, 1996, p.10

5 Shah Waliullah (1703-1762) of Delhi, the capital of the Mughal Sultanate

6 *Ijtihād*: exercise of personal judgment in legal matters

7 Salafī here refers to the first three generations, the Salaf, of Muslims in Madīna

8 Shaykh Abdalqadir as-Sufi, *Root Islamic Education*, Madina Press, London, 1993, p. 3

9 *"You have an excellent model (uswatun ḥasana) in the Messenger of Allah."* (Q. 33:21)

10 *"In this way We have made you a middlemost community (umma), so that you may act as witnesses against mankind and the Messenger as a witness against you."* (Q. 2: 142)

11 Refer to Muhsin, S.M., *Alfarabi and the Foundation of Islamic Political Philosophy*, Oxford University Press, Oxford, 2001, p. 131

12 Ibn Rushd, *Bidāyat al-Mujtahid*, tr. by I.A.K. Nyazee, Garnet Publishing Limited, Reading, 1996, Vol. II, pp. 571-572

13 The practice of the Messenger of Allah ﷺ

14 Al-Bukhārī and Muslim from *An-Nawawi's Forty Hadith*, tr. Ibrahim, E. & Johnson-Davies, D., The Holy Koran Publishing House, Damascus, 1997, p. 34

15 Robert Briffault, *The Making of Humanity*, G. Allen, London, 2007, p. 52

16 Ibn Rushd, *Kitāb faṣl al-maqāl fī mā bayn al-sharī'ati wal-ḥikmati minal-ittiṣāl* (*The Decisive Treatise, Determining the Nature of the Connection Between Religion and Philosophy*), tr. Hourani, G.F., in *Averroes – On the Harmony of Religion and Philosophy*, Luzac, London, 1976

17 Asadullah A. Yate, *Ibn Rushd: Mujtahid of Europe*, Turmverlag, Germany, 1999, pp. 11-12

18 Reported sayings of the Prophet Muḥammad ﷺ

## Chapter 2 The Linkage between Politics and Trade in Islam

1 Shaykh Abdalqadir as-Sufi, *Sultaniyya*, Madina Press, Cape Town, 2002, p. 42

2 Shaykh Abdalqadir as-Sufi, *Sultaniyya*, Madina Press, Cape Town, 2002, p. 41

3 The disbelievers, singular *kāfir*

4 Shaykh Abdalqadir as-Sufi, *Sultaniyya*, Madina Press, Cape Town, 2002, pp. 41, 42

5 Shaykh Abdalqadir as-Sufi, *Sultaniyya*, Madina Press, Cape Town, 2002, p. 42

6 Shaykh Abdalqadir as-Sufi, *Engines of the Broken World: Discources on Tacitus and Lucan*, Budgate Press, Cape Town, 2012, p. 23

7 Shaykh Abdalqadir as-Sufi, *Sultaniyya*, Madina Press, Cape Town, 2002, p. 38

8 Kister, M.J., "The Market of the Prophet", *Journal of the Economic and Social History of the Orient* 8 (1965): 272-276

9 Bashir, Z., *Sunshine at Madina*, The Islamic Foundation, Leicester, 1990, p. 193

10 Abdalhaqq Bewley and Amal Abdalhakim-Douglas, A., *Zakat: Raising a Fallen Pillar*, Blackstone Press, Norwich, 2001, pp.5-6

11 J.M. Hobson, *Eastern Origins of Western Civilisation*, Cambridge University Press, Cambridge, 2009

12 J.L. Abu-Lughod, *Before European Hegemony: The World System A.D. 1250 – 1350*, Oxford University Press, Oxford, 1989

13 A. Anievas and K. Nisancioglu, *How The West Came to Rule*, Pluto Press, London, 2015

14 The Ottoman caliphate was founded by Osman I in 1299 in Anatolia.

15 al-Mawardī, Abū'l Hasan, *al-Aḥkām as-Sulṭāniyyah*, p. 168

16 Zysow, A., *The Encyclopaedia of Islam, Vol. 2, "Zakat"*

17 Trade, which generates most of the wealth in society, has to be conducted in a *ḥalāl* way. *Ḥalāl* trade requires justice (*al-qisṭ*) in transactions and freedom in the market-place.

18 Ibn Khaldūn, *Al-Muqaddima* cited by Umar Vadillo, *The Return of the Gold Dinar*, Madina Press, Cape Town, 1996, p. v

19 Ibn Khaldūn, *Al-Muqaddima*, cited in Umar Vadillo, *The Return of the Gold Dinar*, p. 91

20 Abdalhaqq Bewley and Amal Abdalhakim-Douglas, *Zakat: Raising a Fallen Pillar*, pp. 5-6

21 Abdalhaqq Bewley and Amal Abdalhakim-Douglas, *Zakat: Raising a Fallen Pillar*, p. 4

22 Q. 9: 60

23 https://shaykhabdalqadir.com/2008/09/30/the-collapse-of-the-monetarist-society-part-three/

24 Fractional reserve banking is explained in chapter 3

25 Utsa Patnaik, *Dispossession, Deprivation, and Development: Essays for Utsa Patnaik*, Arindam Banerjee and C. P. Chandrasekhar, editors, Columbia University Press, Palo Alto (USA), 2018

26 See chapter 3 for explanation

27 Shaykh Abdalqadir as-Sufi, *The Sign of the Sword*, Murabitun Publications, Norwich, 1984, p. 74

28 Shaykh Abdalqadir as-Sufi, *The Sign of the Sword*, p. 72

29 being superseded

30 Abdalhaqq Bewley and Amal Abdalhakim-Douglas, *Zakat: Raising a Fallen Pillar*, p. 36

## CHAPTER: 3 CAPITALISM, BANKING AND THE MODERN STATE

1 David Downing, *Capitalism*, Heinemann Library, Oxford, 2002, p. 6

2 R.G. Grant, *Capitalism*, Hodder Wayland, London, 2001, pp. 4,5

3 Pierson, C., *The Modern State*, Routledge, London, 1996, p. 31

4 Shaykh Abdalqadir as-Sufi, *Technique of the Coup de Banque*, Kutubia Mayurqa, Palma De Mallorca, 2000, p. 68

5 https://www.theguardian.com/commentisfree/2014/mar/18/truth-money-iou-bank-of-england-austerity

6 Davies, G., *A History of Money: From Ancient Times to the Present Day*, University of Wales Press, Cardiff, 2002, p. 457

7 Shaykh Abdalqadir as-Sufi, A., *Technique of the Coup de Banque*, p. 68 and J.P. Hirsch, "Revolutionary France, Cradle of Free Enterprise", *American Historical Review* 94 (1989): 1281

8 Umar Vadillo, *"Fatwa on Banking"*, http://www.shaykhabdalqadir.com/content/index.html

9 White, A. D., *Fiat Money Inflation in France*, D Appleton-Century Company, New York, 1933, pp. 1-2

10 The revolutionary government had confiscated large amounts of church property

11 White, A. D., *Fiat Money Inflation in France*, p. 5

12 Land, which like gold and silver possesses intrinsic value and was accepted as collateral upon which currency was issued.

13 White, A. D., *Fiat Money Inflation in France*, pp. 8-9

14 White, A. D., *Fiat Money Inflation in France*, pp. 7-8

15 Davies, G., *A History of Money: From Ancient Times to the Present Day*, pp. 557-558

16 White, A. D., *Fiat Money Inflation in France*, pp. 42-43

17 Jonker, J., "Competing in tandem: Securities markets and commercial banking patterns in Europe during the nineteenth century", *The Origins of National Financial Systems* (ed. Douglas J. Forsyth and Daniel Verdier), Routledge, London, 3003, p. 75

18 White, P.T., "The Power of Money", *National Geographic*, January 1993, p. 83

19 Islamic law

20 Pierson, C., *The Modern State*, pp. 78-79

21 The Saudi riyal is pegged (fixed) to the US dollar at 3.75 riyals equaling 1 US dollar.

22 Imām al-Qurṭubī, *al-Jāmi' li-aḥkām al-Qur'ān*, p. 724

## Chapter 4: The Fall of the Caliphate

1 Wallernstein, I., Decdeli, H., and Kasaba, R., "Incorporation of the Ottoman Empire and the World Economy." *The Ottoman Empire and the World-Economy*, Islamoglu-Inan, (ed). Cambridge University Press, Cambridge, 1987

2 Lewis, B., *What Went Wrong?: The Clash Between Islam and Modernity in the Middle East*, Perennial, New York, 2002, p. 6

3 S. Pamuk, *The Ottoman Empire and European Capitalism*, Cambridge University Press, Cambridge, 1987, p. 56.

4 Going beyond

5 Shaykh Abdalqadir as-Sufi, *The Return of the Khalifate*, Madina Press, Cape Town, 1996, p. 34

6 Shaykh Abdalqadir as-Sufi, *Technique of the Coup de Banque*, p. 107.

7 Mandaville, J.E., "Usurious Piety: The Cash Waqf Controversy in the Ottoman Empire", International Journal of Middle East Studies, 10 (1979): p. 306

8 Schacht, *The Encyclopaedia of Islam, Vol. 2, "Riba"*

9 Umar Vadillo, *Fatwa on Paper-Money*, Madina Press, Granada, 1991, p. 15

10 Yasin Dutton, *The Origins of Islamic Law: the Qur'ān, the Muwaṭṭa' and Madīnan 'Amal*, p. 150

11 Umar Vadillo, *The Return of the Gold Dinar*, p.55

12 R.H. Davison, *The Encyclopaedia of Islam, Vol. 2, "Tanzimat"*

13 Umar Vadillo, *The Esoteric Deviation in Islam*, Madina Press, Cape Town, 2003, pp. 325-326

14 D. Sourdel, A.K.S. Lambton, F. de Jong, P.M. Holt, *The Encyclopaedia of Islam, Vol. 2, "Khalifa"*

15 Shaykh Abdalqadir as-Sufi, *The Return of the Khalifate*, Madina Press, Cape Town, 1996, p. 83

16 Shaykh Abdalqadir as-Sufi, *Sultaniyya*, Madina Press, Cape Town, 2002, pp. 137, 138

17 Qur'ān 40: 64

18 *Ruhi*, meaning spiritual

19 Qur'ān 2: 29

20 Muḥammad al-Ḥajj, the ruler of Songhai

21 Shaykh Uthman dan Fodio, *Handbook on Islam*, Madina Press, Granada, 1996, p. 91

22 "The disaster which overwhelmed the country immediately after the removal of Abdulhamid can only be interpreted as an open warning from Allah and a demonstration that He had tied each and everything, so that when he was removed everything could only collapse. Indeed, Abduhamid was an example of truth and justice confirmed by the Divine. He had a high station with Allah, and his value was clearly demonstrated by Him." Ustad Necip Fazıl, *The Great Ruler: A Study of Abdulhamid Khan II*, tr. Malik Sezgin & Asadullah Yate, Cambridge Publications DE, Stralsund (Germany), 2020, p. 510

23 Sultan Abdulhamid II, quoted by Ustad Necip Fazıl, *The Great Ruler: A Study of Abdulhamid Khan II*, p. 426

24 Ustad Necip Fazıl, *The Great Ruler: A Study of Abdulhamid Khan II*, pp. 235-6

25 *dawla*

26 Ustad Necip Fazıl, *The Great Ruler: A Study of Abdulhamid Khan II*, p. 236

27 Ottoman sultans

28 Ustad Necip Fazıl, *The Great Ruler: A Study of Abdulhamid Khan II*, p. 509

29 Shaykh Abdalqadir as-Sufi, *The Return of the Khalifate*, p. 77

30 Shaykh Abdalqadir as-Sufi, *The Return of the Khalifate*, p. 14

31 Shaykh Abdalqadir as-Sufi, *The Return of the Khalifate*, p. 34

32 Shaykh Abdalqadir as-Sufi, *The Return of the Khalifate*, pp. 20, 21

33 Shaykh Abdalqadir as-Sufi, *The Return of the Khalifate*, p. 15

34 Shaykh Abdalqadir as-Sufi, *The Return of the Khalifate*, p. 20

35 Shaykh Abdalqadir as-Sufi, *The Return of the Khalifate*, p. 22

36 Ustad Necip Fazıl, *The Great Ruler: A Study of Abdulhamid Khan II*, p. 212

37 M. Al-Rasheed, *A History of Saudi Arabia*, Cambridge University Press, Cambridge, 2002, p. 15

38 N.J. Delong-Bas, *Wahhabi Islam: From Revival and Reform to Global Jihad*, Oxford University Press, New York, 2004. pp. 31-32

39 T. Niblock, *Saudi Arabia: Power, Legitimacy and Survival*, Routledge, New York, 2006. p. 29

40 T. Niblock, T., *Saudi Arabia: Power, Legitimacy and Survival*, p. 31

41 Western province of Arabia which includes Makka, Madina and Jeddah

42 Shaykh Abdalqadir as-Sufi, *The Return of the Khalifate*, p. 79

43 G. Troeller, *The Birth of Saudi Arabia: Britain and the Rise of the House of Sa'ud*, Frank Cass, London, 1976, p. 248

44 M. Al-Rasheed, *A History of Saudi Arabia*, p. 42

45 Shaykh Abdalqadir as-Sufi, *The Return of the Khalifate*, pp. 90-91

46 David Johnston, *A Turn in the Epistemology and Hermeneutics of Twentieth Century Usul Al-Fiqh*, Islamic Law and Society, Koninklijke Brill NV, Leiden, 2004, 11, p. 2

47 M. Enayat, *Modern Islamic Political Thought*, p. 78

48 Following the opinion of a *mujtahid* (someone qualified to make legal judgments)

49 Judgments in legal matters

50 Layish, A., "The Contribution of the Modernists to the Secularisation of Islamic Law", *Islamic Law and Legal Theory*, edited by Ian Edge, Dartmouth, Aldershot, 1996, p. 579

51 N.R. Keddie, *An Islamic Response to Imperialism*, University of California Press, Berkeley, 1983, p. xvi

52 E.E. Shahin, "*Salafiyah*", *The Oxford Encyclopedia of the Modern Islamic World*, p. 464

53 Shaykh Abdalqadir as-Sufi, *The Return of the Khalifate*, pp. 2-3

54 Unification

55 Shaykh Abdalqadir as-Sufi, *The Return of the Khalifate*, p. 91

56 A detailed account of scientific materialism follows in Part 2 of this book

57 Shaykh Abdalqadir as-Sufi, *The Return of the Khalifate*, p. 38

58 Shaykh Abdalqadir as-Sufi, *The Return of the Khalifate*, p. 87

59 "According to this doctrine all the religions really worship the same god. God is a symbol common to all religions and each one offers a different perspective, each of which is equally acceptable and valid. From here follows the idea of the 'unity of belief in God of all religions and spiritual paths.'" Umar Ibrahim Vadillo, *The Esoteric Deviation in Islam*, Madina Press, Cape Town, 2003, p. 80

60 Umar Ibrahim Vadillo, The *Esoteric Deviation in Islam*, pp. 273-274

61 Mark Sedgwick, "Freemasonry," *Encyclopaedia of Islam Vol. 3*, Published online 2014

62 Ustad Necip Fazıl, *The Great Ruler: A Study of Abdulhamid Khan II*, p. 26.

63 Mark Sykes, *The Caliph's Last Heritage: A Short History of the Turkish Empire*, https://www.dailysabah.com/arts/revolutionary-young-turks-under-influence-of-italy/news

## Chapter 5: The Rise of Ideology amongst Muslims

1 Shaykh Abdalqadir as-Sufi, *Technique of the Coup de Banque*, Editorial Kutubia Mayurqa, Palma De Mallorca, 2000, pp. 93-94

2 Adjective from Salaf, the early generations of Muslims, especially the Companions

3 Shaykh Abdalqadir as-Sufi, *Root Islamic Education*, Madina Press, London, 1993, pp. 4-5

4 René Descartes, *Principles of Philosophy*, Part 1, Article vii, tr. by John Veitch, http://cat.lib.unimelb.edu.au:80/record=b3987012~S30

5 Ted Benton and Ian Craib, *Philosophy of Social Science: the philosophical foundations of social thought*, Palgrave Macmillan, New York, 2011, p. 232

6 Glyn Davies, *A History of Money: From Ancient Times to the Present Day*, University of Wales Press, Cardiff, 2002

7 Shaykh Abdalqadir as-Sufi, *The Time of the Bedouin: on the politics of power*, Budgate Press, Cape Town, 2006, p. 278

8 Shaykh Abdalqadir as-Sufi, *The Time of the Bedouin: on the politics of power*, pp. 278-279

9 Shaykh Abdalqadir as-Sufi , *For the Coming Man*, p. 80

10 Greek philosophers after Socrates (469 BC – 399BC)

11 Shaykh Abdalqadir as-Sufi, *For the Coming Man*, pp. 85-86

12 Martin Heidegger, *Nietzsche* IV, tr. F.A. Capuzzi, ed. D.F. Krell, Harper and Row, San Francisco, 1982, p. 164

13 "This situation is grounded in the fact that science itself does not think, and cannot think – which is its good fortune, here meaning the assurance of its own pointed course. Science does not think. This is a shocking statement. Let the statement be shocking, even though immediately add the supplementary statement that science always and in its own fashion has to do with thinking, That fashion, however,

is genuine and consequently fruitful only after the gulf has become visible that lies between thinking and science, lies there unbridgeably. There is no bridge – only the leap. Here there is nothing but mischief ties and asses' bridges by which men today would set up a comfortable commerce between thinking and science." Martin Heidegger, *What is Called Thinking*, p. 8

14 Martin Heidegger, *What is Called Thinking*, p. 12

15 Paul Neumarkt, "Martin Heidegger: the Philosopher of Psychological Con-Fusion", *Journal of Evolutionary Psychology*, March 2003, p.36

16 Jünger uses this word in a similar way to how we use the word *fiṭra* in Islam. Muslims believe that human beings are imbued with *fiṭra* which is defined as an inborn natural predisposition which cannot change and which exists at birth in all human beings. The destinies of all things in the universe, including human beings, are predetermined by their life form (*fiṭra*). This way of defining human beings incorporates everything about them; their life-cycles, their habitat, their familial and social relations, their livelihoods and capacity for language.

17 Shaykh Abdalqadir al-Sufi, "The Gestalt of Freedom", *Ian Dallas: Collected Works*, Budgate Press, Erasmia, South Africa, 2005. p. 826

18 Ernst Jünger, cited by Shaykh Abdalqadir al-Sufi, "The Gestalt of Freedom", *Ian Dallas: Collected Works*, p. 831

19 Ernst Jünger, cited by Shaykh Abdalqadir al-Sufi, "The Gestalt of Freedom", *Ian Dallas: Collected Works*, p. 830

20 Ernst Jünger, cited by Shaykh Abdalqadir al-Sufi, "The Gestalt of Freedom", *Ian Dallas: Collected Works*, p. 828

21 Ernst Jünger, cited by Shaykh Abdalqadir al-Sufi, "The Gestalt of Freedom", *Ian Dallas: Collected Works*, p. 835

22 Ernst Jünger, cited by Shaykh Abdalqadir al-Sufi, "The Gestalt of Freedom", *Ian Dallas: Collected Works*, p. 836

23 Ernst Jünger, cited by Shaykh Abdalqadir al-Sufi, "The Gestalt of Freedom", *Ian Dallas: Collected Works*, p. 836

24 According to Karen Armstrong *logos* and *mythos* were two ways of thinking, speaking and acquiring knowledge. "*Logos* ('reason') was the pragmatic mode of thought that enabled people to function effectively in the world. ... *Logos* was essential to the survival of our species. But it had its limitations: it could not assuage human grief or find ultimate meaning in life's struggles. For that people turned to *mythos* or 'myth'. ... But a myth would not be effective if people simply 'believed' in it. It was essentially a programme of action. It could be put into correct spiritual and psychological posture but it was up to you to take the next step and make the 'truth' of the myth a reality in your own life. The only way to access the value and truth of any myth was to act upon it. The myth of the hero, for example, which takes the same form in nearly all cultural traditions, taught people how to unlock their own heroic potential." (Karen Armstrong, *The Case for God*, The Bodly Head, London, 2009, p. 3)

25 Ernst Jünger, http://www.ernst-juenger.org/2009/10/anarch-and-waldganger-1.html

26 Shaykh Abdalqadir al-Sufi, "The Gestalt of Freedom", *Ian Dallas: Collected Works*, p. 837

27 Ernst Jünger, cited by Shaykh Abdalqadir as-Sufi, "The Gestalt of Freedom", *Ian Dallas: Collected Works*, p. 824

28 Ernst Jünger, cited by Shaykh Abdalqadir as-Sufi, "The Gestalt of Freedom", *Ian Dallas: Collected Works*, p. 826

29 Tracy Strong, Foreword in Carl Schmitt, *The Concept of the Political* (based on the 1932 edition), University of Chicago Press, Chicago, 1996

30 Carl Schmitt quoted by Shaykh Abdalqadir as-Sufi, *The Time of the Bedouin*, p. 284

31 Carl Schmitt, *The Concept of the Political* (based on the 1932 edition), University of Chicago Press, Chicago, 1996

32 Tihomir Cipek, https://www.fdv.uni-lj.si/docs/default-source/tip/the-political-versus-the-state-the-relevance-of-carl-schmitt's-concept-of-the-political514ec5304f2c67bc8e26ff00008e8d04.pdf?sfvrsn=0

33 Carl Schmitt, *The Concept of the Political*, pp. 13-14

34 Henning Ottmann quoted by Tihomir Cipek, https://www.fdv.uni-lj.si/docs/default-source/tip/the-political-versus-the-state-the-relevance-of-carl-schmitt's-concept-of-the-political514ec5304f2c67bc8e26ff0000 8e8d04.pdf?sfvrsn=0

35 https://www.thenews.com.pk/print/595752-the-us-has-been-at-war-225-out-of-243-years-since-1776

36 Charles Perkins, *The Secret History of the American Empire*, Plume Printing, New York, 2007, pp. 4-5

37 John Pilger, *The New Rulers of the World*, Verso, 2002. p. 2

38 Roman poet (35-65 AD)

39 Shaykh Abdalqadir as-Sufi, *The Engines of the Broken World: Discources on Tacitus and Lucan*, Budgate Press, Cape Town, 2012, pp. 147-148

40 Law governing human conduct

41 Shaykh Abdalqadir as-Sufi, *The Interim is Mine*, Budgate Press, Cape Town, 2010, p. 127-129

## Chapter 6: Atheistic Capitalism: The Dominant Religion of Our Time

1 https://www.youtube.com/watch?v=XO70G3zrR3g

2 Walter Benjamin, *The Frankfurt School on Religion – Key Writings of the Major Thinkers*, ed. Eduardo Mendieta, Routledge, New York, 2004, p.261

3 Eugene McCarraher, *The Enchantments of Mammon – How Capitalism*

*Became the Religion of Modernity*, Harvard University Press, Cambridge, Massachusetts, 2019, p. 12

4 Eugene McCarraher, *The Enchantments of Mammon – How Capitalism Became the Religion of Modernity*, p. 18

5 Shaykh Abdalqadir as-Sufi, *The Return of the Khalifate*, p. 77

6 Shaykh Abdalqadir al-Sufi, *The Time of the Bedouin: on the politics of power*, p. 166

7 A.C. Grayling, *Towards the Light: The Story of the Struggles for Liberty and Rights that Made the Modern West*, Bloomsbury, London, 2007, p. 59

8 Shaykh Abdalqadir al-Sufi, *The Engines of the Broken World: Discourses on Tacitus and Lucan*, p. 166

## PART 2

### Chapter 7: Politics

1 Shaykh Abdalqadir al-Sufi , *The Interim is Mine*, p. 136

2 Shaykh Abdalqadir as-Sufi, *The Entire City*, Orhan Books, Cape Town, 2015, p. 226

1 Shaykh Abdalqadir al-Sufi , *The Time of the Bedouin: on the politics of power*, p. 238

2 Aisha Abdurrahman Bewley, *Democratic Tyranny and the Islamic Paradigm*, Diwan Press, Bradford, 2015, p. 68

3 Shaykh Abdalqadir al-Sufi , *The Time of the Bedouin: on the politics of power*, p. 181

4 Shaykh Abdalqadir al-Sufi, *Technique of the Coup de Banque*, Kutubia Mayurqa, Palma De Mallorca, 2000, p. 50

5 Shaykh Abdalqadir al-Sufi, *Technique of the Coup de Banque*, p. 53

6 Shaykh Abdalqadir al-Sufi, *Technique of the Coup de Banque*, p. 54

7 Shaykh Abdalqadir al-Sufi, *Technique of the Coup de Banque*, p. 55

8 Shaykh Abdalqadir al-Sufi, *Technique of the Coup de Banque*, p. 56-58

9 The Reign of Terror was a period of the French Revolution, following the creation of the French Republic, when a series of murders, massacres and public executions were carried out by the Committee of Public Safety

10 Shaykh Abdalqadir al-Sufi, *The Time of the Bedouin: on the politics of power*, p. 48

11 Shaykh Abdalqadir al-Sufi, *Technique of the Coup de Banque*, p. 64

12 Shaykh Abdalqadir al-Sufi, *Technique of the Coup de Banque*, p. 92

13 Financial Times, February 6, 2012

14 Financial Times, January 9, 2012

15 Shaykh Abdalqadir al-Sufi, *The Engines of the Broken World: Discourses on Tacitus and Lucan*, p. 104

16 Shaykh Abdalqadir al-Sufi, *The Engines of the Broken World: Discourses on Tacitus and Lucan*, pp. 111-112

## Chapter 8: State Capture

1 Ralph Miliband, *The State in Capitalist Society: The Analysis of the Western System of Power*, Quartet Books, London, 1973, p. 4

2 https://news.ubc.ca/2014/05/25/the-corporation-10-years-later/

3 Joel Bakan, *The Corporation: The Pathological Pursuit of Profit and Power*, Free Press, New York, 2004, p. 103

4 Charles Derber, *People Before Profit*, Souvenir Press, London, 2002, p. 60

5 Charles Derber, *People Before Profit*, p. 71

6 Shaykh Abdalqadir al-Sufi, *Technique of the Coup de Banque*, p. 94

7 http://whistleblowersqld.com.au/wp-content/uploads/2017/06/17.-McMahon-on-CAPTURE-2002.pdf

8 "The tax deductibility of bribes is a practice which the Convention has made easier to abolish. Until recently, offering bribes to foreign public officials as a way of obtaining contracts was a perfectly normal way of doing business in many OECD countries. Companies seeking contracts abroad often expected to have to pay a bribe to foreign officials, just to stay in the race. Several governments saw no reason to disagree and offered favourable tax treatment for bribery payments, which could be written off as expenses. These governments argued that making bribes to foreign public officials non-deductible contradicted the principle that all expenses associated with earning taxable income should be taken into account for tax purposes. A second argument they cited was that non-deductibility would be an ineffective deterrent against bribery of foreign officials anyway, even if it changed the effective cost of a bribe." https://www.oecdobserver.org/news/archivestory.php/aid/245/Writing_off_tax_deductibility_.html

9 https://www.transparency.org/en/press/media-advisory-foreign-bribery-goes-unpunished-by-most-big-exporters1

10 https://www.transparency.org/en/news/exporting-corruption-2018

11 Shaykh Abdalqadir al-Sufi, *The Time of the Bedouin: on the politics of power*, p. 62

12 Joan Didion quoted by Shaykh Abdalqadir al-Sufi in *The Time of the Bedouin: on the politics of power*, p. 62

13 governing.com/topics/politics/ALEC-enjoys-new-wave-influence-criticism.html

14 Alexander Hertel-Fernandez, *State Capture: How Conservative Activists, Big Businesses, and Wealthy Donors Reshaped the American States—and the Nation*, Oxford University Press, New York, 2019, p. x

15 Alexander Hertel-Fernandez, *State Capture: How Conservative Activists, Big Businesses, and Wealthy Donors Reshaped the American States—and the Nation*, pp. 13,14

## Chapter 9: Economics

1 D. MacTaggert, C. Findlay and M. Parkin, *Economics*, Addison-Wesley Publishing Company, Sydney, 1196, p.9

2 https://www.goodreads.com/author/quotes/95227.Ha_Joon_Chang

3 Shaykh Abdalqadir al-Sufi, *The Engines of the Broken World: Discourses on Tacitus and Lucan*, p. 149

4 The people who worship other than Allah or associate partners with Him

5 Shaykh Abdalqadir al-Sufi, *The Sign of the Sword*, Murabitun Publications, Norwich, 1984, pp. 16-17

6 Shaykh Abdalqadir al-Sufi, *The Engines of the Broken World: Discourses on Tacitus and Lucan*, p. 104

7 David Harvey, *A Brief History of Neo-liberalism*, Oxford University Press, Oxford, 2007, p. 2

8 https://www.yesmagazine.org/economy/2016/03/18/more-confessions-of-an-economic-hit-man-this-time-theyre-coming-for-your-democracy/

9 https://www.americanprogress.org/issues/democracy/news/2017/03/29/429442/corporate-capture-threatens-democratic-government/

10 https://scholarlycommons.law.wlu.edu/powellmemo/1/

11 David Harvey, *A Brief History of Neo-liberalism*, p. 48

12 Susan George, *A Fate Worse Than Debt*, Penguin Books, London, 1988, pp. 47,48

13 “Today, poor countries pay over $2 billion each year in interest alone, much of it on old loans that have already been paid off many times over, and some of it on loans accumulated by greedy dictators. Since 1980, developing countries have forked up over $4.2 trillion in interest payments – much more than they have received in aid during the same period. And most of these payments have gone to Western creditors – a direct cash transfer to big banks in New York and London.” Jason Hickel, *The Divide: A Brief Guide to Global Inequality and its Solutions*, Windmill Books, London, 2017, p. 26

14 “Think of all the profits that Shell extracts from Nigeria’s oil reserves, for example, or that Anglo-American pulls out of South Africa’s gold mines. Foreign investors take nearly $500 billion in profits out of developing countries each year, most of which goes to rich countries.” Jason Hickel, *The Divide: A Brief Guide to Global Inequality and its Solutions*, p. 26

15 “A big proportion of this takes place through ‘leakages’ in the balance of payments between countries, through which developing countries lose around $973 billion each year. Another takes place through an illegal practice known as ‘trade invoicing’. Basically, corporations – foreign and domestic alike – report false prices on their trade invoices in order to spirit money out of developing countries directly into tax havens and secrecy jurisdictions. Developing countries lose $875 billion through trade invoicing each year. A similarly large amount flows out annually through ‘abusive transfer pricing’, a mechanism that multinational companies use to steal money from developing countries by shifting profits illegally between their own subsidiaries in different countries. Usually the goal of these practices is to evade taxes, but sometimes they are used to launder money or circumvent capital controls.” Jason Hickel, *The Divide: A Brief Guide to Global Inequality and its Solutions*, p. 27

16 https://www.tni.org/en/article/debt-austerity-devastation

17 To use David Dayen's term, https://prospect.org/coronavirus/how-fed-bailed-out-the-investor-class-corporate-america/

18 https://robertreich.org/post/621202833075781163

19 https://www.reuters.com/article/uk-health-coronavirus-cenbank-graphic-idUKKBN22N2EP

20 Maurizio Lazzarato, *The Making of the Indebted Man*, The MIT Press, London, 2012

21 David Harvey, *A Brief History of Neo-liberalism*, p. 19

22 Jason Hickel, *The Divide: A Brief Guide to Global Inequality and its Solutions*, Windmill Books, London, 2017, p. 17

23 Susan George, *A Fate Worse Than Debt*, p. 257

## Chapter 10: Scientific Materialism

1 John Carroll, *The Wreck of Western Culture – Humanism Revisited*, Scribe, Melbourne, 2004

2 Tom Sorell, *Scientism: Philosophy and the Infatuation with Science*, New York: Routledge, 1991.

3 Ian Hutchinson, *Monopolizing Knowledge: A Scientist Refutes Religion-Denying, Reason-Destroying Scientism*, Fias Publishing, Belmont, MA, 2011.

4 Allan Bullock & Stephen Trombley (Eds), *The New Fontana Dictionary of Modern Thought*, London: Harper Collins, 1999, p.775

5 David Orr, (October 1992), "Environmental Literacy: Education as if the Earth Mattered", Twelfth Annual EF Schumacher Lectures, Great Barrington, MA

6 Quoted by Abdalhaqq Bewley, https://bewley.virtualave.net/darkness.html

7 René Descartes, *Principles of Philosophy*, Part 1, Article vii, tr. by John Veitch, http://cat.lib.unimelb.edu.au:80/record=b3987012~S30

8 Abdalhaqq Bewley, https://bewley.virtualave.net/darkness.html

9 Abdalhaqq Bewley, https://bewley.virtualave.net/darkness.html

10 Massimo Pigliucci, https://blog.apaonline.org/2018/01/25/the-problem-with-scientism/

11 https://shaykhabdalqadir.com/2013/07/28/technique-as-religion/

12 Abdalhaqq Bewley, https://bewley.virtualave.net/darkness.html

13 A very serious event resulting in great destruction and change, *Cambridge Dictionary*

14 Ernst Jünger, cited by Shaykh Abdalqadir as-Sufi, "The Gestalt of Freedom", *Ian Dallas: Collected Works*, p. 835

15 Shaykh Abdalqadir as-Sufi, "The Gestalt of Freedom", *Ian Dallas: Collected Works*, p. 837

## Chapter 11: Public Relations

1 Shaykh Abdalqadir, *Engines of the Broken World*, p. 112

2 Shaykh Abdalqadir al-Sufi , *The Interim is Mine*, p. 136

3 Pamela Thurschwell, *Sigmund Freud*, Routledge, London, 2000, p.1

4 Adam Curtis documentary, "The Century of the Self, 2004, Part 1: Happiness Machines"

5 Adam Curtis documentary, "The Century of the Self, 2004, Part 1: Happiness Machines"

6 A focus group is a small demographically diverse group of people whose reactions are studied in market research or political analysis. The reactions of the participants, in guided and open discussions about new products, for example, can be used to determine the reactions that can be expected from the general public. The focus group is a research

method designed to collect data which offer powerful insights into people's feelings and thoughts and thus a more detailed, nuanced, and richer understanding of their perspectives on ideas, products, and policies.

7 Stewart Ewan, Adam Curtis documentary, "The Century of the Self, 2004, Part 1: Happiness Machines"

8 Herbert Hoover, Adam Curtis documentary, "The Century of the Self, 2004, Part 1: Happiness Machines"

9 She was secretary of the International Psychoanalytical Association from 1925-1934

10 Ellen Herman, Adam Curtis documentary, "The Century of the Self, 2004, Part 2"

11 John Gittinger, Adam Curtis documentary, "The Century of the Self, 2004, Part 2"

12 Robert Reich, Adam Curtis documentary, "The Century of the Self, 2004, Part 4"

13 Robert Reich, Adam Curtis documentary, "The Century of the Self, 2004, Part 4"

14 Herbert Marcuse, Adam Curtis documentary, "The Century of the Self, 2004, Part 3"

## Chapter 12: The Nuclear Family

1 Alexis Martinez, https://medium.com/gender-theory/the-home-and-capitalism-8c4082388603

2 Working Group Report, 1986, p. 13, https://www.dennisfox.net/papers/reagan-family.html

3 Quoted by Shaykh Abdalqadir as-Sufi, *Technique of the Coup de Banque*, p. 86

4 Shaykh Abdalqadir as-Sufi, *Technique of the Coup de Banque*, p. 87

5 Shaykh Abdalqadir as-Sufi, *The Time of the Bedouin: on the politics of power*, pp. 164-165

6 Shaykh Abdalqadir as-Sufi, *The Collaborative Couple*, the title of a lecture delivered by him at the University of Malaya in 1990.

7 Rabea Redpath, Granada Mosque's XVI Anniversary, "The Collaborative Couple: A vision of Shaykh Abdalqadir As-Sufi", talk given on June 30, 2019

8 Shaykh Abdalqadir as-Sufi, *The Collaborative Couple*, 1990.

9 Shaykh Abdalqadir as-Sufi, *The Collaborative Couple*, 1990.

10 Gilles Deleuze and Felix Guattari, *Anti-Oedipus: Capitalism and Schizophrenia*, trans. Robert Hurley, Mark Seem and Helen R. Lane, Continuum, London and New York, 2004, p. 323

11 Timothy Laurie and Hannah Stark, "Reconsidering Kinship Beyond the Nuclear Family" with Deleuze and Guattari, *Cultural Studies Review* volume 18 number 1 March 2012, http://epress.lib.uts.edu.au/journals/index.php/csrj/index pp. 19-39

## Chapter 13: Education

1 Alexander James Ingles (1879-1924) in *The Principles of Secondary Education*, Houghton Mifflin Company, Boston, c1918

2 John Taylor Gatto, "A Short Angry History of Compulsory Schooling", *Educating Your Children in Modern Times*, Kinza Academy, San Ramon, California, 2003, p. 17

3 Philomena Abernathey, Josh Bell, Amanda Chapple, Jodie Claypool and Allen Cobb, "The Six Functions of Education: Adaptive, Integrating, Diagnostic and Directive, Differentiation, Selective and Propaedeutic", Idaho College, 2012, p.6

4 John Taylor Gatto, "A Short Angry History of Compulsory Schooling", *Educating Your Children in Modern Times*, p. 18

5 John Taylor Gatto, "A Short Angry History of Compulsory Schooling", *Educating Your Children in Modern Times*, p. 18

6 John Taylor Gatto, "A Short Angry History of Compulsory Schooling", *Educating Your Children in Modern Times*, pp. 11-12

7 John Taylor Gatto, "A Short Angry History of Compulsory Schooling", *Educating Your Children in Modern Times*, pp. 11-13

8 John Taylor Gatto, "A Short Angry History of Compulsory Schooling", *Educating Your Children in Modern Times*, p. 18

9 Shaykh Abdalqadir as-Sufi, Introduction to *The Meaning of Man: The Foundations of the Science of Knowledge*, Ali al-Jamal, Diwan Press, Norwich, 1977, p. 1

10 Shaykh Abdalqadir as-Sufi, *Oedipus and Dionysus*, Ian Dallas, Granada, 1992 p. 23

11 Shaykh Abdalqadir as-Sufi, *Kufr: An Islamic Critique*, p. 26

12 Shaykh Abdalqadir as-Sufi, *The Book of 'Amal*, Madina Press, Cape Town, 2008, p. 58

13 Shaykh Abdalqadir as-Sufi, *The Book of 'Amal*, p. 40

14 Shaykh Abdalqadir as-Sufi, *The Book of 'Amal*, p. 42

15 Shaykh Abdalqadir as-Sufi, "Discourse on Futuwwa", Cape Town, 2013

16 Abū 'Abd ar-Raḥmān al-Sulamī, *Kitāb al-Futuwwa*, Inner Traditions International, New York, 1983, p. 33

17 Shaykh Abdalqadir as-Sufi, "Talk on Futuwwa", Cape Town, 2007

18 Abū Ḥāmid al-Ghazālī, *Iḥyā 'Ulum ad-dīn*, section translated as *The Duties of Brotherhood in Islam* by Muhtar Holland, The Islamic Foundation, Leicester, 1980, p. 5

19 Shaykh Abdalqadir as-Sufi, *The Book of 'Amal*, p. 54

20 "Renowned Arab knights such as Imru'ul al-Qays and Antar ibn Shadad al-Absi were not officially knighted as in Europe. They became knights by reputation of their courage, dignity, noble deeds and the pursuit of honour, through poetry, tales and legends. Incorporating generosity, forgiveness, and a just and honourable repute as well as advocating justice and freedom, they became the treasure of their people, and a major aspect of Arab poetry. Pride of culture revolved around their adventures and feats." Habeeb Salloum, https://www.newageislam.com/islam-and-the-west/habeeb-salloum/arab-manliness-and-honour-muruah-gave-birth-to-european-chivalry/d/110428

21 Ibn Isḥāq and Ibn Hishām, https://abuaminaelias.com/dailyḥadithonline/2012/08/06/prophet-universal-justice/

22 Al-Jāḥiẓ, *Al-Bayān wa-at-Tabyīn*, (Cairo, 1932) 3:11 as quoted by Shihab al-Sarraf, https://www.scribd.com/document/217703816/Mamluk-Literature-and-Its-Antecedents

23 Umar Faruq Abdallah, http://qadriyya.org/wp-content/uploads/2011/02/Dr_UFA_Lecture_QARS_2011.pdf

24 Jonathan Phillips, "The Image of Saladin: From the Medieval to the Modern Age", https://repository.gei.de/bitstream/handle/11428/129/ED_2011_04_06_Phillips_Reputation_of_Saladin.pdf?sequence=9&isAllowed=y

25 Shaykh Abdalqadir as-Sufi, *The Book of 'Amal*, p. 47

26 Shaykh Abdalqadir as-Sufi, *The Interim is Mine*, Budgate Press, Cape Town, 2010, p. 25

27 Shaykh Abdalqadir as-Sufi, *The Interim is Mine*, pp. 26-27

28 Shaykh Abdalqadir as-Sufi, *The Interim is Mine*, p. 28

29 Shaykh Abdalqadir as-Sufi, *The Interim is Mine*, p. 30

30 Shaykh Abdalqadir as-Sufi, *The Interim is Mine*, p. 30

31 Shaykh Abdalqadir as-Sufi *The Interim is Mine*, p. 54

32 Shaykh Abdalqadir as-Sufi, *The Interim is Mine*, pp. 55, 56

33 The Magna Carta is a "charter of English liberties granted by King John of England on June 15, 1215, under threat of civil war and reissued, with alterations, in 1216, 1217 and 1225. By declaring the sovereign to be subject to the rule of law and documenting the liberties held by 'free men,' the Magna Carta provided the foundation for individual rights in Anglo-American jurisprudence." https://www.britannica.com/topic/Magna-Carta

34 Shaykh Abdalqadir as-Sufi, *The Interim is Mine*, p. 66

35 Shaykh Abdalqadir as-Sufi, *The Interim is Mine*, p. 73

36 Shaykh Abdalqadir as-Sufi, *The Interim is Mine*, p. 111

37 Robert Devereux, the Earl of Essex, quoted by Shaykh Abdalqadir as-Sufi, *The Interim is Mine*, pp. 78, 79

## Chapter 14: Media

1 https://getuplearn.com/blog/functions-of-mass-media/

2 https://getuplearn.com/blog/mass-media-and-society/

3 https://getuplearn.com/blog/functions-of-mass-media/#information

4 Hassim Dockrat, personal communication.

5 Glyn Davies, *A History of Money: From Ancient Times to the Present Day*, University of Wales Press, Cardiff, 2002

6 John Ralston Saul, *The Collapse of Globalism and the Reinvention of the World*, Viking, Australia, 2005

7 Francis Fukuyama, *The End of History and the Last Man*, Penguin, London, 1992, p. 4

8 https://www.dosomething.org/us/facts/11-facts-about-global-poverty

9 https://www.cnbc.com/2017/11/14/richest-1-percent-now-own-half-the-worlds-wealth.html

10 https://shaykhabdalqadir.com/the-collapse-of-the-monetarist-society-part-three/

11 John McMurtry, "The Cancer Stage of Capitalism", *CCPA Monitor*, July/August 1996

12 Hacking is the act of gaining unauthorised access to data in a system or computer.

13 Jason Ferriman, *After Wikileaks: An Assessment of the Wikileaks Phenomenon*, The Dallas House Monographs, Cape Town, 2011, pp. 44-45

14 Jason Ferriman, *After Wikileaks: An Assessment of the Wikileaks Phenomenon*, p. 46

## PART 3

1 https://shaykhabdalqadir.com/2011/09/12/syria-the-end-of-the-world-community/

2 The caliphate

3 https://shaykhabdalqadir.com/2011/06/22/ayyuhal-walad-lesson-nine-here-is-the-*dīn*/

4 The science of the application of the *sharī'a*

5 https://shaykhabdalqadir.com/2011/06/22/ayyuhal-walad-lesson-nine-here-is-the-*dīn*/

6 https://shaykhabdalqadir.com/the-collapse-of-the-monetarist-society-part-three/

7 https://www.youtube.com/watch?v=XO70G3zrR3g

## Chapter 15: The Institutions of Islamic governance

1 Shaykh Abdalqadir al-Sufi, *Oedipus and Dionysus*, Freiberg, Malaysia, 1992, p. 9

2 Shaykh Abdalqadir al-Sufi, *The New Wagnerian*, Freiberg, Granada, 1990, p. 15

3 Q. 59: 6,7

4 Abū'l Hasan al-Mawardī, *al-Aḥkām as-Sulṭāniyyah*, tr. Asadullah Yate, Ta-Ha Publishers Ltd., London, 1996

5 B. Tibi, "Authority and Legitimation", *The Oxford Encyclopedia of the Modern Islamic World,* Oxford, 1995, pp. 155-160

6 Abū'l Hasan al-Mawardī, *al-Aḥkām as-Sulṭāniyyah*, p. 28

7 *Kharaj* is a tax levied on land by the Caliph 'Umar. He had decided not to divide conquered land among the soldiers but rather to leave it to its owners in return for a payment of a tax on the land.

8 Imām al-Ghazālī, *Naṣīḥat al-Mulūk*, tr. as *Counsel for Kings* by F.R.C. Bagley, Oxford University Press, London, 1964, p. 114

9 Abū'l Hasan Abū'l Hasan al-Mawardī, *al-Aḥkām as-Sulṭāniyyah*, p. 362

10 S.M Ghazanfar, "Medieval Public-Sector Economics", in *Medieval Islamic Economic Thought*, ed. S.M. Ghazanfar, Routledge Curzon, London, 2003, p. 241

11 Qur'ān 4: 104

12 A.R.I. Doi, *Shari'ah: The Islamic Law*, Ta Ha Publishers, London, 1984, p. 14

13 Shatzmiller, M, Bosworth, C.E., Heffening, W., *The Encyclopaedia of Islam, Vol. 2, "Tidjara"*

14 R.P. Buckley, *The Book of the Islamic Market Inspector*, Oxford University Press, Oxford, 1999, p. 3

15 S.M. Ghazanfar, *Medieval Islamic Economic Thought*, Routledge Curzon, London, 2003, pp. 229-230

16 Ibn Taymiya, *Public Duties in Islam: The Institution of the Ḥisba,* tr. Muhtar Holland, The Islamic Foundation, Leicester, 1982, pp. 29-33

17 A-K. Rafeq, "Craft Organisation, Work Ethics, and the Strains of Change in Ottoman Syria", *Journal of the American Oriental Society* p. 497

18 B. Lewis, "The Islamic Guilds", *The Economic History Review,* Vol.8 No. 1,(Nov., 1937) pp. 20-34

19 A-K. Rafeq, "Craft Organisation, Work Ethics, and the Strains of Change in Ottoman Syria", *Journal of the American Oriental Society,* Vol. III. No. 3 (Jul.-Sep., 1991) p. 497

20 M. Maksudoğlu, "Waqf", *Sultaniyya,* Madina Press, Cape Town, 2002, p. 52

21 M.G.S. Hodgson, *The Venture of Islam: Conscience and History in a World Civilisation,* University of Chicago Press, Chicago, 1974, p. 124

22 M. Hoexter, "Waqf Studies in the Twentieth Century: The State of the Art", *Journal of the Economic and Social History of the Orient,* Vol. 41, No. 4. (1998), p. 476

23 T. Kuran, "The Provision of Public Goods Under Islamic Law: Origins, Impact, and Limitations of the Waqf System", *Law and Society Review,* Vol. 35. No. 4, 2001, p. 849

24 M. Maksudoğlu, "Waqf", pp. 58-59

25 A popular collection of prayers on the Prophet.

26 Celebration of the birth of the Prophet.

27 T. Kuran, "The Provision of Public Goods Under Islamic Law: Origins, Impact, and Limitations of the Waqf System", p. 850

## Chapter 16: Trade & Commerce in the Qur'ān

In the following chapters, unreferenced translations are by Abdassamad Clarke

1 Mujāhid was the great Follower who was a student of the Companion 'Abdullāh ibn 'Abbās ﷺ, who had been singled out for his exceptional grasp of the explanation of Qur'an, and to whom Mujāhid had read out the Qur'ān numerous times, a number of times going through the meanings as well.

2 'Abdalwāḥid ibn 'Āshir said in his *al-Murshid al-Mu'īn:* "The first thing which is incumbent upon the legally capable person – as long as he is capable of reflection – is that he know Allah and the Messengers by the attributes and qualities set out in the *āyats*."

3 al-Qurṭubī, *al-Jāmi' li aḥkām al-Qur'ān,* (51:56).

4 It is important to note that spending must be from legitimate wealth from *ḥalāl* sources. In other words, the philanthropy that has been the mark of the guilt-ridden usurer since at least the time of the Medici banking family is unacceptable. Ill-gotten gains are only to be restored to those they were taken from, not disbursed in very public displays of philanthropy.

5 Cicero, in the second book of his treatise *De Officiis*

6 Ar-Rāghib al-Aṣfahānī (d. c. 1109 CE), *al-Mufradāt fī gharīb al-Qur'ān*

7 *Tafsīr al-Qurṭubī, Vol. 1, Juz' 1: Al-Fātiḥah & Sūrat al-Baqara 1-141,* Translated by Aisha Bewley, Diwan Press.

8 *ibid*

9 See: Abdalhaqq Bewley with Amal Abdalhakim Douglas, *Zakat – Raising a Fallen Pillar,* Diwan Press.

10 Exponential growth was first discovered by mathematicians in their studies of compound interest.

11 Here we see the correct use of *maqāṣid,* not as self-sufficient sources of legislation, but providing an understanding of its deeper purposes.

12 Qāḍī Abū Bakr ibn al-'Arabī, *Aḥkām al-Qur'ān*

13 *Tafsīr al-Qurṭubī, Vol. 3, Juz' 3: Sūra al-Baqarah 254 – Sūrah Āli 'Imrān 95*, p.89, translated by Aisha Bewley, Diwan Press

14 *Tafsīr al-Qurṭubī, Vol. 3, Juz' 3: Sūra al-Baqarah 254 – Sūrah Āli 'Imrān 95*, p.144-6, translated by Aisha Bewley, Diwan Press

15 Imām Mālik ibn Anas, *al-Muwaṭṭa'*, 31.23 General section on selling food, 1899, tr. Aisha Bewley, Diwan Press.

16 'Fruits' here mean agricultural produce and not necessarily those that are sweet.

17 *Ṣaḥīḥ al-Bukhārī, Bāb as-salām ilā ajalin mā'lūm....*

18 Ibn Mājah with a *ḥasan isnād*. Al-Ḥākim says it is *ṣaḥīḥ*.

19 Niall Ferguson, *The Ascent of Money – A Financial History of the World*, Penguin, 2008.

20 Muslim narrated it in his *Ṣaḥīḥ*, and here it is from *The Complete Forty Hadith* of Imām an-Nawawī. Ta-Ha Publishing Ltd., London 3rd revised edition.

21 Ar-Rāghib al-Aṣfahānī, *al-Mufradāt fī gharīb al-Qur'ān.*

22 He was the sixth person in Islam, and one of the very few who had memorised the entire Qur'ān directly from the Prophet ﷺ. The *fiqh* of the people of Kufa, i.e. Ḥanafīs, relies a great deal on his narrations.

23 Imām Mālik ibn Anas, *al-Muwaṭṭa'*, 31.44 What is not permitted of free loans, No. 94, tr. Aisha Bewley, Diwan Press.

24 *Tafsīr al-Qurṭubī, Vol. 4, Juz' 4: Sūrah Āli 'Imrān 96 – 200 & Sūra an-Nisā' 1 – 23*, p.65, translated by Aisha Bewley, Diwan Press,

25 *alladhīna hādū* – the Jews, refers specifically to the descendants of Yahūdhā (Judah), one of the twelve sons of Ya'qūb ﷺ.

26 Ammar Fairdous, *A Convergence of Civilisations – The Ascendancy of Usury over Judaeo-Christian and Muslim Commerce*, Diwan Press 2023.

27 Shaykh Dr. Abdalqadir as-Sufi, "Ta Sin Mim – Today", https://shaykhabdalqadir.com/ta-sin-mim-today/

28 *ibid*

29 Crops and cattle are not hidden but exposed to view (*ẓāhir*) before people. But people's money and debts are hidden (*bāṭin*) and only known to them themselves.

30 Shabbīr 'Usmānī, "*Kitāb al-īmān,* (8) – The chapter on the command to fight people until they say *lā ilāha ill'Allāh Muḥammad rasūlu'llāh* – there is no god but Allah and Muḥammad is the Messenger of Allah", *Fatḥ al-mulhim bi sharḥ Ṣaḥīḥ al-Imām Muslim.* To be published by Turath Publishing.

31 "On payment of *zakāt* to the Imām whether he is just or unjust", the *Mudawwana.*

32 *ibid*

33 Ibn Juzayy al-Kalbī, *al-Qawānīn al-fiqhiyya – The Judgments of Fiqh, Vol.2 – 'Ibādāt,* translated by Asadullah Yate, Diwan Press

34 al-Qurṭubī, *al-Jāmi' li aḥkām al-Qur'ān.*

35 Ibn Juzayy al-Kalbī, *Kitāb at-tashīl li 'ulūm at-tanzīl.*

36 Abū Dāwūd and an-Nasā'ī narrated it from Ibn 'Umar.

37 The *mudd* is what two cupped hands can contain, defined by the People of Madīna by the hands of the Messenger of Allah ﷺ. They had made vessels for the *mudd* and the *ṣā'* according to this definition.

38 Four *mudds*.

39 A major student of Saḥnūn whose *Mudawwana* is the pillar of Mālikī *fiqh* after the *Muwaṭṭa'*.

40 The earliest work in Islam dedicated to the rulings governing the market. It was transmitted in *al-Mi'yār al-Mughrib* of al-Wansharīsī (d. 1508 CE).

41 Yaḥyā ibn 'Umar, *Aḥkām as-Sūq*, unpublished translation by Abdassamad Clarke

42 The *ṣā'* is a volumetric measure and the *riṭl* is a weight, and yet Imām Mālik defined one in terms of the other even though the same volume of different substances will have different weights. It is understood that what is implicit here is that the substance in this case is wheat, since that was the dominant staple among the people of Madīna.

43 Al-Qāḍī 'Iyāḍ, *Tartīb al-madārik*

44 Abdalhaqq Bewley, "The Prophet ﷺ as Ruler", *MFAS Journal 1.1*, Diwan Press.

45 Ibn Khaldūn, *al-Muqaddima*.

46 *ibid*

47 Shaykh Abdalqadir as-Sufi, "The Islamic Dinar – A Way-stage Passed," https://shaykhabdalqadir.com/the-islamic-*dīnār*-a-way-stage-passed/

48 *ibid*

49 Ibn Juzayy al-Kalbī, *al-Qawānīn al-fiqhiyya – The Judgments of Fiqh, Vol.2 – Mu'āmalāt and other matters,* p.119, translated by Asadullah Yate, Diwan Press

50 McGrath, James F., "Jesus and the Money Changers (John 2:13-16)" https://digitalcommons.butler.edu/cgi/viewcontent.cgi?article=1887&context=facsch_papers

51 4th Muslim Lawyers' Conference in Potsdam 29th June – 1st July 2001, http://www.bogvaerker.dk/wordpress/?p=662 (accessed 9/8/23).

52 Umar Vadillo, "Living Islam: Muamalat and Sufism, Rethinking Islamic Banking, EP 30", https://open.spotify.com/episode/6oTDJpuTU1IuPRHXLa6KLm

53 The mint is a service to anyone who wishes to change their gold and silver – whether other coinage, jewellery, cutlery, clippings, or raw metals –

into gold *dīnārs* and silver *dirhams*. It is supervised by the judiciary on behalf of a leader. It is not a leader's duty to 'issue a currency'. Moreover, unlike contemporary minting which is a highly technological process and thus very capital intensive, the main expense of traditional minting is the production of the dies for the obverse and reverse sides of the coins. The rest of the process requires nothing more than a firm setting for one die, an implement for the other die and a strong hammer.

54 Edward Lane, *Arabic-English Lexicon.*

55 Ibn Juzayy al-Kalbī, *Kitāb at-tashīl li 'ulūm at-tanzīl*

56 Sa'īd ibn Manṣūr in his *Sunan* as a *mursal* [*ḥadīth* narrated by a Companion or Follower without mention of the Companion who had heard it directly from the Prophet ﷺ].

57 Aṣ-Ṣāwī, *al-Ḥāshiyah 'alā al-Jalālayn.*

58 *ibid.*

59 At-Tirmidhī narrated it from Abū Hurayra.

60 Even though 'martyr' is literally a witness as is *shahīd*, one hesitates to use the word in translation because of its cultural appropriation by christianism and because it is thus overlain with the sense of passive suffering and pain, far from the joyous sense of the word *shahīd.*

61 At-Tirmidhī and al-Ḥākim narrated it from Abū Sa'īd al-Khudrī

62 Al-Munāwī, *Fayḍ al-Qadīr*

63 As-Suyūṭī, in *Tārīkh al-Khulafā'*, translated as *The History of the Khalifahs who took the Right Way* by Abdassamad Clarke, Ta-Ha Publishers Ltd., London

64 al-Qurṭubī, *al-Jāmi' li aḥkām al-Qur'ān*i

65 Ibn Juzayy al-Kalbī, *Kitāb at-tashīl li 'ulūm at-tanzīl*, the commentary on the *āyat*, *"They were only ordered to worship Allah, making their dīn sincerely His as people of pure natural faith..."* (Sūra al-Bayyina – The Clear Sign 98:5).

1 *ibid*

1 *ibid*

## CHAPTER 17: TRADE AND COMMERCE IN THE SUNNA AND SĪRA

1 *Ṣaḥīḥ Muslim*

2 The winter and summer caravans are referred to in Qur'ān 106:2. The winter caravan is said to have gone to the Yemen and Abyssinia, and the summer one to Syria. Ghassān were an Arab tribe on the southern border of the Byzantine empire in alliance with it.

3 Ammar Fairdous, *A Convergence of Civilisations – The Ascendancy of Usury over Judaeo-Christian and Muslim Commerce*, Diwan Press 2023, citing: M. Van De Mieroop, "The invention of interest. Sumerian loans", *The Origins of Value – The Financial Innovations that Created Modern Capital Markets*, Oxford University Press, Oxford, p. 17-30.

4 Ammar Fairdous, *A Convergence of Civilisations*, citing B. Bromberg, "The origin of banking: religious finance in Babylonia" 2, *The Journal of Economic History* 77

5 Michael Hudson, *And Forgive Them Their Debts: Lending, Foreclosure and Redemption From Bronze Age Finance to the Jubilee Year,* ISLET (October 30, 2018)

6 Ammar Fairdous, *A Convergence of Civilisations – The Ascendancy of Usury over Judaeo-Christian and Muslim Commerce*, p.17

7 Prof. Benjamin Nelson, *The Idea of Usury, from Tribal Brotherhood to Universal Otherhood,* Princeton University Press; First Edition (January 1, 1949).

8 Al-Ḥasan al-Baṣrī counts the Divine name al-Khāliq – the Creator among those names that, like ar-Raḥmān – the All-Merciful, may not be used for a created being.

9 Narrated by Imām Aḥmad in his *Musnad*, Abū Dāwūd, and Imām Muslim in his *Ṣaḥīḥ*.

10 Edward Lane, *Arabic-English Lexicon*. Something to note here is that these definitions are Edward Lane's scrupulous translations of entries from dictionaries written in Arabic about the Arabic language by the most famous lexicographers.

11 *ibid*

12 *Tafsīr al-Qurṭubī, Vol. 3, Juz' 3: Sūrat al-Baqara 254 – 286 & Sūrah Āli 'Imrān 1 – 95*, translated by Aisha Bewley, Diwan Press.

13 *ibid*

14 Abdalhaqq Bewley, "The Prophet as Ruler", *MFAS Journal 1.1*, Diwan Press

15 Ad-Dārimī, "Chapter on the departure of knowledge," *as-Sunan*,

16 See Ibn Abī Zayd al-Qayrawānī, *Kitāb al-Jāmi'*, Chapter 1, Sunnahs the opposite of which are innovations, on being led and following, the merits of the Companions and about shunning the people of innovation. Translated by Abdassamad Clarke, Diwan Press.

17 Shaykh Muḥammad ibn 'Alawī al-Mālikī responded to works that Imām Muḥammad ibn al-Ḥasan ash-Shaybānī and Imām ash-Shāfi'ī wrote critical of Imām Mālik and the school of Madīna in his book *Faḍl al-Muwaṭṭa' wa 'ināya al-umma al-Islāmiyya bihi*.

18 It ought to be noted that this treatment did not stem from partisanship, for Imām Muḥammad, may Allah have mercy on him, treated the *Kitāb al-Āthār* of Imām Abū Ḥanīfa in a similar fashion. See my translation published by Turath Publishing of London.

19 *Tārīkh Dimashq* by Ibn 'Asākir as well as *Tārīkh Baghdād*, and *Dhamm al-kalām wa ahlihi* by al-Harawī.

20 "Madīna the New Matrix", Abdassamad Clarke, from the module, "Early Madīna", The Muslim Faculty of Advanced Studies.

21 Shaykh Abdalqadir as-Sufi, *The Time of the Bedouin: on the politics of power,* Budgate Press, p.288.

22 *ibid*, p.275

23 Dean of the College of Islamic Studies at Hamad Bin Khalifa University

24 Ibn Kathīr, *al-Bidāya wa an-Nihāya*.

25 Abdalhaqq Bewley, "The Prophet ﷺ as Ruler", *MFAS Journal 1.1*, Diwan Press

26 *Sunna* comprises what the Messenger of Allah ﷺ did (*fi'lī*), his words of instruction, prohibition and advice (*qawlī*), and his endorsements (*iqrārī*).

27 Al-Bukhārī and Muslim from Abū Hurayra

28 Abdalhaqq Bewley, "Futuwwa" https://www.youtube.com/watch?v=oKhoRfOSszw

29 Al-Bukhārī and Muslim, at-Tirmidhī and Ibn Mājah narrated it from Anas

30 Ibn Mājah narrated it from Abū Usayd.

31 Aṭ-Ṭabarānī narrated it in *al-Kabīr* from Abū Usayd.

32 Ibn Shabbah, *Tārīkh al-Madīna*.

33 *ibid*.

34 al-Qurṭubī, *al-Jāmi' li aḥkām al-Qur'ān* on *āyat* 25:7.

35 At-Tirmidhī narrated it from Abū Hurayra.

36 Riyad Asvat, "*Mu'āmalāt* as the Way Forward" a lecture from the module "The Question Concerning Economics", the Muslim Faculty of Advanced Studies, 2014.

37 *Al-Muwaṭṭa',* Imām Mālik ibn Anas, tr. Aisha Bewley, Diwan Press.

38 Ibn Sa'd, *aṭ-Ṭabaqāt al-kubrā.*

39 Abdassamad Clarke and Dr. Tobias Andersson, "Introduction to the History of the Khalifahs", from the module, "The History of the Khalifahs", the Muslim Faculty of Advanced Studies.

40 Shaykh Dr. Abdalqadir as-Sufi, "Discourse: Britain-Money-Muslims-Monarchy – Part 1 of 5", https://www.youtube.com/watch?v=rB5bYk3Z2Ns

41 Abū Dāwūd and at-Tirmidhī narrated it and he [at-Tirmidhī] said, "A good *ṣaḥīḥ ḥadīth.*" No. 28 in Imām an-Nawawī's foundational collection, *The Complete Forty Hadith*, translated by Abdassamad Clarke. Ta-Ha Publishers Ltd., London

42 *Jāmi' at-Tirmidhī*

43 She was from Quraysh and emigrated to Madīna, where the Prophet ﷺ assigned her a house in which she lived with her son.

44 Ibn Ḥajar al-'Asqalānī, *al-Iṣāba fī tamyīz aṣ-Ṣaḥāba.*

45 *Mughnī al-muḥtāj* 2:22

46 In addition to local government help, the Muslims of Norwich in England even received a commendation from the Prime Minister's office for the perceived benefit to the local community from their initiative.

47 *Sunan Ibn Mājah*

48 At today's prices (30/8/2022) the debt was more than £150,000.

49 'Amr ibn Maymūn narrated it, according to as-Suyūṭī in *Tārīkh al-Khulafā'*, translated as *The History of the Khalifahs who took the Right Way* by Abdassamad Clarke, Ta-Ha Publishers Ltd., London

50 £89,858,000 in today's prices (30/8/2022).

51 Al-Bukhārī narrated it.

52 *Mawlās* are both the freed slaves, often non-Arabs, and those who had taken an affiliation to an Arab tribe.

53 'Abd al-Ḥayy al-Kattānī, "Chapter on 'Umar being upset at the Companions for their abandoning trade to other ordinary people and the rabble", *at-Tarātīb al-idāriyya.*

54 Qāḍī 'Iyāḍ, *Tartīb al-Madārik.*

55 1302/1884 – 1382/1962

56 'Abd al-Ḥayy al-Kattānī, *at-Tarātīb al-idāriyya.*

57 *ibid*

58 Shaykh Dr. Abdalqadir as-Sufi, *Root Islamic Education*

59 *Oxford Dictionary*

60 Perennialism acknowledges the fact of the universal human experience of the Divine and Prophethood but ignores or denies the abrogation by the last revelation of Sayyiduna Muḥammad ﷺ of all other religions. In his magisterial work, *The Esoteric Deviation in Islam,* Umar Vadillo treats this movement among Muslims in considerable depth, examining it against the *uṣūl ad-dīn*, the *uṣūl al-fiqh* and the *fiqh* itself, especially of the *mu'āmalāt.*

## Chapter 18: Transactions – *Mu'āmalāt*

1 Ilyās Qabalūn, "Introduction on *Mabādi' uṣūl al-fiqh*" to *al-Manār fī uṣūl al-fiqh* by Imām an-Nasafī, Dar al-Kotob al-Ilmiya, Beirut 1971.

2 Ad-Dārimī and at-Tirmidhī.

3 See as evidence the thesis that Prof. Benjamin Nelson develops in his work *The Idea of Usury – from Tribal Brotherhood to Universal Otherhood,* a thesis neatly summarised in the book title.

4 In a footnote, Ibrahim Lawson writes: "I use the word 'technik' (pronounced: tekneek) in place of the more conventional 'technique' or 'technology'. It refers to what Heidegger calls Gestell, which is normally translated as 'enframing' However, both of these alternatives have their

drawbacks, the German is too unfamiliar and the English neologism, while more technically correct, does not have the same immediate resonance as 'technik', in which we hear something more of the original Greek *techne* while at the same time seeing it somehow twisted into a strange and ugly new expression. Technik is the essence of modern technology; it is neither a piece of equipment nor a procedure but a way of Being which has grown out of the European tradition and become effectively global.

5 Ibrahim Lawson, "The Question Concerning Money", from "The Question Concerning Economics", the Muslim Faculty of Advanced Studies, https://themuslimfaculty.org/2-question-concerning-money/

6 Shaykh Dr. Abdalqadir as-Sufi, *The Book of 'Amal, Discourses*, p. 297, Dallas House (Pty) Ltd.

7 Abū Nu'aym narrated it from Anas

8 The *fuqahā* understand the Divine command here as recommendation.

9 John A. Makdisi, "The Islamic Origins of the Common Law," North Carolina Law Review, Vol. 77, pp.1687-1696.

10 Abdassamad Clarke, "Money: from Fiat to the Gold Dīnār", from the module, "The Question Concerning Economics", the Muslim Faculty of Advanced Studies.

11 Jörg Guido Hülsmann, *The Ethics of Money Production*,

12 *ibid*

13 Under the direction of Umar Vadillo, the Gold Dinar Movement minted dinars and dirhams and implemented their use in many different settings, most notably in the state of Kelantan in Malaysia, where they were used to settle utilities and in ordinary transactions, and where people used them to pay their *zakāt* with.

14 Imām Mālik ibn Anas, *al-Muwaṭṭa', 31.45.96,* tr. Aisha Bewley, Diwan Press

15 William Blackstone, *Commentaries on the Laws of England,* (1769), Vol. 4, p.91.

16 Al-Bayhaqī, *Shu'ab al-Īmān*

17 Al-Munāwī, *Fayḍ al-Qadīr, ḥadīth* 9385

18 Imām Mālik ibn Anas, *al-Muwaṭṭa',* 31.24 "Hoarding and raising prices by stockpiling", tr. Aisha Bewley, Diwan Press

19 Imām Mālik ibn Anas, *al-Muwaṭṭa',* 17.6 "*Zakāt* on the property of orphans and trading for orphans", tr. Aisha Bewley, Diwan Press

20 Humaira Shahid became a Member of the Punjab Provincial Assembly from 2002 where she fought for women's rights and then introduced the Punjab Private Money Lending Act, 2007, prohibiting interest-based private money lending in Punjab, Pakistan, and her law was replicated and adopted by the Provincial Assembly of the North-West Frontier Province. She earned an MPhil in English from the University of the Punjab. Humaira is author of the autobiographical *My Journey in Love, Faith and Politics.*

21 Humaira Shahid, *The Praxis of Prosperity,* "The public markets".

22 William Blackstone, *Commentaries on the Laws of England,* (1769)

23 Imām Mālik ibn Anas, *al-Muwaṭṭa',* 31.13.35

24 Yaḥyā ibn 'Umar al-Kinānī al-Andalusī, *Aḥkām as-Sūq.* My unpublished translation

25 *ibid*

26 *ibid*

27 Ivan Illich, "Beauty & The Junkyard", Whole Earth Review, Winter 1991.

28 Imām an-Nawawī, *ḥadīth* No. 9, *The Complete Forty Hadith,* translated by Abdassamad Clarke, Ta-Ha Publishing Ltd., London

29 "As for sales, they are of three kinds: 1. The sale of *'ayn*, by which we mean gold or silver, for *'arḍ*, anything other than these..." Ibn Juzayy al-Kalbī, *al-Qawānīn al-fiqhiyya – The Judgments of Fiqh, Vol.2 – Mu'āmalāt and other matters*, translated by Asadullah Yate, Diwan Press

30 Edward Lane, *The Arabic-English Lexicon,* in which Lane translates from one of the most famous Arabic dictionaries, *Tāj al-'Arūs* of az-Zabīdī, "[*īmān*]'s primary meaning is the becoming true to the trust with respect to which God has confided in one, by a firm believing with the heart; not by profession of belief with the tongue only, without the assent of the heart."

31 *ibid*

32 Humaira Shahid, *The Praxis of Prosperity,* "The public markets."

33 Imām al-Ghazālī, *On the Duties of Brotherhood,* translated by Muhtar Holland

34 Humaira Shahid, *The Praxis of Prosperity,* "The public markets."

35 See Chapter 18, pp.288-9 for Ivan Illich's account of Aristotle's observations on supply and demand.

36 https://www.brais.ac.uk/conferences/inaugural-conference-2014

37 James C. Scott, *Against the Grain,* p. 31.32

38 Imām Mālik ibn Anas, *al-Muwaṭṭa',* 31.13 *muzābana* and *muḥāqala,* tr. Aisha Bewley, Diwan Press

39 Paul Oliver, *The Story of the Blues,* , Oxford University Press, 1997

40 "Bitcoin: A Second Chance for the Muslim World" by Asif Shiraz and "How Bitcoin Can Help Muslims Follow the Teachings of the Quran" by "Muslim Bitcoiner"

41 Shoshana Zuboff, *The Age of Surveillance Capitalism, The Fight for a Human Future at the New Frontier of Power,* 2019, Public Affairs.

42 Aisha Bewley, "The Colonialisation of the Deen", *Reweaving Our Social Fabric,* Diwan Press.

43 Shoshana Zuboff, *The Age of Surveillance Capitalism,* 2019, Public Affairs.

44 https://open.spotify.com/episode/48kjIbpqn9IA7E5su5f1NG

45 Mustafa Özdamar, "Kitablar Kutubhaneler ve Vakiflar", Vakiflar, p.49, Istanbul Vakiflar Basmudurlugu, Istanbul 1984.

46 Prof. Mehmet Maksudoğlu, "Waqf", in *Sultaniyya* by Shaykh Dr. Abdalqadir as-Sufi.

47 Narrated by al-Ḥākim in his *Tārīkh* from Anas.

48 Also narrated by al-Ḥākim in his *Tārīkh* from Anas.

49 Clearly scholars of the *sharī'a* must number in the hundreds of thousands, from *madrasa*s and pesantren or pesantren pondoks in the East, İmam Hatip schools in Turkey, the Azhar in Egypt, the Zaytuna in Tunis, the Qarawiyyīn and other scholarly centres in Morocco, and the Dar al-Ulums in England.

50 https://www.reuters.com/article/finance-islamic-scholars-idUSL5E8DG31N20120229#

51 "HSBC is a key player in the arranging of Sukuk." https://www.sukuk.com/whos-who/hsbc-158/

52 Reuters *op cit*: "Last October Goldman announced it would issue as much as $2 billion in sukuk or Islamic bonds, making it one of the first top Western banks to raise money in that way."

53 Originally from a *khuṭba* delivered at the Ihsan Mosque, Norwich, UK, on 2/3/12, which was subsequently filmed as a talk: https://www.youtube.com/watch?v=nHE61NO2f-c. Here the original text has been greatly expanded upon.

54 Ibn Juzayy al-Kalbī, *al-Qawānīn al-fiqhiyya – The Judgments of Fiqh, Vol.2 – Mu'āmalāt and other matters,* p.119, translated by Asadullah Yate, Diwan Press

55 *ibid*

56 Imām Mālik ibn Anas, *al-Muwaṭṭa',* 31.33 Prohibition against two sales in one. At-Tirmidhī provided an *isnād* and said that it is *ḥasan ṣaḥīḥ,* as did an-Nasā'ī from Abū Hurayra.

57 *ibid*

58 A major feature of modern banking that loomed large during the pandemic is the Repo market, whereby the American Fed, in the new era of the "magic money tree", extended its reach – and the reach of the new debt – far beyond any sane limits and allegedly lent a total of $46 trillion. Repo is that one bank sells another bank some asset, for example treasury bonds, for $100 million with an agreement to purchase them back in a very short time for $110 million. In essence what has taken place is a loan of $100 million with $10 million paid in interest. The timescale is generally very small and so the interest rate is astronomically high.

59 Mufti Taqi Usmani, *An Introduction to Islamic Finance,* p.72

60 Usmani, *op cit,* p.67

61 Narrated by at-Tirmidhī, 1232; an-Nasā'ī, 4613; Abū Dāwūd, 3503, Ibn Mājah, 2187, Aḥmad, 14887, as cited by Ammar Fairdous in *A Convergence of Civilisations – The Ascendancy of Usury over Judaeo-Christian and Muslim Commerce,* "Chapter 4: Evading the Taint of Usury." Diwan Press 2023.

62 Imām Mālik ibn Anas, *al-Muwaṭṭa'* 31.19.45

63 Imām Mālik ibn Anas, *al-Muwaṭṭa'* 31.19 Buying on delayed terms and re-selling for less on more immediate terms

64 "Is Islamic Banking Really Islamic? An Insider's view with Harris Irfan". https://www.youtube.com/watch?v=f13mgKVjJsU&t=1677s Here an Islamic banker with decades of experience of the industry admits

clearly that it is usurious from top to bottom and entirely dependent on fractional reserve banking. Regrettably, after the splendid diagnosis he then moves on to a cure that is arguably worse than the disease.

65 Umar Vadillo, "Living Islam: Muamalat and Sufism, Fallacy of Islamic Banking", "Murabahah." Ep.32, https://open.spotify.com/episode/6ap8IiUCOP9IZtZwcipXVK in which he examines in much greater depth the issues involved in this transaction.

66 Ammar Fairdous, *A Convergence of Civilisations – The Ascendancy of Usury over Judaeo-Christian and Muslim Commerce*, "Chapter 4: Evading the Taint of Usury," Diwan Press 2023

67 'Abdullah ibn Sulaymān ibn Māni', *Baḥth fī ar-ribā wa aṣ-ṣarf*, Majallah al-Buhuth al-Islamiyyah, Vol. 46.

68 Yaḥyā ibn 'Umar al-Kinānī al-Andalusī, *Aḥkām as-Sūq*, my unpublished translation

69 *The Oxford Dictionary of English*

70 *ibid*

71 Ibn Juzayy al-Kalbī, *al-Qawānīn al-fiqhiyya – The Judgments of Fiqh, Vol.1 – 'Aqīdah and 'Ibādāt*, p.318-9, translated by Asadullah Yate, Diwan Press

72 Umar Vadillo, "Transforming Islamic Banking to Overcome Imminent Challenges", a document summarising the much fuller treatment in the podcast: "How to Transform Islamic Banking," Ep. 34, https://open.spotify.com/episode/019xuwDxTCIb1VP9g0Tf4H

73 For one example where this is already happening see the Local Zakat Initiative in the UK: https://localzakat.co.uk.

74 Yaḥyā ibn 'Umar, *Aḥkām as-sūq*, unpublished translation by Abdassamad Clarke

## Part 4 – Conclusion

1 Capitals are in the original

2 Shaykh Abdalqadir as-Sufi, *The Interim is Mine*, pp. 135-136

3 Q. 51:56

4 Shaykh Abdalqadir al-Sufi, *The Engines of the Broken World: Discourses on Tacitus and Lucan*, p. 166

5 Shaykh Abdalqadir as-Sufi, *The Sign of the Sword*, p. 25

6 *Ribā* is from the root *rabā* meaning to increase, to swell. Its technical meaning is usury and interest signifying "any unjustified increase of capital for which no compensation is given." (Schacht, *The Encyclopaedia of Islam*, Vol. 2, *Ribā*). Commenting on Qāḍī Abū Bakr ibn al-'Arabī's statement: "*Ribā* is any unjustified increment over the countervalue (*'iwaḍun*)", Umar Vadillo says: "Another way of expressing the same is '*Ribā* is any unjustified increment between the value of the goods given and the counter value of the goods received.'" Value is correct only if the transaction is equivalent. This equivalency is referred to in the Qur'ān as *qisṭ*. (Q. 5: 8)

7 Shaykh Abdalqadir as-Sufi, *The Sign of the Sword*, p. 19

8 Q. 2: 277,278

9 Shaykh Abdalqadir as-Sufi, *The Sign of the Sword*, p. 21

10 Shaykh Abdalqadir as-Sufi, *The Sign of the Sword*, pp. 23-24

11 Q. 48: 23

12 Jalāl ad-dīn al-Maḥallī and Jalāl ad-dīn as-Suyūṭī, *Tafsīr al-Jalālayn*, tr. Aisha Bewley, Dar Al Taqwa, London, 2007, p. 1102

13 https://shaykhabdalqadir.com/the-collapse-of-the-monetarist-society-part-three/

14 Chris Hedges, *America – The Farewell Tour*, Simon and Schuster, New York, 2018, p. 295

15 Chris Hedges, *America – The Farewell Tour*, p. 20

16 Shaykh Abdalqadir as-Sufi, *The Sign of the Sword*, p. 12

17 "Islam: its New Beginning", https://www.youtube.com/watch?v=XO70G3zrR3g

18 *Al-Muwaṭṭa'*, the first book on *ḥadīth* and Islamic law, was written by Imām Mālik ibn Anas

19 Qur'ān 4: 58

20 Imām Mālik, *al-Muwaṭṭa'*, Diwan Press, tr. Aisha Bewley and Ya'qub Johnson, Norwich, 1982, p. 434

21 Yasin Dutton, *Origins of Islamic Law: the Qur'ān, Muwaṭṭa', and Madīnan 'Amal*, Curzon, Richmond, Surrey, 1999, p. 1

22 Shaykh Abdalqadir as-Sufi, *Root Islamic Education*, Madina Press, London, 1993, p. 155

23 Yasin Dutton, *Origins of Islamic Law: the Qur'ān, Muwaṭṭa', and Madīnan 'Amal*, p. 2

24 Yasin Dutton, *Origins of Islamic Law: the Qur'ān, Muwaṭṭa', and Madīnan 'Amal*, p. 3

25 The Mālikī *madhhab* grew out of the texts compiled by students on Imām Mālik's legal decisions like the *Mudawwana* of Imām Abū Sa'īd Saḥnūn (776-854)

26 Qāḍī 'Iyāḍ, *ash-Shifā' bi ta'rīf ḥuqūq al-Muṣṭafā, al-qism ath-thānī fīmā yajibu 'alā al-anām min ḥuqūqihi 'alayhi as-salām, al-bāb ar-rābi' fī ḥukm aṣ-ṣalāti 'alayhi wa at-taslīm wa farḍ dhālika wa faḍīlatihi, al-faṣl at-tāsi' fī ḥukm ziyārati qabrihi* ﷺ *wa faḍīlati man zārahu wa sallama 'alayhi wa kayfa yuṣallī wa yad'ū*, aphorism translated by Abdassamad Clarke.

27 Shaykh Abdalqadir as-Sufi, *Root Islamic Education*, p. 96

28 Shaykh Abdalqadir as-Sufi, *Root Islamic Education*, p. 96

29 Imām Muslim, from Fazlul Karim, *Al-Hadis Vol. II*, The Book House, Lahore, p. 592

30 *Ḥaqīqa* means reality and refers to the inward illuminations of knowledge which flood the heart of the seeker on the Path of Sufism

31 Shaykh Abdalqadir as-Sufi, *Root Islamic Education*, p.3

32 Imām Mālik ibn Anas, cited in Aisha Bewley, *Islam: The Empowering of Women*, Ta-Ha Publishers, London, 1999, p. 48

33 Qāḍī 'Iyāḍ, ibn Mūsā al-Yaḥṣubī, *Tartīb al-Madārik*, cited in Shaykh Abdalqadir as-Sufi, *Root Islamic Education*, 1993, pp. 123-125

34 Shaykh Abdalqadir as-Sufi, *Root Islamic Education*, 1993, p. 125

35 Shaykh Abdalqadir as-Sufi, *Root Islamic Education*, 1993, p. 113

36 Az-Zabīdī, *Itḥāf as-Sādat al-Muttaqīn bi sharḥ Iḥyā' 'ulūm ad-dīn*, vol. 3 pg. 118. Az-Zabīdī does not ascribe this as a Prophetic *ḥadīth* but nevertheless says that the meaning is sound and true.

37 Abul-Qasim al-Junayd, *al-Rasail*, tr. A.H. Abdel-Kader in *The Life, Personality and Writings of al-Junayd*, Luzac, London, 1976, p. 172

38 Ahmad ibn 'Ajība, *The Basic Research*, p. 26

39 Abul Qasim al-Junayd, *Al-Rasail*, p.172

40 Abū Bakr al-Kalabādhī, *The Doctrine of the Sufis*, p. 3

41 Muḥyī al-Dīn ibn al-'Arabī, M., *Futuḥāt al-Makkiyah*, (section on "The Mysteries of Bearing Witness to the Oneness of God and Prophethood of Muḥammad", p. 26

42 Shaykh Abdalqadir as-Sufi, *The Hundred Steps*, p. 80

43 *Ḥaqīqa* means reality and refers to the inward illuminations of knowledge which flood the heart of the seeker on the Path of Sufism

44 Shaykh Abdalqadir as-Sufi, *The Entire City*, Introduction

45 The Divine Presence

46 Shaykh Abdalqadir as-Sufi, *The Moussems 1992 & 1993 Gatherings of Light*, Black Stone Press, London, 1994, p. 17

47 Shaykh Abdalqadir as-Sufi, *The Moussems 1992 & 1993 Gatherings of Light*, p. 19

48 Shaykh Abdalqadir as-Sufi, *An Interview with Shaykh Dr. Abdalqadir as-Sufi*, by Riyad Asvat, Iqra Agencies, Erasmia, 2013, p. 4

49 Shaykh Abdalqadir as-Sufi, *An Interview with Shaykh Dr. Abdalqadir as-Sufi*, pp. 3-4

50 Caliphate

51 https://shaykhabdalqadir.com/2011/06/22/ayyuhal-walad-lesson-nine-here-is-the-deen/

52 The science of the application of the *sharīʿa*

53 https://shaykhabdalqadir.com/2011/06/22/ayyuhal-walad-lesson-nine-here-is-the-deen/

54 https://shaykhabdalqadir.com/2011/09/12/syria-the-end-of-the-world-community/

55 Q. 59: 7

56 Shaykh Abdalqadir as-Sufi, *The Time of the Bedouin*, p. 266

57 Shaykh Abdalqadir as-Sufi, *The Interim is Mine*, p. 127

58 Q. 59: 6,7

59 Shaykh Abdalqadir as-Sufi, *Root Islamic Education*, pp. 7-8

60 Q. 14: 26-31

61 Q. 3: 110

62 Q. 2: 142

63 Q. 33:21

64 Shaykh Abdalqadir as-Sufi, *Root Islamic Education*, p. 3

65 Shaykh Abdalqadir as-Sufi, *The Entire City*, p. 307

66 Shaykh Abdalqadir as-Sufi, *The Book of Safar*, p. 31

67 "Self-manifestation, presencing, self-disclosing, the unveiling of a reality in the realm of vision, a showing forth of the secrets of the One in existence." Aisha Bewley, *Glossary of Islamic Terms*, p. 224

68 Shaykh Abdalqadir as-Sufi, *The Book of Safar*, p. 31

69 Conformity with the *sharīʿa* as revealed by Allah in the Qur'ān and as practised by the Prophet Muḥammad ﷺ.

70 Uthman Dan Fodio, *Handbook on Islam, Iman and Ihsan*, Diwan Press, Norwich, 1978, p. 29

71 Shaykh Abdalqadir as-Sufi, *The Book of Safar*, p. 47

72 Q. 2: 208

73 Shaykh Abdalqadir as-Sufi, *The Moussems 1992 & 1993 Gatherings of Light*, p. 38-39

74 "The bohemian who came to lead a crusade against the West," The Sunday Age, February 21, 2010 and "Ian Dallas gave Eric Clapton a book – and Layla was born," The Australian, August 7, 2021

75 Q. 37:96

76 Shaykh Abdalqadir as-Sufi, *The Book of Safar*, p.83

# INDEX


**A**

'Abbād [ibn az-Zubayr] 264
al-'Abbās 166
the Abbasids 11, 22, 24, 190-1
  the Abbasid caliphate 21, 165-6
  the Abbasid economy 22
  the Abbasid family 165
  the Abbasid state 21
*'abd* 28
'Abd al-Azīz Ibn Sa'ūd 53-54, 59
Amal Abdalhakim-Douglas 359-60
Umar Faruq Abdallah 380
'Abd al-Malik ibn Marwān 226
'Abd al-Qādir al-Jīlānī 166-7
'Abd al-Wahhāb Khallāf 56
'Abd ar-Raḥmān ibn Fayṣal 54
'Abd ar-Razzāq Sanhūrī 56
'Abd Manāf 242
'Abd Shams 242
Prince Abdulhalim 61
Abdulhamid II 363
'Abdullāh ibn 'Amr ibn al-'Āṣ 220
'Abdullāh ibn az-Zubayr 264-5
'Abdullāh ibn Ja'far 210, 265-6
'Abdullāh ibn Jud'ān 165
'Abdullāh ibn Rashīd 54
'Abdullāh ibn Sa'ūd 53
'Abdullah ibn Sulaymān ibn Mānī' 400
'Abdullāh ibn 'Umar 220, 264, 307, 337
Philomena Abernathey 378
ability to conceptualise, think and judge 67
ability to draw valid conclusions 67
abrogation
  abrogation by Islam of all other religions 394
  abrogation of Judaism and Christianity 3
absolutist states 34
abstention from tyranny 8
Abū az-Zinād 283
Abū Bakr 11, 20, 26, 265
  the first caliph 334
  the first caliph, Abū Bakr 196
Abū Dāwūd 334, 387, 391, 393, 399
Imām Abū Ḥanīfa 224-5, 391
Abū Hurayra xix, 203, 220, 252, 283, 290, 389, 392, 399
J.L. Abu-Lughod 359

Abū Najīḥ al-'Irbāḍ ibn Sāriya 262
Abū Nu'aym 395
Abū Qatāda 220
Abū Qilāba 204
Abū Sa'īd al-Khudrī 220, 296, 389
Imām Abū Sayf 229
Abū Sufyān 296
Abū Ṭālib 19
Abū Usayd 392
Abū Yūsuf 224-5
Abyssinia 21, 242, 350, 390
academia 105
  academic achievement 153
  academic research into education 158
accountability to Allah 350
accumulation of capital 158
accumulation of wealth 346
acquiescent society 160
acquisitions and mergers
  controls on 102
acquisitiveness 278
action/behaviour 86
acts of God 83
acts of obedience 216
acts of worship and ordinary transactions 227
  acts of worship 221, 252
addiction to drugs 331
Aden 19, 21
adequate access to clean drinking water 180
*adhān* (the call to prayer)
  arrangements for 193
adjustive or adaptive function 152-3
*'adl* 222
  *'adl*, plural *'udūl* – "just" 275
administration
  administration of justice 45
  administrative acts 57
  administrative and financial matters 192
  administrative branches of government 156
  administrative elites 101
  administrative measures 20
advanced democracies 105
adversarial parties 92, 95
advertising 84, 326
  advertising agencies 138
aerospace 106
affairs of everyday life 252
Jamāl ad-Dīn al-Afghānī 55, 57-58, 62
Afghanistan 21, 59, 90, 132, 323
  occupation of 80
Africa 18, 22, 68, 329
  African Americans 297
  African and Asian economy 21
  African and European caliphates 11
  African Muslim 250
  Central Africa 21
  sub-Saharan Africa 21
"After Wikileaks: An Assessment of the Wikileaks Phenomenon" 382
*Against the Grain* 397
agencies of socialisation 159
agent 290
agents of imperialism 49
*The Age of Surveillance Capitalism* 397
ages
  age of enlightenment xvii
  age of faith 86
    end of the age of faith 325

age of the corporation and bank 173
*agora,* institution of the 244
agreement of persons 217
agriculture xxii, 12, 20, 144
agricultural produce 196
agricultural products 22
agricultural work 145
agriculturist 234
*ahilik* 294
*al-Aḥkām as-Sulṭāniyyah* 357, 359, 383
*Aḥkām as-Sūq* 223, 388, 396, 400
*Ahl al-Futuwwa* 170
Imām Aḥmad 391, 399
AI 300
AIDS 118
air pollution 103
'Ā'isha 220, 247
the *ākhira* 236
al-'Āḍid li-Dīn Allah 166
al-Ahsa 53
*al-Bidāya wa an-Nihāya* 392
alchemy 14
alcohol 331
ALEC 109-10
Aleppo 166
aletheia 72
Alexandria 20, 23
Alexandria–Cairo–Red Sea complex 23
*Alfarabi and the Foundation of Islamic Political Philosophy* 358
algebraic amounts 215
Algeria 59, 199
algorithms 309
'Alī ibn Abī Ṭālib 11, 21, 194, 237, 263
*'ālim* 55
Ali Pasha 62, 64
Allah
Allah's absolute unity 163
Allah's caliph 10
Allah's Sunna 331
Allah's uncompromising power 163
annihilation in Allah 342
consciousness of Allah 342
direct knowledge of Allah 342
experience of Allah's Presence 340
allegiance 47, 337
Salvador Allende 115
The Almagest 166
alternative currency 298
*'amal* 3, 9, 259, 348
the *'amal ahl al-Madīna* 293, 333, 338-40
the new nomos 347
*'amal* (practice) 258, 334
*'amal* – work, deed, action and practice 274
the *'amal* of the People of Madīna 254
*'āmala* 275
*amāna* – trustworthiness 234-35, 290
America 80, 133, 137
American civic project 79
American Civil War 157
American consumerism 133
American culture 79
American empire, coming to an end 329
American Express 99
American Fed 399
the American Fed 399
American global primacy, twilight of 211
the American Historical Review 361

American Legislative Exchange Council (ALEC) 108
American life 136
American policy 183
American Psychiatric Association 137
American recording industry 290
Americans 138
American silver 42
American soldiers 136
American Tobacco Corporation 134
Americas 68
America's billionaires 120
*America – The Farewell Tour* 402
history of America 79
*The Secret History of the American Empire* 369
*amīr* 26, 28, 53, 226, 228, 337, 354
a governor of a province or a town 191
*amīr al-mu'minīn,* authority of 337
amirate xvi, 191, 253, 355
*amīr* of Hā'il 54
*amīr*s 196, 228
*amīr*s (governors) 9
an appointed *amīr* 226
ample provision 324
*amr* [command/authority] xviii, 335, 354
'Amr ibn Maymūn 393
'Amr ibn 'Uthmān 266
analysis of contemporary society 356
analytical framework 356
anarchist 75
Anas ibn Mālik 220, 259, 287, 392, 395, 398
Anatolia 24, 59, 64, 294
Anatolian Osmanlı land 296
ancient and natural ethos 171
ancients 247
ancient society 289
Andalus 293
Andalusian guilds 293
Dr. Tobias Andersson 393
*And Forgive Them Their Debts* 390
Anglo-American jurisprudence 381
A. Anievas 359
annual temple tax 228
anonymous sources 182
the *Anṣār* 224
*'an tarāḍin minkum – by means of mutually agreed trade* 280
Antar ibn Shadad 380
anthropologists 123
antibiotics
overuse of 103
anti-democratic 137
*Anti-Oedipus: Capitalism and Schizophrenia* 378
anti-poverty campaigns 141
anti-public interest practices 105
anxiety 152
apartheid xvi
apostates 208
apotheosis of modernity 130
an app 231
the appearance of piety 236
the appetites 277
applying the law 191
appointing judges and magistrates 191
apprentice (*al-ājir or al-mubtadi'*) 197
*'aqīda* 14, 86, 271
Ash'arī theology 353
classical/orthodox Asha'rī position 56

Arabia 267
the Arabian coast of the Gulf 55
the Arabian Peninsula 18-19, 22, 52, 54, 64
the Arabian Sea 21, 23
Arabian society 165
Arabistan 56
bloodlines of Arabian horses 166
pre-Islamic Arabia 35
Arabic 22, 166, 285
Arabic poetry 166
Arabic term 295
the Arabic-English Lexicon 389, 391, 397
arable land 295
Arab poetry 380
the Arabs 18, 54, 256, 268
the Arabs despised commerce 267
Arab tribes 267
the Arab world 199
Assembly of Arabs 253
biographies and histories of the Arabs 166
al-A'raj 283
*Der Arbeiter* 76
arbitrage trading 98
arbitrary manipulation of the market 196
arbitration systems 210
archbishops 105
archery 165
architecture 12, 14, 243
architectural style 243
arena of staged social debate 161
aristocracy 168, 351
aristocratic leadership of Europe 170
arithmetic 166
the Ark of Nūḥ 254
armaments 42
Armenia 21
Karen Armstrong 368
the army 20, 178
army generals xix
army (*jaysh*) 190
management of the army 191
aromatics 19
arson 10
art 14, 74
artisans 53, 234, 288
artisan guilds 197
*'aṣabiyya* 4, 255-6
kinship 351
Asad ad-Dīn Shirkuh 166
*The Ascent of Money – A Financial History of the World* 386
ar-Rāghib al-Aṣfahānī 385-6
Ashhab 267
Asia 18, 22-23, 25, 29, 68, 329
Central Asia 22, 24
East Asia 30
South Asia xix
South Asian caliphates 11
Southeast Asia 19, 21, 23, 30
'Asīr 54
*aṣnāf* (guilds) 190, 197, 348
aspirational classes 139
Julian Assange 177, 182-3
Swedish rape trial 183
asset bubbles xxiii, 120
Assyrians 19
Vincent Astor 158
astronomy 12, 14
Riyad Asvat 392, 404
'Aṭā' ibn Yasār 220, 260
atheism 63, 86, 324-5

atheistic capitalism 82
atheists 88, 326
victory of atheism over religion 88
Athens 244, 288
'Ātika bint Murra as-Sulamiyya 242
the atom
the billiard-ball solidity of the atom 70
auditors 105
Sultan Aurangzeb 29
Australia xvii, 105
Australian newspapers 354
Australia's private sector organisations 106
Austria 48
Austrian Empire 45
Austrian School of Economic 277
Austrian Sudbahn 51
"Authority and Legitimation" 383
authority/legitimacy 34
authorisation 337
authoritarianism 157
authoritarian command 156
authority figures 153
automation
automated future 300
automating the process of earning money 217
automatons 138
*Averroes – On the Harmony of Religion and Philosophy* 358
Awdaghast 21
*awliyā* 164
*awqāf* (endowments) 18, 20, 190, 193, 228, 296, 300, 302, 332, 348
deed of trust (*waqfiyya*) ratified by the *qāḍī* 198
Axum Empire 246
*āyats* 15, 202-6, 209, 249
*Āyat al-Kursī* 206
*āyats* on spending 208
longest *āyat* in the Qur'ān 208
*'ayn* 397
the Ayyubid dynasty 166
Azerbaijan 21
al-Azhar 60, 398
Egypt's control of the 301
independence of 302

## B

Babylonia 243-4
Babylon 20, 211
Babylonians 246
Babylonian shrines 244
Francis Bacon 87, 125
*badaniyya* (physical partnership) 292
Baghdad 21-22, 80, 166-7
F.R.C. Bagley 383
Bahrain 53
*Baḥth fī ar-ribā wa aṣ-ṣarf* 400
bailouts xxiii, 97, 120
Joel Bakan 101, 371
the balanced human being 14
balanced income 198
the balance of society 171
the Balkans 24, 199
the ballot box 94
banditry 24
Arindam Banerjee 360
Banī 'Adī 264
Banī Qaynuqā'
market of 260
banking xxiv, 10, 33, 43, 45-46, 58, 65, 82, 96, 212, 243-4, 298, 332, 346

banker-governor 55
bankers 51, 62, 286
Baring family 55
court banker 51
banking and corporate classes 301
banking and financial services 104
banking cartels 35, 50
banking elite 65
banking entity 327
banking-finance 147
banking houses 212
banking job 302
banking system 60, 112, 327
bank loans 210
banks 131, 160, 217, 243, 266
Agricultural Bank 58
Anglo-Austrian Bank 51
Bank of America 99
Bank of England xxii, 36
Bank of New York Mellon 99
banks and corporations 120
banks and stock exchanges 294
Barclays 212
Baring's Bank 58
Bischoffsheim and Goldschmidt 51
central banks xxiii, 35, 50, 113, 120-1, 286, 294
Citigroup 99
La Banque de France 34, 38
Morgan Stanley 99
central banking 38
foundation of capitalism 85
modern banking xx, 147, 294, 399
private bankers 96
private banking 38
privately owned banking cartels 50
reserve banking 38
bankruptcy 44, 244, 299
bankruptcy let-out clauses 235
Banū Hāshim 241
Banū Qaynuqā' 19
*baqā* 343, 345
subsistence in Allah 342
barley 29
José Manuel Barroso 120
barter 196, 264
*barzakh* (interspace) 343
Z. Bashir 359
basic health services 107
*The Basic Research* 403
basic technique 65-66
Basra 53, 265
the Battle of the Camel 264
the Battle of Uḥud 213
*bay' al-'īna* – sale [known as] *'īna* 305
*bayān* (explication) 202
*al-Bayān wa at-tabyīn* 380
*al-Bayān wa at-taḥṣīl* 267
*bay'at* (pledge of allegiance) 28
al-Bayhaqī 396
the *bayt al-māl* 20, 26, 190, 196, 213, 262, 348
gathering of the *zakāt* in a the *bayt al-māl* 227
*beatius dare quod accipere* [it is more blessed to give than to receive] 173
"Beauty & the Junkyard" 396
becoming true to the trust, the primary meaning of *īmān* 290
Bedouin 52, 250, 255-7, 351
Bedou 256
Bedouinism 256, 351
Bedouin tribal confederations 52
coalesce into a group 351

*Before European Hegemony: The World System A.D. 1250 – 1350* 359
Beglerbegi 48
*Der Begriff des Politischen* 76
behaviour 187, 248-9
behaviour/action 12
behavioural regulation 159
Being 71-72, 75
*Being and Time* 141
Being-itself 128
Being of beings 72
encounter with Being 128
Belgium 25
belief in the Divine 172
loss of belief in God 71
Josh Bell 378
Benjamin/McCarrarher narrative 83-84
Walter Benjamin 84, 369
Ted Benton 366
Berlin 80
Edward Bernays 132-3, 134-6, 138
Bertelsmann 182
best community (*umma*) 350
best of forms 47
betraying trusts 10
better living conditions 175
bewildered herd 135
Abdalhaqq Bewley 27, 32, 129, 205, 225, 252, 258, 359-60, 375-6, 385, 388, 391-2
Aisha Bewley 91, 299, 370, 385-6, 391-2, 396-8, 401-3, 405
bicameral parliamentary assembly 93
*Bidāya [al-mujtahid wa nihāya al-muqtaṣid]* 13, 358
Big Brother 178
big business 140
the biggest crime in the history of mankind 179
the big idol 163
billionaires xxiii
bi-metallic currency, integrity of 346
biological phenomena 349
biotechnology 182
Birgevi Mehmed Effendi 44
*birr*, true right action 163
*The Birth of Saudi Arabia: Britain and the Rise of the House of Sa'ud* 364
Bitcoin 298
"Bitcoin: A Second Chance for the Muslim World" 397
Bitcoin network 300
"How Bitcoin Can Help Muslims Follow the Teachings of the Quran" 397
Muslim Bitcoiner 397
neither anonymous nor privacy-friendly 300
black American recording artists 291
the Black-Scholes model 98
Black Sea 24
William Blackstone 396
Tony Blair 139
Lloyd Blankfein 99
blind imitation 56
blockchain 299-300, 347
a register of transactions 299
public and open to inspection 299
blogging 177
blueprint xviii
blueprint for an illuminated city 253

blueprint pattern 11
body/mind dichotomy 126
Bombay 21, 30
bondholders' returns 117
bond of brotherhood 292
the Book of Allah and the Sunna of His Prophet 331, 333
*The Book of 'Amal* 379-80, 395
*The Book of Righteousness* 162
*The Book of Safar* 405
*The Book of the Islamic Market Inspector* 383
bookshops 14
boom-and-bust cycles 179
booty 15-16, 18, 28
distribution of 191
Bosworth 383
bourgeois society 76
bourgeois marriage 149
brainwashing the public 141
BRAIS – British Association of Islamic Studies 295
BRAIS conference, Edinburgh 2014 295
Louis Brandeis 98
bravery 172
bravery (*shajā'a*) 165
Brazil 330
Brazilian construction conglomerate 107
breach in the armour of the capitalist agenda 177
bread and circuses 148
breaking the idols 163
bribery, a tax deductible expense 106
bridges 20
*A Brief History of Neo-liberalism* 373, 375
Robert Briffault 358
A.A. Brille 134
Britain 30, 48, 55-56, 60, 101, 114, 144
British 55
British agent 54
British army 30
British Consulate 62
British Crown 30
British crown agents 54
British East India Company 29
British government 182
British housewives 138
British imperialism 55
British-installed Saudis 56
British occupation of India 30
British colonial rule 272
B. Bromberg 390
the Bronze Age 234
brotherhood 168, 243, 256, 292
brotherhood and guardianship (*muwālāt*) 163
brotherhood elite 170
brotherhood of mankind 60
for the sake of Allah 292
brothers 274
R.P. Buckley 383
budget cuts 114
building 253
building mosques, schools or hospitals 221
al-Bukhārī 209, 392-3
*Ṣaḥīḥ al-Bukhārī* 386
al-Bukhārī and Muslim 290, 334, 358
bullion 29
Allan Bullock 375
bureaucracy 45, 71, 92
the Bureau of Labor in the USA 146
Lord Burghley 171

George W. Bush 330
business 155, 187
a good business climate
creation of 118
business and political state
authority of 158
business corporations 141
business journalism 84, 326
businessmen 274
business writers 84, 326
bus ticket 209
butter 29
buying and selling 207, 211, 281
buyer and seller 280
buying 252
buying back stock 120
Byzantine Empire 23
Byzantines 19
Byzantium 350

## C

C+ programming 293
Caesar 354
Cairo 23, 55, 58
Calcutta 30
the caliphate [see also khalifate] 6, 21, 27, 47, 63, 166, 190, 261, 267, 332, 348
abolishment of the sultanate and caliphate 46
Allah's representative (caliph) 8
authority of a caliph 337
the caliph 9, 20, 47, 195-6
caliphate of 'Umar ibn al-Khaṭṭāb 189
caliphates 85, 190
caliphate/sultanate 26
caliphs 6, 9, 191, 324
*The Caliph's Last Heritage: A Short History of the Turkish Empire* 365
functions of the caliph 191
judgements of the caliphs 335
not simply a collaborator of caliph and *wazīr* 192
John Calvin 60
the Cambridge Dictionary 376
camels 15, 19
Ewan Cameron 137
campaign contributions 110
campus 161
Canada 291
canals 20, 24
"The Cancer Stage of Capitalism" 382
capacity to receive sensory data 67
Cape Town 357
capitalism xxiv, xxv, 33, 45, 57-58, 60, 65, 81, 86, 131, 142, 145-6, 150-1, 178, 212-3, 325, 348, 360
abolition of capitalist supermarket distribution 188, 332
a danger to the human species 329
a life-threatening disease 181, 329
an end to 187
a psychosis 85
a religion 84
a technique of enchantment 84
cancerous form of 181
cancer stage of 328
capital 33, 203, 211, 213, 236, 290, 327
the Great, the Universal, Creditor 121
capital accumulation 114
capital flight 119

capitalism's icons 326
capitalism's priests 326
capitalist economy 121
capitalist entity 213
capitalist ideology 329
capitalist modalities 82, 332
currency, banking, taxation 187
capitalist modality 281
capitalist mode of production 43
capitalist-organised media and information systems 181
capitalists 37, 298
capitalist society 84, 146, 328
capitalist system 56, 69, 94, 154
capitalist technic xix
capitalist world order 178, 355
chicanery 111
collapse of 346
crony capitalism 105
economic system of 298
failure of 131
grasping, mean and miserly character of capitalism 259
ground-rules of capitalism 213
ills of capitalism 216
its moral codes 326
its psychotic nature 329
predatory oligarchic capitalism 215
prism of 323
the rise of capitalism 34
the religion of modernity 326
usurious religion of 202
war against 345
captured women and children 28
caravans 16, 18-19, 242, 282, 285, 291, 293-4
a guild of traders 291
caravan routes 19
caravanserais 199, 285
the first guild 291
carefully structured free-space 161
Andrew Carnegie 158
John Carroll 375
cartels 287
cartel of traders 261
fixing prices 288
cartoons 175
catalyst to development 174-5
catastrophic collapse 298
categorical imperative 70
cattle 19, 25
causes of unemployment 111
the cave (*kahf*) 162
CCPA Monitor 382
the Cecils 171
Robert Cecil 171-2
cemeteries 199
central government 159
centralised state planning 114
the centrality of leadership in the *dīn* 221
C.E.O.s 99
challenging male power 134
C. P. Chandrasekhar 360
Ha-Joon Chang 111
Amanda Chapple 378
"Chapter on the departure of knowledge" 391
character 248
excellence of character 344
charity (*ṣadaqāt*) 8
Charles V 24
chemistry 14
Ken Chenault 99
cheques 295

children
childcare 145
childhood 133
childishness 158
child labour laws 145
childlike people 152
child's earliest experiences 150
controlling the environment of children 159
safety for 347
Children of Ismā'īl 241
the Children of Israel 240, 246
Chile 115
China xxiv, 19, 21-23, 30, 35, 82, 106, 181, 209, 246, 291, 330, 355
China International Fund 106
China Sonangol 106
Chinese 18
Mandarin Chinese 22
Chinese capitalism 355
Chinese Muslim 250
chits 209
chits (*ṣukūk*)
sale of 308
chivalry 170, 256
chivalric age
end of 169
chivalric ethos 168
chivalric honours and courtesies 171
chivalric obligation 171
chivalric order 169
chivalric orders 170
chivalric values 171
chivalrous knight 167
chivalry in European civilisation 168
chivalry of the Christians 169
Christian rules of chivalry 168
rites and practices of 169
the chocolate market 309
chocolate prices 308
cocoa beans 309
cocoa crops 309
the cocoa market 308
Christendom 215
cathedrals 243
the Catholic Church 60, 243
Catholic philosopher 83
celibate and misogynistic priesthood 170
tyranny and irrationality of the Catholic Church 124
Christian 168, 212, 235
Christian context of understanding 124
Christian doctrines 71
christianism 389
Christianity 3, 31, 60, 87, 241, 326
changed itself into capitalism 84
Christians 61, 251
metaphysics of 250
Christians and their ilk 202
Christian theological orthodoxy 87
Christian theological thinking 124
Christian traditions 214
hegemony of the Church 87
the Church 37, 168-70, 183
churches 243
clergy 63
demise of Christian theism 71
chronic malnutrition 180
Winston Churchill 95
the CIA 115, 136-7
the CIA's chief psychologist 137
Marcus Tullius Cicero 385
Roman statesman and orator 111

cigarettes 134
cinema 174-5
Tihomir Cipek 77, 369
circles of teaching 164
circulation of wealth 17-18, 189-90, 346, 350
cisterns 199
citizen merchants 288
citizenship 34
  citizen 131, 245-6
  civil engineering 20
  civil revival 80
  civil rights 141
  civil service 92
  civil situation 244
  civil society 105
the city 242, 244, 254, 295
  cities 285
    innovation of cities 243
  city bonds 117
  city budget 117
  city dwellers 16
  city forms 248
  city moulded by revelation 249
  city/state-based order 250
  city tax revenues 117
  civic model 246
  civic model for mankind 237
  civic order 248
  civic reality 90, 131
  civic revival xxiv, 347
  civil and municipal functions (public safety) 194
  civil authority 205
  physical environment of 194
  public order and governance of 192
City University of New York 117
civic resistance
  to capitalist modalities 329
civilisation 11, 133, 170, 191, 243-4, 268, 281
  civilisational forms 248
  *Civilisation and Its Discontents* 142
  cyclical nature of 255
  origin of 243
  revitalisation of the 257
civil war 54, 78-80
clan-based society 243
Eric Clapton 405
clarification (*bayān*) 202
classification-structuralism 183
classified media 182
Clause Four 139-40
Clausewitz 16, 274
Jodie Claypool 378
clean water 79, 107
Clear *Fatḥ* (opening) 263
climate change 103, 119, 330
Bill Clinton 140, 330
clothes for the poor at Eid 200
coarse food 339
Allen Cobb 378
coercion 276, 331
*cogito ergo sum* 67-68, 126
a coherent existential methodology
  to activate Islam 356
the Cold War 183
  end of 179
  "The Collaborative Couple: A vision of Shaykh Abdalqadir as-Sufi" 378
the collapse of *futuwwa* 173
*The Collapse of Globalism and the Reinvention of the World* 381
the collapse of society 296

collateral 34, 38, 290
the collection of taxes 45
collective bargaining power 309
collective psychosis 331
collectivising the population 157
"The Colonialisation of the Deen" 398
colonialism 43, 112
colonial era 319
colonial rebellion against Europe 55
colonisation 74
Columbia Teachers College 158
Columbia University 289
combat against enemies 274
combination of transactions 306
*Commentaries on the Laws of England* 396
commerce 20, 225, 246, 281
commercial cartels 287
commercial contracts 18
commercial exchange of goods and services 195
commercial/industrial economy 158
commercial interests 301
commercialisation and commodification of economic relationships 34
commercial life of the Muslims 209
commercial practice 258
commercial property 303
commercial structures
Muslims adapted existing 294
commercial transaction 195, 210, 243
commercial world 209
Commission of Enquiry 105
the Committee of Public Safety 371
the Committee of Union and Progress (CUP) 46, 62
commodities 10, 17, 26, 41, 230, 276-7, 306, 309, 326
commodity elites 114
(including the military industrial complex) 82
Commodity Futures Modernisation Act 98
commodity wealth 230
common denominator, lack of 196
common fund 292
the common good 302
Common Law 272, 275
offense at 283
common liability 291
the commons 293, 296, 300
common land 296
national ownership of 301
common values 175
communal harmony 174
communism 65, 82, 113
communist economy (state capitalism) 69
Communist Party 35
community 189-90, 247, 251, 337
communities 103, 150
community leaders 221, 261, 319
community – nearest thing to a bank 264
Companions 366
the Companions and Followers 3, 219, 224, 226, 237, 247-8, 254, 258, 261, 264, 297, 308, 333, 337, 339, 391
age of the 226
consensus of the 262
their extensive interconnectedness financially 266
companions in the way of Allah 204

Companions of the Cave 170
keeping company 169
compassion 31
competence 158
"Competing in tandem: Securities markets and commercial banking patterns in Europe during the nineteenth century" 361
competition 155
complete blueprint pattern for human societies 190
*The Complete Forty Hadith* of Imām an-Nawawī 386, 393, 396
complete restoration of the *Dīn* 218
complex transactions 281
compound interest 385
compulsory schooling 157
computers 104, 143
the concentration camp 31
*The Concept of the Political* 368-9
the concept of things 66
*The Idea of Usury – from Tribal Brotherhood to Universal Otherhood* 394
concerted action of governments 223
*Confessions of an Economic Hit Man* 115
confiscated property 37
conflicting emotions 133
conflict of interest divestment requirements 115
congregational prayers
  leading 191
conquest 168, 212
conscripted army 60
consensus 56, 226
  consensus in practice 224
  consensus of the Companions 219
consequence-free environment 106
conservative 279
  the Conservative Party 139
considerateness 292
conspiracy 123
  conspiracy theory 35
Constantinople 23, 63
constitutionalism xx, 45, 57-58, 60, 62
  Constitution 79
  constitutionality 34
  constitution of 1876 46
construction 106
construction and maintenance of the water system 199
construction of consent 116
consumer and production community 78
consumerism 116, 134, 136, 141-2, 156, 347
  conspicuous consumption 158
  consumer products 135
  consumers 121, 138, 158, 299
  consumer spending 138
  consumptionism 134
  consumption of alcohol 193
contamination of foodstuff 194
contemporary financial dealings 280
contemporary society xiii
context of understanding 83
continent-wide civil war 79
continuous supply of workers 146
contracts 197, 216, 291, 293
  contract of brotherhood 292
  contract of marriage 292
  nature of contracts 217

"The Contribution of the Modernists to the Secularisation of Islamic Law" 365
control and regulation 301
conveniences or comforts 196
conventional morality
had to be banished 158
*A Convergence of Civilisations – The Ascendancy of Usury over Judaeo-Christian and Muslim Commerce* 386, 390, 399-400
convergence of world views 123
cooperation culture 294
Copernicus 127
copper 23
Cornwall 234
the Corona virus pandemic xxiii, 120-1
corporations xxiii, 92, 101, 103, 108, 131, 133, 135-6, 142, 158, 177, 217, 288, 292, 326
accelerating control of multinational capital conglomerates 181
Airbus 106-7
Amazon xxiii, 109, 121
Anglo-American 374
BP Amoco 104
Chevron 121
Comcast 182
corporate boardrooms 113
corporate capitalism 102
corporate debt xxiii, 121
corporate donations 103
corporate drafted priorities 110
corporate economy 157-8
corporate financing 101
corporate financing of elections 103
corporate form 101
corporate-friendly priorities 108
corporate-government relations 103
corporate intelligentsia 84, 326
corporate interventions 109
corporate investments 102
corporate law 102
corporate looting 121
corporate political spending 109
corporate profits 156
corporate society 101
corporate sponsors 157
corporate state 101, 324, 331
corporate takeover of global governance 330
corporate world 217
corporation-financiers 173
corporations' culture 103
corporations' iconography 103
corporations' ideology 103
*The Corporation: The Pathological Pursuit of Profit and Power* 371
corporatisation 346
corporatocracy 326, 352
political system of 355
custodians of society 330
Daimler/Chrysler 104
East India Company xx, 30
Enron 159
Enron scandal 105
Exxon 104
FedEx 109
Ford 104
Fox Corporation 182
GE (General Electric) 104

General Motors 104
Global Crossing 159
GM 104
Goldman Sachs 99
Grupo Globo 182
Halliburton 121
Hearst Communications 182
HSBC 398
IBM 104
interests of the corporations 133
Islam does not grant legal standing to corporations 346
Kraft Foods 109
Lagardere Group 182
Lehman Brothers 133
Lloyds 212
McDonald's 109
Mobil 104
most profitable corporations in America 121
multinational corporations 119, 355
Netflix 121
News Corp 182
Northern Trust 99
Odebrecht 106-7
Rio Tinto 106
Royal Dutch/Shell 104
Shell 374
Sinopec 106
Sony Group Corporation 182
State Street 99
Time Warner 182
Toyota 104
transnational corporations 104
coalition of transnational corporations 330
UBS AG 99
UPS 109
Walmart xxiii, 104, 109, 121
Walt Disney Company 182
Wells Fargo 99
World.com 159
corruption probe 107
the cosmos 70
cost plus profit 288-9
cotton 25, 29-30
cotton textiles 29
counsel xxi
Counsel for Kings 383
counterculture 141-2
countervalue 38
countryside 285
courage xiv, 234
course of action 176
courtesy 169
court of law 197
courts 244, 332
covert operations 115
the Covid pandemic 95, 309
cowboy novels 95
"Craft Organisation, Work Ethics, and the Strains of Change in Ottoman Syria" 384
craftsmen 198, 234
craft guilds 197
craftsmen and workers 293
Ian Craib 366
crashes 299
creation of awareness 176
credit and debt 266, 276, 297, 307
credit and debt transactions 209
complex web of 264
credit and trading activities 243
credit default swaps 98
credit money 35, 41
creditor 235

credit profile 148
credit terms 209
credit transactions 209-10, 235, 281
endebtment 44
proper management of 216
Credit Suisse report 180, 329
criminal investigators 105
crippling depression 329
crisis 94
crisis management 94
crisis policies 94
critical analysis 160, 161
critical judgment 153
critical thinkers 152
*The Critique of Pure Reason* 68
Lord Cromer 55, 58
crops 209
cropsharer 297
cropsharing 297
cropsharing agreements 296
crucifixes 170
the Crusades 169-70, 212
Crusader ethos 169
Crusaders 166-8
the Third Crusade 167
Cuba 80
Cui bono? Who benefits? 111
cultivator 209
cult of personality 66
cult of system 160
the Cultural Studies Review 378
cultures 153
cultural consensus 174
cultural traditions 175
cultural transmission 174-5
cuneiform 243
cure 302
currency
paper and digital currencies 229
curriculum of public schools 153
Adam Curtis 376-7
"The Century of the Self, Part 1: Happiness Machines" 376-7
"The Century of the Self, Part 2" 377
Lord Curzon 59
custodianship of teachers 159
customers 234
customs 153
customs of a land (*'urf/'āda*) 259
cutbacks 117
cyber security 330
Cyprus 21

## D

aḍ-Ḍaḥḥāk 204
daily lives 133
the *Dalā'il al-Khayrāt* 200
Ian Dallas 379, 392, 405
*Ian Dallas: Collected Works* 367-8, 376
*The Interim is Mine* 369-70, 376, 380-1, 401, 404
*The New Wagnerian* 383
*Oedipus and Dionysus* 379, 383
Dallas House 182
*The Engines of the Broken World: Discources on Tacitus and Lucan* 359, 369-71, 373, 376, 401
*The Entire City* 370, 404-5
Shaykh Dr. Abdalqadir as-Sufi
"The Collaborative Couple" 148-9, 378

"Discourse: Britain-Money-Muslims-Monarchy – Part 1 of 5" 393
"Discourse on Futuwwa" 379
*Discourses* 395
*The Hundred Steps* 403
"An Interview with Shaykh Dr. Abdalqalqadir as-Sufi", 404
Introduction to *The Meaning of Man: The Foundations of the Science of Knowledge* 379
"Islam: its New Beginning" 3, 402
"The Islamic Dinar – A Way-stage Passed" 388
*Root Islamic Education* 338, 357, 366, 394, 402-4
*The Time of the Bedouin: on the politics of power* 255, 366, 368, 370-2, 378, 392, 404
Damascus 20
dams 20
Uthman Dan Fodio 405
danger to the human species 181
Dante Alighieri 169
*dār al-ḥarb* 327
*Dār al-Islām* 13, 27
*Dar al-Ulums* 398
ad-Dārimī 391, 394
Charles Darwin 68, 127, 154-5
Darwinian terms 323
*Dasein* (being-there) 71-72
data 157
date-palms 296
date-palm groves 297
dates 53
dates, olives and water
in mosques at the time of breaking the fast of Ramadan 200
G. Davies 360-1, 366, 381
R.H. Davison 362
Richard Davis 99
*dawla* 332
*ad-dawla al-Islāmiyya* 10, 15, 17, 20, 164
*dawla* (dynasty) 17
*Devlet* 48
*dawla* means rotation, turn of fortune, and dynasty 349
dawn prayer 228
Dāwūd ibn al-Ḥusayn 296
David Dayen 375
the Days of *Jāhiliyya* [Days of Ignorance prior to Islam] 337
dearth and famine in Madīna 287
death and life instincts 142
death of the Days of Ignorance 47
death sentence 38
debasement 196
debased coins 198
debt and credit 44, 112, 148, 187, 235, 243-4, 281, 399
*dayn* – credit/debt 208
debt 228
'Debt, austerity, devastation: it's Europe's turn' 119
debt, both commercial and personal 266
debt crisis 119
debtors 121, 244
debt receptor 160
debt-related deaths 120
debts and interest payments 243, 264
high yield debt 98
indebtedness 296
overdue debts repaid 193

personal debt 208
private debt 121
public debt 121
reckless indebtedness 266
scourge of debt 119
stern warnings against debt 210
substantial debts 264
those in debt 27
worldwide debt xxiii, 120
debt and credit transactions 208
debt-based monetary systems 210
debt leveraging 34
debtor-creditor relation 121
H. Decdeli 362
the deceased's estate 215
decision-making processes 101, 105
*The Decisive Treatise, Determining the Nature of the Connection Between Religion and Philosophy* 358
declared principles 108
dedicated practice 340
deep relationships
deprived of 157
defence structures and functions 113
defending a town 200
defend the nation 191
deferrals 282
deferred transactions 275-6
deficit 117
Primavera De Filippi 300
defrauding customers 10
de-industrialisation 117
F. de Jong 362
delay in delivery or payment 281
Gilles Deleuze 378
Deleuze and Guattari 150-1
Delhi 357
deliberate deprivation 30
delivering water to a locality 200
N.J. Delong-Bas 364
Delos, the greatest bank of the Greek world 244
Delphi 244
M. Van De Mieroop 390
democracy 18, 57-58, 60, 65, 82, 86, 91, 95, 131, 135, 137, 140, 160, 325, 352
an interface between corporate power and the people 179
a palliative 135
capitalism's public relations interface 179
democracies 94, 179
democratic capitalism 147
democratic citizens 137
democratic institutions
undermined 115
democratic-pluralist perspective 101
democratic political process 108
democratic regime 108
democratic rule xiii
democratic state 94
democratic system 178
*Democratic Tyranny and the Islamic Paradigm* 370
democratisation 34
democricity 136
the real history of democracy 108
true nature of 95
demographic transition 34
demonstrative reasoning 13
Deng Xiaoping
embrace of capitalism 77
Denmark 104

the gross domestic product of Denmark 104
*De Officiis* 385
the department of amenities 20
department stores 133
dependence on centralised management 158
dependency habits
inculcation of 157
depoliticisation 76-77
deposits 40, 50, 294
depositors 294
depreciation 37
The Depression of 1873 51
depriving others of their inheritance 10
Charles Derber 103, 371
deregulation 114
deregulation doctrines 98
derivatives 98
desert
ubiquity of the desert 245
design 324
desire 150-1
desire for wealth and power 114
desires culture 133, 156
despotism 253
despot 244
destinies 47
the destitute 27
determinants of income 111
determinants of prices 195
devaluation 37
unilateral devaluation 36
to develop full potential 178
developing countries 374
development 86, 325
developing countries 119, 355
developing world 114, 118
development models 122
Robert Devereux, the Earl of Essex 171-2, 381
devolution 323-4
John Dewey 158
*Dhamm al-kalām wa ahlihi* 391
*Dhāt* – Essence 274
*dhawq* (tasting) 345
taste 342
*dhikr* (invocation and remembrance of Allah) 342
*dhimma*
contract of 251
diagnostic and directive function 152-3
dialectics
dialectic of "freedom" versus a controlling state 301
dialectical method 160
dialectical tension 77
dust of 161
*Dialogue Concerning the Two World Systems* 68
diarrhoea 79, 180
dictatorships 94-95, 113, 179
dictionaries of the Qur'ān 203
Joan Didion 372
different classes 153
differentiated man 149
differentiating function 152, 154
digital equivalents 278
digital media 174
dignity xiv
digression on terminologies 295
Jamie Dimon 99
*dīn* 3-5, 13, 48, 187, 216, 252, 258, 268, 274, 327

beginning of the *dīn* 238
*Dīn al-Fiṭra* 219, 271-2
*dīn* IS *mu'āmala* 186, 345
Dīn of Truth 32
*dīn* (religion) 9
protection of the *dīn* from modification and deviation 191
restoration of the *dīn* 268
the *dīnār* and the *dirham* 20, 26-28, 204, 224, 227, 229, 231, 265, 279, 292, 299, 306
weights from the system of weights 223
common *dirhams*
common *dirhams* had a known weight and known value 225
the *dīnār* and *dirham* are standardised weights 230
the *dīnār* and *dirham* of the *sharī'a* 226
*dīnārs* or *dirhams* 297
the *dirham* 265
the *dirham* of the *sharī'a* 226
*dirhams* 20, 27, 224, 231, 264
the implementation of the *dīnār* and *dirham* in Kelantan, Malaysia 229
standardised weights 230
diphtheria 180
diplomatic agreements 169
direct taxes 50
Dir'iyyah 53
dirty money 50, 51
disagreements with their Prophets 290
disciples of the Messenger of Allah 'Īsā 170
discovery 182
"discovery" of the Americas 42
discrediting the great masters 159
disease 125
disenchantment 326
dishonesty 10
dishonest scheme (scam) 179
disinheritance of heirs 215
dismantling the *nafs* (self) 161, 163, 164
disorder 253
disparities 282
disposal of treasury funds 191
*Dispossession, Deprivation, and Development: Essays for Utsa Patnaik* 360
distinction between *'ibādāt* and *mu'āmalāt* 186
distinction between politics and the political 77
distribution 40, 290-1
distribution channels 283, 291
Districtism 256
diversified consumerism 118
*The Divide: A Brief Guide to Global Inequality and its Solutions* 374-5
divide between rich and poor countries 122
the Divine 76, 290
Divine commands and prohibitions 271
Divine contract xxiv
Divine Contract 33
Divine intervention 127
Divine Presence 341, 343
Divine protection (*'iṣma*) 247
Divine purpose 324
Divine religion 256

Divine Self-disclosure 343
Divine transaction 170
Divinity 326
divinity as idea 129
dynamic opening to the 326
final Divine Revelation 32
lack of recognition of 88
recognition of the 326
division between mind and matter 67
divorce 252
*dīwāns* and correspondence
*dīwān* [register of the Muslims] 262
*dīwāns* (registers) 20
management of the *dīwān* 191
maintenance of the *dīwān* 192
DNA 352
dockets 209
Hassim Dockrat xiv, 177, 381
doctor 302
Doctor Honoris Causa of Literature 76, 130
*The Doctrine of the Sufis* 403
A.R.I. Doi 383
the dollar
dropped as world's reserve currency 329
domestic production 144
domestic violence
high rates of 146
dominant class 156
dominant development model 123
dominant group 155
dominant majority 252
dominant paradigm 202
domination of the world 59
donkeys 200
double-coincidence of wants 196
doubt 87
Amal Abdalhakim Douglas 385
David Downing 360
dowries 279
Derek Draper 140
dreams, daydreams and slips of the tongue 132
Dresden 80
drug addiction 118
*du'ā* 251
*dūlatan* 17
*dunyā* [world] 354
duties of brotherhood
*The Duties of Brotherhood in Islam* 379
eight duties of brotherhood 164
personal aid 164
Yasin Dutton 9, 335, 362, 402
dyes 19
dynastic change 351
dystopia
dystopian Orwellian future 299
dystopian reality 179

## E

Ralph Anstruther Earle 52
earlier revelations 250
earliest writing 243
early modern period 112
earning a living 150
the earth
the stationary centre 127
the East 48
easterners 247
East Africa 21
East African coast 21
East China Sea 22
Easter day parade 134

*Eastern Origins of Western Civilisation* 359
the East Hungarian Railway 51-52
eating, sleeping, sexual intercourse 239
e-books 177
ecclesiastical real estate 37
ecologists 123
The Economic History Review 384
economics 14, 17, 34, 49, 90, 179, 373
  administration of economic matters 196
  an ideology 111
  a political argument 111
  a political argument not a science 123
  a science 111, 122
  capitalism's theology, philosophy and cosmology 326
  classical economic theories 113
  economic activity 40, 197, 233
  economically developing countries 115
  economic and political self-interest 123
  economic and political theory 64
  economic boom in the 15th century 24
  economic/business activities 195
  economic circumstances 220
  economic class 154
  economic classes 154
  economic considerations 192
  economic crisis 138
    the economic crisis of 2020 xxiii, 120
    Corona virus pandemic 120
  economic elites 101, 122
  economic freedom 148
  economic free market 127
  economic growth 122
  economic growth and development 122
  economic institutions 116
  economic lifeblood of the planet 234
  economic milieu 197
  economic philosophy 138
  economic policies 115
  economic power 114
  economic principles 196
  economic progress 136
  economic prosperity 179
  economic pursuits 195
  economic regulations 108
  economic ruin 37
  economics and politics 132
  economic status and occupation 153
  economic system 122, 286
  economic terms 189
  economists 84, 123, 326
  economy 131
  economy and workforce 153
  economy – a system resting on scarcity 289
  false parameters of 232
  ideological tool 111
  no objective truths in 111
  not a science 111
  social science 111
economy
  agrarian and handicraft economy 144
  agrarian economy 297
ecosphere
  defending from destruction, pollution and over-exploitation 347

ecstasy 326, 343
Ecuadorian embassy 182
Ian Edge 365
Edinburgh 295
Edirne 51
education 14, 45, 49, 90, 102, 107-8, 113, 117, 155, 174, 176, 199, 302, 324
educating a slave girl 31
*Educating Your Children in Modern Times* 378, 379
educational circumstances 167
educational content 174
educational institutions 116, 157
educational performance 154
educational system 178
education in Islam 161
education system 153-4
formal education 174
purpose of education 153
six principles or functions of 152
transformation of education methodology 158
effective citizen rights 100
efficient market hypothesis 98
the Ego and the Id 68
Egypt 19-20, 23, 26, 53, 59, 64-65, 69, 166, 196, 199, 241, 265, 301
Ancient Egyptians 18
cultivated soil in 199
Egyptian forces 54
Egyptian reformers 57
Egyptians 246
gulf of Egypt 24
'Eids 28
arrangements for Eid-prayer 193
*Der Einzelne*, the isolated one 74
electoral process 103
elected democratic governments 173
electoral roll 92
electoral system 103
electricity 180
electricity consumers 73
electronic currencies 38
elimination of laws and religions 74
elites 137
elite brotherhood of warriors 170
elite group 135
elite group of caretakers 155
elite of bankers 161
elite power 122
e-mail 177
emasculated Islam 331
emergency powers 94
emotional symbols 134
empire 78-80, 96, 245, 250
the [Roman] Empire 245
empiricism 12, 87, 325, 340
employment
employees 158, 223
employer 223
employment market 223
employment outside the home 145
employment status 153
M. Enayat 364
enchantment 84
capitalism, a technique of enchantment 326
*The Enchantments of Mammon – How Capitalism Became the Religion of Modernity* 369-70
*The Encyclopaedia of Islam* 362, 365, 383, 401
the end of history 179

*The End of History and the Last Man* 381
the end of metaphysics 128
the end of privacy 178
the end of secrecy 178
endowments 199
enemies 274
the enemy
identify the enemy 331
energy xxii, 108
'enframing' [see also *Gestell*] 394
engineering of consent 132, 135
England 24-25, 29, 101-2, 172, 398
English apple-growers 291
English East India Company 29
English history 168
English language 79
English people 291
English society 168
English spy 55
engrossing 286
the Enlightenment 240
enslavement 244
enslaved system 150
entertainment 174-6
entities 66
entrenched interests 140
entrenched power domains 182
entropic forces of humanness 170
environmentalism 108, 141
environment 103
environmental damage 103
environmental pollution 113
environmental protection authorities 105
environmental regulations 108
"Environmental Literacy: Education as if the Earth Mattered" 375
envy 152
epistemology
epistemic and social practices 128
epistemic sources 340
epistemological foundations 68, 127, 340
epistemological sources 12
equipment 197
equipment and materials 292
equity 189
equitable distribution xxv
equity, freedom and justice in trade and commerce 348
Dr. Erbakan xxi
*Eros and Civilisation: A Philosophical Inquiry into Freud* 141
*The Esoteric Deviation in Islam* 226, 362, 365, 394
esprit de corps 256
essence 273
essential services 107
Robert Devereux, the Earl of Essex
the Essex coup d'état 173
execution of 172
establish *ṣalāt* 164
estates of deceased persons 26, 197
*The Ethics of Money Production* 395
Ethiopia 21
ethnicity 153
ethnic immigrants 118
ethos of *futuwwa* 168
Euclid 166
Euphrates 267
Eurasia 23
Eurasian trade routes 22
Euro-Asian trade 24
Europe 18, 22-25, 34, 43, 59, 68, 83, 169, 226, 283, 329

eurocentric worldview 69
Eurocentrism 69
European aerospace manufacturer 107
European civilisation 168
European culture 215
European discourse 159
European imperialism 112
European Middle Ages
squalor, disease, poverty, starvation and brute labour of 124
European mould 76
European Papal Christendom 169
European powers 42
Europeans 46, 49, 61
European wars 173
the European tradition 395
Being as Event 128
everyday items 280
everyday transactions 221
every-man-for-himself approach 309
evolutionary theory 68, 127
evolution of civilisation 142
evolution of Islamic civilisation 199
evolution of media platforms 178
Stewart Ewan 135, 377
excess gold 284
exchange 40
exchange rates 230, 282
exchange rates 231, 287
excommunication 171
execution of punishments 191
the executive 35
executive branches of government 156
executives 326
exegeses xvii
existence
"from *ex-* 'out' + *sistere* 'take a stand" 298
existence of God 83
existential attractiveness 278
expeditionary forces 194
expeditions 265
expenditure 187, 203
experiencing reality 163
experimentation 87, 325
explanation of reality 71
exploitation of people 103
exploration 74
exponential growth 206, 385
exponential growth powers 212
exponential processes 206
export trading 291
expose corruption 175
extending the period of childhood 159
extermination of indigenous peoples 74
externalities 102-3
extradition 182
extravagant borrowing 117
extreme wealth 215
eye of revelation 248

## F

fables and romances 125
Facebook xxiii, 109, 121
the Face of Allah 214
face value 306
factories and mills 145
factories 29, 60
"facts" 235
*Faḍl al-Muwaṭṭa' wa 'ināya al-umma*

al-Islāmiyya bihi 391
Ammar Fairdous 214, 244, 386, 390, 399-400
fairness and justice 222
fair and equal opportunity 178
fair trader 283
faith 74
fake news 331
the fall of the caliphate xxv, 33, 42
fallow land 11
false dialectic 65
false interpretation 213
false scriptures
the data-banks of figures 327
falsification (clipping)
guarding against their 195
fame 163
the family 203, 243
abolition of the family 147
a unit of production 144
break-up of the family unit 147
familial strife 215
family expenditure 147
family identity 168
family relations 133
family system 150
family tradition 158
family wage 145
the family and Companions 248
famine 289
*fanā fillāh* (annihilation in Allah) 163, 343, 345
fantasy 133
fantasy numbers system 187
*faqīh* (jurist) 339
al-Fārābī 8
*farā'iḍ* (obligations) xx, 331
*farā'iḍ* – the fixed shares of inheritance 215-6
*fāris* (horseman) 165
farmers 53, 234
farmers' markets 264
fascism 113
fashions 175
fastest wealth creation 181, 329
fasting 12, 216, 337
beginning and end of fast of Ramadan 337
supervision of fast of Ramadan 193
*fatā* – young man 161-2, 165
*A Fate Worse Than Debt* 373, 375
*Fatḥ al-mulhim bi sharḥ Ṣaḥīḥ al-Imām Muslim* 387
*Fatḥ* of Makka 204
*Fātiḥa* 201
Fatimid caliph 166
*fatra* (gap) 246
*Fatwa on Banking* 361
*Fatwa on Paper-Money* 362
*fatwās* 55, 225, 302
William Faulkner 79
*fay'* 28
*Fayḍ al-Qadīr* 389, 396
Fayṣal ibn Turkī 54
Shaykh al-Faytūrī 344
Ustad Necip Fazıl 49, 62, 363-5
fear 152
fear of Allah 167
federal income tax 159
federal lobbying expenditures 110
the Federal Reserve xxiii, 97, 120-1
the Federal Reserve System 35, 50
federal taxes 121
feet of monarchs 224
female infanticide 10

Niall Ferguson 210, 386
Jason Ferriman 182, 382
Fertile Crescent 19
feudalism 34
fiat currencies 26, 38, 41, 211, 286, 298
fiat money xxii, 35, 39, 50, 105, 228, 309
*Fiat Money Inflation in France* 361
fiduciary event 187
fiduciary metaphor 345
fifty percent of the world's wealth 179
fighting forces 20
fighting in the streets 95
finance 62
finance capital 97
finance capitalism 34
finance elites 114
finance sector 327
financial and monetary transactions 244
financial circumstances 167
financial collapse of 2008 99, 131
financial crisis of 2008 xxiii, 105, 120
financial crisis xxiii, 36
financial dealings 8
financial elite 98, 183
financial elites 82, 120
financial functions 191
financial institutions 113
financial manipulation 157
financial matters 20
financial oligarchs 35, 96
financial oligarchy 91, 98, 112
financial recklessness 119
financial slavery 148
financial system 35
financial turmoil 42
financiers 51, 158
without recourse to the financial instruments and institutions of capitalism 227
financial crisis 211
The Financial Times 371
C. Findlay 373
*fiqh* 27, 47, 186-7, 202, 227-9, 231, 253, 262, 267, 275, 282, 297, 306, 345, 354
the division of *fiqh* into *'ibādāt* and *mu'āmalāt* 238
*fiqh* for traders 267
*fiqh* of caliphate 47
*fiqh* of commercial transactions 210
*fiqh* of *mu'āmalāt* 276
*fiqh* of purification 276
formal *fiqh* 227
methodology 335
Taṣawwuf without learning 338
teaching of 193
*uṣūl al-fiqh* – principles of *fiqh* 272
firewood 301
*firman* (royal edict) 29
Imperial Firman 51, 55
the First Amendment 103
first born 215
the first caliphs 194
first cities 242, 296
first generations 319
first Sa'udi state 54
the first *sūra* revealed in Madīna 238
fiscal government xx
fiscal responsibility 97
fiscal state xxi, 18, 212
abolition of 189

*fiṭra* (natural condition) 47, 245, 249, 336, 353, 367
inborn natural predisposition 324
five daily prayers
arrangements for 193
five year plan 149
fixed exchange rate for the purposes of *zakāt* 231
fixed terms 70
flagrant tax avoidance 131
flawless ruby 247
flocks and herds 301
*flous* 228
*flous* for gold or silver 282
*flous* (*fulūs* singular *fals*) – small copper coins 231, 280
focus groups 138-9, 376
the Followers 254, 258
the Followers of the Followers 254, 258
food xxii
food hampers for the poor 200
foodstuffs 209, 281-2, 308
force of the law 196
Henry Ford 158
foreign bond-holders 51
foreign bribery 107
*Foreign Bribery Rages Unchecked in Over Half of Global Trade* 107
foreign domination 58
foreign laws 56
the Foreign Office 55
foreign traders 285
the Forest 75
forestalling 283
forfeiture of the goods or their value 286
forgiveness 164, 292
formalities 306
Douglas J. Forsyth 361
*For the Coming Man* 366
fortitude 173
Fortune 500 companies 110
fortune-telling 193
fossil fuel energy 158
foundation of a market 259
foundation of faith 159
foundation of science 67
foundations 108
fountains 199
fractals 269
fractional reserve banking xxii, 26, 29, 31, 34, 38-39, 41, 44, 50, 85, 105, 211, 327, 355, 360, 400
fractional reserve generation of money supply 346
fragmentation of control 157
France 24-25, 37, 48, 56, 60
French government 37
French institutions 45
French language 45
French prosecutors 107
French railway engineers 61
French Republic 36
French Revolution 36, 38, 45, 68, 183, 224, 243
French Third Republic 61
franchise 169
*The Frankfurt School on Religion – Key Writings of the Major Thinkers* 369
frankincense 18
fraud 179
fraudulent business practices 196
fraudulent transactions monitoring of 194

Freddie Mac 99
free and regular elections 100
freedom 130, 160, 301
freedom and justice in trade and commerce 189
freedom of assembly 141
freedom of expression 149
freedom of speech 141
the basis of true choice 217
free exchanges 82, 187, 332
freeing slaves 27, 31, 204
free markets 18, 33, 68, 112, 140, 253, 263, 291
"free market" doctrine 97
free market economy management of a 191
free market principles 113
Freemasonry 59, 60-61, 365
20th century Masonic lodges 62
*fatwā* against 62
[free]mason 55
masonic state 49, 62
masons 62
the first lodge in Jaffa 61
the Grand Lodge of London 60
grand lodges of India 59
Grand Master of all Mesopotamian freemasonry 59
lodge in Cairo 55
lodges of Basra 59
free men
gathering of 244
free political culture 100
free trade 112, 190, 292
Freiburg 141
*Freiheit ist Existenz* 76, 130
French Flanders 25
the French Republic 371
the French Revolution 240, 371
fresh legal rulings 56
Anna Freud 132, 136
Sigmund Freud 68, 127, 132, 135, 138, 140, 142-3, 148, 150, 376
Freudians 141, 150
Freud's writings 133
Friday *jumu'a* prayer 221
arrangements for 193
friends of Allah (*awliyā-Allah*) 343
friend of Allah (*walī-Allah*) 343
frugality 158
fruits 209
*fu'ād* – heart 274
Fuad Pasha 62, 64
Francis Fukuyama 381
full measure and weight 196
fun 161
fundamental building blocks 67
funds 294
*funduq* (in modern Arabic a hotel) 285
funerals 200
*fuqahā* (jurists) 27, 395
divisions among the *fuqahā* and *'ulamā* in India 254
*fuqahā* ruling the amīr 66
*fuqahā*'s maxim 276
*fuqarā* 344, 353
furnishings 297
*furūsiyya* (*futuwwa*) 165-6
fusion and fission 70
al-Fusṭāt 166
*Futuḥāt al-Makkiyah* 403
future of mankind 190
futures markets 308-9
futures contracts 209
futures markets in foodstuffs 209

*futuwwa*, noble brotherhood 161-2, 165, 167-8, 172, 197, 256, 344, 392
essence of 163
*futuwwa* institutionalised 164
*futuwwa* of the Muslims 169
*futuwwa* – the noble qualities of character 258
noble qualities of 292
fuzzy mathematics 70

## G

the G10 xxiv
the G10 plus China 121
gain 187
Galileo Galilei 68, 87, 127-8
Galilean telescope 129
gallantry (*shahāma*) 165
Francis Galton 155
gambling 11, 193, 298, 331
game developers 175
the gap between poor and rich 132
gap (*fatra*) 246
gas xxii
Pierre Gassendi 87
gatheredness 343
John Taylor Gatto 155, 156, 378-9
GDPs 104
gems 19
genealogies 166
genealogical hegemony 168
general welfare 303
generosity 168, 172
generosity (*sakhā*) 165
genetic re-engineering 178
gentrification 118
genuine factual knowledge 125
geography 12, 14
Susan George 118-9, 373, 375
German Muslims 250
Germany 48, 60, 137
Gestalt 73, 75
Gestalt of the worker 73-74
"The Gestalt of Freedom" 367-8, 376
*gestell* – "enframing" 274, 394
al-Ghāba 265
*ghanīma* – spoils 28-29, 31, 196, 297
*gharar* – uncertain and risky transactions 286
Ghassān 242, 390
Imām Abū Ḥāmid al-Ghazālī 164, 192, 292, 379, 383, 397
S.M. Ghazanfar 195, 383
John Gittinger 137, 377
the giving/spending culture 206
the global banking crisis of 2008 211
the global banking system 38
global capitalism 69, 77, 179, 329-30
global capital accumulation 122
global capitalist network 58
global corporatocracy 103
global corporate totalitarianism 330
global corporation 104
global economy xxiii, 120-1
global financial crisis 95
global GDP xxiii, 120
global hegemony 206
global holocaust 90, 132, 323
globalisation 60, 179
globalisation of poverty 79
global markets 120, 179
global media and entertainment companies 104
global media ownership 182

global order 250
global power of technique 129
global rules 104
global state 78
global super-market 78
global world state 69
global village 225
*The Glossary of Islamic Terms* 405
glossary of Qur'ānic terms 211
gluttony 114
God 125-6
the death of God 70
idea of god 326
Johann Wolfgang von Goethe 73, 159
going out to meet the caravans – forestalling 282
gold 19, 23, 26, 28, 36-37
gold standard 287
gold and silver 228, 235, 276, 278, 286, 298-9, 346-7, 388
attractiveness of 280
gold and silver coins 280
to different standards and weights 231
tangible commodities 230
well-established gold and silver coins 230
the gold *dīnār* xxi, 41, 225
gold (*dīnār*) coins 195
the Gold Dīnār Movement 279, 395
gold *dīnārs* and silver *dirhams* 227, 229, 290, 389
the "Golden Age" of Islam 21
gold for gold 230, 281
gold for silver 282
the gold Islamic *dīnār* 188, 332
good and evil 78
good behaviour 192
good business climate 117
good character 163
don't waste a good crisis 95
goods and paper money 188
goods and services 33, 194
Google xxiii, 109, 121
the Gospels 228, 320
Phillip Gould 139
governance xxiv, xxv, 5-6, 18, 269, 332
a social capacity 187
central function of 189, 347
governance and administration 252
governance of the city 118
governing 15, 189
institutions of 190
problems of 190
government 17, 46, 100, 325
government agencies 135, 177
government borrowing 42
government councils 45
government fiat 44
government functions 45
government legislation 41
government post 265
government regulation or law 50
governments 121, 179
governments and corporations 152
legitimacy of a 350
local and national 301
role of government 111, 117
the absolute authority 126
the Government of India Act 30
governors 9, 195
governor for Ireland 172
governor of Madīna 308
judgements of the 335
the Gramm-Leach-Bliley Act 98

the Granada Mosque 378
Grand Mufti 58
Grand Wazīr 62
Grand Wazīr Ali Pasha 52
Grand Wazīr Mahmud Nedim Pasha 52
R.G. Grant 360
grapes 18
graphic designer 293
A.C. Grayling 370
grazing land 301
great capitalist fortunes 215
great classical scholars 253
greater concentration of ownership 98
Greater Syria 167
the Great Negus 242
the great numbers of questions 290
the Great Reset
a coup d'état 330
*The Great Ruler: A Study of Abdulhamid Khan II* 363-5
great writers of Europe 169
the Greco-Roman world 241
Greece 104, 199, 241
Ancient Greece 124
expropriated *waqf* land 199
greed 114, 152
greed in human affairs 195
greedy dictators 374
Greek 22
Greek learning 250
Greek model 246
Greek mythology 132
Greek philosopher 67
Greek thought 241
Greek world 244
the Greeks 12, 19, 244
sciences and philosophies of the Greeks 250
speculation of the Greeks 250
Alan Greenblatt 108
"Greetings are for Allah..." 251
groceries 207
group membership 155
growing complexity of modern life 56
guarantees of immunity 242
guardianship of minors 193
guardianship of women 193
Felix Guattari 150, 378
guidance 201, 208, 211, 247, 257
guidance (*hudā* and *hidāya*) 202
guilds 18, 60, 164, 197, 285, 291, 293, 332, 346
economic functions performed by the guilds
inhibiting monopoly capitalism 198
protecting the integrity of the bi-metallic currency 198
providing social security 198
medieval revival of guild culture in Europe 294
Persian models 293
guilt-ridden usurer 385
Gulags 31, 323
Gulkhane Hatti-Cherif 60
Antonio Guterres, UN Secretary General 330

## H

habit-control schooling 157
hacking 382

*ḥadd*-punishments (specific fixed penalties laid down in the *sharī'a*) 192
*ḥudūd* 27, 347
legal parameters and the punishments for infringement of *ḥudūd* 226
living within the *ḥudūd* 348
*al-Hadis Vol. II* 403
*ḥadīth* 14, 186, 200, 225, 233, 254, 258, 262, 264, 266-9, 334, 337
codification of *ḥadīth* 335
collation of *ḥadīth* 334
*ḥadīth* literature 258
teaching of *ḥadīth* 193
the *ḥaḍra* 344
*ḥaḍrat ar-Rabbānī* 344
*ḥāfiẓ* (knowing by heart) 339
Ḥafṣa [bint 'Umar ibn al-Khaṭṭāb] 334
the ḥajj 10, 216, 252
dates of the 337
ḥajj festival 266
al-Ḥakīm [at-Tirmidhī] 236
al-Ḥākim 389, 398
Ḥakīm ibn Ḥizām 265
the *ḥalāl* and *ḥarām* 216
*ḥalāl* and *ḥarām* food 252
*ḥalāl* functioning community 227
*ḥalāl* livelihoods 233
*ḥalāl* [permitted] 344, 353
*ḥalāl* purposes 294
*ḥalāl* trade 10
*ḥalāl* transactions in commerce 261
the *ḥarām* [prohibited] xx, 50, 344, 353
*ḥāl* (state)
the states he is passing through 353
Hamad Bin Khalifa University 392
Ḥamāsah of Abū Tammām 166
Hamburg 80
Ḥanafī [*fiqh*] 335, 337
Ḥanafī dynasties 333
Ḥanafī *madhhab* 225
Ḥanafīs 336, 386
Ḥanafī *'ulamā* 267
Ḥanbalī [*fiqh*] 335, 337
Ḥanbalī scholar 167
*The Handbook on Islam, Iman and Ihsan* 363, 405
the hands of the Messenger of Allah 387
hand to hand trade locally 188
restoration of 332
happiness machines 136
the Hapsburg Empire 24
the *ḥaqīqa* – reality 338, 403
al-Harawī 391
hard cash (*naḍḍ*) 220
Hareket Army 49
a harmonious society, how to establish 326
the harmony between philosophy and religion 13
Harvard University 152
harvests 209
harvest time 296
David Harvey 112, 373, 375
[David] Harvey's definition 122
al-Ḥasā 54
al-Ḥasā province 52
Ḥasan al-Bannā 55, 57
al-Ḥasan al-Baṣrī 390
Hāshim ibn 'Abd Manāf 242
*al-Ḥāshiyah 'alā al-Jalālayn* 389
Ḥassān ibn Thābit 247

Ḥātib ibn Abī Balṭa'a 261
Hatti-Sherif Gulkhane 46
Hawaii 80
heads of state xix, 115
health 108
health bureaucrats 105
health care 104, 113, 330
healthcare 107
healthcare systems 69
health of the race 155
health regulations 108
health system 178
the heart 236, 273
cleaning the 344
perception of the 340
the heart of Qur'ān 273
hedge funds 298
Chris Hedges 329, 402
W. Heffening 383
Werner Heisenberg 70, 80
held wealth 26, 229
heliocentrism 68
*Heliopolis* 75
helping people have their rights and claims fulfilled 193
heraldry 168
heraldic displays 170
Ellen Herman 137, 377
hermeneutics of a restored human discourse 128
hermeneutic strategy 56
Alexander Hertel-Fernandez 108-10, 372
Jason Hickel 122, 374-5
*hidāya* (guidance) 202
a hidden elite 92
the hidden hand of the market 114
the hidden (spiritual) xiii, 356
hidden wealth 219
hides 25
hierarchy 223
the higher echelons of business 156
higher learning 182
higher price items 280
the higher spiritual task 148
high moral behavioural values 168
high prices xxii, 287
high standard of work ethics 198
high transaction fees 119
highway robbery 10
the Hijaz 52, 54
the Hijra (the Prophet's migration to Madīna) 204, 237, 336
*Ḥilf al-Fuḍūl* 165
Ḥimyar 242
hindu empire xxi
hinterland 295
Hiroshima 80
Hirsch
J.P. Hirsch 361
Joel Hirsch 51
Joseph Hirsch 51
Maurice de Hirsch 51
Moses Hirsch 51
the *ḥisba* 192, 332
*ḥisba* (administration of the city) 190, 348
Hishām ibn Muḥammad 242
history 150, 175
cyclical view of 255
the historical beginning of Islam 237
historiography xvii, 14
historians 123
historical record 175, 243

*The History of the Khalifahs who took the Right Way* 389, 393
*A History of Money: From Ancient Times to the Present Day* 360-1, 366, 381
*A History of Saudi Arabia* 364
Adolf Hitler 95
HIV/AIDS 180, 329
hoarding [monopoly] 10, 286
hoarding foodstuffs 284
hoarding money 196, 284
hoarding necessities 196
hoarding or engrossing 283
prohibition of 346
Thomas Hobbes 68, 126
J.M. Hobson 359
M.G.S. Hodgson 384
M. Hoexter 384
holding one's tongue 164
Muhtar Holland 379, 384, 397
P.M. Holt 362
holy places
Stock Exchanges 327
homo economicus 324
homo sapiens 324
homosexuality
decriminalisation of 60
honesty 168
Hong Kong 106, 211
honour 168
honour given to women 170
hooligans 95
Herbert Hoover 377
Hormuz 22
the horror of this modern age 90, 132
the horse 15
horsemanship 165
hospitality 285
hospitality to the guest 164
hospitals 199
G.F. Hourani 358
house arrest 47, 182
household table 147
the House of Hapsburg 24
house utensils and bride's trousseaus for poor girls 200
how business shapes policy 109
*hudā* (guidance) 202
a Hudaybiyya moment 263
Ḥudhayfah ibn al-Yamān 220
Michael Hudson 390
huge amounts of wealth 196
*al-ḥukm far' at-taṣawwur* 276
Jörg Guido Hülsmann 277, 395
the human being 126, 248
dimensions of human personality 340
goal of 341
human collective behaviour 330
human dignity 113
human experience 235
Humanism 31, 65, 83, 148, 248
human life 9
human mind 132
human psyche 132
human reason 71, 126
human resources 152
human rights 60, 141, 160
human virtue 8
human welfare 123
inner and outer aspects of human personality 338
protection of human beings 347
what is a 326
the humane conditions of Islamic law 31

Humayun 46
Ḥunayn 204
the hundred biggest economics 104
hunger 125
number one cause of death 180
hunting 165
Robert Hurley 378
Edmund Husserl 141
Ian Hutchinson 375
the hybrid state 78
hygienic function 155
hypotheses 87, 325
hypotheses of scientists 86

## I

*'ibāda* 8, 221
expressed in fiduciary metaphor 187
*'ibāda* for Allah 164
*'ibādāt* and *mu'āmalāt* 227, 319
*'ibādāt* and *mu'āmalāt* inextricably joined together 319
*'ibādāt* (devotional and ritual acts) xxvi, 57, 187, 238
*'ibādāt* (worship) 186, 345
Ibn 'Abbās 203, 207, 209, 222, 238, 252, 264, 385
Ibn Abī Aḥmad 296
Ibn 'Ajība 342, 403
Ibn al-'Arabī
Muḥyī al-Dīn ibn al-'Arabī 403
Shaykh al-Akbar Ibn al-'Arabī 343
Qāḍī Abū Bakr ibn al-'Arabī 385, 401
Ibn al-Ḥājj 267-8
*al-Madkhal* 267
Ibn al-Humām 219
'Abd ar-Raḥmān ibn al-Qāsim 220
Ibn 'Asākir 391
'Abdalwāḥid ibn 'Āshir 385
Ibn 'Aṭiyya 214
Ibn Ḥajar al-'Asqalānī 393
Ibn Hishām 165, 380
Ibn Isḥāq 257, 380

Ibn Juzayy al-Kalbī 216, 220, 222, 228, 232, 239, 290, 305-6, 387, 388, 397, 399-400
Ibn Kathīr 392
Ibn Khaldūn 22, 27, 44, 219, 224, 255-6, 351, 359, 388
Ibn Khuwayzimandād 208
Ibn Mājah 334, 386, 392, 399
*Sunan Ibn Mājah* 393
Ibn Mas'ūd 203, 213, 234
Ibn Rajab 167
Ibn Rashīd 54
Ibn Sa'd 393
Ibn Sa'ud 55
criminal family of Ibn Saud 55
Ibn Saud family 55
reneged on allegiance 55
Ibn Shabbah 392
Ibn Taymiyya 384
Ibn 'Umar 47, 387
Ibn Wahb 220, 255, 287
Ibn Zam'a 266
Ibrāhīm 162-3, 237, 242, 245
E. Ibrahim & D. Johnson-Davies 358
Ibrāhīm Hakki 303
Ibrahim Pasha 53
Carl Icahn 115-6
iconography 103, 168

*'idda* (a period after the death of her husband or divorce during which a woman must wait before re-marrying) 193
*iddikhār* – buying enough grain at harvest time for the year 283
ideas 67, 72
idea of democracy 136
idea of god 88
ideas and ideals 64
ideal state 8, 149
ideology 64, 83, 123
ideologies 66
idhn xiii
idolatry 246
idolaters 32
idols 162
*'Īds* 252
Ihsan Mosque, Norwich 398
*iḥtikār* – hoarding, monopoly 284
*Iḥyā 'Ulum ad-dīn* 379
*ijmā'* (consensus), 333
*ijtihād* [independent reasoning] xviii, 7, 56, 192, 335
*ijtihād*: exercise of personal judgment in legal matters 357
*ijtihād* judgments 221
*mujtahid* (someone capable of *ijtihād*) 192
*mujtahid* (someone qualified to make legal judgments) 364
*mujtahids* 56
*ikhlāṣ* – sincerity 239
illegal and fraudulent sales/transactions 194
Ivan Illich 288, 396-7
illuminated order 253
illumination 162
*'ilm* (knowledge/science) 275
*'ilm al-aḥwāl* (science of states) 340-1, 344
*'ilm al-'aql* (the science of the intellect) 340
*'ilm al-asrār* (the science of the innermost consciousness) 340-1, 344
*'ilm al-kalām* 86

*'ilm al-ladunī*, direct knowledge from Allah 162
*'ilm an-nafs* 344
'Imād ad-Dīn Zanjī 167
image in the eyes of others 134
"The Image of Saladin: From the Medieval to the Modern Age" 380
imamate
examine the *imām* who leads the prayer 193
Imamate (leadership) 5
*Imām* (leader) 220
*imāms* who take prayer 187
the just Imām 221
*İmam Hatip* schools 398
*īmān* – trusting, or confiding, or having trust or confidence 290, 300
immigrant workers
remittances 119
imperialist penetration 43
Imperial prestige and tradition 63
impersonal power 34
imprisonment
at the king's pleasure 286
improper gain 196
inadequate drinking water 180

inborn natural predisposition 47
incarnation (*ḥulūl*) 342
the Incense Road 19, 22
"Incorporation of the Ottoman Empire and the World Economy" 362
independent check on power 183
independent contractors 121
independent judiciary 100
independent livelihood 157
have to surrender the dream of 158
India xviii, xx, xxi, 19, 21-22, 29-30, 53, 59, 106, 209, 234, 246, 254, 330
Indian Independence 30
Indian Rebellion 30
Indian subcontinent 30
Indian Ocean 22, 23-24, 30
the indigenous community 79
indigenous peoples 250
indigo 30
the individual 248, 253
individualism 86, 324
individuality 143
individuality had to be banished 158
individual's personal satisfaction 138
realm of the 285
the semblance of individuality 178
indivisibility
lack of indivisibility 196
Indonesia 209
inductive methods of the natural sciences 125
industrial capitalism 151
industrial centres of the north 297
industrial economy 297
industrial farm animal production 103
industrialisation 29, 34, 145
industrialisation and its effects on the environment 141
industrialism 145
industrialists 158
industrial mass production 156
the Industrial Revolution 42, 66, 68, 144
industrial society 31, 133, 142
industrial titans 158
industrial utopia 158
industry 20, 71, 125
industry and machine manufacturing 144
supervision of industry (product standardisation, arbitration, minimum wages, etc.) 194
inflation xxii, xxiii, 37, 39, 41, 79, 284, 309, 355
hidden tax 79
informality 164
information 174, 176-7
information overload 177
infrastructure 102, 151
infrastructure for business 118
infrastructure projects 120
Alexander James Ingles 152, 155, 378
inheritance 168, 215
arbitrary designation or disinheritance 215
inheritance shares 215
inherited capital 212
laws of inheritance 212, 215, 346
inner lives 152
inner drives 143
innovation 391

instant financial trading 79
instant interaction 177
institutions 34, 187, 190, 328
  institutional framework 112
  institutional investors 298
  institutional schooling 157
instrument of revenue 159
instruments of the bankers 65
insurance regulators 105
integrated society 175
integrating function 152-3
integrity 275
intellect 162, 342
  intellectual bankruptcy 160
  intellectual exchange 169
  intellectuals 135
the intention 239
intention to circumvent the law 306
interest 34-35, 40, 42, 44, 46, 50, 148, 399
  interest-based economy 245
  interest-based financing 43
  interest-bearing loans 243
  interest charges 281
  interest debt 149
  interest debt mechanisms and institutions 50
  interest rates 148, 399
  interest rate swaps 98
  interest transactions 244
  lending money on 327
  prohibition of 294
  simple interest 213
interest groups 175
intermediary steps 228, 306
the International Commission 51
the international community 106
international economic balances 179
international institutions 160
International Journal of Middle East Studies 362
the International Monetary Fund (IMF) 35, 69, 77, 85, 112-3, 117-9, 179
the International Monetary System 58
the International Psychoanalytical Association 377
the Internet 177-8, 347
  Internet Protocol Television 177
  Internet radio 177
the interregnum [in the khalifate] 46
the inter-state system 43
intrinsic value 10, 26, 41, 131, 278
"Introduction on *Mabādi' uṣūl al-fiqh*" 394
*An Introduction to Islamic Finance* 399
the invention of the telescope 127
investment 114, 236
  Investment Bank Division of UBS AG 99
  investment banker 98
  investment bankers 118
  investment banker, the dominant element in the financial oligarchy 112
  investors 290
  powerful cabal of investment bankers 117
inward and outward sciences 338
the inward (psychological) xiii, 356
IOU 36
Iran 22, 55, 355
  cultivated soil in 199
  Irani 58

Iraq 21, 53, 90, 132, 236, 242, 323
Conquest of Iraq 297
Ireland 172
Irish Muslims 250
the irrational function
the irrational function ... was usury 189
the irrational self 136
irrational fears and desires 135
irrigation 296
*irshād* (guidance) 202
'Īsā 246
*al-Iṣāba fī tamyīz aṣ-Ṣaḥāba* 393
*'Ishā* 303
*ishtirā'* (legislation) 57
*islāḥ* (reform) 57
Islam 212, 250
a filter for culture 241
a private "religion" 208
*arkān al-Islām* (the pillars that support the edifice of Muslim society) 10
as *dīn* and social nexus 170
a totally functional, social reality 355
beginning of 226
description of the original Islamic phenomenon 356
five steps of Islamic revival 332
has no priesthood 187
II Islamic Countries Conference on Statistical Sciences 128
is a market movement 186
Islamic banking
Islamic finance industry 295
Islamic brotherhood and leadership 169
Islamic coins 21
Islamic conduct in war and peace 168
Islamic *dawla* xxv, 189-90, 347
Islamic governance 9, 66, 251
fractal of Islamic governance 263
institution of Islamic governance 355
Islamic guilds
developed spontaneously from the craftsmen themselves 198
membership was not restricted to Muslims 198
possessed an inner spiritual life 198
the dominant economic and social institutions in Muslim lands 198
the masters, journeymen and apprentices did not develop into different economic and social classes 198
Islamic Khalifate 52
destruction of the Islamic Khalifate 52
Islamic lands 52
Islamic law 18, 25, 44, 50, 55, 190, 327, 334, 346, 348
abandonment of Islamic law 57
Islamic legal history 335
primary sources of Islamic law 333
secondary sources of Islamic law 333
wisdom of Islamic law 293
Islamic market 20
Islamic model 169
Islamic modernism 64-66, 81
Islamic modernist *'ulamā* 68-69
Islamic Movement 59

Islamic political thought 190
Islamic polity 17
*Islamic Response to Imperialism* 57
Islamic revival xiii, 187, 356
'Islamic' revolution in Iran xvi
Islamic society 199
Islamic socio-political and economic order 335
the Islamic state 66
Islamic states 40
Islamic traditions 214
islamisation 58
is transactional 186
no priesthood 332
not a political movement 186
reestablishing 187
revival of 332
structuralism in 334
superstructure of 332
the so-called Islamic state 355
three realms in Islamic cosmology 340
very source of 336
Islamic banking xix, 295
"Is Islamic Banking Really Islamic? An Insider's view with Harris Irfan" 399
Islamic bank 292
Islamic bankers 294
Islamic Banks 59
Islamic finance 295
Islamic bonds 398
"The Islamic Guilds" 384
Islamic law 402
*Islamic Law and Legal Theory* 365
Islamic markets 229
"The Islamic Origins of the Common Law" 395
Islamic Republic of Iran 355
*An Islamic Response to Imperialism* 365
Islamic revival
steps for Islamic revival 356
Islamoglu-Inan 362
*Islam: The Empowering of Women* 403
Ismā'īl 241
*al-ism al-a'ẓam* (the Supreme Name i.e. Allah) 342
*isnād* 253
*al-Isrā* 341
Israel 56
Israelites 246
Istanbul 47, 49, 51-52, 62, 294
*istiḥsān* (juristic preference) 333
*istiṣlāḥ* (public interest) 57
Italy 48
Italian city-states 24
Italian Muslims 250
*Itḥāf as-Sādat al-Muttaqīn bi sharḥ Iḥyā' 'ulūm ad-dīn* 403

## J

the *jabarūt* (kingdom of power or lights) 341
Jābir ibn 'Abdullāh 220
Jacobinism 63
al-Jāḥiẓ 166, 380
Jakarta 226
[*Tafsīr*] *al-Jalālayn* 233
*jamā'a*/community 187, 253, 331
*jamā'at* 344
Sidi Ali al-Jamal 379
*al-Jāmi' li aḥkām al-Qur'ān* 362, 387, 389, 392
Japan 181
jealousy 152

Jeddah 364
Jerusalem 3, 20, 166-7, 199, 341
Roman destruction of Jerusalem 241
Jesus 241
drove the money changers from the Temple 228
"Jesus and the Money Changers (John 2:13-16)" 388
jewellery 388
Jews 18-19, 49, 61, 214, 235, 251, 264
Jewish [banking] families 212
Jewish traditions 214
the Jews and the hypocrites 211
the Jews and their ilk 202
Judaism 3, 60
ritualism and legalism of the Jews 250
shelter for Jews, Christians and others 250
Jibrīl 208, 222, 251
*jihād fī sabīlillāh* (war in the way of Allah) 16, 233, 252, 267, 327, 331, 348
*jihād an-nafs* 344
*jizya* 25, 28-29, 31-32, 196, 213
Ya'qub Johnson 402
David Johnston 56, 364
joint-stock companies 29, 101
J. Jonker 361
Jordan 19
journalists 135, 175
journalistic profession 61
Journals
The Journal of Economic History 390
The Journal of Evolutionary Psychology 367
The Journal of the American Oriental Society 384
The Journal of the Economic and Social History of the Orient 359, 384
journeyman (*aṣ-ṣāni'*) 197
jousting 169
J.P. Morgan 158
J.P. Morgan Chase 99
Judaeo-Christian tradition 196
Judaeo-Christian worldview 240
Judaism 241
Judaism, Christianity and Islam
agreement between 214
judgments 252
judiciary 35, 156, 190, 196, 348
judges 20, 194
judicial authority 194
judicial fines 26, 197
judicial powers 194
jumu'a 28, 252
*jumūd* (stagnation) 58
Imām Abū al-Qāsim al-Junayd 342, 353, 403
Imām al-Junayd's five rules 353
Junaydī Sufism 353
Ernst Jünger 70, 73-76, 81, 129-30, 367-8, 376
Jünger's mythology 75
junta of financiers 111
juridical acts 57
jurists 339
jury system 275
Just Balance 222
justice (*'adl*) 6, 168, 172, 217, 222, 354
establishment of justice 190
justice and equity in financial affairs 189, 347

the just man of authority 224
jute 29

K

Ka'b ibn al-Ashraf 19
al-Kabīr 392
*kāfir* 358
Abū Bakr al-Kalabādhī 343, 403
Immanuel Kant 67, 68, 127, 128
Heidegger's dismantling of the Kantian frame 128
the Kantian world 70
Karbala 53
Fazlul Karim 403
*karuma* – to be noble and generous 258
R. Kasaba 362
*kātib* (scribe or secretary) 192
'Abd al-Ḥayy al-Kattānī 267-8, 394
Nikki R. Keddie 57, 365
Kelantan, Malaysia 229, 395
state government of 226
Robert Kelly 99
Kent State 161
Khadīja bint Khuwaylid 19, 257
the khalifate (*khilāfa*) xviii, 5, 27, 48, 54, 186, 345
a *farḍ* of our religion 261
"Khalifa" 362
*khalīfa* – successor 5, 16, 226, 237, 261
*khalīfa* Hārūn ar-Rashīd 224
*khilāfa* of 'Uthmān 262
*al-Khulafā' ar-Rāshidūn* (the Rightly-Guided Caliphs) 11, 258, 261
the Rightly-Guided Caliphs Abū Bakr, 'Umar, 'Uthmān and 'Alī) 190
the Last *Khalīfa* 48
political dismemberment of 54
rebellion against Khalifate 55
resistance to the Khalifate 59
the return of the Khalifate 46
suspension of the 257
*al-Khāliq* – the Creator 390
*khalwa* (withdrawal from the world in the concentration of invocation) 342
*kharāj* – a share of the crops 25, 196, 213, 297, 383
collection and distribution of *kharāj* and *zakāt* 191
Kharj 53
al-Khaṭīb 268
Khatt-I Humayun 60
Khaybar
Conquest of Khaybar 297
Khubayb [ibn az-Zubayr] 264
*khuṭbas* 166, 221, 398
al-Khwārizmī 215
Kilwa 21
Kināna 241
kings xix
death of Louis XVI 93
king and aristocracy 171
Henry IV of France 172
Kingship 351
kings of England
Elizabeth I 29, 171-2
the Elizabethan Age 173
Elizabeth the Virgin Queen 171
Henry VII 168
Henry VIII 171

King James I (King James VI of Scotland) 29, 172
King John 171, 381
King Richard I 168
kings ruled in the name of God 83
Ludwig I 51
kinship 256
M.J. Kister 19, 359
*Kitāb al-Āthār* 391
*Kitāb al-Futuwwa* 379
*Kitāb al-Jāmi'* 391
*al-Kitāb al-mukhtaṣar fī ḥisāb al-jabr wa-l-muqābala* 215
*Kitāb at-tashīl li 'ulūm at-tanzīl* 387, 389
*Kitāb faṣl al-maqāl fī mā bayn al-sharī'ati wal-ḥikmati minal-ittiṣāl* 13, 358
*"Kitablar Kutubhaneler ve Vakiflar"* 398
*Kitāb wa Sunna* 65, 339
knights 169-70
knightly elite 173
knowledge 11, 13, 20
knowing about Allah 86
*'ilm al-kalām* or *'aqīda*, theology 340
knowing Allah
the subject of Sufism 340
knowledge of Allah 86, 340
the knowledge of texts 334
the knowledge of the ancients 12
man of knowledge 163
Koch brothers 109
Kohan 21
John Koskinen 99
Kuala Lumpur 128
Kufa 265, 386
*kufr* 62, 187
the *kāfir* 348
*kāfir* hegemony xx
*kāfir* ideas and organisations 65, 68
*kāfir* model 18
*kāfir* slaving 31
*kāfirūn* (unbelievers) 349
*kuffār* [disbelievers] 16, 30, 188
*Kufr: an Islamic Critique* 161, 379
refusing to submit to the *kuffār* [disbelievers] 354
the hypocrisy of the *kuffār* [disbelievers] 332
turning away from *kufr* 332
*kül vakfi* (*waqf* of ash) 303
T. Kuran 200, 384
Kurdish 166
*kuttāb* (secretaries) 192, 332
Kuwait 54
the Shaykh of Kuwait 59

L

labour 297
labour market 155
Labour Party 139, 140
Labour Party constitution 140
a *lafīf* of lesser witnesses 275, 299
R. D. Laing 150
lakes 199
A.K.S. Lambton 362
land 11, 37, 113, 191, 227
agricultural land 303
agricultural land in Algeria 199
agricultural land in Tunisia 199
collection of land-tax (*kharāj*) 265
land grabs 119
landlords 11

land ownership 296
landowner 296-7
land surveying 20
land that has been irrigated 196
land usage 295
management of the land-tax (*kharāj*) 191
a piece of land 265
pieces of land 265
plot of land 297
someone who works the land 296
Edward Lane 231, 389, 391, 397
Helen R. Lane 378
largesse 169
the Last Day 222, 253
the Last Messenger 246
the late Middle Ages 243
Latin 22, 155
Latin America 329
Laudium xiv
Timothy Laurie 378
law 13, 14, 45, 325
the Law and Society Review 384
law court 197
a law-governed society 347
a law-governed society, a nomocracy 190
laws criminalising foreign bribery 107
laws governing commerce 214, 257
legal contractual matters 217
legal currency 226
legal decisions 339
legal entity 187, 331
legal institutions 116
legalisation of usury and banking 60
legalism 250
legalists 75
legality of contracts 196
legal methodologies 56
legal persons
corporations transformed into legal persons 102
legal punishments 208
legal recourse 290
legal redress 210
legal structures and functions 113
legal system 178
legal tender 44
legislation 57, 178
legislation in the *mu'āmalāt* 57
legislative process 109
liability for mistakes and errors of judgment 302
limited liability 102
litigation 217
man-made legislation 57
law of universal gravitation 127
laws of gravity 70
Ibrahim Lawson 394-5
A. Layish 57, 365
layoffs 109
Maurizio Lazzarato 121, 375
leadership 47, 136, 140, 247, 252, 337
centrality of leadership and rulership 252
leader 28, 261
leaderless 47
leader of the Muslims 208
leadership of an imām 221
the aim of leadership 350
leap into Islam 73
leap into thinking 73
leather goods 19
left wing 92

legitimacy 168
length of contract 197
Levant 24
*Leviathan* 68
B. Lewis 362, 384
Ken Lewis 99
Wyndham Lewis 147
lexicographers 249
liberal democracy 35, 45, 69, 77
liberal market forces 86, 325
liberals 61
liberation of the self 142
libertarianism 116
libido 150
libraries 14, 199
Libya 21, 132
life imprisonment 182
*The Life, Personality and Writings of al-Junayd* 403
life project 149
linking products to emotional desires and feelings 134
Walter Lippmann 135
Eric Lipton 115
literature 14
  literary skills 178
livestock 53, 233
living conditions of underprivileged people
  betterment of 175
living expenses 209
living organisms 67
*livres* 37
loans 213, 265-6
  loans at interest 281
lobbying 103
the local
  local authorities 263
  local Chambers of Commerce 116
  local community 234
  local elite groups 115
  local governance 186
    local government 263
  local governance an open matter 345
  local industries 157
  local leaders 187, 332
  local market 263
  local strongman 114
  The Local Zakat Initiative 400
locus of the self-disclosure of Truth 72
logic 13, 325
  logical empiricism 128
  logical processes 70
  logic and reason 87
  logistic infrastructure 291
*Logos* ('reason') 368
Ronald Logue 99
London 182
  London merchants 29
loopholes 121
looting 10
Lord of Existence
  face to face meeting with the Lord of Existence 251
loss of billions of dollars 131
loss of economic freedom 147
love 74, 133
Benjamin Loveluck 300
love of the Messenger 164
Low Countries 25, 172
low prices 287
low-skilled jobs 155
loyalty 168-9, 292, 300
  loyalty and sincerity 164

loyalty to Allah 167
*lubb* – core 274
Lucan 79
Lucius 75
lucrative overseas contracts 107
Martin Luther 60
Luxembourg 25

M

*al-mā'ash* and *al-mā'ad* – the Muslim's material and spiritual life
unity between 192
machine culture 65-66
machine society 31
machine guns 55
John Mack 99
D. MacTaggert 373
Madagascar 21
*madhhabs* 336
emergence of the *madhhabs* 271
*madhāhib* 27, 337
*madhhab* (legal school) 335
*madhhab* of Madīna 335
*madhhab* of Mālik 228, 306
*madhhab 'Umarī* (*madhhab* of 'Umar) 336
Madīna al-Munawwara – The Illuminated City 7-9, 11, 19, 52-53, 163, 190, 194-5, 209, 224-5, 233, 236-8, 246, 249, 253-4, 257, 260, 265, 267, 287, 292, 337-8, 340, 350, 354, 364, 393
a garden city 295
complete blueprint pattern for Islamic societies 351
Madīnan agreement 297
Madīnan *āyat* 233
Madīnan model 190, 348
Madīnan model is nomocratic 347
Madīnan order 290
Madinans 9, 238
Madīnan state 11
Madīnan years 248
Madīna of the Messenger of Allah 264
Madīna of the *Salafī* community 351
market in 260
market of 262
primary model 190
the model of government without state 189
Madras 30
*madrasas* 199, 398
magazines 159
Muḥammad ibn 'Abdu'l-Karīm al-Maghīlī 47
magic 246
magic money tree 399
The Magna Carta 171, 381
Jalāl ad-dīn al-Maḥallī 401
al-Mahdī 165
mainstream media 177, 182
a protector for established powers 177
maintenance of family 205
maintenance of mosques and public baths 193
maintenance of the armed forces 45
major construction projects 107
major institutions of society
assault on 116
*makārim al-akhlāq* – the noble qualities of character 258
John A. Makdisi 275, 395

Makḥūl 220
*The Making of Humanity* 358
*The Making of the Indebted Man* 121, 375
Makka 165, 195, 233, 237, 242, 341, 364
  centre of Quraysh's commercial network 350
  *sūq* of Makka 261
Makka and Madīna
  upkeep of Makka and Madīna 199
Mehmet Maksudoğlu 199, 303, 384, 398
*malakūt* (the kingdom of unseen forms) 5, 341
Curzio Malaparte 70
malaria 180, 329
Malaysia 226, 229, 395
  Malay Sultanates 11
male sexual power 134
malicious deception (hoax) 179
Imām Mālik ibn Anas 7, 9, 209, 220, 224-5, 228, 253-5, 258, 267, 281, 283-4, 286-7, 296-7, 306, 332, 340, 344, 386, 391-2, 396-7, 399, 402
  Imām Mālik's clarifications 258
  Mālikī 335, 337
  Mālikī existential methodology 347
  Mālikī *fiqh* 275, 293, 387
  Mālikī legal methodology 353
  Mālikī *madhhab* 402
  Mālikīs 293
  methodology of 336
  statement on Sufism and the law 338
  teachings of 340
management
  management theory 84, 326
  managerial elite 108
  managers 326
  managing the masses 135
*mā'nā* – meaning 274
*al-Manār fī uṣūl al-fiqh* 394
mandats 38
J.E. Mandaville 362
Peter Mandelson 139-40
*Manfūḥah* 54
the man in authority 219, 221, 223, 253, 263, 288
mankind's ideological evolution 179
manliness (*murūwwa*) 165
Roger Manners, the 5th Earl of Rutland 172
man's desires 133
Al-Manṣūr 165
manufacturing 33, 145
  manufacture 227
  manufactured goods 22
  manufacturers 234
*maqāṣid* 385
  *maqāṣid* (primary goals) 8
  *maqāṣid* – the purposes of the *sharī'a* 272
Maqrīzī 20
Herbert Marcuse 141-2, 150, 377
*ma'rifa*, knowledge of deeper levels of being 338
maritime transportation 20
the market 9-10, 19-20, 26, 77, 194, 257, 332, 344
  a place for the market 260
  establishment of the market of Madīna 259
  existing markets 263

hypermarkets 283
if you abandon the market 267
Islam is a market movement 345
maintenance of markets 194
market-driven approach 300
market economy 39
market-forces monetarism 160
marketing 84, 134, 156, 326
marketing agencies 138
marketing and public relations 132
marketing technique 289
the market of Nabīṭ 259
market overseers 261
market participants 277
market people 288
the market-place xix, 194, 228, 236, 238, 253, 257, 268, 274, 283
market-places 230, 301
market practice 257
the market price 287
markets 16, 18, 197, 228, 282, 293
network of markets 350
markets as a *ṣadaqa* 260
[the market's] ground rules 259
markets in Norfolk 291
proper functioning of markets 113
state interventions in markets 113
the market of Madīna 259
markup 279, 294
Christopher Marlowe 169-70
marriage 27, 216, 243, 252, 292, 347
marriages 226
marriage settlement 278
marrying idolatresses 246
the core of society 292
Marseilles 25
martial training 169
Alexis Martinez 377
martyrs 161, 233-4, 389
Marwān ibn al-Ḥakam 308
Karl Marx 114
critique of capitalism 76
Marxists 39
Masjid al-Aqṣā 199
*maṣlaḥa* (considerations of public interest) 57
*al-maṣāliḥ al-mursalah* (public interest) 333
mass communications 182
mass communication media 174
mass incarceration 331
mass instruments of communication 159
massive foreign bribery scheme 107
mass killings 137
mass society 149, 159
mass media 133, 174-5
functions of mass media 174
mass produced object 150
mass production business empires 157
mass schooling 158
mass surveillance 159
master (*al-mu'allim* or *al-ustādh*) 197
to master nature 125
Master of az-Zubayr! 265
material assistance 164
materialism 63, 86, 324, 337, 347
material culture of production and consumption 326
mathematics 12, 14, 243
compound interest 206
mathematical entity 298
mathematical formulation of the mechanistic view 67

mathematical logic 128
Maududi 55
Abu'l Ḥasan al-Mawardī 5, 25, 357, 359, 383
*mawlās* 243, 267, 296, 393
*Mawlid* 200
mayor of a Western city 260
Eugene McCarraher 84, 369-70
James F. McGrath 388
G. McMahon 105
John McMurtry 181-2, 382
meadows for weak cattle and sheep to graze 199
meaningless competitions 159
*The Meaning of Man: The Foundations of the Science of Knowledge* 379
meanness (*bukhl*) 8, 280
means of exchange 276
means of production 40
means of transport 291
measurement 12
Mecca 3, 10, 18-19, 52-53
mechanico-materialism 126
mechanics 127
  mechanical science 68, 325
  mechanical system 67
  mechanisation 33
  mechanism 86, 324
  mechanistic view of nature 67
the mechanism of mass surveillance 159
mechanisms of exploitation and domination 121
the media xx, 49, 90, 92, 159, 174-5, 324
  agenda-setting ability of 175
  media and publishing institutions 116
  media elites 82, 114
the Medici 385
medicine 14, 18, 302
  medical researchers 105
  medical studies 302
  medical treatment 302
the medieval 68, 87
  medieval scholastics 277
  medieval sports 168
  modes of thought and practices 325
*Medieval Islamic Economic Thought* 383
"Medieval Public-Sector Economics" 383
the Mediterranean 21-22
  Mediterranean region 19
  a Muslim Lake 21
medium of exchange 39, 40, 44, 148, 277, 284
  media of exchange 278
mega-capital fortunes 212
mega-entities 217
Mehmed Ali Pasha 62
Mehmed II 23
Paul Meiser 133
Eduardo Mendieta 369
mental apparatus 132
mental illness 137
merchants 53, 248, 346
  mercantilism
    modern capitalism 112
  merchandise 45, 283
  merchant communities 22
  merchant oligarchy 350
  merchant woman 257

merits
merit of chastity 8
merit of courage 8
merit of generosity 8
merit of justice 8
Angela Merkel 120
Marin Mersenne 87
Mesopotamia 24, 53, 245, 296
Mesopotamian model 245
Mesopotamian plain 22
the Messenger of Allah 203, 208, 209, 210, 219, 223, 233, 241, 246, 247, 250, 252, 257, 258, 259, 262, 264, 273, 283, 286, 287, 290, 292, 296, 306
after he alighted in Madīna 238
birth or the death of the 237
character of 246
hijra of 237
life of 247
the hands of 224
the Messengers
three core attributes of the 234
metal product 19
raw metals 388
metalware 29
metaphor 211
metaphor of a good word 349
metaphysics 71, 72, 250
method 327
method of experiment 12
methodologies 161
methodology 160
methods of investigation 12
ossification, complexification, and structuralisation of 334
Mexico 118
MGM Holdings Inc. 182
microscopic conditions of scrutiny 177
the Middle Ages 168
the Middle East 21, 23, 25, 65, 69, 114, 118
middlemen 51
the middlemost community (*umma*) 350
Midhat Pasha 62
Ralph Miliband 371
the military 164, 165
large military 78
military acts 57
military force 115
military *furūsiyya* (*al-furūsiyya al-ḥarbiyya*) 165, 166
military machine 329
military rule xiii
military structures and functions 113
millionaires xxiv, 329
mind
an immaterial substance 126
minimum of competition 198
mining 106
mines 145
mining rights 107
Ministries of *Awqāf* 301, 302
the mint 26, 190, 195, 332, 348, 388
minting *dirhams* and *dīnārs* 252
office of the mint 195
miracle 250
the *Mi'rāj* 251, 341
mis-classifying employees 121
miserliness 278, 280
misguidance 211
Mishārī 54
Mithat Pasha 62, 64

*mithqāl* – the weight of the gold *dīnār* 223
mithqāls of gold 226
*al-Mi'yār al-Mughrib* 387
mob-rule (ochlocracy) 352
mobs (corporations) 352
mode of being 274
*Modern Egypt* 58
*Modern Islamic Political Thought* 364
modernity 34, 49, 52, 59, 68, 83, 84, 86, 240, 324, 325, 326
beginning of modern philosophy 126
modern age 323
modern capitalist dystopia 354
modern courts 210
modern employment contract 223
modern industrialism 31
modernisation 60, 61, 86, 87, 356
modernisation plans 95
modernisation process 325
modernisers 139
modernism 48, 59, 65, 66, 68, 69, 160
modernist dismantling 66
modernist epistemology 86, 324
modernist Muslims 56
modernist paradigm 124
modernists xviii, xix, 58, 80, 247, 261
modernist thought and practice 127
modernist *'ulamā* 60
modernist visions 69
modernist worldview 83
modern *kufr* 82
modern men and women entrapped within a "somnambulistic helplessness" 333
modern modes of thought and practices 325
modern money 131
modern Muslim 129
modern nation states 34
the modern period 12, 34
modern science 127
modern science and philosophy 326
modern society 130, 153, 176
the modern state xxiv, 33, 36, 76, 94, 100, 183, 186, 189
development of the modern state 171
modern states 50
modern technique 65, 66, 68
the 127
the modern worldview 83, 86, 124, 125, 324, 325
outmoded modernism 68, 69, 80
science and philosophy of 80
transition to modernity 34
*The Modern State* 361
modern structuralist defence 128
the Moghuls 333
mohair 25
molestation of children 148
monarchy 18, 45, 351
monarchical rule xiii
money 276, 277, 344
animating spirit of capitalism 326
as a medium of exchange 196
as pure electronic stored units of numbers 332
*'ayn* (cash) 281
bogus money 131
cash 276
cash transactions 281

coinage 42, 194
the coinage in use in Madīna 225
coins
coins of the Romans and Persians 230
different types and qualities of 231
standardising the quality of 195
counterfeiting 196
creation of currency 50
creation of money xxii, 36
creation of money supply 327
cryptocurrencies 297, 298
cryptocurrency exchanges 299
cryptocurrency market 298
currencies 10, 17, 22, 26, 35, 39, 40, 44, 50, 52, 82, 195, 276, 278, 279, 332
Assignats 34, 37, 38
currency of the Muslims xxi
digital-currencies 210
issuing a currency 389
nature of currencies 294
paper-, digital- and crypto-currencies 347
currency
one currency 69
one currency, the US dollar 179
*ex-nihilo* money xxiv
fabricated money 120
is useless and sterile 196
monetarist (money *ex nihilo*) practice 187
monetarist social model 160
monetarist system 181, 187, 328
monetary system 65, 66, 112
money-changer 231
money created out of nothing xxii
money substitutes 26
money supply 35, 38, 39, 44, 85, 281
money system 36
nature of money 217
pieces of money 231
pure electronic stored units of numbers 188
quality and integrity of 113
substitutes of money 46
the Mongols 24
the Mongol invasion 22
*Pax Mongolica* (peace and stability across the Mongol Empire) 23
monitored environment 161
*Monopolizing Knowledge: A Scientist Refutes Religion-Denying, Reason-Destroying Scientism* 375
monopoly 29, 30, 34, 44
monopoly and control over the means of violence 34
monopoly capitalism 346
monotony of daily life 175
morality xxi, 78, 325
moral and Divine imperatives 347
moral character of rulers 221
moral codes 84
Morocco 21, 209, 398
Moroccan Mālikī *fuqahā'* 275
Moroccans 207
Phillip Morris 104
mortgage 37
mortgage bank 51
mosques 199, 200, 263, 301
establishment of mosque 259
markets attached to 263
mother 149
mother (*umm*) 249

motion picture companies 175
a mount in the way of Allah 204
*The Moussems 1992 & 1993 Gatherings of Light* 405
movement of wealth 15, 189, 190, 347
movements against military intervention in South-East Asia 141
Mozambique 21
*mu'addib* (schoolmaster)
  assesses the abilities of 193
*mu'adhdhin* (one who calls to prayer)
  assesses the abilities of 193
Mu'ādh ibn Jabal 194
*mu'allim* (teacher or master of a craft)
  assesses the abilities of 193
*mu'āmala* – behaviour 186, 274
*mu'āmalāt* (social transactions) xix, xxv, xxvi, 57, 186, 187, 218, 238, 252, 274, 285, 291, 292, 295, 300, 345, 394
  *mu'āmalāt at-tijāriyya* – ordinary commercial transactions 253
  *mu'āmalāt māliyya* (financial transactions) 259
  *mu'āmalāt* of trade and commerce 186, 276
  standard topics of 282
Mu'āwiya ibn Abī Sufyān 266
*muḍāraba* 236, 257
*al-Mudawwana* 219, 387, 402
*mudd* 223, 224, 387
*al-Mufradāt fī gharīb al-Qur'ān* 385, 386
the Mughals 11, 29
  the Mughal *dawla* 29, 30
  Mughal India 29
  Mughal Sultanate 357
*Mughnī al-muḥtāj* 393
*al-Muhadhdhib*
  commentary on 225
the *Muhājirūn* 224, 292
Muḥammad 'Abduh 55, 56, 57, 58, 129
Muḥammad Abū Zahra 56
Muḥammad al-'Amrāwī 228, 229
Muḥammad al-Ḥajj 363
Muḥammad Ali Pasha 53, 61, 62
Muḥammad Hāshim Kamālī 56
Muḥammad ibn 'Abd al-Wahhāb 53, 54
Muḥammad ibn 'Abd al-Wahhāb al-Baskarī 268
Muḥammad ibn 'Abdullāh ibn Ḥasan 260
Muḥammad ibn al-'Arabī xvii
Muḥammad ibn 'Alawī al-Mālikī 391
Muḥammad ibn al-Ḥasan ash-Shaybānī 225, 254
  Imām Muḥammad's commentaries 254
Muḥammad ibn al-Munkadir 220
Muḥammad ibn Ka'b al-Quraẓī 220
Muḥammad ibn Sa'ūd 52, 53
*muḥāqala* – renting land in exchange for wheat 296, 397
*muḥaqqiqūn* – scholars who investigate carefully and verify things 226
S.M. Muhsin 358
the *muḥtasib* 192, 193
  checking weights, measures, quality and prices 197
  civil and municipal duties of 194
  *muḥtasib* – market inspector 258, 260
  *muḥtasib* (municipal governance) 9
  *muḥtasib*s 196

*muḥtasib*'s duties 193
supervised the guilds 197
*al-Mujabbarūn* – "those made mighty" 242
Mujāhid 201, 220, 222, 385
*mujāhid* king 167
*mujāhidūn* 233, 267
the *mulk* 5, 341
*mulk* (the kingdom of forms) 340
multi-confessionalism 60
the multiple wife family 148
multiplicity 342
multipolar world 330
multistakeholder initiatives (MSIs) 330
the *mūmin* (true believer) 164
the *mūminīn* 319
*mūminūn* (believers) 164
*mūminūn wa-l-mūmināt* [believers male and female] 354
'Abd ar-Ra'ūf al-Munāwī 236, 284, 389, 396
al-Mundhir ibn az-Zubayr 266
Munich 51
municipal unions 117
*al-Muqaddima* 27, 255, 359, 388
Pléiade Edition 256
*murabāḥa* 294
the Murabitun World Movement xiv, xvi, xviii, 355
Prince Murad 61
murder mystery fiction 215
*mursal ḥadīth* 389
Mürseli Aga 303
*al-Murshid al-Mu'īn* 385
Musa Adam xiv, xv
*muṣallas* (places set aside outside the towns for Eid) 199
*musāqā* (cropsharing) 296
*Muṣḥaf 'Uthmānī* 334
*mushāraka* – partnership 11, 292
*mushrik* anthropology 112
music 14, 159
music firms 175
Imām Muslim 391, 403
Muslim
authentically Muslim 250
meetings between Muslims and Christians 170
the Muslim Brotherhood (*al-Ikhwān al-Muslimūn*) 57
Muslim civilisation 303
Muslim civilisations 8
Muslim commerce 289
Muslim communities 264
the Muslim community 169, 228, 263
Muslim countries 58, 355
Muslim culture 215
the Muslim *dawla* 25, 26, 28
the Muslim diaspora xix
Muslim governance 27
Muslim growth
post-terrorist and post-political stage of
Muslim institutions 45
Muslim mainstream 66
Muslim markets 259
Muslim masons 61
Muslim practice 260
Muslim rule 29
Muslims 61
Muslim ships 21
Muslim societies 190, 302
Muslim society 83, 165, 210, 285, 303, 324

Muslim Turks 303
Muslim *umma* 58, 319
*Muslimūn wa-l-muslimāt* [muslims male and female] 354
Muslim world 197
the Muslim world community shattered and in need of restoration 336
*Ṣaḥīḥ Muslim* 390
The Muslim Faculty of Advanced Studies MFAS 392, 393, 395
"Early Madīna" MFAS 392
"Introduction to the History of the Khalifahs" MFAS 393
"The Question Concerning Economics" MFAS 392, 395
"The Question Concerning Money" MFAS 395
"The History of the Khalifahs" MFAS 393
"Madīna the New Matrix" MFAS 392
*MFAS Journal 1.1* 388, 391-2
"Money: from Fiat to the Gold Dīnār" MFAS 395
"Mu'āmalāt as the Way Forward" MFAS 392
Imām Muslim 203
4th Muslim Lawyers' Conference 388
the Muslims of Norwich 393
*Musnad* 391
Mussolini 95
*al-Mustaḍī' ibn Yūsuf al-Mustanjid* 166
Mustafa Rashīd Pasha 61, 62
al-Musta'ṣim 22
al-Muṭṭalib 242
mutually agreed price 280
*al-Muwāfaqāt* 272
muwahid doctrines 59
*muwālāt* 164
*al-Muwaṭṭa'* 7, 9, 213, 253, 255, 258, 262, 281, 284, 296, 297, 332, 334, 335, 338, 386, 392, 396, 397, 399, 402
*Muwaṭṭa'* the first *ṣaḥīḥ* work 254
*muzābana* 397
selling fresh dates for dried dates while still on the trees 296
*muzāra'a* 11
My Journey in Love, Faith and Politics 396
myrrh 18
mythos or 'myth' 368
myth of research 160
myth of the hero 368
mythologies 150
myths for our culture 133
removal of the mythic subject 128

## N

Nabateans 267, 268
*Nabawiyyat* 28
*naḍḍ* (hard cash) 220
*nafaqa* 203
*nafs* (the body and psyche of the human being) 340
annihilation (*fanā*) of *nafs*, *rūḥ* and *sirr* 342
*nafs* (ego) 353
struggle against *nafs*, *hawā*, *shayṭān* 344
Nagasaki 80
Najd 52, 54
the *Vilayet* of Najd 55

naked cultural colonisation 128
Namik Kemal 61, 62, 64
Napoleon Bonaparte 34, 38, 94, 95, 183
Napoleonic law 272
Napoleonic state 34, 36, 68
narratives 83
narrative of public life 108
Imām an-Nasafī 394
an-Nasā'ī 334, 387, 399
*Naṣīḥat al-Mulūk* 383
Nasser 56
the nation 78
National Amusements 182
national banks 244
National Chamber of Commerce 116
the National Debt 48
nationalisation of monarchism 173
nationalism 58, 86, 325
national legal systems 231
National Mental Health Act 137
the national state 35
the nation-state xx, 78, 179, 250
the nation-state model 302
nation-states 255
the nation (umma) 249
National Geographic 361
natural bonds of sociability 159
natural condition (*fiṭra*) 249
natural justice 212
the natural order 195
Islamic law only recognises natural persons 346
the natural nomos (*dīn al-fiṭra*) 347
the natural pattern (*fiṭra*) 277
natural philosophy 125, 171
natural predisposition 47
natural processes 129, 206
the natural religion 187
natural resources 355
natural science 125
natural selection 154, 155
natural time 352
the natural world 83
the natural religion
submitting to natural religion 332
naval ports 21
navy 21
Imām an-Nawawī 225, 358, 386, 396
An-Nawawi's *Forty Hadith* 358
Nawfal 242
the Nazi party 95
Nazi Death Camps 90, 323
near relatives 16, 215
necessities 196
ensuring the supply of necessities (foodstuffs, etc.) 194
the needs culture 133, 156
the needy and the poor 285
negotiation of the price 280
the Negus 242
neighbourhoods
neighbourhood associations 157
neighbourhood restoration 118
Benjamin Nelson 245, 390, 394
*The Idea of Usury, from Tribal Brotherhood to Universal Otherhood* 390
neo-colonialism 112
neo-liberalism 77, 112, 113, 116, 122
neo-liberal xxv
neo-liberal argument 122
neo-liberal doctrine 114
neo-liberal fundamentalists 120
neo-liberal ideology 77

neo-liberal paradigm 117
neo-liberal practices 117, 118
neo-liberal principles 122
neo-liberal project 121
neo-liberals 39
Netherlands 24, 25
networking 80
Paul Neumarkt 367
neurotic condition 149
new beginning xxiv
new civic force 256
a new elite in politics, business and social sciences 137
a new elite of bankers 173
a new emergent model of human society 171
*The New Fontana Dictionary of Modern Thought* 375
a new form of hieroglyphics 178
a new generation of Muslims 166
a new interpretations of Islam 57
new lifestyles 175
newly freed slaves 296
new media 177
a new model of humanity 68
new Muslims 271
a new nomos 80, 82, 216, 347
a new political class 171
*The New Rulers of the World* 369
news leaks 182
a new social ethos 164
new socio-political conditions 56
newspapers 159, 175
newspaper tycoons 92
news reports 175
new technologies 210
Isaac Newton 67, 127
Newtonian mechanistic universe 129
Newtonian model 70
new values 175
a new way of thinking 72
a new world economy 43
a new world order 159, 160
a new worldview 159
New York 132, 134, 136
New York banks 133
New York City fiscal crisis 117, 118
New York investment bankers 118
New York investment banks 114, 118
New York's World Fair 136
New York Times 115
T. Niblock 364
Nietzsche 70, 72, 73, 88, 128, 325, 366
Nigeria's oil reserves 374
the Night Journey 341
the Night Journey and *Mi'rāj* 208
night prayers 233
nihilism xvii, xxiv, 70, 71, 72, 80, 276, 347
overcoming of nihilism 72
the rise of nihilism 71
nine-tenths of provision 233
K. Nisancioglu 359
Richard Nixon 115
nobility xiv, 162, 168
nobility and generosity 258
nobility of character 256
noble chivalric qualities 172
noble *furūsiyya* (*al-furūsiyya an-nabīla*) 165
noble qualities of character 258
noblesse oblige 212
*The Noble Qur'ān* 246, 250
the Noble Book 215, 252

no fixed return 293
noise pollution 103
nomadism 256
  nomads 250
  partially nomadic 250
*nomos* 212
  nomocracy (law-governed society) 190, 338
  nomocratic society 7, 8
non-academic behaviour 153
non-familial attachments 150
non-monetary services (for its own sake) 277
non-Muslims 216, 263
  non-Muslim countries 64
  non-Muslim minorities 45
non-Oedipal man 148, 149
non-*shārīʿī* currencies 44
  non-*shārīʿī* [*dīnārs* and *dirhams*] 27
non-usurious economy 263
non-Western societies 69
North Africa 20, 24, 25

North America and Europe
  most corrupt countries 105
North Carolina Law Review 395
northern Nigeria 31
notary publics 275
not-for-profit organisations 135
novelists 152
nuclear disarmament 141
the nuclear family 49, 90, 144, 145, 150, 151, 324
  nuclear family structure 146
nuclear physics 70
*nudāwiluhā* 17
  etymological root of 349
  "We deal out" 349
Nūḥ 222, 254
numerical traces 131
Amīr Nūr ad-Dīn Zanjī 166, 167
I.A.K. Nyazee 358

## O

Barack Obama 331
obedience 252, 253
  obedience to His Messenger 252
  obedience to the *amīrs* 252
objectives of mass media 176
objectivity 68, 325
  no objective truths in economics 123
  objective experience 127
  objective/separate world 126
  objects of the mind 298
object of trade 290
obligations
  obligation to service 172
  obligation to stand in prayer at night 233
  obligatory shares of inheritance (*farāʾiḍ*) 215
observation 12, 87, 325
the observer of the phenomena 126
ochlocracy (mob-rule) 352
Ödemish, western Anatolia 303
the OECD 372
  OECD Convention on Combating Bribery of Foreign Public Officials in International Business Transactions 106
Oedipus complex 148
  Oedipal model 149
  Oedipal/primal drama 149

the offender shall forfeit all his goods 286
office-bearers 275
officers of the court 105
official bureau 20
official history 108
oil xxii, 36, 106
oil and gas reserves 55
oil producing countries 114, 118
oil producing states 40
oils 29
old economy 157
*The Old Testament* 246
oligarchy xiii, xxv, 11, 17, 18, 35, 65, 131, 190, 346, 348, 352
masquerades as democracy 82
masquerading as democracy 132
obscenely wealthy oligarchs 216
oligarchic capitalism 215
oligarchic chiefs 99, 131
oligarchic elites 39
oligarchic governance 7
oligarchs 212, 213
the oligarchic 161
Paul Oliver 397
*The Story of the Blues* 397
Oman 22
ombudsman 194
once-Muslim lands 215
Hugh O'Neill, the Earl of Tyrone 172
one percent of the world's population 179
one worldism
one global world state 179
one world bank 160
one world currency 160
one-world currency 77
one-world economic order 77
one world government 69
one world government (UNO) 179
one world state 77, 79, 161
*On the Duties of Brotherhood* 397
ontology 72
OPDA 43
OPEC oil price hike 114, 118
open democratic societies 300
the open family 148
operating commuter ships 200
oppression
the oppressed 165
the oppressed, exploited, stateless, homeless and poverty-stricken 351
the oppressor 165
optimum control and regulation of information 177
orchards 295
orchards in Suffolk 291
order, design... 324
Orders
Order of the Garter 169
Order of the Golden Fleece 169
Order of the Star 169
ordering the armies and provisioning them 191
an organised way of work 198
organising picnics for a designated guild 200
the Orient Railway 51
original cultures 250
the original Islamic phenomenon xiii
the original sources of the law 56
original tribes 246
"The origin of banking: religious finance in Babylonia" 390

*The Origin of Species by Means of Natural Selection or the Preservation of Favoured Races in the Struggle for Life* 68, 154
*The Origins of Islamic Law: the Qur'ān, Muwaṭṭa', and Madīnan 'Amal* 362, 402
the origins of usury
among the Jews 214
*The Origins of Value – The Financial Innovations that Created Modern Capital Markets* 390
Orkney 234
orphans 16
David Orr 375
orthodoxy 161
orthodoxic *'aqīdas* xvi
Orthodox Seminary 95
the Osmanlıs 44, 256, 257, 302, 303
the demise of the Ottoman caliphate 45
the Osmaniya 84
Osmanlı Padishas 49
Ottoman authority 52
the Ottoman caliphate 359
the Ottoman Caliphate 24, 43, 49, 52
the Ottoman Caliphs 47
the Ottoman Dawla 51, 52, 59, 60, 61, 64
the Ottoman Empire 199, 294
the Ottoman Empire and European Capitalism 362
the Ottoman Empire and the World-Economy 362
Ottoman finances 43
Ottoman foreign debt 42
Ottoman History 43
the Ottoman Khalifate 61
Ottoman masonry 61
Ottoman modernists 58
Ottoman overlordship 54
the Ottoman period 194
Ottoman Public Debt Administration (OPDA) 42
Ottoman raw materials 25
Ottoman reformers 61
the Ottomans 11, 23, 24, 25, 42, 55, 190, 333
the Ottoman state's total revenue 199
the Ottoman Sultan 53, 55
Ottoman traders 25
Ottoman *waqf*s 199
Pax Ottomana (peace and stability across the Ottoman Empire) 24
the other 243
Henning Ottmann 369
ounce 224
outflow of wealth
from poor countries to the rich 119
outward (physical) xiii, 356
outward sciences 339
overpricing 287, 288
over-production
over-production of goods 133
problem of 133
over-the-counter (O.T.C.) derivatives 98
overviews of trade and commerce 186
Oxfam 180
*The Oxford Dictionary of English* 394, 400

*The Oxford Encyclopedia of the Modern Islamic World* 365, 383
Mustafa Özdamar 398

## P

a pact of justice 165
Pakistan 59
Palestine 22, 167
Orhan Pamuk 43
S. Pamuk 362
Panama 80
the pandemic 399
Vikram Pandit 99
the Papacy
  abolition of Papal rule 171
  the Papal Church 169
  Papal Rome 170
  the Papal system 171
paper money xx, xxii, 34, 38, 39, 41, 44, 45, 46, 50, 228, 229, 326, 332
  evolution of paper money 36
  paper banknote 278
  paper money (*Caime-i-Muthebere-i-Nakdiye*) 60
  paper receipts 10
paradigms 122
paradox 70
paralysis 323
parasitical class of speculators 209
parasitic capitalism 290
Paris 93
  Paris Peace Conference 136
M. Parkin 373
parliamentarianism 58
  parliamentary democracy 301
  parliamentary regime 46
  parliamentary sessions 92
particles and forces 127
particles and waves 70
partnerships 25, 292
party democracy 91
passage of measured time 170
passive smoking 103
pastoral land 295
patents 104
  patent payments 119
William Paterson xxii, 36
the Path of Sufism 403
the path to Truth 162
Utsa Patnaik 30, 360
patricians 244
paying a neighbourhood's taxes 200
paying taxes 139
"On payment of *zakāt* to the Imām whether he is just or unjust" 387
payment in advance 209, 276
payment of the soldiers 191
payments on debt 119
peace-time budget deficits 97
peace treaty 28
peer review 128
Peking Academy 160
pension funds 117, 119
"the people" 301
People Before Profit 371
people in authority 219
people of integrity 217
people of Iraq 224
the People of Madīna 209, 224, 238, 259, 319, 387, 388
  ethos and the practice of the People of Madīna 268

practice of the People of Madīna 258
people of standing and probity 223
people of *tafsīr* 222
people of taste (*dhawq*) and penetrating inner sight 342
People of the Book 213, 251
people of the cities 320
people's representatives 92
people's suffering 302
peppers 29
perennialism 394
perfumes 19
Charles Perkins 78, 369
John Perkins 115
permanent lie 330
permanent record
of all transactions 299
permissible 202
Persia 20, 22, 26, 59, 196, 242, 350
Persian Empire
Persians 246
the Persian Empire 17
Persian emperors 242
Persian models of state 18
Persian Gulf 22, 30
personal identity 178
personality politics xx
personal liberty
had to be banished 158
personal loan (*qarḍ*) 281
personal network 177
personal relations 8
personal relationships 206
personal rule xiii, 190
the person in authority 252
persuasion 176
pertussis 180
pesantren 398
petrodollars
recycled 118
recycling 114
pharaonic tower 327
pharmaceuticals 119
phenomena 13
phenomenon of technology 129
philanthropy 385
Jonathan Phillips 380
philosophy 12, 13, 14, 66, 70, 72, 141
classical philosophical tradition 124
phenomenological ontology 128
philosophers 152
Aristotle 8, 126, 128, 288, 289, 397
René Descartes 67, 68, 71, 87, 125, 126, 366, 376
Cartesian dualism 129
Hegel 70
Martin Heidegger 70, 71, 72, 73, 76, 80, 128, 141, 366, 367, 394
"Martin Heidegger: the Philosopher of Psychological Con-Fusion" 367
*Sein und Zeit – Being and Time* 70, 128
the Nietzsche book 70
*What is Called Thinking* 367
Heraclitus 72
Ibn Rushd 8, 12-13, 358
*Ibn Rushd: Mujtahid of Europe* 358
Parmenides 72
Socrates 366
post-Socratic philosophers 71
pre-Socratic philosophers 72
Benedict Spinoza 67
philosophical thinking 71

philosophy of science 128
*Philosophy of Social Science: the Philosophical Foundations of Social Thought* 366
Plato 8, 67, 72, 126, 152
Plato's metaphysics 72
*Principles of Philosophy* 68
the speculation of philosophers 86, 340
Stoicism 158
the task of philosophy 72
Western philosophy 67
Western philosophical thinking 72
the Phoenicians 234
photography 174
physical and military opposition 82
lifeblood of capitalist atheism 187, 332
physical existence 202
physical infrastructure and public works
construction and maintenance of 191
physical localisation of each profession 197
a physical market 346
physical reality 235
physical scales 222
physical world 125
C. Pierson 33-34, 3601
piety 167
Pigalle night club 96
Massimo Pigliucci 128, 376
John Pilger 79, 369
pilgrimage 12, 19, 337
pilgrims 199
protection for pilgrims 191
pillory 286
piracy 24
plague 119
planetary movements 352
planned anarchy 161
planners 135
the Plantagenet period 171
plantations 297
planting crops 209
plastic and electronic currencies 10
Plebeians 148, 244
Plovdiv 51
pneumonia 180
podcasts 177
poetry 14, 159
poets 167, 248
Poland 104
Polanyi 289
police 105, 178
policeman 160
police structures and functions 113
police terror 331
policing 20
politics xiii, xviii, xxiv, 8, 12, 14-16, 34, 49, 90, 139-40, 150, 155, 175, 179, 244, 288, 324
a political emissary xix
failure of 80
friend-enemy relation 78
phase of the political cycle 351
policy-making 175
policy of the *umma* [society] 191
policy proposals 110
policymaking process 110
the polis 244
political action committee contributions 110
political activism xvi
political acts 57

political analysis xvii
political and economic
methodology 58
political authority 190
political awareness 174
political circumstances 167
the political class 80, 132, 301
political considerations 192
political democracy 93, 96
political democracy is a machine
92
political despotism 58
political distinction 78
political doctrines 80
political donations 103
political elites 77, 101
political freedom 113
political ideals 113
political ideology 66
political institutions 116
political leaders 175
political monopoly 77
Islam is not a political movement
345
political parties 92
political philosophy xiii, xv, xvii,
xviii, xxi, 58, 172
political power 15, 160, 168
cyclical nature of political power
348
political process 108
political processes 178
political professionals 108
political reform 61
political scientists 101, 109
political state 18
political structures 34
political system 101, 175
political theorist 76
political theorists 40
political theory 68, 76, 126
political theory and policy 64
political will 182
political writer 135
political writings 3
politicians xix, 131, 135
politics and social life 147
polities 242
polity xxv, 208
polity of estates 34
poll-tax riots 95
pollution 141, 194
Polybius, Greek historian 351
pondoks 398
the poor 27
poor families 156
poor person 204
popes 147
Pope Innocent III 171
popular revolt 329
pornography 331
the Porte 45-46, 51
Portugal 22
Portuguese 24
positive commands 290
post-COVID pandemic 329
post-Imām ash-Shāfi'ī scholars 334
the post-modern era xvii
Post-Office Savings Bank 58
post-usury culture 227
post-war history 179
Potsdam 228
the pound (lb) 224
poverty 122
extreme global poverty 180
extreme poverty 180, 329

Lewis Powell 116
memo sent by 118
power 163
a fissure crack in the power nexus 183
power of God 88
"The Power of Money" 361
practical implementation 196
practical security 37
the practice of the people of Madīna 319
prayer 164, 292
the obligation to stand in prayer at night [at the beginning of Islam] 233
prayer times 12
pre-adolescent 197
precedent 230
precedent and custom 272
precious metals 282, 286
objective physical characteristics of 277
precipitous loss in value 298
precision 70
pre-industrial society 144
pre-Islamic times 165
the pre-modern 83
pre-modern Christian society 83
pre-modern Europe 124
pre-modern Islamic society 85, 324
pre-modernity 240
the Presence of Allah 324
His Presence 251
the Presence of God 83
President Hoover 136
President Truman 137
Pretoria xiv, xv
preventable diseases 180
previous religions and ways 248
prices and values 280
origins of increases in level of prices 111
price fixing 287
price setting 287
prices of *dīnārs* and *dirhams* 287
pricing mechanism 279
the priesthood of the doctorate 160
priests 243
the primary model of governance Madīna 350
primary sources
understanding of the 356
prime minister of the state 191
the Prime Minister's office 393
primitive leadership 351
primitive technology 65-66
primogeniture 212, 215
*Principles of Philosophy* 366, 376
*The Principles of Secondary Education* 152, 378
print media 174
prioritising profits over principles 107
prison 182
prisoners 169
prisoners of war 28
private arena xxi
private armies 30, 104
private business interest
merging with government affairs 115
private education 154
private individuals 298
private ownership 39
private practice in medicine 302
private property rights 112-3

private transactions and experience 299
privatisation of state programs and agencies 109
the Privy Council 172
the problem of production 158
processed foods 103
products and services 134
producers 121, 234
product design 84, 326
production lines 133
production of necessities 195
production of textbooks and educational resources 182
professions 197
professional elites 101
the profession of money changing 231
profits 33, 187, 211, 236, 288, 290, 306
not to be 'excessive' 195
profitable and unprofitable 78
programmer 293
progress 86
progressive world history 69
prohibitions 282
attempts to evade the prohibitions of interest 214
evading the prohibitions of usury 283
promised victory 331
promissory notes xxiii, 28, 36, 39, 44, 50, 229
propaedeutic function 153, 155
propaganda 159
property
properties of apostates 26, 197
properties with no known owner 25, 196
property of orphans 284
the Prophet ﷺ 163-5, 186, 190, 194-6, 209, 211, 224-5, 235, 242, 245, 247-8, 251-2, 257, 259-60, 265, 297, 308
abolished the state 189
biography of the Prophet 165
commands of our Prophet 320
goals and functions held by the Prophet 191
had many scribes and secretaries 192
"The Prophet as Ruler" 388, 391-2
Prophethood 236, 242
the Prophetic era 230
Prophetic ḥadīth 254
the Prophetic heritage 246
Prophetic values 225
the Prophetic weights and measures 224
the Prophet Muḥammad
Allah's caliph (representative) on earth 338
the Prophet of Madīna 248
the Prophet of the time 245
"The Prophet as Ruler" 225
the Unlettered Prophet 249
the Prophets 162, 235, 246, 343
the Prophets and Messengers 248
the Prophets and Messengers
the Prophets and Messengers sent to the Children of Israel 246
prosperity for society 190
a protected *tasawwuf* 339
protecting women 172
protecting women from danger and slander 170
Protestantism 60

the Protestant Church 87
protocols 187, 328
protocols and contracts 52
provinces 194
the Provincial Assembly of the North-West Frontier Province 396
provision 201, 232
two types of 232
"The Provision of Public Goods Under Islamic Law: Origins, Impact, and Limitations of the Waqf System" 384
psychoactive drugs 141
psychoanalysis 132, 137, 141
psychoanalyst 134
psychoanalysts 136, 141, 150
psychoanalytic terminology 132
psychoanalytic theory 148
psychology 14
psychological building blocks 127
psychological identity 148
psychological lives 136
psychological manipulation 156
psychological techniques 135
psychological theory 133
psychology departments 137
psychosis 90, 323-4
the psychosis of capitalism 90
the public arena xxi
free access to public thoroughfares 194
maintenance of public order 191
public banking 38
public bureaucracy 34
the public educational system 154
public health 117
public institutions 101
public markets 285
public medicine 302
public or municipal services 199
set up, financed and maintained by *awqaf* 346
public programs 108
public records 20
public safety and hygiene 194
public spaces 296
public utility 301
*Public Duties in Islam: The Institution of the Ḥisba* 384
public interest (*maṣlaḥa*) 56
public opinion 103, 175
public relations 49, 84, 90, 136, 156, 324, 326
public relations campaigns 103
public relations exercise 179
public relations interface 82
public schools 154
public school environment 153
publishing 174
Puerto Rico 80
punishments for misdemeanours 192
Punjab Private Money Lending Act 2007, 396
Punjab Provincial Assembly 396
puppet dictators 112
purchases 264
purchases made online 209
purchase tax 148
pure original nature, *fiṭra* 170
puzzles 175

## Q

Ilyās Qabalūn 394
Qāḍī 'Iyāḍ 388, 394, 402
*qāḍī* (judge) 9, 193, 197, 257, 301

Qāḍī Ibn Rushd al-Jadd 267
*qadr*
decree of Allah 352
al-Qaida 355
*qalb* – heart 274
al-Qa'qā' ibn Ḥakīm 220
*Qarawiyyīn* 398
*qarḍ ḥasan* (a goodly loan) 208
*qaṣīda* 247
Qasīm 53
al-Qāsim 220
Qatāda 208, 222
Qatar 53
*al-Qawānīn al-fiqhiyya – The Judgments of Fiqh* 387-8, 397, 399-400
Ibn Abī Zayd al-Qayrawānī 391
Imru'ul al-Qays 380
*qibla* 3
*qinṭār* 223, 224
*qirāḍ/muḍāraba* profit-sharing trade investments 11, 236, 246, 290-1
*qisṭ* (justice) 359, 401
*qiyās* (analogical deduction) 333
qualitative bonding 170
quality of life 125
quantitative easing xxii, xxiii, 120
quotidian social nexus
a psychosis 131
the Qur'ān xxi, 3, 9, 13, 27, 63, 186, 194, 200-1, 214-7, 242, 247, 253, 257, 267, 320
Makkan *Sūra* 222
Qur'ānic terminology 324
the Qur'ān walking 247
the Qur'ān and Sunna 324
Qur'ānic and Islamic pattern 170
Quraysh 241-2, 246, 264, 267, 292, 349-350, 393
Imām al-Qurṭubī 26, 186, 203-4, 207, 213, 222, 238, 252, 345, 362, 387, 389, 392
'Abd ar-Raḥīm ibn 'Abd al-Karīm al-Qushayrī 205
Sayid Quṭb 55
the *Quṭb* 167
Quṭb ash-Shaykh xvii

## R

*rabā* 401
Rabī'a ibn Abī 'Abd ar-Raḥmān 220
racism 118
race riots 95
radio 159, 174
A-K. Rafeq 198
ar-Rāghib al-Aṣfahānī 203, 211
Ragusa 25
*ar-Raḥmān* – the All-Merciful 390
railways 301
construction of railways 101
raising up the poor 172
raisins 261, 288
Rajab, 27th of 341
Ramadan 10
*al-Rasail* 403
*ra's al-māl* (capital) 212
M. Al-Rasheed 364
the *Rasūl* 164
ratio legis [reason for the law] 56
rational critique 181, 187, 328
rationalism 12, 59, 87, 325, 340
the rational animal 72
rationalism and empiricism 124, 127
rationalist educated Egyptians 129

rationalists 67
rationality 126
rational methods 68, 325
rational minds 138
rational principles 91
rational thinking 12
ar-Rāzī 353
re-adoption of the *Shari'at* 28
Ronald Reagan 114, 117, 120, 138
real estate 37
reality 130, 235, 274
real-value exchange system xxiv, 187
real wealth
gold, silver and commodities 188, 332
the real world of trade and the marketplace 238
reason 12-13, 67, 325, 340
reason and logic 125
reason and sense perception 124
reasoning 87
reasoning about facts 128
receipts 40, 50
recession 117
recommended and approved practices 289
reconciling people's hearts 27
"Reconsidering Kinship Beyond the Nuclear Family" 378
recording transactions 299
record labels 291
red camels 165
redefining man 128
the 'red ones' 267
Rabea Redpath 149, 378
the Red Sea 21, 23, 52
reductionism 337
re-educated society 149
re-establishment of Islam xvii
the Refah Party xxi
refinements or luxuries 196
reflection 13
the Reformation 59-60, 84, 240
reformism 58
reform 57
reformist *'ulamā* 66
reforms 45
refugee crisis 132
refusal to submit to other than Allah 161-2, 164
the region 295
regional development 20
a register (*sijil*) 198
the regular price 261
regulatory capture 105
regulatory obligation 294
Robert Reich 121, 138, 140, 377
reigning paradigm 123
the Reign of Terror 68, 371
relations of power 136
religion 86, 88, 133, 158
action/behaviour 340
religious faith 159
religious houses 244
religious leaders 152
religious versus secular dichotomy 186
religious worldview 86, 325
religious zone of prayer and worship 238
remuneration 197
the Renaissance 240
renewal of trade 231
a renewed world order 70
rent xxii, 260
rent-extraction 34

renting 252
renting land for crops – *muḥāqala* 296
renting land for gold or silver 296
repatriated profits 119
repatriation of profits from foreign investors 119
replacement of broken crockery 200
the Repo market 399
a repo – repurchase agreement 307
representation
representative democracy 146
representative government 45
representative institutions 100
representatives of the people 92
repression 142
republic 8, 18, 79
the Republic of Turkey
founding of the Republic of Turkey in 1923, 199
repudiation of value 71
research and development 102
resentment 244
reservations
indigenous community enslaved in 79
*res fungibilis et primo usu consumptibilis* (a thing that is fungible and primarily used in consumption) 277
resistance of the masses against injustice 352
resourcefulness 158
resources 15, 74
production, distribution and consumption of 189
respect for good women 170
retailing 104
retirees 121
*The Return of the Khalifate* 51, 362-5, 370
Reuters 398
the revealed Books 343
revelation 13, 242, 247-8, 254, 257
revelation and existence 271
the beginning of 237
revenues 196
revenues from state lands 26, 197
revivers of the *dīn* of Islam 354
revolution 34, 93
revolutionary activity 161
revolutionary dialectic xx
revolutionary government 37
revolutionary leaders xix
revolutionary political activity 62
the Revolutionary State 34
the revolution of 1908 62
"Revolutionary France, Cradle of Free Enterprise" 361
the revolving door 96
*Reweaving Our Social Fabric* 398
*ribā* (usury) xxii, xxiv, 10, 18, 38-41, 44, 50, 196, 202-3, 205, 213-4, 281, 289, 306, 327-8, 331, 346, 355, 401
elimination of *ribā* 194
inextricably enmeshed in *ribā* 263
ways for Muslims to become free of *ribā* 299
David Ricardo 114
rice 25, 29
rich men 286
Rashid Rida 55-57
the Riegle-Neal Act 98
right-acting first generations (*salaf*) 267-8, 276

right and left 40
rights
the right of free association 100
the right of free opposition 100
the right of free speech 100
the Rights of Man 65
the rights of slaves 193
Rainer Maria Rilke 159
riots in Paris 38
risk
is shared 293
risks 234
*riṭl* 223-4, 388
ritual 74
ritualism 250
ritual objects 278
Riyadh 53-54
*riyā'* – showing-off 239
roads 24, 199
John D. Rockefeller 158
Sir Thomas Roe 29
James Rohr 99
Rome 148, 248
as a civic model 244
the Roman Church 169
Roman citizens 250
Roman models 293
Romans 18-19, 246, 250
the Romans 240
Roman subjects 245
Rome (Constantinople) 242
the Holy Roman Emperor 24
the Roman Empire 17
the Roman republican model 246
the rope of Allah 47
the Rothschilds 51
rough garments 339
Jean Jacques Rousseau 152
royal and aristocratic families 212
royal palaces 221
*rubūbiyya* (Lordship) 331
governance of the universe 352
ordering and commanding of the universe 328
the *rūḥ* (soul) 6, 340
*ruḥānī* (spiritual) openings/ illuminations 343
the rule of law 347
establishment of 191
the ruler 191, 252, 257
rulership 253
rules of exception 94
the ruling class 137, 150
the ruling class in the US 141
the ruling power structure 142
Russia xxii, 24, 48, 330
Russia and China 122
the Russian Empire 45
the Russian Revolution 135
the Russian university system 160

## S

the *ṣā'* 223-4, 264, 287, 387
*ṣā'* [measuring vessels] 224
the *sābiqūn wa-s-sābiqāt* [those who outstrip each other in drawing near to Allah, male and female] 354
sacraments 84
sacred precincts (Ḥaram) of Makka 242
sacrifice 204
sacrificing fundamental principles 139

*sadaka tashlari* (stones/pillars for the poor) 303
*ṣadaqa* 25, 205, 279, 303
*ṣadaqāt* 8
*sadd adh-dharā'i'* – blocking the means to arrive at something to arrive at something illegal 306
saddle 242
Sa'd ibn Abī Waqqāṣ 220
the *ṣādiqūn wa-ṣ-ṣādiqāt* [those who are sincere, male and female] 354
*safar*, wayfaring 352
Safar (the month) 356
safe roads 107
safety regulations 108
*ṣaḥīḥ ḥadīth* 254, 319
*Ṣaḥīḥ al-Bukhārī* 264
*ṣaḥīḥ* books 254
*Ṣaḥīḥ Muslim* 47
Sahl ibn 'Abdullāh at-Tustarī 252
Abū Sa'īd Saḥnūn 219, 339, 387, 402
Sa'īd ibn Manṣūr 389
Sa'īd ibn Sa'īd ibn al-'Āṣ ibn Umayya 195, 261
Saints-days 170
the *Salaf* 366
*salafī* 357
the *salafī* community 7
the *salafī* movement 58
the *salafī* phenomenon 339
"*Salafiyah*" 365
Ṣalāḥ ad-Dīn Ayyūbī 166, 167, 170
*salam* contracts 209

the *ṣalāt* (prayer) 10, 201-4, 221, 337, 341, 344
a societal act of worship 221
establish the *ṣalāt* 202
*ṣalāt* and *zakāt* 28
sales 216, 264
monitoring of unlawful sales and collusion 194
sale of jewellery online 282
sales tax 188
abolition of sales tax 332
the *sālik* (the seeker on the path of truth) xix
Sālim ibn 'Abdullāh ibn 'Umar 220
Habeeb Salloum 380
Salonika 59, 64
Salonika lodges 60
saltpeter 30
Samarkand 22
Samra bint Nuhayk al-Asadiyya 195
sanctions xxii
sanitation 180
Sarajevo 51
Shihab al-Sarraf 380
Saudi Arabia 40, 52, 355
the Kingdom of Saudi Arabia 53-54
Kingdom of Najd, Hijaz and its Dependencies 54
the Sa'ūd dynasty 53
Sa'ūd ibn 'Abd al-'Azīz 53
Saudi Arabia: Power, Legitimacy and Survival 364
Sa'ūdī authority 54
the Sa'ūdī clan 53
Saudi riyal 361
Sa'ūdīs 53
Sa'ūdī states 53
Saudi usurpers 59
the Saudi-Yemeni war of 1934 54
the second Sa'ūdī-Wahhābī state 54

John Ralston Saul 381
savings 279
Aḥmad ibn Muḥammad aṣ-Ṣāwī 233, 389
ṣawm (fasting) 10
ṣayrafī 231
skilled in recognising the different types and qualities of coins 231
SBM Offshore 106
scales (*mīzān*) 222
universal image of justice 223
scandals 299
scarcity 142
scepticism 87
Schacht 362, 401
Carl Schmitt 70, 76-77, 80, 368, 369
scholars 9, 248
judgements of the 335
scholasticism 124
school 153
a conditioning laboratory 156
school administrators 157
schools 244
school system 156-7
the school of Madīna 391
Klaus Schwab 330
science 13, 71, 74, 87, 125, 128
outlines of scientism 125
physical sciences 69
physics 68, 182
positive sciences 48
science and philosophy of modernity 70
science and technology 11, 68, 86, 325
science does not think 72
science of algebra (*al-jabr*) 215
science of management 157
science of marketing 157
sciences of Islam 166
scientific causality 206
scientific management 159
scientific materialism 49, 59, 90, 124, 127, 129, 324
scientific method 87, 111, 126
the scientific revolution of the 16th and 17th centuries 125
scientific thinking 66
scientism 124-5
critique of 127
end of scientism 129
roots of scientism 125
*Scientism: Philosophy and the Infatuation with Science* 375
scientistic thinkers 128
scientists' hypotheses 340
the universality of scientific knowledge 68
universality of scientific knowledge and method 325
Scotland 234
James C. Scott 397
scribes 333
scripture xvii
scrutiny of circumstances 191
sea routes 42
secondary causes 125
secondary causation 129
the second caliph 'Umar 196
the second century AH 9
the Second Interregnum 257
the second-son problem 212
second and third sons 212
secularism 57, 60, 64-66, 81, 86, 187, 324

secularisation 45, 83
secular institutions 45
secularisation of Islamic law 58
secularists 80
secularist *'ulamā* 68-69
secular law 60
securitisation 98
security 291
Mark Sedgwick 365
seeking Allah's bounty 233
Mark Seem 378
Selanik (Thessaloniki) 47
self-actualising individuals 142-3
the Self-disclosure of Allah 342
the Self-disclosure of Truth 73
self (nafs) 163
self-image 134
self-perpetuating oligarchic families 216
self-reliance 158
the Seljuks 190
the Seljuk governor of Aleppo 166
selling 252
the seller 279
selling food before taking possession 308
the Senate 79
Senator Phil Gramm 98
sense experience 325
Recep Şentürk 256
separation 343
Serbia 51
serfdom xxi
sermon 221
servant of Allah 162
service 161, 163-4
services 145
supervision of services (professional services – medical practitioners, pharmacologists, teachers, etc.) 194
service/worship 324
the seventh century 21
sexuality 133, 141
high rates of sexual abuse against women and children 146
sexual drives 150
sexual liberty 147-8
Malik Sezgin 363
Imām ash-Shāfi'ī 280, 391
the Shāfi'ī [*madhhab*] 335, 337
the *shahāda* 4, 10, 337
the double *shahāda* 348
Humaira Shahid 285, 291, 293, 396-7
*shahīd* (martyr) 167, 389
E.E. Shahin 365
Shakespeare 55, 169
Shām 257, 267
share-cropping
a usurious scheme 296
share-cropping peonage 297
shareholders 330
liability of 102
a share of someone else's profit 236
the *sharī'a* xvii, xviii, xxiii, xxv, 7-8, 13, 18, 20, 27, 39, 50, 57, 189, 191, 202, 204, 208, 212, 225, 231, 235, 246, 248, 257, 259, 275-6, 281, 284, 290, 293, 296, 338, 341, 346, 348, 382, 398, 404
aims of the Law (*maqāṣid ash-sharī'a*) 56
analogical reasoning (*qiyas*) 56
application of 190
establishment of the 343

the *sharī'a* and *ḥaqīqa* 343
the *sharī'a* and *taṣawwuf* are inseparable 340
the relationship between *sharī'a* and *taṣawwuf* 338
*Shari'ah: The Islamic Law* 383
*sharī'a* limits 66
*sharī'a* rights 226
the *shari'at* 31
conformity to 342
the Sharīf of Mecca 53
[*sharika*] *māliyya* – financial partnership 292
sharing wealth 15
ash-Shāṭibī 272
M. Shatzmiller 383
Shawar 166
Imām Muḥammad ibn al-Ḥasan ash-Shaybānī 391
shaykh (master) of instruction (*tarbiya*)
taking a shaykh of instruction 342
Shaykh of *ṭarīqa* xvii
*shayṭān* 277
sheep 19
Shetland 234
the Shī'a 4, 29, 53, 58
a Shī'ī activist 58
a Shī'a activist 55
Shī'ī modernists 58
ash-Shifā' bint 'Abdallāh 195, 262
*ash-Shifā' bi ta'rīf ḥuqūq al-Muṣṭafā* 402
Shinasi 62, 64
ship 254
Asif Shiraz 397
shops 283
shopkeepers 280
"A Short Angry History of Compulsory Schooling" 378-9
shorter working days 145
shorting stocks and shares 298
short runs of consumer goods 143
short-sighted policies 119
showing someone the way (*irshād*) 202
shrines 244
*Shu'ab al-Īmān* 396
*shuhadā'* (martyrs) 235
*shurṭa* (police) 190
Sicily 21
the sick 233
the Sick Man of Europe 43
*ṣidq* – truthfulness and honesty 234
the *ṣiddīqūn* (utterly truthful) 235
*The Sign of the Sword* 360, 373, 401
Sijilmassa 21
silk 19, 25, 29-30
the Silk Road 22, 285
silver 23, 26, 28, 36-37, 42
the silver *dirham* xxi, 41, 225, 281
silver (*dirham*) coins 195
the silver Islamic *dirham* 188, 332
silver exchanged for silver 281, 230
simple trade 289
*simsar* (brokerage) 25
*simsar* (brokerage) associations 25
sincerity 292
Singapore 106
SIPRnet program 183
*sīra* 186, 242, 263, 266
Siraf 21-22
the *Ṣirāṭ al-Mustaqīm* 5
the *sirr* (innermost consciousness) 341
Sistan 21
"The Six Functions of Education:

Adaptive, Integrating, Diagnostic and Directive, Differentiation, Selective and Propaedeutic" 378
six months imprisonment 286
*siyāsa shar'iyya* (administrative regulations) 58
skill of communications 192
slavery 30, 31, 79, 296, 309
  abolitionism 31
  new system of 297
  slavery of debtors 296
  slaves 53, 74, 129
    respect for slaves 31
    setting slaves free 200, 216
  slave-society 31
small change 281
small traders 291
  smaller companies 288
  small farms 297
Adam Smith 68, 114, 127, 156
sobriety 343
socialism
  traditional socialists 39
social welfare 228
society
  destruction of social groups and nations 74
  social change
    coherent vocabulary of 161
  social context 149
  social contract 68, 75, 126, 277, 338
  social control 147, 331
  social development 13
  social distress 244
  social/economic institutions 285
  social elites 101
  social field 150
  social freedom 148
  social identity 73, 129
  social immune system 181
  social inequality 114
  socialisation 174
  socialising the population 157
  socialism 301
  social life 9
  socially structured psychosis 90, 131
  social media 178
    agent for positive change 177
    social media platforms 177
  social networking 177
  social networking sites 177
  social orders 254
  social reality 161, 268
  social responsibility 212
  social sciences 68, 70, 77, 137, 325
  social security 113, 346
  social status 155
  social trust 300
  a societal act of worship 221
  society and the environment 194
  a society based on trust 290
  society of children 152
  society's welfare function 195
  socio-financial system 187, 345
  sociologists 123
  socio-political and economic order 332
  socio-political models xvii
Sofia 51
software 104
solar systems 74
solidarity 163
soma 132

somnambulistic helplessness 90, 132, 323
song 150
Songhai 363
Tom Sorell 375
soul 132
a sound currency 253
soup kitchens 200
sources of growth 111
D. Sourdel 362
South Africa 104, 291, 330
  South Africa's gold mines 374
South China Sea 22
southern route 23
sovereignty 34
  of "the people" 301
  sovereign integrity xx
  sovereign power xxi
the Soviet Union
  collapse of the Soviet Union 77
Soweto xiv
space, time and phenomena 341
Spain 21, 23
speaking out 164
special adviser to the President 115
special exemptions 121
special supplements 175
specific injunctions of the text (*juz'iyyāt*) 56
speculators 309
spending 202-5
  spending in the Way of Allah 27, 205
  spend on your family 204
spices 19, 22, 25, 29-30
spinning 145
spirit of inquiry 12
spiritual considerations 192
  spiritual dimension 126
  spiritual journey 250
  the spiritual life of the city 193
  the spiritual outsider 75
  spiritual time 352
  spiritual transaction 187
spontaneous convergence 277
sports 155
stability of economic and social life 198
stagnation of wealth 18
stakeholders 330
Stalin 95
  Stalin's Gulags 90, 323
the standard for mankind 8
standing capital 213
standing reserve 274
Hannah Stark 378
stars 74
stasis 149
the state 46, 74, 160, 169, 212, 217, 244, 287, 299
  the controlling state 301
  debt collector state 160
  despotism of the state 302
  functions of the state 77
  a service industry of the bank 160
  State and Federal public sector authorities 106
  the state and regulatory capture 108
  the state as machine 94
  state capitalism 82
  state capture xxv, 90, 100, 105
    *State Capture How Conservative Activists, Big Businesses, and Wealthy Donors Reshaped the American States – and the Nation* 108, 372
  state control 94

state education departments 157
State Farm Insurance 109
state governments 109
statehood 9
*The State in Capitalist Society: The Analysis of the Western System of Power* 371
state institution 165
state intervention 113
state interventionist theories 114
state-isation 46
State Law 36-37
state legislators 109
state legislatures 109-10
a state that surveils 219
statism 49, 58
the structuralist state 173
states (*aḥwāl*) 342
stations (*maqāmāt*) 342
*Statistical Procedures and Human Values* 128
statute 286
steel 29
steep rise in value 298
stimulus xxiii, 121
stinters 237-8
stipends 262, 267
stocks and shares 293
stock exchanges 112
stock-market boom 135
stocks and bonds 52
stored wealth 187, 345
store of value 277-8
storks 200, 303
the stranger 243-4, 246
strangers xix, 274
Tracy Strong 76, 368
structuralism 86, 160, 171, 183, 324-5, 337
antidote for structuralism 340
inherent structuralism 183
structured information system 149
structure of power 132
student life 161
John Stumpf 99
subject and objects 67
subjective evaluation 280
subject/observer 126
subjects 252
subjugation of nature 71
submitted to destiny
the literal meaning of muslim 352
sub-Shīʻa modernism 55
subsidies and tax incentives 118
subsidising the cultivation of rare roses 200
suburbanisation 117
subversion of religion 59
success 206
successful careers 154
Sufalah 21
suffering and death 152
Sufism 86, 339, 352
Sufi commentaries (*tafsīr*) 163
Sufis 163
Sufi Shaykh 166
*Sufism: The Living Tradition* xiii
Sufyān 267
sugar 29
Suhar 21
suicide xxiv, 80, 331
*ṣukūk* 295, 398
*ṣukūk* instrument 295
the *ṣukūk* mentioned in the *Muwaṭṭa'* 295

Abū 'Abd ar-Raḥmān al-Sulamī 162, 379
Sulaymān ibn Abī Ḥathma 262
Sulaymān ibn Mūsā
Suleyman I 24
sultan 52, 208
  authority of a sultan 337
  Sultan Abdalaziz 62
    the murder of Sultan Abdalaziz 62
  Sultan Abdulmajid 60, 61, 62
  Sultan Abulhamid II 47-49, 52, 62
    dethronement of Sultan Abulhamid II 52, 64
  sultanates 85, 190
  *sulṭāniyya* xviii, xix
  *Sultaniyya* 48, 357, 359, 363, 384, 398
  Sultan Jahangir 29
  Sultan Mahmud 60
  the sultan of Egypt 166
  sultans 339
Sumatra 24
Sumeria 243, 244
  Sumerian cuneiform 243
  Sumerians 234
  Sumerian writings 243
The Sunday Age 405
the Sunna xxi, 3, 9, 27-28, 31, 186, 235, 248, 250, 254-5, 257-9, 261, 266, 272, 320, 392
  definition of the the Sunna 334
  the Sunna of the rightly guided *khulafā'* 262
  *sunan* (practices) 8-9
  *sunna fi'lī*, demonstrated in action and in practice 248, 392
  *sunna iqrārī*, his endorsement 248, 392
  *sunna qawlī*, the words of instruction, counsel and wisdom 248, 392
  Sunna, the normative practice of the Prophet
    authentication of the Sunna, the normative practice of the Prophet 334
  Sunnī 27, 58
    Sunnī modernists 58
*sunnat Allah* 328
*Sunshine at Madina* 359
Sun Tzu 274
super-currencies 160
supermarkets 283
supernatural being 247
super-wealthy 219
supply and demand 156, 288-9, 294, 397
  supply and demand forces 195
supplying fruits to the children of a community 200
support for each other 163
supporting retired sailors 200
support right against wrong 167
supranational nexus 330
the Supreme Court 103, 116
supreme governance 186
the Supreme Porte 62
the *sūq* (market) 190, 195, 293, 348
*Sūras*
  Sūra al-Baqara 202, 205-6, 211, 213, 275
  Sūra Āli 'Imrān 213
  Sūra al-Hashr 17
  Sūra al-Anbiyā 162

Sūra Āli 'Imrān 276
Sūra al-Isrā' 216
Sūra al-Kahf 162
Sūra al-Mā'ida 216
Sūra al-Muṭaffifīn 237
Sūra al-Muzzammil 217, 232
Sūra an-Nisā' 214-5
Sūra ar-Raḥmān 222
Sūra ar-Rūm 214
Sūra ash-Shūrā 222
Sūra aṭ-Ṭalāq 232
Sūra at-Tawba 204, 218-9
Sūra Yā Sīn 273
Surat 29
surveillance 132
surveillance and communication organs 181
surveillance capitalist techno-elite 299
surveillance of affairs 191
survival and escape 129
survival of humanity xvii
sustainable incomes, benefits and pensions 120
Jalāl ad-dīn as-Suyūṭī 237, 389, 393, 401
Swedish judiciary 183
swing voters 139-40
Switzerland 60
the sword and the pen 192
Mark Sykes 365
British spy 62
symbolism 132
symbol of the penis 134
Ronald Syme 17
Syria 19, 20, 22, 24, 26, 132, 196, 241-2, 390
systems
systemic disorder 181
systemic political corruption 105
system of banks and megabanks 112
system of credit 25
system of justification and legitimation 122
system of technique 73
systems concept 66
systems control 65
systems of belief 64
systems of governance xiii
system's perpetuation 151
system technique 65-66

## T

*aṭ-Ṭabaqāt al-kubrā* 393
aṭ-Ṭabarānī 392
aṭ-Ṭabarī 242
the *tābi'i-t-tābi'īn* (Followers of the Followers) 336, 340
the *tābi'ūn* (Followers) 337, 339
*tablīgh* – transmission 234
taboo against women smoking 134
Tabūk 204
*tafsīr* (commentary and explanation of the meaning of the Qur'ān) 193, 208, 232-3, 238
*Tafsīr al-Jalālayn* 328, 353, 401
*Tafsīr al-Qurṭubī* 385-6, 391
Ṭā'if 53, 261
a *ṭā'ifa* (party) 197
*ṭā'ifas* 198
*Tāj al-'Arūs* 397
*tajalliyāt*, illumination into the heart 162, 352

takeover of governments by oligarchs 189
*talfīq* (legal eclecticism) 57
"Talk on Futuwwa" 379
Tamīm ad-Dārī 253
tangible commodities 230
Tanzania 21
the Tanzimat (era of modern reform) 45-46, 61
  Tanzimat reforms 60
*taqlīd* 56
  shackles of *taqlīd* 56
  *taqlīd* (blind imitation) 58
*taqwā* (fearful awareness) of Allah 16, 164, 213, 232, 262
  people of *taqwā* 202
*tarāḍin – "mutually pleasing"* 280
*at-Tarātīb al-idāriyya* 267, 394
*tarbiya* 344
*Tārīkh* (history) 398
  *Tārīkh al-Khulafā'* 389, 393
  *Tārīkh al-Madīna* 392
  *Tārīkh aṭ-Ṭabarī* 242
  *Tārīkh Baghdād* 391
  *Tārīkh Dimashq* 391
*ṭarīqa* xvii, 343
  *ma'rifatullāh* 344
  not *wird*, or *waẓīfa*, or *bay'a* or *silsila* 344
  *ṭarīqas* (Orders) 164, 341
*Tartīb al-madārik* 388, 394, 403
*taṣawwuf* xvi, xvii, 162, 338, 342-4
  *fiqh* without practising *taṣawwuf* 338
  purification of the self 345
"Ta Sin Mim – Today" 387
tasteless apples 291
*tawba* 224, 327
*tawḥīd* 129, 162
  confirmation of *tawḥīd* 129
taxation 18, 20, 34, 82, 173, 332
  abolition of value added tax 188, 332
  tax 25, 259
  taxation on income 25
  tax breaks xxiii, 120
  tax cuts 97, 114
  taxes 79, 285
    collection and distribution of taxes 191
    income tax 39
    taxes on wealthy individuals 108
  tax farms 199
  tax gathering powers 212
  tax havens 121
  tax holidays 119
  tax on the trade 228
  tax policy 108
  tax revenue
    US loses tax revenue 121
tax deductibility of bribes 372
Charles Taylor 83
tea 30
teaching 205
  teachers 153, 199
team of historians 289
technical bankruptcy 117
technical resemblance to *ijtihād* 57
*Technique of the Coup de Banque* 360-2, 366, 370-1, 377
technique/technology 49, 73-74, 76, 84, 394
  *techne* 395
  technical ability 96
  technical banking culture 206
  the technical project 50

technical projects 52
technic society 90
'technik' 394
'technique' 394
technique or technology
a new power 129
technique society 323
techniques of dialectical method 160
technological advances 51
technological change
the impact of technological change 111
technological innovations 33
technological knowledge 25
technological procedures 74
technological process 65-66, 68
technological project investment 35, 51
technological society 31
technologies 119, 326
technology 49, 71, 73-74, 125
techno-socio-projects 13
withdrawal from 129
telecommunications 118
telephone company 301
television 159, 174-5
temple accounts 243
temples 243-4, 278
the banks 327
the ten Companions of the Prophet Muḥammad 170
terminology 66
terminologies 295
terms and conditions 217, 223
territorial integrity of the polity
defence of 191
territoriality 34
territorial nationalism 60
the territory of Islam (*dār al-Islām*) 9
the Terror 94-95
the Reign of Terror 38
terrorism xxiv, 80, 95
tetanus 180
textiles 29
textual sources 9
Thābit al-Banānī
Margaret Thatcher 114, 120, 138-9
Thawbān 204
theatre groups 175
the theatre of the political class 132
*The Case for God* 368
theft xxii, 10
"The invention of interest. Sumerian loans", 390
theism 88, 326
theocracy xiii, 63
theocratic 7
theologians 63
dogmas of theologians 340
theology 84, 86, 125
*The Market of the Prophet* 359
*The Modern State* 360
*The Moussems 1992 & 1993 Gatherings of Light* 404
*The Origins of National Financial Systems* 361
theory
theoretical foundations 181, 187, 328
theoretical utopianism 122
theory and practice are inseparable 338
theory and practice become separated 337
the theory of evolution 154
thinking 71, 73, 159

think-tanks 108
Third Pillar of Islam 28
third world 115
those in authority 252
thread 29
three fundamental laws of mechanics 127
Pamela Thurschwell 376
B. Tibi 383
the Tigris River 22
*tijāra* – trade 211
  "Tidjara" 383
timber 25
time of destiny 352
timocracy 7
Timur 23
tin 234
at-Tirmidhī 334, 389, 392-4, 399
tombs 199
too big to fail 97
tools and seed 296
top secret security clearances 183
the Torah 320
"torches of freedom" 134
torture 323
total culture module 160
totalitarianism xiii, 69
  total indoctrination 161
  totalitarian edict 95
  totalitarian state 149
total wealth 329
the total wealth in the world xxiv, 180
*Towards the Light: The Story of the Struggles for Liberty and Rights that Made the Modern West* 370
Townshipism 256
Townsville, Australia 182
trade xxiv, 15-16, 20, 169, 205, 211, 227, 233-4, 236, 238, 246, 249, 257
  offence against public trade 283
  progressive abandonment of 268
  regulation of trade 257
  trade and commerce 10, 40, 194, 215, 222, 266, 276, 283
    trade and commerce in the Qur'ān 201
  trade and exchange 227
  trade guilds 197
  trade routes 22, 30, 285
  traders 233-4, 236, 257, 263, 283, 285, 288, 291
  trade unions 92, 187, 332
    attacks on trade unions 114
  trading horses 282
  trading licences 291
  trading practices
    supervision of trading practices 194
tradition xvii
  traditionalists xix
  traditional modes of authority 141
transactions 186, 280, 290, 302, 319
  transactions – *mu'āmalāt* 271
  transactions particularly over distances 299
transfer of funds 294
transformation of conceptions of reality 34
transformation of modes of communication 34
transformative force 74

"Transforming Islamic Banking to Overcome Imminent Challenges" 400
transmission 9
  transmission of the Message (*tablīgh*) 235
Transoxiana 22
Transparency International 106-7
transportation 12, 104
  transport services 117
  transport technologies 42
transvaluation of the scientific evaluation 128
trapeza 147
travellers 16, 27
travelling in the land 233
treacherous Turks 49
the Treasury 26, 96-97
  of the Muslim *dawla* 196
  treasury bonds 399
  Treasury Department xxiii, 96, 120
  treasury departments 113
treaties 242
  treaty with Britain 55
treat the neighbour with kindness 164
tribes 244
  tribal affiliation 243
  tribal-based society 243
  Tribal Brotherhood 245
  tribal relations 250
tribute-taking empires 34
trillion dollar bailout 97
tripartite hierarchy
  of mutually reinforcing individual and social utilities 196
triumph 256
G. Troeller 364
the Trojan Horse 49
Stephen Trombley 375
true equivalence 223
true knowledge about man and society 125
the Trump administration 115
  Trump's cabinet 116
trust 290, 299
  a trustworthy completely truthful trader 235
  trustworthiness (*amāna*) 210, 217, 235
truth
  Truth (*aletheia*) 72
  truthfulness 168, 217
  truthfulness (*ṣidq*) 235
tuberculosis 180, 329
the Tudor Dynasty 168, 170-1
Tunis 398
Turkestan 59
Turkey xviii, xx, 22, 51, 199, 330
  Turkey's arable land 199
Turkī ibn 'Abdullāh 54
Turks 55
*A Turn in the Epistemology and Hermeneutics of Twentieth Century Usul Al-Fiqh* 364
turn of fortune 17
Twelfth Annual EF Schumacher Lectures 375
twentieth century 8, 70
two free contracting parties 217
two fundamental doctrines of political power 171
two *khalīfas* 219
two months' imprisonment 286
two sales in one 227, 306

two yearly caravans – those of winter and summer 242
tyranny 351
tyrannical statism 189
tyranny of speculation 160
tyranny of the majority 91
Tyrian shekel, 228

## U

*'udūl* witnesses of integrity, knowledge and competence 299
Uḥud 214
the UK 138, 181, 301
the United Kingdom 61
the constitution of the the United Kingdom 61
Ukraine xxii
'Umar ibn 'Abd al-'Azīz 253, 260
'Umar ibn al-Khaṭṭāb 11, 20, 26, 189, 194, 224, 237, 252, 260, 262, 264-6, 268, 284-5, 288, 297, 383
the second caliph 334
'Umar's long caliphate 262
the Umayyads 11, 190
the *umma* xviii, xx, 27, 242, 246, 249, 250-1, 334, 350
*umma ad-da'wa*
the community comprising those who are invited to the *dīn* 251
*umma al-ijāba*
comprising those who have responded to the invitation (*da'wa*) 251
*umm al-madhāhib* (mother/core of the *madhhabs*) 335
*ummī* – "unlettered" 249
*ummiyyīn* – the unlettered Arabs 245
*umm* (mother) 249
Umm Salama 220
the UN 330
the UN Convention against Corruption 106
United Nations agencies 179
United Nations General Assembly 330
United Nations Organisation 58, 69, 85, 179
the UNO 77
the Secretary General Antonio Guterres 330
unacceptable behaviour 192
unanimity (*ijmā'*) 306
uncompromising success 331
the unconscious 132, 138
store of instinctual desires and needs 132
unconscious drives 142
unconscious feelings of the masses 135
unconscious irrational forces 135
undercutting 261, 288
undercutting and overpricing 287
understanding of *tawḥīd* 129
un-elected elite 65
un-elected personnel 173
unemployed 121
unfit 155
union (*ittiḥād*) 342
unions 223
unit of consumption 146
units of account 278
universal ethical principles (*kulliyyāt*) 56

universal forced schooling 159
universalisation of Western liberal democracy 179
Universal Otherhood 245
universal suffrage 100
the universe a giant machine 125
the university 161
the University of Bilbao 76, 130
the University of Chicago 158
the University of Melbourne xvii, 182
University of Malaya 378
unjust distribution 142
the unjust structuralist state 189
unnecessary procurements 107
unpayable debts 120
the Unseen 202, 204
unveiling of Allah 353
upper-classes 154
upward mobility 154
the *ūqiyya*
consists of forty silver *dirhams* 223, 226
urbanisation 34
urban city dwellers 250
the urban community 256
the urban individual 148
the urban system 256
'Urwa ibn az-Zubayr 220
the US xxii, xxiv, 38, 78-79, 101-2, 114, 118, 121, 133, 138, 157, 181-2, 296
the citadel of capitalism 328
the United States 329
the United States of America 79
US Bank 99
US-based transnational corporations 115
US businesses 110
US capital 114
the US Chamber of Commerce 116, 118
US corporations 115
US democracy 134
the US dollar 36, 40, 69, 77, 79, 361
the world's reserve currency 355
the US empire 79
the US Federal Reserve Bank 114
US foreign military interventions 79
the US government 114, 136
US hegemony 355
US imperial tradition 114
US interests 115
the US Secretary of Labour 140
the US Senate 98
the US State Department 183
US Supreme Court Judge 98
the US war in Vietnam 141
use of weapons 165
*'ushr* – one tenth of the harvest 25, 196
Mufti Taqi Usmani 399
Shabbīr 'Usmānī 387
the USSR
the fall of the USSR 179
*uṣūl* principles 259
*uṣūl ad-dīn* 394
*uṣūl al-fiqh* 56, 333, 394
"Usurious Piety: The Cash Waqf Controversy in the Ottoman Empire" 362
usury xviii, xxv, 44, 149, 187, 196, 208, 214, 243-4, 246, 253, 267, 274, 292, 319
adoption of usury among the Christians 214

as much as a handful of grass 213
charging interest on a loan 243
compound interest 213, 244
fundamental principle of capitalism 346
no scruples about 268
predatory interest rates 120
the prohibition of usury 213
strict prohibition of usury 214
the gravity of usury 208
ubiquity of 245
unjustified increase xxiii, 44
unjustified increment 44
usurers 210
usurious banking xxv
usurious capitalism 319
usurious central principle 327
usurious clearinghouses 35
usurious debt 296
usurious intent 214
usurious paper money xx
usurious power control 112
usurious transaction 230
usury banking 59
usury capitalism 216
usury economics 211
usury edifice 327
usury finance 44
usury-free container caravans 188, 332
usury system 105
*uswatun ḥasana* 351, 357
*al-'Utbiyya* 267
Uthman dan Fodio 47, 363
'Uthmān ibn 'Affan 11, 21, 219, 253, 265
*khilāfa* of 'Uthmān 262
the third caliph 334
utility 276

## V

vaccines
three recommended doses of vaccine 180
Umar Vadillo 37, 38, 46, 61, 229, 359, 361-2, 365, 388, 394-5, 400-1
"Living Islam: Muamalat and Sufism, Fallacy of Islamic Banking" 400
"Living Islam: Muamalat and Sufism, Rethinking Islamic Banking, EP 30" 388
*The Return of the Gold Dinar* 359, 362
value of a currency 275
Commodore Vanderbilt 158
vassal systems
so-called democratic governments 112
vast majority of employees 223
vegetarian 95
John Veitch 366, 376
Venice 25
*The Venture of Islam: Conscience and History in a World Civilisation* 384
Daniel Verdier 361
the very poor 16
vessels 224
a vibrant democracy 175
the vibration of the atom 74
victory 129
Vienna 51-52, 132
virtual currencies 347
*The Virtuous City* 8

Visa 109
the vision of Allah 342
Paul Volker 114
the Voyages of Discovery 68
vulnerability 138
vulnerable nations 115

## W

Rick Waddell 99
wage freezes 117
wage theft 121
waging war 208
Wagner 159
Wahhabism 64, 65, 66, 81
the Wahhābī Amīr 55
Wahhābī doctrine 53
*Wahhabi Islam: From Revival and Reform to Global Jihad* 364
Wahhābī modernists 58
Wahhābīs 80
Wahhābī *'ulamā* 68, 69
*waḥy* – revelation 162
Wā'ila ibn al-Asqa' 240
*Der Waldgäng* 76
Waldgänger 75
*walī* (singular of *awliyā*) 164
Shah Waliyullāh ad-Dahlawī 7, 254, 357
I. Wallernstein 362
Wall Street 96-97
Wall Street bank 133
Wall Street/Treasury alliance 97-98
al-Wansharīsī 387
want for your brothers what you want for yourself 164
*waqf* (a charitable endowment) property 197-8, 253, 259, 300, 303, 346
for arranging the funerals of the poor and destitute without relations 303
for feeding birds in winter 303
for looking after poor and orphaned children 303
for poor girls 303
for providing nurses to look after the children of working women 303
for providing replacements for pitchers broken by children and servants 303
for the benefit of non-humans, including donkeys and storks 200
for the slaves 303
for travellers 303
for widows 303
objectives for 200
to purchase brides' trousseau 303
"Waqf" 384, 398
*waqf* administrators 44
*waqfiyya* 199
*waqf* 300
"Waqf Studies in the Twentieth Century: The State of the Art" 384
the *waqf* system 199
Islamic society financed through the *waqf* system 346
Wāqida 242
*waqt*
the time that he is living in 353
war 16, 74, 78
the mis-named war on terror 263
war against the enemy 191

war from Allah and His Messenger 40, 207, 327
war from Himself and from His Messenger 319
war in Iraq, Syria, Libya, Afghanistan 132
the war on terror 183
warriors 248
World War I 24, 136
World War II 133, 136
world-wide civil war 77, 80
the Warburgs 212
warehouses 291
The Washington School of Psychiatry 141
water 113, 191
purity of water 276
water pollution 103
water utilities 301
watersheds in mankind's story 243
waves of trade 179
wayfarers 200
wayfaring 352
Divine Self-unveiling 352
the Way of Allah 15, 16, 204
person fighting in the Way of Allah 233
*wazīr* 166
the deputy and representative of the caliph 191
wazirate (vizierate) 190-1, 332, 348
*wazīrs* 192
wealth 163, 186, 204
wealthiest 1 percent xxiv, 180
wealthy merchants of Arabia 11
*The Wealth of Nations* 68
weaponry 42
weapons 104
weather changes 352
weaving 12
web-design 293
Weber/Taylor narrative 83
web of interconnected finance 210
websites 159, 177
weights and measures 10, 222-4, 226, 252, 281
control of weights and measures 194
measures of the people of Madīna 223
unity on weights and measures 225
weighed, measured, and counted 125
weights of the coins 225
weights of the currency 20
the weights of the people of Makka 223
welfare 25, 199
of Muslims and non-Muslims 213
welfare distribution 16
welfare recipients 121
the wellbeing of citizens 117
wells 199
the West 48-49, 241, 245-6
the Western academic community 160
Western civilisation 70
Western-controlled political institutions 123
Western engineers 42
Western Europe 21
Western European states 45
Western historians 167
Western imperatives 55
Western imperialism 62
westernisation 45, 46, 60-61

Western liberal democracy 179
Western models 45
Western nations 48
Western Powers 51
Western rationalism 76
Western technology 44
Western universities 159
Western worldview 301
West Africa 21, 31, 209
Western Mediterranean 23
*What Went Wrong?: The Clash Between Islam and Modernity in the Middle East* 362
wheat 19, 25, 29, 388
wheat for barley 282
wheat for wheat 281
whirling matter 70
A.D. White 361
P.T. White 361
Whole Earth Review 396
Wikileaks 177, 182-3
*wilāyat* xix
winter and summer caravans 390
wisdom 13
wisdom – *ḥikma* 247
the wisdom of elders 158
the wisdom of historians 152
witnesses 275
"*witnesses against mankind*" 350
witnessing 236
women 244
fair treatment of 168
respect for 347
women and children 276
women and the weak
protecting women and the weak 167
women's rights 141
wool 25
work 74
the worker 74
workers 103, 121
workers are slaves in all but name 223
work ethic 147
workforce 155
working class 117
working class families 145
working class women 145
the work of women 144
workshops 197, 293
Working Group Report, 1986 377
the world
world civilisation 250
the world crisis 346
world culture 209
the World Economic Forum (WEF) 330
world empires 104
worldly appetites 276
the world monetary system
the bedrock of the world monetary system 118
the world press 183
the world's millionaires 181
the world's reserve currency 36, 79
the world's resources 79
the world state 73, 78, 129
world superpower 79
the world's wealth 173
world trade 106, 148
the World Trade Organisation 69, 85, 113, 179
worldview 141, 160
worldview in Europe 124
the worldview of scientific

materialism 129
worldviews 122
the World Bank 35, 77, 85, 112-3, 179
the World Wide Web 177
worship
obligatory acts of 337
worship of Allah 11
worship of other-than-Allah 162
*The Wreck of Western Culture – Humanism Revisited* 375
write-offs 121
writing 242-3, 249
to record debts 246
writing and recording 209
writing of Qur'ān and other books 200
written record 217, 293
wrongdoing
countless examples of wrongdoing 193
wrongdoers (*ẓālimūn*) 349
the wronged person 165
*wuḍū'* 276, 344

## Y

Yahūdhā (Judah) 386
Yaḥyā 246

Yaḥyā ibn 'Umar 223, 287, 320, 388, 396, 400
Yaḥyā [ibn Yaḥyā] 296, 306
Ya'qūb 386
yard 224
yarn 29
Asadullah Yate 13, 228, 358, 363, 383, 387-8, 397, 399-400
Yathrib 8, 19
Yemen 19, 22, 52, 242, 350, 390
Yemenis 246
Yemeni territory 54
Yersinia pesti 120
Young Azharis 60
Young Ottomans 61
Young Turks 49, 60, 62
Young Turk coup d'état 60
youthful energy 161
*yunfiqūn* 203

## Z

az-Zabīdī 397, 403
*zāhid* (doing-without) 339
*zakāt* xx, xxvi, 8, 10, 16, 18, 20, 25-27, 186, 196, 203-5, 213-5, 220, 225-9, 279, 284, 319, 337, 347, 395
abolition of *zakāt* 28
as personal charity 228
a Taken Zakāt 226
categories of recipients
the poor and needy 229
collected and assessed amount of 226
dates and raisins 229
eight categories who are eligible to receive *zakāt* 204
fallen pillar of the *dīn* 218
gold and silver 229
grains and pulses 229
immediate distribution of the 227
livestock 229
minting *dīnārs* and *dirhams* to pay *zakāt* 229
obligations of *zakāt* 204
pay the *zakāt* 164, 218, 221
the person who "pays *zakāt*" 218

the pillar has fallen 345
recipients of *zakāt* 27
restoration of 319
restoration of the pillar of *zakāt* 28, 227
a taken *ṣadaqa* 218
"take!" *zakāt* 218
those who collect [*zakāt*] 27
*zakāt al-fitr* 193
*zakāt* collectors 26-28, 219-20, 228, 319, 345
  *amīr*'s appointment of *zakāt* collectors 226
  appointment of *zakāt* collectors 191
  authority of *zakāt* collectors 193
*zakāt* is taken from actual held wealth 229
*zakāt* is the right of the poor and needy and other categories 229
*Zakat – Raising a Fallen Pillar* 205, 359-60, 385
Thierry Zarcone 62
*zāwiyas* (gathering places for Sufis) 199
Zaytuna 398
zenith of spiritual achievement 343
zero interest loans 97
zero-sum game 274
Zimbabwe 21
Ziya Pasha 62, 64
*zoon logon echon* 72
az-Zubayr ibn al-'Awwām 264-5
Shoshana Zuboff 299, 397
A. Zysow 359

Printed in the USA
CPSIA information can be obtained
at www.ICGtesting.com
LVHW091210171123
764118LV00003B/44

9 781914 397257